Modern
SPANISH
Grammar

Second Edition

Routledge Modern Grammars

Series concept and development – Sarah Butler

Other books in the series:

Modern Spanish Grammar Workbook by Juan Kattán-Ibarra and Irene Wilkie
ISBN 0–415–12099–3

Modern French Grammar
Modern French Grammar Workbook

Modern German Grammar
Modern German Grammar Workbook

Modern Italian Grammar
Modern Italian Grammar Workbook

Modern SPANISH Grammar

A practical guide

Second Edition

Juan Kattán-Ibarra
and Christopher J. Pountain

 Routledge
Taylor & Francis Group

LONDON AND NEW YORK

First published 1997
by Routledge

Second edition published 2003
by Routledge
2 Park Square, Milton Park, Abingdon, Oxon, OX14 4RN

Simultaneously published in the USA and Canada
by Routledge
711 Third Avenue, New York, NY 10017

Routledge is an imprint of the Taylor & Francis Group, an informa business

© 2003 Juan Kattán-Ibarra and Christopher J. Pountain

Typeset in ITC Stone Serif/Sans by RefineCatch Limited, Bungay, Suffolk

The authors assert their moral right to be identified as the authors of this work

British Library Cataloguing in Publication Data
A catalogue record for this book is available from the British Library

Library of Congress Cataloguing in Publication Data
A catalog record for this book is available from the Library of Congress

ISBN10: 0–415–27303–X (hbk)
ISBN10: 0–415–27304–8 (pbk)

ISBN13: 987–0–415–27303–9 (hbk)
ISBN13: 978–0–415–27304–6 (pbk)

Contents

Contents

Contents

PART B Functions

I Social contacts and communication strategies

Contents

Contents

Contents

Note to the Second Edition

The bi-partite approach we took when producing the first edition of *Modern Spanish Grammar* has proved popular with students and tutors alike. For the second edition we went back to the people that use the *Grammar* and asked what they would like to see improved.

As s result, we have taken the opportunity to make some changes to Part A (Structures) and to carry out revisions and make additions to Part B (Functions), as well as making some general corrections and updatings.

Thank you to all our readers – we hope that they find this new edition as stimulating as the first.

Juan Kattán-Ibarra
Christopher J. Pountain
April 2003

Introduction to the First Edition

This book is divided into two major parts: *Structures* and *Functions*.

Part A – Structures is a concise grammar of Spanish organized in the familiar traditional way, describing the forms of Spanish in turn. This section should be used for quick reference when you want to know something about a form or structure you can identify (e.g. the subjunctive forms of a particular verb, how adjectives agree with nouns, when to use **ser** or **estar**, etc.).

Part B – Functions is newer in concept, and the larger of the two. It is organized according to the kinds of things you might want to say in particular situations in Spanish, and here you can look up such things as how to apologize, how to ask the time, how to describe a person, etc. You will find that sometimes the same ground is covered in both parts, although it is organized in a different way (we have, however, tried to keep exact overlap between the two sections to a minimum).

INTRODUCTION

You will need constantly to refer back and forth between the two parts of the book, and so there are a lot of *cross-references* between them indicated in the text or by arrows in the margin. Do not be content with consulting just one section, therefore, but follow up the cross-references given – that way you will understand both the structures of Spanish and the way in which they are used. There is also an *index* of words and topics so that you can find information again quickly and easily.

Third person verbs, pronouns and possessive adjectives are often potentially ambiguous in Spanish: an extreme case is **su**, which can mean 'his', 'her', 'your', 'its' or 'their'. In this book we have given the most likely translation for examples rather than the full range of options which are theoretically possible.

We have not hesitated to use traditional grammatical terms, especially in the Structures part. It is worth spending a little time getting to grips with these: understanding the terms will help you understand the structures better, even if they may appear a bit daunting at first. We have described terms with which you are likely to be unfamiliar in the *Glossary*.

The following abbreviations and symbols have been used:

App.	Appendix
esp.	especially
fam.	familiar
f.	feminine
ger.	gerund
inf.	infinitive
L. Am.	Latin America
lit.	literally
m.	masculine
p.p.	past participle
pers.	person
pl.	plural
pol.	polite
R. Pl.	River Plate
sg.	singular
*	denotes that the grammatical construction is unacceptable in Spanish

We hope that readers will find our approach interesting and useful: we will be delighted to receive opinions on the book and details about the ways in which it has been used in teaching and learning Spanish.

Juan Kattán-Ibarra
Christopher J. Pountain
December 1995

Glossary

Small capitals indicate that the word is described elsewhere in the Glossary.

Active see **Voice**

Adjectives (see **2**, **3** and **5**)
Adjectives are words which describe NOUNS, and they agree in NUMBER (singular or plural) and GENDER (masculine or feminine) with the noun they describe:

> **Es un lugar muy *bonito*.**
> It is a very nice place.

> **Las habitaciones son muy *cómodas*.**
> The rooms are very comfortable.

Adjectives in Spanish also function as NOUNS (see **5.3**) and as ADVERBS (see **14**).

Adverbs
Adverbs are words which tell you something about a VERB, an ADJECTIVE or another adverb:

> **Me llaman muy *a menudo*.**
> They call me very often.

> **Ana María era *increíblemente* bella.**
> Ana María was incredibly beautiful.

> **Hablaba *tremendamente rápido*.**
> He/she was speaking tremendously fast.

Agent
The performer of a verbal action: in an ACTIVE sentence, the agent is typically the SUBJECT of the sentence; in a PASSIVE sentence, the agent (the subject of the corresponding active sentence) is usually introduced by 'by' in English and by **por** in Spanish.

Antecedent (see especially **18.2.5**)
This is the noun to which a RELATIVE CLAUSE pertains, and which usually stands immediately before the relative PRONOUN:

> ***El muchacho*** **que está con Pedro es amigo mío.**
> The boy who is with Pedro is a friend of mine.

> *La casa* que compramos es estupenda.
> The house we bought is very good.

Articles (see 4)

There are two kinds of article in Spanish: definite articles: **el, la, los, las** 'the'; indefinite articles: **un, una** 'a', 'an':

> *El* **hotel no está lejos.**
> The hotel is not far.

> **¿Hay *un* restaurante por aquí?**
> Is there a restaurant nearby?

Auxiliary verbs

This is the name given to certain very common verbs which regularly combine with other verb forms. In Spanish, **haber** is the perfect auxiliary and combines with the past participle to make the compound tenses (see **16.1.1.7**); **poder, deber, saber** and **querer**, which are followed by an infinitive, are the principal modal auxiliaries (see **21**) corresponding to English 'can', 'may', 'might', 'will', 'would', etc.

Clause

A clause is a sentence within a sentence, recognizable because it contains a verb of its own. Main clauses do not depend on other elements within the sentence for their meaning. Subordinate clauses are dependent on another clause:

> **No creo que venga.**
> I don't think he/she will come.

> **Espero que aparezca.**
> I hope it appears.

In the previous sentences, **No creo** and **Espero** are the main clauses, while **que venga** and **que aparezca** are subordinate clauses.

Complement (see 26)

A CLAUSE, INFINITIVE or GERUND which functions as the SUBJECT or OBJECT of a verb, or as the object of a PREPOSITION. Examples are:

> **Me gusta *bailar*.**
> I like to dance. (lit. 'dancing pleases me')
> (**Bailar** is the subject complement of **gusta**.)

> **Estoy seguro de *que no lo hará*.**
> I'm sure he/she won't do it.
> (**Que no lo hará** is the object complement of **de**.)

> **Siguió *silbando*.**
> He/she carried on whistling.
> (**Silbando** is the object complement of **siguió**.)

Conjunctions (see 27)

Conjunctions join words or groups of words. They are words like **y** 'and', **o** 'or', **pero** 'but', **aunque** 'although':

> **Iré mañana *o* pasado.**
> I'll go tomorrow or the day after tomorrow.
>
> **Habla español *pero* no muy bien.**
> He/she speaks Spanish but not very well.

Demonstratives (see **9**)
Demonstratives indicate proximity or remoteness, e.g. **este** 'this', **aquel** 'that'.

Diphthong (see **1.2**)
A diphthong is a group of two vowels in the same syllable.

Direct object see **Object**

Gender (see **2**)
Spanish has two genders, masculine or feminine. For example **la oficina** 'the office' is feminine, while **el coche** 'the car' is masculine. ADJECTIVES, ARTICLES, DEMONSTRATIVES, POSSESSIVES and PRONOUNS must agree in gender when they relate to one another.

Gerund (see **17.12**)
Gerunds are forms like **estudiando** 'studying', **haciendo** 'doing'.

Hiatus (see **1.5.2**)
Where two vowels together belong to different syllables, they are said to be in hiatus.

Imperative see **Mood**

Indicative see **Mood**

Indirect object see **Object**

Infinitive (see **17.11**)
This is the base form of the Spanish verb, as it normally appears in a dictionary, for example, **cantar** 'to sing', **beber** 'to drink'.

Intransitive
An intransitive verb is one which cannot take a direct OBJECT, e.g. **salir** 'to go out', **cenar** 'to dine'.

Mood
In Spanish it is usual to refer to the indicative (see **17.1–17.10**), the subjunctive (see **18**) and the imperative (see **17.13**) as different moods of the verb:

> **José *vive* en Barcelona.**
> José lives in Barcelona. (indicative)
>
> **Ojalá *vuelva* pronto.**
> I hope he/she comes back soon. (subjunctive)
>
> ***Abre* la ventana, por favor.**
> Open the window please. (imperative)

As a rough guide, the indicative is associated with statements and assertions, the imperative with orders and commands, and the subjunctive with a wide range of subordinate CLAUSE usages.

Nouns
Nouns typically denote things, people or animals, or abstract concepts, e.g. **mesa, Ramón, niña, cocodrilo, belleza, razón.**

Number
Spanish, like English, distinguishes singular and plural number. For example **el niño** 'the child' (singular), **los niños** 'the children' (plural).

Object
It is usual to distinguish between direct objects and indirect objects. A direct object is a noun, pronoun or noun phrase which undergoes the action of the verb. An indirect object is a noun, pronoun or noun phrase which is more indirectly affected by the action of the verb:

> **Antonio compró *un coche.***
> Antonio bought a car. (**un coche** is the direct object of **compró.**)

> **Le escribí a *María.***
> I wrote to María. (**María** is the indirect object of **escribí.**)

Object pronouns (see 8.2)
These are words which take the place of a noun or noun phrase which is functioning as an OBJECT. Like objects, object pronouns can be direct or indirect and they can be found together in the same sentence:

> **Leí el libro.**
> I read the book. (**el libro**, the thing read, is the direct object of **leí**)

> ***Lo* leí.**
> I read it. (direct object pronoun: **lo**)

> **Dejó todo el dinero a su hermana.**
> He/she left all the money to his/her sister. (**su hermana**, the person who was given the money, is the indirect object, with **el dinero** acting as direct object.)

> ***Le* dejó todo el dinero.**
> He/she left him/her all the money. (indirect object pronoun: **le**)

> ***Se lo* dejó todo a su hermana.**
> He/she left it all to him/her. (the indirect object pronoun **le** has become **se** before a direct object pronoun, see **8.2.2.2.**)

Passive see Voice

Past participles
A past participle is that part of the verb which is used to form compound tenses (see **16.1.1.7**), for example:

> **Hemos *terminado.***
> We have finished.

No te había *visto*.
I hadn't seen you.

Past participles can also function as ADJECTIVES, in which case they must agree in GENDER and NUMBER with the noun they qualify:

Estábamos muy *sorprendidos*.
We were very surprised.

El trabajo está *terminado*.
The job is finished.

Person

A category of personal pronouns (see **8**), POSSESSIVES (see **10**) and verb forms (see **16**) indicating relationship to the speaker ('I' = first person, 'you' = second person, 'they' = third person).

Possessives (see 10)

Adjectives or pronouns which indicate to whom or what something or someone pertains or belongs, e.g.:

***nuestros* amigos**
our friends

Madrid y *sus* museos
Madrid and its museums

Estos libros son *míos*.
These books are mine.

Predicate

The predicate is that part of the sentence which tells you something about the subject:

El tren para Sevilla *sale del andén número cuatro*.
The train for Seville leaves from platform four.

Su último libro *ha tenido un gran éxito*.
His/her last book has been very successful.

Prepositions (see 25)

Prepositions are words like **a** 'to', **con** 'with', **en** 'in', 'on', 'at', **entre** 'between', 'among', and which can give you information such as location, time, direction:

Están *en* casa.
They are at home. (place)

Irán *a* España.
They'll go to Spain. (direction)

Se quedará *hasta* el lunes.
He/she will stay until Monday. (time)

Pronouns

Pronouns are words which take the place of a noun or a noun phrase. For example:

Felipe nada muy bien.
Felipe swims very well.

Él nada muy bien.
He swims very well. (subject pronoun)

No conozco a Elvira.
I don't know Elvira.

No *la* conozco.
I don't know her. (object pronoun)

Este libro es de Enrique.
This book belongs to Enrique.

Este libro es *mío*.
This book is mine. (possessive pronoun)

Reflexive (see 23)
In its literal use, a reflexive verb form involves the use of an OBJECT PRONOUN which refers back to the SUBJECT of the verb, e.g. **Pilar se lavó** 'Pilar washed herself'. However, the reflexive verb form has a wide variety of functions in Spanish, which are described in **23**.

Relative clause
A relative clause is a group of words within a sentence, containing a verb, and introduced by a RELATIVE PRONOUN, which refers back to a preceding noun or pronoun (the ANTECEDENT).

Las personas *que fueron a la reunión* estaban de acuerdo.
The people who attended the meeting were in agreement.

El pueblo en que se establecieron está muy lejos.
The town in which they established themselves is very far away.

Relative pronouns (see 11)
Relative pronouns are words like **que**, **el que/el cual** and **quien**, which introduce a RELATIVE CLAUSE:

La mujer a *quien* verdaderamente quiere es Alicia.
The woman he really loves is Alicia.

Éste es el colega *que* te presenté ayer.
This is the colleague I introduced to you yesterday.

Relative pronouns can be missed out in English, as the above translations show, but they can never be omitted in Spanish.

Subject
This is a word or group of words within a sentence, which shows the person or thing performing the action denoted by the verb:

El español no es difícil.
Spanish is not difficult.

Gabriel y Victoria vendrán conmigo.
Gabriel and Victoria will come with me.

Tense

Tenses are different forms of the verb which, amongst other things, refer to different times (the present, imperfect, future, etc., are traditionally known as the tenses of the verb):

> **Elena *vive* en la Argentina.**
> Elena lives in Argentina. (verb in the present)

> **Elena *vivió* antes en París.**
> Previously Elena lived in Paris. (verb in the past)

Transitive

A transitive verb is one which has a direct object, e.g. **ver (el campo)** 'to see (the countryside)', **escribir (una carta)** 'to write (a letter)'.

Verbs

Verbs often denote actions or states, but they can also convey other ideas, for example transformations:

> **Trabajé en Madrid.**   I worked in Madrid.
> **Están muy contentos.**   They are very happy.
> **Se puso a llover.**   It started to rain.

Voice

The active and passive voices of the verb are usually distinguished in both English and Spanish. Only TRANSITIVE verbs can be passivized. In the active voice the SUBJECT of the verb is also its AGENT, whereas in the passive voice the subject of the verb is the transitive verb's OBJECT, and the agent is introduced by a preposition (normally **por** in Spanish and 'by' in English).

There are some important differences between English and Spanish in this area, which are described in **24**.

Part A

Structures

1
Pronunciation and spelling

Pronunciation is described here using the symbols of the International Phonetic Alphabet.

The Spanish alphabet

Letter	Name	Pronunciation	Examples	
a	a	[a]	**ama**	[ama]
b	be	[b] after a pause or after **n** or **m**; otherwise the fricative sound [β] (like [b] but with the lips not quite together).	**bueno** **imbécil** **la bota** **hablaba**	[bweno] [imbéθil] [laβota] [aβlaβa]
c	ce	[k] before **a**, **o** or **u** or a consonant,	**caro** **ocre**	[karo] [okre]
		[θ] (like *th* in English 'thin' – standard Peninsular pronunciation) or [s] (Latin America and much of Andalusia) before **e** or **i**.	**encía**	[enθía] / [ensía]
		cu before a vowel is pronounced [kw]	**cuando**	[kwando]
(ch)[1]	(che)	[tʃ] (like *ch* in English 'church')	**hecho**	[etʃo]
d	de	[d] after a pause or after **n** or **l**;	**duro** **molde**	[duro] [molde]
		otherwise the fricative sound [ð] (like *th* in English 'rather').	**la dama** **lado** **verde**	[laðama] [laðo] [berðe]
		[ð] is prone to be weakened to the point of disappearing altogether in a number of styles of speech, so pronunciations like [aβlao] for **hablado** are very common.		
e	e	[e]	**merece**	[mereθe] / [merese]
f	efe	[f]	**fama**	[fama]
g	ge	Before **a**, **o** or **u**: [g] after a pause or **n**;	**gama** **angosto**	[gama] [angosto]

		otherwise the fricative sound [ɣ] (like [g] but with the contact between tongue and soft palate not quite made).	haga	[aɣa]
		Before **e** or **i**:		
		[x] (like *ch* in Scots 'loch' or German *acht*)	genio	[xenjo]
		gu before **a** or **o** is pronounced [gw] after a pause or **n**;	guardia	[gwardja]
		and otherwise [ɣw].	fragua	[fraɣwa]
		gu before **e** or **i** is pronounced [g] after a pause or **n**;	guerra	[gerra]
		otherwise [ɣ].	ruegue	[rrweɣe]
		gü before **e** or **i** is pronounced [gw] after a pause or **n**;	pingüino	[pingwino]
		and otherwise [ɣw].	argüir	[arɣwir]
h	hache	always silent in standard pronunciation.	haba	[aβa]
i	i	[i] Also used before or after a vowel to make different diphthongs (see **1.2** below).	mito	[mito]
j	jota	[x] (see **g**)	eje	[exe]
k	ka	[k] In Spanish this sound is not 'aspirated' (accompanied by a short puff of air) before a vowel as in English.	kilo	[kilo]
l	ele	[l] In standard pronunciation [l] is always the alveolar, or 'clear' *l* of English 'flee', never the velar, or 'dark' *l* of English 'cool'.	leche	[leʃe]
(ll)[1]	(elle)	The standard pronunciation is [ʎ] (like *lli* in English 'million'), but this is very commonly weakened to [j] (like *y* in English 'yet'). Il is also pronounced [ʒ] or [dʒ] (like *s* in English 'pleasure' or *j* in English 'judge') in some regions, notably the Río de la Plata.	calle llegar	[kaʎe] / [kaje] / [kaʒe] [ʎeɣar] / [jeɣar] / [dʒeɣar]
m	eme	[m]	madre	[maðre]
n	ene	[n]	vano	[bano]
ñ[2]	eñe	[ɲ] (like *ny* in English 'canyon')	señor	[seɲor]
o	o	[o]	ojo	[oxo]
p	pe	[p] In Spanish this sound is not 'aspirated' (accompanied by a short puff of air) before a vowel as in English.	paso	[paso]
q	cu	always appears with **u**: **qu** has the value [k] (see **k**).	queso	[keso]
r, rr	ere, erre (erre doble)	**r** between vowels or after **p, b, t, d, c, g,** is pronounced as a 'flap' [r] (with a single flick of the tongue);	pero abre	[pero] [abre]

		after other consonants it is pronounced [rr].	**enredar**	[enrreðar]
		rr is pronounced as a 'trill' or 'roll' [rr] (with vibration of the tongue).	**perro**	[perro]
		r at the beginning of a word is pronounced [rr]; at the end of a word it is pronounced [r] and often loses its voiced quality in this position.	**rojo**	[rroxo]
			dar	[dar]
s	ese	[s] The [s] of standard Castilian is pronounced as an apico-alveolar sound, that is, with the tongue slightly curled back. The [s] of Latin American Spanish is more like the [s] of English. Before a voiced consonant, it is often pronounced [z]. In many regional pronunciations, **s** before a consonant or at the end of a word is aspirated (pronounced [h]) or tends to disappear altogether.	**paso** **mismo** **huevos**	[paso] [mismo] / [mizmo] / [mihmo] [weβos] / [weβoh] / [weβo]
t	te	[t] In Spanish this sound is not 'aspirated' (accompanied by a short puff of air) before a vowel as in English.	**teme**	[teme]
u	u	[u] Also used before or after a vowel to make different diphthongs (see 1.2). See also **c**, **g** and **q**.	**fuma**	[fuma]
v	uve	Pronounced as **b**.	**vuelo** **lavar**	[bwelo] [laβar]
w	uve doble	Relatively rare in Spanish, and exists only in borrowed words. Its pronunciation varies between [b], [β] and [w].	**water** **whisky** **software**	[báter] [(g)wiski] [sofwer]
x	equis	Either [ks] or [gz] between vowels;	**examen**	[eksamen] /[egzamen]
		before a consonant, pronounced as [ks] in careful speech, but more often as [s], especially in Peninsular Spanish.	**extra**	[ekstra] / [estra]
		In Mexican Spanish, **x** is pronounced [x] (like *ch* in Scots 'loch' or German 'acht') in a number of words of Amerindian origin, including the name of the country **México** (the spelling used in this book).	**Oaxaca**	[oaxaka]
y	i griega	Between vowels, after a consonant and at the beginning of a word, **y** is pronounced [j] (like *y* in English 'yet'), often strengthened to [ʒ] in some regions.	**trayendo** **yate**	[trajendo] / [traʒendo] [jate]/[ʒate]
		It is also used before or after a vowel to make different diphthongs (see 1.2). In the conjunction **y**, it is pronounced [i].		

| z | zeta | [θ] (like *th* in English 'thin' – standard Castilian pronunciation) or [s] (in Latin America and much of Andalusia). | **zona** | [θona] / [sona] |

[1] **ch** and **ll** were considered to be separate letters in their own right until recently.
[2] **ñ** is still considered a separate letter.

NOTE   Since Spanish spelling attempts to reflect pronunciation, spelling changes often take place in related words:

feliz	**felices**	preserving the sound [θ] or [s]
ataca	**ataque**	preserving the sound [k]
rige	**rija**	preserving the sound [x]
carga	**cargue**	preserving the sound [ɣ]
agua	**desagüe**	preserving the sound [ɣw]

 16.1.2.2 (p. 66)

1.2   Diphthongs

a, **e** and **o** are thought of as 'strong' vowels in Spanish, and **i** (**y**) and **u** are thought of as 'weak' vowels, or 'semivowels'. A combination of strong + weak, or weak + strong, forms a diphthong.

a + i	aire	[ajre]
a + u	áureo	[awreo]
e + y	ley	[lej]
e + u	Europa	[ewropa]
o + y	hoy	[oj]
o + u	not very common, mainly in abbreviations, e.g. COU, or proper names, of Galician origin, e.g. **Couceiro**	[ow]
i + a	enviar	[embjar]
i + e	bien	[bjen]
i + o	serio	[serjo]
u + a	Guatemala	[gwatemala]
u + e	bueno	[bweno]

The combinations **i** + **u** and **u** + **i** also form diphthongs: **viudo** [bjuðo], **ruido** [rrwiðo].

1.3   Syllabification

Syllables in Spanish consist of at least one vowel.

A diphthong counts as one vowel for the purposes of syllabification. A non-diphthongal vowel sequence ('strong' vowel + 'strong' vowel) counts as two syllables:

> **tra-er**
> **a-ho-ra**
> **fe-o**

A single consonant followed by a vowel is grouped into the same syllable as the following vowel.

> **bue-no**
> **a-la**

A consonant group between two vowels is split between the two syllables, except that the groups **pl**, **pr**, **bl**, **br**, **fr**, **fl**, **tr**, **dr**, **cl**, **cr**, **gl**, **gr** are never split:

> **ad-qui-rir**
> but
> **re-gla**
> **a-cre**

A major difference between English and Spanish is that **s** is never considered to belong to the same syllable as a following consonant:

> **Es-pa-ña**
> **ex-tra-ño**
> **as-que-ro-so**

ll and **rr** count as single consonants and are never divided between syllables:

> **hue-lla**
> **pe-rro**

NOTE | Spanish words are hyphenated in writing only at syllable divisions.

1.4 *Sinalefa*

When one word ends in a vowel and the next word begins in a vowel (unless there is a break between the words involved), the two vowels are considered to belong to the same syllable, even though they may not naturally form a diphthong. This phenomenon, which is a striking feature of Spanish pronunciation, is called **sinalefa**:

hasta_hoy	[as-taoj]
entre_ellos	[en-tre-ʎos]
tengo_hambre	[ten-goam-bre]

Even groups of three or more vowels may be treated in this way:

culta_Europa	[kul-taew-ro-pa]

1.5 The written stress accent

1.5.1 Use of the written stress accent in Spanish assumes that Spanish words are stressed on the next to the last syllable if they end in a vowel, **n** or **s**, and on the final syllable if they end in a consonant other than **n** or **s**. Such words are not written with an accent.

> pa-*pel*
> a-rre-ba-*tar*
> *ha*-blan
> mu-*je*-res
> com-*pra*-mos
> ter-*mi*-na
> e-qui-va-*len*-te

Any departure from this situation is marked by the writing of an accent on the vowel in the stressed syllable:

> can-*tá*-ba-mos
> te-*rrá*-que-o
> *ár*-bol
> a-*sí*
> fran-*cés*
> a-za-*frán*

1.5.2   The written accent is also used (even when the word is stressed regularly according to **1.5.1**) to indicate when a combination of vowels which would be expected to form a diphthong (as in **1.2**) in fact does not, but forms two separate syllables. Such groups of vowels are said to be in hiatus.

> Examples of irregularly stressed words (i.e. those words which would need a written accent on the stressed syllable in any case):
> a-*hí*
> re-*í*

> Examples of regularly stressed words (the written accent marks the hiatus and hence the syllable division but would otherwise be unnecessary):
> co-*mí*-a
> ba-*úl*
> re-*ú*-ne

> Contrast
> se-*rí*-a/*se*-ria
> con-ti-*nú*-o/con-*ti*-nuo

1.5.3   The written accent is also used to achieve a different spelling for some pairs of words which sound the same:

el	definite article	él	'he', 'him'
mi	'my'	mí	'I', 'me'
se	reflexive pronoun	sé	'I know'
si	'if'	sí	'yes'
solo	'only', 'alone' (adjective)	sólo	'only' (adverb)
tu	'your'	tú	'you'

como, **cuando,** etc.	**cómo, cuándo,** etc. (used in questions, indirect questions and exclamations, see **12**)
este, ese, **aquel,** etc.	**éste, ése aquél,** etc. (the accent is used optionally here)

1.5.4 **Adverbs** (see **14.1**)

Adverbs formed from a feminine adjective + **-mente** preserve any written accent that normally is used with the adjective:

Adjective	Adverb
fácil	**fácilmente**
magnánima	**magnánimamente**

1.6 # Punctuation

Spanish and English share many features of punctuation. The chief differences are:

(a) Inverted question marks and exclamation marks are used to introduce questions and exclamations. This sometimes means that the inverted marks come in the middle of a sentence (see **28.2**):

¿Cuándo llegaste?	When did you arrive?
¡No me fastidies!	Don't annoy me!
Y María ¿dónde está?	And where's María?

(b) The punctuation of direct speech is quite different in the two languages. Spanish uses a dash to set apart quoted speech in a dialogue, or various forms of inverted commas (traditionally «», though increasingly "" or '') for short quotations within a narrative passage:

> **–¿Qué pasa aquí? –preguntó asombrado –.No sabía que había un problema.**
> 'What is happening here?' he asked, astonished. 'I didn't know there was a problem.'

> **Y con un «no» rotundo, se marchó.**
> And with a definite 'no', he/she went off.

(c) Other differences between English and Spanish punctuation are more a question of degree. Spanish tends to use exclamation marks only for genuine exclamations and not simply to call attention to statements (a common feature of informal letters in English), especially when the 'exclamation' is a subordinate clause:

> **Carmen nos dijo que se bañaron a medianoche.**
> Carmen told us they went for a swim at midnight!

(d) Topicalization in Spanish (see **24.5, 28.1**) produces Spanish word orders which are relatively unusual in English, so English punctuation is not a guide. Short topics are not normally separated from the rest of the sentence by commas:

> **La verdad es que yo mi infancia y mi adolescencia las recuerdo, como una época muy feliz.**
> The truth is that I remember my childhood and adolescence as being a very happy time.

However, longer topics do usually have a comma:

> **Los otros niños que conocía en aquel entonces y en cuyos juegos no me gustaba participar, creía que me detestaban.**
> I thought that the other children I knew at that time, whose games I did not like joining in with, hated me.

1.7　Capital letters

Spanish does not use capital letters in certain cases where English does:

(a) With days of the week and months of the year:

> **Los martes visito a mi abuela.**
> On Tuesdays I visit my grandmother.

> **En agosto suele hacer mucho calor.**
> In August it is usually very hot.

(b) With adjectives and nouns expressing nationality or other affiliation:

> **Juan es francés.**
> Juan is French.

> **No sé si es católica, protestante, judía o musulmana.**
> I don't know whether she is a Catholic, a Protestant, a Jew or a Muslim.

> **Voté por los nacionalistas.**
> I voted for the Nationalists.

(c) In titles of books, etc., Spanish capitalizes only the first word:

> *El amor en los tiempos del cólera*
> *Love in the Time of Cholera*

2
Gender and gender agreements

2.1 **Masculine and feminine**

All nouns in Spanish belong to either the masculine (m.) or the feminine (f.) gender. By 'gender' we mean a grammatical property which applies to animate and inanimate notions alike: gender does not necessarily have anything to do with biological gender or sex. Pronouns must reflect the gender of the noun for which they stand. Adjectives, articles, possessives and demonstratives must agree in gender with the noun or pronoun to which they relate.

> **un chico** (m.) **alto** (m.)   a tall boy
> **La casa** (f.) **está limpia** (f.).   The house is clean.

It is important to remember to make such agreements even when the noun is not overtly present:

> **¡Está muy rica** (f.)**!** (a comment on a **paella** (f.))
> It's quite delicious!

> **Encantada** (f.) **de conocerle.** (when the speaker is female)
> Pleased to meet you.

● 29.4.2 (p. 156)

> **¿Listas** (f. pl.) **ya?** (speaking to a group of girls)
> Ready?

2.2 **Plural**

Complications may arise with agreements in the plural (pl.) when agreement has to be made with a group of nouns of different genders. Normally, the masculine plural is used if the group refers to or involves one or more masculine nouns:

> **hombres** (m.) **y mujeres** (f.) **muy viejos** (m. pl.)
> very old men and women

> **Tengo muy buenos amigos** (m. pl.).
> I have very good friends. (the friends may be male, or a mixture of male and female)

However, because the juxtaposition of a noun and adjective of different genders sounds odd in Spanish, this rule is sometimes broken:

> **un antiguo sillón de brazos** (m. pl.) **y patas** (f. pl.) **doradas** (f. pl.)
> an antique armchair with gilded arms and feet

In practice, Spanish speakers tend to avoid such constructions if possible.

2.3 General rules for gender

Although a number of rules for the gender of nouns can be given to help learners, genders of Spanish nouns which refer to inanimate things are essentially arbitrary. It is best to learn the gender of a noun along with the noun itself, by remembering the form of the definite article that goes with it: **la cárcel** (f.) 'prison', **el avión** (m.) 'aeroplane'. Here are some of the more general rules, but note that they do have exceptions.

- Nouns referring to males are masculine.
- Nouns referring to females are feminine.
- Nouns ending in **-o**, **-or**, **-aje**, **-men**, **-gen** are masculine.
  But note **la mano** (f.) 'hand'.
- Nouns ending in **-a**, **-ad**, **-ed**, **-ud**, **-ión**, **-umbre**, **-ie** are feminine.
  But a large number of nouns in *-a* which refer to males, e.g. **el artista** (m.) 'artist', **el policía** (m.) 'policeman', and many abstract nouns ending in *-ma* are masculine, e.g. **el problema** (m.) 'problem', **el tema** (m.) 'topic', 'theme'.

2.4 Words which are both masculine and feminine

Quite a large number of nouns may be either masculine or feminine, and vary in meaning accordingly, e.g.:

el guía (m.) 'guide' (person)	**la guía** (f.) 'guide' (book)
el corte (m.) 'cut'	**la corte** (f.) 'court', 'capital'
el orden (m.) 'order' (sequence)	**la orden** (f.) 'order' (command)
el margen (m.) 'margin' (of a page)	**la margen** (f.) 'river bank'

2.5 Nouns which vary in gender

A relatively small number of nouns vary in gender. Two of the most frequently used are:

- **mar** 'sea', which is normally masculine, but is often used as a feminine by those who work on or by the sea.
- **radio** 'radio', which is feminine in Spain but masculine in many parts of Latin America (**el radio** also means 'radius').

2.6 Agreement classes of adjectives

There are several diferent patterns of agreement for adjectives in Spanish:

Class 1. Masculine singular ending in **-o**:

	Singular	Plural
Masculine	**bueno**	**buenos**
Feminine	**buena**	**buenas**

Class 2. Masculine singular ending in **-e**, a consonant or a stressed vowel (but there are many exceptions, constituted by Group 3 below):

	Singular	Plural
Masculine	**triste**	**tristes**
Feminine	**triste**	**tristes**

	Singular	Plural
Masculine	**feliz**	**felices**
Feminine	**feliz**	**felices**

	Singular	Plural
Masculine	**israelí**	**israelíes**
Feminine	**israelí**	**israelíes**

Class 3. A large number of adjectives ending in a consonant in the masculine singular, especially those ending in **-or** when this denotes an agent, **-án**, the suffixes **-ón** and **-ín**, and adjectives denoting nationality or membership of another grouping. The common link is that such adjectives are typically used of people, and are very often used as nouns in their own right:

	Singular	Plural
Masculine	**español**	**españoles**
Feminine	**española**	**españolas**

	Singular	Plural
Masculine	**inglés**	**ingleses**
Feminine	**inglesa**	**inglesas**

	Singular	Plural
Masculine	**hablador**	**habladores**
Feminine	**habladora**	**habladoras**

Class 4. An increasing number of words used adjectivally in modern Spanish have no distinct agreement forms. Among these are:

- Many 'modern' colour terms (e.g. **rosa** 'pink', **malva** 'mauve') and colour adjectives modified by **claro** 'bright' and **oscuro** 'dark' (e.g. **libros azul claro** 'bright blue books').
- **Macho** 'male' and **hembra** 'female'.
- Nouns used adjectivally in fixed expressions: **horas** *punta* 'rush hours', **preguntas** *clave* 'key questions', **horas** *extra* 'overtime'.

2.7 The neuter

A 'neuter' gender is traditionally distinguished in Spanish, though no noun belongs to this category. The definite article (and arguably the personal pronouns), demonstratives, possessives and relatives have distinct 'neuter' forms:

Definite article	**lo**
Personal pronoun	**ello, lo**
Demonstratives	**esto, eso, aquello**
Possessives	**lo mío, lo tuyo, lo suyo, lo nuestro, lo vuestro**
Relatives	**lo cual, lo que**

Neuter elements refer to propositions, facts or general ideas expressible as sentences, never to specific nouns:

Lo suspendieron en matemáticas.
He/she failed maths.

Eso me extraña.
That (i.e. the fact that he/she failed maths) surprises me.

but:

Ésta es mi idea.
This (i.e. the idea) is my idea.

Entonces empezó a llorar, lo que me sorprendió bastante.
Then he/she began to cry, which (i.e. the fact that he/she began to cry) surprised me greatly.

but:

Entonces nos propuso otra teoría, con la que no estaba de acuerdo.
Then he/she proposed another theory to us, with which (i.e. the theory) I did not agree.

Sólo me ocupo de lo mío.
I bother only about things that concern me. (general idea)

but:

Sólo me ocupo del mío.
I bother only about mine. (e.g. a book)

El niño no había comido en cuarenta y ocho horas. La madre parecía no hacer caso de ello/él.
The child had not eaten for forty eight hours. The mother appeared not to notice this (i.e. the fact that he had not eaten)/him (i.e. the child himself).

2.8 *Lo*

(a) **Lo** + adjective (always m. sg.) corresponds to such notions in English as 'the . . . thing', 'the . . . aspect':

> **lo bueno y lo malo**
> the good and the bad

> **Lo gracioso fue que entonces no sabía qué decir.**
> The funny thing was that he/she didn't know what to say then.

> **en lo arriba expuesto**
> in what has been said above

> **lo mejor de Madrid**
> the best aspects of Madrid

(b) **Lo** + adjective (variable according to noun referred to) corresponds to 'how . . .' (see **12.1**):

> **No sabes lo bonitas que son las flores.**
> You don't know how beautiful the flowers are.

(c) **Lo** + **de** is equivalent to English 'the matter of', 'the business of' (the expression often has a rather pejorative overtone):

> **en lo del tráfico de intereses**
> in the insider dealing business

(d) **Lo que** is sometimes used as an alternative to **qué** in indirect questions (see **12.2**):

> **Pregúntales lo que/qué quieren.**
> Ask them what they want.

3
Plurals and number agreement

Plural forms

Spanish nouns and adjectives form their plurals as follows:

Class 1. Singulars ending in an unstressed vowel add -s:

la mesa 'table'	**las mesas** 'tables'
el banco 'bank'	**los bancos** 'banks'
valiente 'brave' (sg.)	**valientes** 'brave' (pl.)

Class 2. Singulars ending in a consonant add -es:

el lápiz 'pencil'	**los lápices** 'pencils'
inglés 'English' (sg.)	**ingleses** 'English' (pl.)
el rey 'king'	**los reyes** 'kings'; 'king and queen'

Class 3. There is some inconsistency with singulars ending in a stressed vowel: those ending in -**í** add -**es**; those ending in other stressed vowels tend increasingly simply to add -**s**, although some older words ending in -**ú** add -**es**:

iraní 'Iranian' (sg.)	**iraníes** 'Iranian' (pl.)
el sofá 'sofa'	**los sofás** 'sofas'
el menú 'menu'	**los menús** 'menus'
el café 'café'	**los cafés** 'cafés'
el tabú 'taboo'	**los tabúes** 'taboos'

Class 4. Singulars ending with -s in an unstressed syllable do not change in the plural:

el martes 'Tuesday'	**los martes** 'Tuesdays'

Class 5. There is quite a lot of variation in the formation of the plural of foreign words, and no hard and fast rule can be given. In particular, English loanwords sometimes keep the English form of the plural, and Latin words ending in -**m** are treated similarly:

el córner 'corner' (in football)	**los córners** 'corners'
el referéndum 'referendum'	**los referéndums** 'referendums'/'referenda'

but those words which are very firmly established in the language are adapted to the rules for Spanish words:

el dólar 'dollar'	**los dólares** 'dollars'
el film 'film'	**los filmes** 'films'

Some Latin loanwords do not change in the plural:

el déficit 'deficit'   **los déficit** 'deficits'

3.1.2 In all the above cases, the stress pattern of the singular is kept in the plural (and so adjustments in spelling sometimes have to be made, e.g. **el origen** 'origin'/**los orígenes** 'origins'. However, there are three words in which the stress is changed in the plural:

el carácter 'character'   **los caracteres** 'characters'
el régimen 'régime'; 'diet'   **los regímenes** 'régimes', 'diets'
el espécimen 'specimen'   **los especímenes** 'specimens'

3.1.3 Compound nouns which are written as one word follow the rules given in **3.1.1**:

el altavoz 'loudspeaker'   **los altavoces** 'loudspeakers'
el sacacorchos 'corkscrew'   **los sacacorchos** 'corkscrews'

3.1.4 Many nouns used adjectivally (see **2.6** *Class 4*) are invariable in the plural.

3.1.5 When surnames are used in the plural to indicate a family, they are usually left in the singular form:

los Moreno 'the Morenos'
los Pérez 'the Pérez family'

3.2 Number agreement

3.2.1 Adjectives agree in number (i.e. they are singular or plural) with the noun or noun phrase to which they relate:

unas cuestiones (pl.) **candentes** (pl.)
some burning questions

distintas (pl.) **interpretaciones** (pl.) **de las cifras**
various interpretations of the figures

A combination of two singular nouns in a noun phrase is equivalent to a plural:

el lápiz (sg.) **y el bolígrafo** (sg.) **rojos** (pl.)
the red pencil and biro

If the adjective precedes a combination of singular nouns, however, it is usually left in the singular to avoid an odd-sounding sequence:

con enorme (sg.) **cuidado** (sg.) **y precisión** (sg.)
with enormous care and precision

3.2.2 **Agreement between subject and verb**

3.2.2.1 The verb agrees in number with its subject, whatever its position:

El tren llega a las ocho.   The train arrives at eight.
Cantan los pájaros.   The birds are singing.

3.2.2.2 There is some variation with subjects which function as collective nouns, such as **la mayoría** 'the majority', **la mitad** 'half', **el resto** 'the rest', etc. Strictly speaking, since these nouns are singular, they take a singular verb; but because they denote a plural idea, there is a strong tendency to use a plural verb instead, especially when a plural noun is involved too:

> **La mayoría no estaba(n) de acuerdo.**
> The majority did not agree.

> **La mitad de los jóvenes no querían salir.**
> Half the young people did not want to go out.

3.2.2.3 When **haber** is used in the sense of 'there is', 'there are', it is always singular, no matter whether the noun that goes with it is singular or plural (you may sometimes hear a plural used by speakers from some regions, but this is not regarded as grammatically 'correct'):

> **Habrá muchos invitados.**   There will be many guests.

▶ **38.1** (p. 226)

3.2.2.4 **Ser** agrees with the noun that follows it rather than with its subject:

> **El problema son los otros.**
> The problem is other people.

4
The articles

Definite article

The definite article forms of Spanish (corresponding to English 'the') are:

	Singular	Plural
Masculine	**el**	**los**
Feminine	**la**	**las**

The article agrees with its noun in number and gender:

> **el árbol** (m. sg.) 'the tree'
> **el policía** (m. sg.) 'the policeman'
> **la carta** (f. sg.) 'the letter'
> **la mano** (f. sg.) 'the hand'
> **los muchachos** (m. pl.) 'the boys'
> **las manifestaciones** (f. pl.) 'the demonstrations'

Before singular feminine nouns beginning with stressed **a-** or **ha-**, **el** is used instead of **la**:

> **el agua** (f. sg.) 'water'
> **el hambre** (f. sg.) 'hunger'

But:

> **las armas** (f. pl.) 'arms', 'weapons'

NOTE These nouns remain *feminine*, and other agreements are made accordingly:

> **el agua fría**
> 'cold water'

If the article does not directly precede the noun, then it reverts to **la**:

> **la siempre aborrecida hambre**
> 'ever-loathed hunger'

There are also some exceptions to this rule, most notably **la a** 'the letter "a"' and **La Haya** 'The Hague'.

See also **2.7–2.8** for the 'neuter' article **lo**, which is not used with nouns.

4.2 ## Principal differences between the use of the definite article in Spanish and English

The Spanish definite article is used:

(a) With abstract nouns:

¿Qué es la verdad? What is truth?

(b) With plural nouns used generically:

Las ovejas son animales mansos.
Sheep are gentle creatures.

(c) With singular nouns which denote a substance ('mass' nouns):

El vino es caro.
Wine is expensive.

Me sienta mal el café.
Coffee doesn't agree with me.

Contrast:

Tenemos vino. We have (some) wine.

With these may be included names of colours (which have no article after a preposition):

El negro es un color de mala suerte.
Black is an unlucky colour.

but:

una película en blanco y negro
a black and white film

(d) With titles and similar expressions:

El señor Sánchez no está.	Sr. Sánchez isn't in.
el Rey Alfonso X	King Alfonso X
en el capítulo once	in chapter eleven
en la página 23	on page 23

(e) With days of the week and seasons:

Llegó el martes pasado.
He/she arrived last Tuesday.

La primavera es la estación más hermosa del año.
Spring is the most beautiful season of the year.

(f) With names of countries which are qualified, or which are masculine:

There is a strong tendency today not to use the definite article with names of countries unless the country is qualified with an adjectival phrase. But formerly names of countries which were masculine took the definite article, and there is accordingly some variation in usage in this area. An exception to this general trend is **la India** 'India'.

en España	in Spain
en (el) Perú	in Peru

but:

en la España de la posguerra	in postwar Spain

The article is retained in names of countries which have a complex title, though **los Estados Unidos** may drop the article (in which case it is treated as singular):

en los Emiratos Árabes Unidos
in the United Arab Emirates

en (los) Estados Unidos
in the United States

Estados Unidos ha declarado que . . .
The United States has said that . . .

(g) With names of languages:

The definite article is used with names of languages except after **hablar** 'to speak', **saber** 'to know' and the preposition **en** 'in':

El japonés es muy difícil.
Japanese is very difficult.

¿Sabes español?
Do you know Spanish?

Traducir al inglés.
Translate into English.

but:

Hablo japonés.	I speak Japanese.
en ruso	in Russian

After **aprender** 'to learn', **entender** 'to understand' and **estudiar** 'to study', the definite article is also usually omitted.

▶ **37.3** (p. 224); **40.3** (p. 240)

4.3 Definite article + *que* and *de*

The forms of the definite article are also used with **que** and with **de**.

4.3.1 **El que, la que, los que** and **las que** form one of the relative pronouns (see **11**); they also have the meaning of 'he, (etc.) who':

Los que habían perdido el bolígrafo no podían escribir.
Those who had lost their pens could not write.

Este niño es el que viste entrar ayer.
This little boy is the one you saw coming in yesterday.

El que, etc., also has the meaning 'the fact that':

> **El que no hubiera contestación me sorprendió.**
> The fact that there was no reply surprised me.

4.3.2 **El de, la de, los de** and **las de** have the meaning 'the one(s) belonging to':

> **Los de Barcelona se juntaron en el pasillo.**
> Those from Barcelona gathered in the corridor.

> **¿Me dejas otra máquina de escribir? La de mi hermano no funciona.**
> Can you lend me another typewriter? My brother's isn't working.

4.4   The indefinite article

The indefinite article forms of Spanish (corresponding to English 'a(n)' in the singular and 'some' in the plural) are:

	Singular	Plural
Masculine	**un**	**unos**
Feminine	**una**	**unas**

As with the definite article (see **4.1**), the indefinite article agrees with its noun in number and gender:

> **un niño** (m. sg.) 'a child'
> **una mesa** (f. sg.) 'a table'
> **un problema** (m. sg.) 'a problem'
> **unos libros** (m. pl.) 'some books'
> **unas mujeres** (f. pl.) 'some women'

Un is used instead of **una** before singular feminine nouns beginning with stressed **a**- or **ha**- in the same way as **el** is used instead of **la** (see **4.1**).

NOTE   The full form **uno** may be used before an adjective: it may be thought of as a numeral in such cases and always has the meaning 'one'. Contrast:

> **Un valiente rescató a la princesa.**
> A brave man rescued the princess.

> **Entre los muchos soldados que lucharon sólo había uno valiente.**
> Amongst the many soldiers who fought there was only one brave one.

4.5   Principal differences between the use of the indefinite article in Spanish and English

The indefinite article is *not* used:

(a) With nouns following **ser** which denote a profession, rank, religion or political affiliation, unless they are qualified by an adjective or adjectival phrase:

Elena es profesora.	Elena is a teacher.
Es general de ejército.	He is an army general.

but

Es un socialista tradicional.	He's a traditional socialist.

34.6 (p. 208)

(b) With **tal** and **cierto** 'a certain', and **otro** 'another':

Nunca he visto tal cosa.
I've never seen such a thing.

con cierta ironía
with a certain irony

(there is, however, an increasing tendency to use the indefinite article with **cierto**)

Me trae otra cerveza, por favor.
Bring me another beer, please.

(c) When a class of noun is implied:

No tenemos coche.	We don't have a car.

but:

Tenemos un coche en Francia.	We have a car in France.

4.6 Use of the plural *unos, unas*

(a) **Unos, unas** is used as the equivalent of English 'some' (also rendered by Spanish **algunos, algunas**, see **13.3**), especially when 'some' is stressed contrastively:

Unas personas se levantaron mientras que otras quedaban sentadas.
Some people stood up while others remained seated.

(b) **Unos, unas** may have the meaning 'approximately':

Unos treinta jóvenes estaban platicando en el pasillo.
About thirty youngsters were chatting in the corridor.

(c) **Unos, unas** also has the meaning of 'a pair of' with nouns which permit such an interpretation:

Llevaba unas gafas de sol muy de moda.
He/she was wearing a pair of very trendy sunglasses.

5
Adjectives

Adjectives agree in number and gender with the noun to which they relate (for examples see **2.6, 3.1.1, 3.2.1**).

5.1 Shortening of adjectives

Some adjectives are shortened when used before a singular masculine noun or before another adjective which precedes a singular masculine noun, e.g.:

> **el primer día del verano** 'the first day of summer'
> **tu primer gran éxito** 'your first great success'

But:

> **de primera clase** 'first-class'

Such adjectives are:

Full form	Shortened form
alguno	algún
bueno	buen
malo	mal
ninguno	ningún
primero	primer
tercero	tercer

(a) **Grande** is shortened to **gran** before any singular noun:

> **un gran error** 'a great mistake'
> **la gran sala** 'the large hall'

But sometimes in literary style the full form is used in the meaning of 'great', 'highly regarded':

> **Fue obra de aquel grande escritor.**
> It was a work by that great writer.

(b) **Cualquiera** is shortened to **cualquier** before any singular noun (see also **13.5**):

> **cualquier día** 'any day'
> **cualquier chica** 'any girl'

(c) **Santo** is shortened to **san** before male names unless such names begin with **To-** or **Do-**:

> **San Andrés** 'Saint Andrew'
> **Santo Tomás** 'Saint Thomas'

5.2 Adjective position

36.1 (p. 212)

Adjective position in Spanish generally depends on the relation between the noun and the adjective. It is very extensively manipulated for stylistic effect, and so adjective placement is rarely 'right' or 'wrong'.

5.2.1 Adjectives placed *after* the noun:

(a) Denote a distinctive or contrastive attribute of the noun; adjectives denoting nationality, place of origin, shape, substance, purpose, colour, etc., therefore very often follow their noun:

> **el gobierno francés** 'the French government'
> **una costumbre asturiana** 'an Asturian custom'
> **una venda triangular** 'a triangular bandage'
> **pintura metálica** 'metalic paint'
> **el año escolar** 'the school year'
> **una casa verde** 'a green house'

(b) Denote a sub-group or particular type of the noun concerned:

> **los libros técnicos** 'technical books'
> **un rasgo geográfico** 'a geographical feature'
> **flores silvestres** 'wild flowers'

NOTE If in English an adjective is stressed, the corresponding adjective in Spanish usually follows the noun, e.g. 'Bring me the *red* pencils (not the *green* ones)', **Tráeme los lápices rojos (no los verdes)**.

5.2.2 Adjectives placed before the noun:

(a) Usually express a non-distinctive property of the noun, especially a feature that is expected or well-known:

> **los feroces tigres de la selva** 'the fierce jungle tigers'
> **mi linda amiga** 'my pretty girlfriend'
> **la madrileña calle de Serrano** 'the Calle Serrano in Madrid'
> **la dura vida de los mineros** 'the hard life of miners'

(b) May have a non-literal or ironical meaning:

> **ni un triste céntimo**
> not (even) a miserable cent

¡Valiente amigo eres tú!
You're a fine friend! (ironical)

5.2.3 **Some contrasting examples:**

los blancos cisnes
'white swans' (implies whiteness is a natural attribute of swans)

los cisnes blancos
'the *white* swans' (a sub-group of swans in general, as opposed to, say, black ones)

la prestigiosa institución
'the prestigious institution' (an institution which is known to be prestigious, e.g. the Spanish Academy)

la institución prestigiosa
'the *prestigious* institution' (singling one institution out in contrast to others which are not prestigious)

la trágica muerte de Lorca
'Lorca's tragic death' (Lorca's death is known to have been tragic.)

Lorca tuvo una muerte trágica.
'Lorca had a tragic death.' (distinguishing the kind of death Lorca had)

Es un auténtico enigma.
'It's a real enigma.' (intensifying, not literally 'real')

Es un diamante auténtico.
'It's a real diamond.' (real as opposed to fake, the literal meaning of 'real')

5.2.4 Adjectives denoting a number or quantity normally precede the noun:

de todas maneras 'in any case'
muchísimas preguntas 'very many questions'
en determinados casos 'in certain cases'
numerosas familias 'numerous (i.e. many) families'

contrast:

familias numerosas 'large families'

5.2.5 Other adjectives normally placed before the noun are:

dicho 'the aforementioned'
llamado 'so-called'
mero 'mere'
otro '(an)other'

5.2.6 There are a number of adjectives which have a rather different meaning according to whether they precede or follow the noun:

	Following	Preceding
antiguo	old	former
cierto	sure	certain
diferentes	different	several
distintos	different	several
grande	big	great
medio	average, middle	half
mismo	self	same
nuevo	brand new	new, another
pobre	poor (i.e. not rich)	miserable
propio	of one's own	very
puro	pure	sheer
simple	simple	mere
único	unique	only
varios	varied	several

36.1 (p. 212)

5.3 Adjectives used as nouns

In Spanish, adjectives are frequently used as nouns:

> **Saludé al viejo.**
> I greeted the old man.

> **¿Quieres un blanco o un tinto?**
> Do you want a white (wine) or a red (wine)?

> **Los más valientes no se dejaron pasmar.**
> The bravest (people) didn't let themselves be frightened.

5.4 Adjectives used as adverbs

English adverbs can often be translated by adjectives in Spanish: see **14.1** (p. 55).

6
Comparative forms of adjectives and adverbs

▶ 37 (p. 219)

6.1   Lack of distinction between 'more . . .' and 'most . . .'

Spanish does not distinguish in quite the same way as English between 'more . . .' (or '. . . -er') and 'most . . .' (or '. . . -est'); both these notions are conveyed by putting **más** before an adjective or adverb. The definite article + **más** + adjective corresponds to English 'the more' ('the . . . -er'), 'the most . . .' ('the . . . -est').

> **ciudades más bellas**
> more beautiful cities

> **las ciudades más bellas del mundo**
> the most beautiful cities in the world

> **¿Cuál es la ciudad más bella?**
> Which is the more/most beautiful city?

> **edificios más altos**
> higher buildings

> **los edificios más altos del mundo**
> the highest buildings in the world

> **¿Cuál es el edificio más alto?**
> Which is the taller/tallest building?

> **¡Habla más despacio!**
> Speak more slowly!

> **Escuché más atentamente.**
> I listened more attentively.

> **¿Quién escucha más atentamente?**
> Who is listening more/most attentively?

Some adjectives and adverbs, however, have special forms:

Adjective	Comparative
bien	**mejor** (**más bien** means 'rather')
bueno	**mejor** (**más bueno** is sometimes used in the sense of 'better in character or behaviour')
grande	**mayor** (always used if the sense is 'older', 'oldest') or **más grande**
mal	**peor**
malo	**peor** (**más malo** is sometimes used in the sense of 'worse in character or behaviour')
mucho	**más**
pequeño	**menor** (always used if the sense is 'younger', 'youngest') or **más pequeño**
poco	**menos**

6.2 For the syntax of comparative constructions, see **37**.

7 Numbers

Cardinal numbers

cero	0
un(o)/-a	1
dos	2
tres	3
cuatro	4
cinco	5
seis	6
siete	7
ocho	8
nueve	9
diez	10
once	11
doce	12
trece	13
catorce	14
quince	15
dieciséis	16
diecisiete	17
dieciocho	18
diecinueve	19
veinte	20
veintiuno (veintiún)/-a	21
veintidós	22
veintitrés	23
veinticuatro	24
veinticinco	25
veintiséis	26
veintisiete	27
veintiocho	28
veintinueve	29
treinta	30
treinta y un(o)/-a	31
cuarenta	40
cincuenta	50
sesenta	60
setenta	70
ochenta	80

noventa	90
cien, ciento	100
ciento un(o)/-a	101
ciento treinta y cinco	135
doscientos/-as	200
trescientos/-as	300
cuatrocientos/-as	400
quinientos/-as	500
seiscientos/-as	600
setecientos/-as	700
ochocientos/-as	800
novecientos/-as	900
mil	1.000
mil un(o)/-a	1.001
mil quinientos/-as treinta y seis	1.536
dos mil	2.000
un millón (de)	1.000.000
dos millones (de)	2.000.000

NOTE In numbers, Spanish practice is to use a full stop to mark off thousands where English uses a comma, e.g. **1.987.656 habitantes** (**un millón novecientos ochenta y siete mil seiscientos cincuenta y seis habitantes** '1,987,656 inhabitants'), and a comma as the decimal point where English uses a full stop, e.g. **97,4 grados** (**noventa y siete coma cuatro grados** 'ninety-seven point four degrees').

(a) Forms involving **un(o)/-a** and **cientos/-as** agree in gender with a following noun. **Un(o)** shortens in the same way as when it is an indefinite article (see **4.4**).

> **doscientas cincuenta liras** 'two hundred and fifty liras'
> **veintiuna libras** 'twenty-one pounds'
> **cincuenta y un libros** 'fifty-one books'

(b) **Ciento** is shortened to **cien** immediately before a noun; **cien** is the form also often used in isolation:

> **cien páginas** 'a hundred pages'
> **el número cien(to)** 'the number one hundred'
> **veinte por ciento** 'twenty per cent'

7.2 Ordinal numbers

primer(o)/-a (see **5.1**)	1st
segundo/-a	2nd
tercer(o)/-a (see **5.1**)	3rd
cuarto/-a	4th
quinto/-a	5th
sexto/-a	6th
séptimo/-a	7th

octavo/-a	8th
noveno/-a	9th
décimo/-a	10th

Although there are ordinal numbers above ten, they are only used in very formal Spanish. In case of need, the cardinal number is used, though an alternative expression can often be found:

el cincuenta aniversario de la revolución 'the fiftieth anniversary of the revolution'

en la página (número) cuarenta y dos 'on the forty-second page'

7.3 Expressions involving numbers

7.3.1 The time

¿Qué hora es?
What time is it?

Es la una; es mediodía; es medianoche.
It's one o'clock; it's midday; it's midnight.

Son las dos.
It's two o'clock.

Son las tres y media.
It's half past three.

Son las cuatro y cuarto.
It's quarter past four.

Son las cinco menos cuarto.
It's quarter to five.

Son las ocho y/menos diez (minutos).
It's ten (minutes) past/to eight.

7.3.2 The date

el dos de mayo 'the second of May'
el (día) uno/el primero de setiembre 'the first of September'
el año mil novecientos ochenta y cuatro 'the year nineteen eighty-four'
el año dos mil (2000) 'the year two thousand'
el siglo diecinueve (XIX) 'the nineteenth century'
el siglo quinto (V) 'the fifth century'

NOTE Roman numerals are always used with centuries in Spanish, unlike in English.

▶ **29.9** (p. 165)

7.3.3   **Kings and queens**

> **Juan Carlos Primero (I)** 'Juan Carlos the First'
> **Alfonso Décimo/Diez (X)** 'Alfonso the Tenth'
> **Luis Catorce (XIV)** 'Louis the Fourteenth'

8
Personal pronouns

► 34 (p. 204)

Spanish distinguishes three persons in both singular and plural: the first person singular ('I', 'me'), the first person plural ('we', 'us'), the second person singular ('you' (only one person)), the second person plural ('you' (more than one person)), the third person singular ('he', 'him'; 'she', 'her', 'it') and the third person plural ('they', 'them').

Most complicated for English speakers is the second person. Not only does Spanish distinguish singular and plural here, but there is also a distinction between *polite* and *familiar* forms of the second person which varies considerably between Spain and Latin America. In Spain, **tú** is extremely common, and tends to be used even between relative strangers unless there is some reason for marking respect. It is not at all unusual to be addressed as **tú** by a shop assistant or a bank clerk if you are the same age or younger than they are, and **tú** is often used in TV interviews in much the same way as first names are used in the English-speaking world. However, such prodigality in the use of the familiar form is not found in some parts of Latin America. You should therefore try and develop a sensitivity to how and when **tú** or **vos** are used here.

8.1 Subject pronouns

8.1.1 The Peninsular system

	Singular	Plural
1st person	**yo**	**nosotros/-as**
2nd person familiar	**tú**	**vosotros/-as**
2nd person polite	**usted**	**ustedes**
3rd person	**él/ella**	**ellos/ellas**

8.1.2 Latin-American systems

These are the same as the Peninsular system except in the second person. There are two different systems:

(a) The *voseo* system (used in many different areas, but particularly in the Río de la Plata area, i.e. Argentina and Uruguay):

	Singular	Plural
2nd person familiar	**vos**	**ustedes**
2nd person polite	**usted**	**ustedes**

(b) The ***tuteo*** system (this is the 'standard' usage in most other Latin-American countries):

	Singular	Plural
2nd person familiar	**tú**	**ustedes**
2nd person polite	**usted**	**ustedes**

Usted and **ustedes** are often abbreviated to **Vd.**, **Vds.** or **Ud.**, **Uds.** in writing. They take a third person verb form everywhere (see **16.1**).

> **Usted no es de aquí, ¿verdad?**
> You're not from here, are you?

> **¡Salgan ustedes!**
> Go out! (pl.)

Vos in the Río de la Plata area has its own special set of verb forms (see **16.1**).

> **Y vos ¿a qué hora comés?**
> And what time do *you* eat?

> **(Vos) sos un ingrato.**
> You're an ungrateful wretch.

In all of Latin America and in many parts of Andalusia, the **vosotros/-as** form is not used, and so the polite/familiar distinction is not made in the plural: **ustedes** (with a third person plural verb form) is the only way of expressing the second person plural. Because **vosotros/as** is nowadays quite frequently used in Spain, this is a major difference between Latin America and Spain. Latin American speakers often sound very formal to Peninsular speakers (and conversely, the **vosotros** forms of Peninsular Spanish sound archaic in Latin America).

8.1.3 The endings of Spanish verbs are sufficient in themselves to indicate the person of the subject, and subject pronouns do not always need to be used:

> **Acabamos de llegar.**
> We've just arrived.

They are used for emphasis and contrast, to avoid ambiguity (especially with third person verb forms, which may be understood as having **él**, **ella** or **usted** as their subject), or, especially with **usted**, to add a nuance of politeness (see **34**):

> **Soy inglés, pero él es escocés.**
> I'm English, but he's Scottish.

> **¡Que conteste ella!**
> Let *her* answer!

> **Él es de Madrid.**
> He's from Madrid.

> Usted no es español, ¿verdad?
> You're not Spanish, are you?

8.2 Object pronouns

Spanish has two kinds of object pronouns:

- Unstressed pronouns: these never receive emphasis, and always appear with a verb.
- Stressed pronouns: these may be stressed, and often duplicate unstressed pronouns to achieve emphasis (see **8.3**). They always follow a preposition.

In the table in **8.2.1** a distinction is made in the third person between direct and indirect object. This important notion is best illustrated by looking at full nouns:

- The direct object undergoes the action of the verb, e.g. **Juan** in **Vi a Juan** 'I saw Juan'.
- The indirect object is, as the term suggests, more indirectly affected by the action of the verb, e.g. **Juan** in **Di un libro a Juan** 'I gave a book to Juan', where **un libro** is the direct object.

However, the distinction between the two is sometimes difficult to perceive in Spanish, where **a** is used with 'personal' direct object nouns (see **25.1.1.1**) as well as with indirect object nouns. In the use of the personal pronouns too there is much variation in usage in the Spanish-speaking world.

8.2.1 Forms

The system which is regarded by many as the standard is given here. If you use the forms given in this table you will not sound especially odd, but you will hear a great deal of variation in the polite form of the second person and in the third person (even from the same speaker!).

	Unstressed pronouns		Stressed pronouns
	Direct object	Indirect object	Prepositional object
1st person sg.	me	me	mí
2nd person sg. informal (see below for **voseo** forms)	te	te	ti
2nd person sg. polite	lo (m.)/la (f.)	le	usted
3rd person sg.	lo (m.)/la (f.)	le	él (m.)/ella (f.)
1st person pl.	nos	nos	nosotros (m.)/ nosotras (f.)
2nd person pl. informal (not in Latin America: see 8.1.2)	os	os	vosotros (m.)/ vosotras (f.)
2nd person pl. polite	los (m.)/las (f.)	les	ustedes
3rd person pl.	los (m.)/las (f.)	les	ellos (m.)/ellas (f.)
Reflexive sg. and pl. (see **23**)	se	se	sí

NOTE | **Ti** does not have a written accent.

In **voseo** areas:

	Direct object	Indirect object	Prepositional object
2nd person sg. informal	**te**	**te**	**vos**

Variations:

(a) **Lo(s)** and **la(s)** are often replaced by **le(s)** when referring to people (see **29.4.2**), especially in central Spain; this is known as **leísmo**. However, **lo(s)** and **la(s)** are generally used for all direct object forms in the south of Spain and in Latin America in preference to **le(s)**, as in the above table; this is known as **loísmo**, and represents the vast majority of speakers. However, there is a great deal of variation in the Spanish-speaking world in this area, especially in Spain, and the use of **le(s)** for **lo(s)** (but not for **la(s)**) is considered an alternative standard.

(b) Not all prepositions take the prepositional forms given here. With **con** 'with', the special forms **conmigo** 'with me', **contigo** 'with you', **consigo** 'with oneself' are used. With **como** 'like', **excepto** and **salvo** 'except' and **según** 'according to', **yo** and **tú** are used instead of **mí** and **ti**. Yo and **tú** are also used in combinations of pronouns, e.g. **entre tú y yo** 'between you and me'.

(c) When **nos** follows a first person plural form in imperative constructions, the verb-form loses the final -**s**:

| **¡Sentémonos!** | Let's sit down! |
| **¡Vámonos!** (see **17.13**) | Let's go! |

(d) When **os** (Peninsula only) follows the second person plural imperative, the verb-form loses the final -**d**:

| **¡Callaos!** | Be quiet! |

8.2.2 Position of object pronouns

8.2.2.1 | ***With respect to the verb***
Object pronouns *precede* finite verb forms (i.e. forms with endings which in themselves indicate the notion of a subject).

| **Me siento cansado.** | I feel tired. |
| **¿Qué le dijiste?** | What did you tell him/her? |

They *follow* infinitives, gerunds and positive imperatives:

antes de saberlo	before knowing it
pensándolo bien	thinking it over
¡Dime!	Tell me!

but:

| **¡No me lo digas!** | You don't say! |

The object pronoun of the infinitive, and gerund complements of a number of common verbs, may be placed before the main verb rather than after the infinitive:

> **No lo quiero recordar,** *or* **No quiero recordarlo.** (see **45.1**)
> I don't want to remember it.

> **Se lo tienes que dar,** *or* **Tienes que dárselo.**
> You have to give it to him.

> **Siempre se está maquillando,** *or* **Siempre está maquillándose.**
> She's always putting on make-up.

To this group of verbs belong:

> **acabar de** + infinitive 'to have just'
> **comenzar a** + infinitive 'to begin to'
> **conseguir** + infinitive 'to succeed in -ing'
> **deber** + infinitive 'must, ought to'
> **dejar de** + infinitive 'to stop -ing'
> **empezar a** + infinitive 'to begin to'
> **estar** + gerund 'to be -ing'
> **intentar** + infinitive 'to try to'
> **ir** + gerund 'to keep on -ing'
> **ir a** + infinitive 'to be going to'
> **lograr** + infinitive 'to succeed in -ing'
> **pensar** + infinitive 'to intend to'
> **poder** + infinitive 'to be able to'
> **querer** + infinitive 'to want to'
> **saber** + infinitive 'to know how to'
> **soler** + infinitive 'usually to'
> **tener que** + infinitive 'to have to'
> **tratar de** + infinitive 'to try to'
> **venir** + gerund 'to have been -ing'
> **volver a** + infinitive 'to do again'

8.2.2.2

With respect to one another
The order of object pronouns is:

1	2	3	4
se	te, os	me, nos	lo, la, le, los, las, les

- **Se** must always stand first. Only one **se** per group can be used, whatever its function (see **23** and **24.4**).
- An indirect object pronoun must always precede a direct object pronoun.
- When **le** or **les** are used in combination with another pronoun of the fourth group, they become **se** and stand in initial position.

Examples:

> **¡Dámelo!**
> Give it to me!

> **Se me olvidó traértela.**
> I forgot to bring it for you.

Se (= **le** *or* **les**) **la entregamos.**
We handed it over to her/him/them/you.

8.3 Reduplicated pronoun structures

(a) Spanish sometimes uses both an unstressed pronoun (e.g. **me**) and an equivalent prepositional phrase with a stressed pronoun (e.g. **a mí**) in order to avoid ambiguity, or for emphasis:

> ¡Dá*selo a ella*!
> Give it to her! (**se** is otherwise ambiguous between 'him', 'her', 'them', 'you')

> *Me* critico a *mí* mismo.
> I'm criticizing *myself*.

(b) An unstressed indirect object pronoun is often used with a full noun indirect object which refers to a person:

> **Dil***e* **a** *Paco* **que se ponga (al teléfono). (29.8.2)**
> Ask Paco to come to the phone.

> **¿Qué** *le* **parece a tu** *padre***? (55.3)**
> What does your father think?

(c) An unstressed pronoun must be used if a direct or indirect object noun or stressed pronoun *precedes* the verb:

> **A** *mis primos* **no** *les* **gustan los deportes.**
> My cousins don't like sports.

> **A** *mí me* **parece que sería peligroso.**
> It seems to *me* that it would be dangerous.

> *Este libro lo* **leí la semana pasada.**
> I read this book last week.

9
Demonstratives

9.1 ## Forms

Spanish distinguishes three demonstratives in contrast to the two of English:

masc. sg.	este	ese	aquel
fem. sg.	esta	esa	aquella
masc. pl.	estos	esos	aquellos
fem. pl.	estas	esas	aquellas
'neuter'	esto	eso	aquello
	'this'	'that'	

All forms except the neuter (see **2.7**) function as both adjectives and pronouns; it is usual (though not obligatory) to mark the pronouns with a written accent (see **1.5.3**):

> **Este** (adjective) **chico me habló ayer.**
> This boy spoke to me yesterday.

> **Éste/Este** (pronoun) **es el chico que me habló ayer.**
> This is the boy who spoke to me yesterday.

► **29.4.2** (p. 156); **35.1** (p. 210)

9.2 ## Order

Demonstrative adjectives *precede* the noun in 'neutral' usage; but they may be placed *after* the noun (in which case the definite article precedes the noun) with an overtone of irony or disrespect, and this is heard very often in speech:

> **Aquel día fue muy difícil.**
> That day was very difficult.

> **La chica esa acabó casándose con un tío muy rico.**
> That (crafty) girl ended up marrying a very rich guy.

Usage

9.3.1 **Este** corresponds more or less to English 'this', i.e. 'relating to me, near to me'. The difference between **ese** and **aquel** is a subtle one; broadly speaking, **ese** relates to notions which are nearby and **aquel** to notions which are more remote. In a conversation, it is often appropriate to think of **ese** as meaning 'relating to us' (the speakers involved) and **aquel** as meaning 'relating to neither of us'. **Aquel** is the more 'marked' of the two, and tends to be used to indicate a notion of remoteness, often in contrast with **ese**.

> **–Me da un kilo de manzanas.**
> 'A kilo of apples, please.'
> **–¿Ésas?**
> 'Those?' (near to you)
> **–No, aquéllas.**
> 'No, those.' (over there)

> **¿Te acuerdas de ese día que pasamos juntos en Benidorm?**
> Do you remember that day (shared experience) we spent together in Benidorm?

> **En aquella noche murieron muchas personas en el bombardeo.**
> That night (remote from our experience) many people died in the bombing.

9.3.2 **Éste** and **aquél** also denote 'the latter' and 'the former' respectively:

> **Juan salió primero, seguido de Pedro. Éste saludó con entusiasmo al público, mientras que aquél no dijo palabra.**
> Juan appeared first, followed by Pedro. The latter greeted the audience enthusiastically while the former did not say a word.

NOTE **Este** is used as a filler in Latin American Spanish (see **30.8.4**).

10
Possessives

10.1 ## Forms

Spanish has two sets of possessives, one *unstressed* and the other *stressed*.

10.1.1 Possessive adjectives which *precede* the noun (unstressed forms):

	Singular		Plural	
	Masculine	Feminine	Masculine	Feminine
1st pers. sg.	mi	mi	mis	mis
2nd pers. sg. familiar	tu	tu	tus	tus
2nd pers. sg. polite	su	su	sus	sus
3rd pers. sg.	su	su	sus	sus
1st pers. pl.	nuestro	nuestra	nuestros	nuestras
2nd pers. pl. familiar	vuestro	vuestra	vuestros	vuestras
2nd pers. pl. (polite form in Spain)	su	su	sus	sus
3rd pers. pl.	su	su	sus	sus

10.1.2 Possessive pronouns and possessive adjectives which *follow* the noun or are freestanding (stressed forms):

	Singular		Plural	
	Masculine	Feminine	Masculine	Feminine
1st pers. sg.	mío	mía	míos	mías
2nd pers. sg. familiar	tuyo	tuya	tuyos	tuyas
2nd pers. sg. polite	suyo	suya	suyos	suyas
3rd pers. sg.	suyo	suya	suyos	suyas
1st pers. pl.	nuestro	nuestra	nuestros	nuestras
2nd pers. pl. familiar	vuestro	vuestra	vuestros	vuestras
2nd pers. pl. (polite form in Spain)	suyo	suya	suyos	suyas
3rd pers. pl.	suyo	suya	suyos	suyas

The 2nd person singular familiar forms are used even in **voseo** areas (see **16**):

¿(Vos) tenés tu libro?   Have you got your book?

Vuestro, etc., are often used to refer to the second person plural, despite the absence of **vosotros**:

> He recibido *vuestro* saludo de fin de año. Siempre es grato tener noticias de *ustedes*.
> I've received your New Year greeting. It's always nice to hear from you.

The gender of the person to which the possessives pertain is irrelevant to their agreement with the noun to which they relate:

> Esos lápices (m.) son suyos (m.).
> Those pencils are hers/his/theirs/yours.

10.2 Usage

10.2.1 Since **su** and **suyo** can refer to a number of different notions, **de** + stressed personal pronoun (see **8.2.1**) is sometimes used instead in cases of potential ambiguity:

> Este es el libro de ella.   This is her book.
> ¿Estas maletas son de usted?   Are these cases yours?

10.2.2 The stressed forms are used as follows:

10.2.2.1 *As pronouns:*
The definite article is used except when the pronoun is introduced by the verb **ser** or understood as such.

> Me gusta tu casa, pero la nuestra es más grande.
> I like your house, but ours is larger.

> La responsabilidad fue mía.
> The responsibility was mine.

> –¿Esta casa es de tu padre?
> 'Is this house your father's?'
> –No, (es) mía.
> 'No, mine.'

10.2.2.2 *As adjectives:*
(a) Corresponding to English 'of mine', etc. An indefinite article or a demonstrative, used in the normal way, may precede the noun:

> Un colega mío me contó . . .
> A colleague of mine told me . . .

> Ese problema tuyo no es tan fácil de resolver.
> That problem of yours is not so easy to solve.

> Es pariente nuestro.
> He's a relation of ours.

(b) In forms of address:

> Pero, amigo mío . . .   But, my friend . . .
> Muy señor mío (see **29.9**)   Dear Sir (beginning a letter)

10.2.2.3   Special uses:

(a) **Suyo** has the meaning of 'particular', 'of one's own':

> **Tiene una estructura muy suya.**
> It has a structure all of its own.

(b) The stressed form of the possessive is sometimes used in place of **de** + stressed pronoun, especially in Latin-American spoken Spanish and in some idioms:

> **alrededor mío** (Latin American) (= **alrededor de mí**) 'around me'
> **a pesar suyo** (idiom) 'in spite of him/her/them'

(c) See also the neuter use of the possessives (see **2.7**).

11
Relative pronouns

There is a fair amount of flexibility in the choice of relatives in Spanish, and preferences rather than rules often govern this choice.

11.1 Que

Que is invariable. It is the most 'neutral' of the relatives, and is used freely as a subject and object relative pronoun, as well as often being used with the 'short' prepositions **a**, **con**, **de** and **en**, especially when the pronoun refers to something *inanimate*:

> **el chico que me saludó**
> the boy who greeted me

> **el chico que vi ayer**
> the boy I saw yesterday

> **el acuerdo a que llegaron**
> the agreement they came to

> **la escopeta con que le amenacé**
> the shotgun I threatened him with

> **el libro de que te hablaba**
> the book I was talking to you about

> **la ciudad en que vives**
> the town you live in

11.2 El que/el cual, etc.

	Singular	Plural
Masculine	**el que**	**los que**
Feminine	**la que**	**las que**

	Singular	Plural
Masculine	**el cual**	**los cuales**
Feminine	**la cual**	**las cuales**

45

(a) **El que**, etc. can also mean 'he who', 'the one which', etc. (see **4.3.1**). **El que** (but none of the other forms given here) is also used as a complementizer (see **26.1.1**).

(b) **El que/el cual** etc. are preferred

● when there is a break in intonation (a comma in print) between the antecedent noun and the relative clause:

> **Llegó otro turista, el cual se quejó de los precios.**
> Another tourist, who complained about the prices, arrived.

● when the relative pronoun refers to a specific person or object:

> **Esta es la iglesia en la que nos casamos.**
> This is the church we got married in.

(c) **El que/el cual** etc. are *not* normally used when they immediately follow their antecedent noun and there is no break in intonation (no comma in print):

> **El chico que conociste en México era mi hermano.** (el cual or el que would sound very odd here)
> The boy you met in Mexico was my brother.

(d) **El que/el cual** (or **quien(es)**) *must* be used after a preposition other than those mentioned above, or with **a** and **de** when these have a directional meaning such as 'to(wards)', 'from':

> **Yo escuchaba lo que decía mi tío, según el cual la empresa podría ser muy peligrosa.**
> I was listening to my uncle, according to whom the enterprise could be very dangerous.

> **A lo lejos divisé una iglesia, a la que me dirigí con paso alegre.**
> In the distance I made out a church, to which I made my way happily.

(e) See also neuter **lo que, lo cual** (see **2.7**).

11.3 *Quien(es)*

(a) **Quien** (pl. **quienes**) refers only to *people*, and may be used in more or less the same circumstances as **el que/el cual**.

> **la chica a quien quiere**
> the girl he loves

> **Isabel quería ir a ver a su madre, quien estaba muy enferma.**
> Isabel wanted to go and see her mother, who was very ill.

> **el estudiante hacia quien ibas**
> the student you were going towards

(b) **Quien(es)**, like **el que**, etc. (see **4.3.1**), also has the meaning of 'he who', etc.

> **Quien no tenga dinero no puede entrar.**
> Those who have no money cannot come in.

▶ 18.2.5 (p. 90)

11.4 *Cuyo* (adj.)

Cuyo corresponds to English 'whose', 'of which':

> **el chico cuyo libro pedí prestado**
> the boy whose book I asked to borrow

> **el atentado, cuyo motivo desconocemos todavía**
> the outrage, the motive for which we still do not know

> **la niña a cuyo lado dormía un cachorrito**
> the girl at whose side a little puppy was sleeping

Cuyo agrees with the noun following it, not with its antecedent noun:

> **la empresa cuyos productos comprábamos**
> the firm whose products we used to buy

12
Interrogative and exclamatory forms

NOTE | Interrogative and exclamatory elements always carry a written accent, whether in direct or indirect questions and exclamations (see **1.5.3**).

▶ 29.3 (p. 155); 30.3 (p. 172); 31.2 (p. 187); 36.2 (p. 214); 43.1 (p. 253)

12.1 ¿Cómo?/¡Cómo!

¿Cómo está usted?
How are you?

¿Cómo es tu novia? (see **36.2**)
What is your girlfriend like?

¿Cómo no me lo advertiste? (see **43.1**)
Why didn't you warn me?

¡Cómo trabaja mi hermana!
How my sister works!

Pedro me preguntó cómo lo sabía.
Pedro asked me how I knew.

Of all the interrogatives/exclamations, English 'how' + adjective is the one which offers most complexity in Spanish. Often Spanish has a completely different structure from English:

¿Cómo es de grande?
How big is it?

¿Cuánto tiene de largo/ancho/alto?
How long/wide/high is it?

¡Qué cansado estoy!
How tired I am.

No sabía lo atrevida (note agreement, see **2.8**) **que era.**
I never knew how daring she was.

12.2 ***¿Cuál? and ¿Qué?/¡Qué!***

 35.3 (p. 211)

In standard usage, **cuál** is used only as a pronoun (although it is sometimes found with adjectival force, this is not generally regarded as correct). **Qué** may be a pronoun or may be used with a noun rather like an adjective. **Cuál** has a more specific reference than **qué**, and the distinction often corresponds to English 'which/what'.

> **¿Cuál quieres?**
> Which (one) do you want?
>
> **¿Qué quieres?**
> What (indefinite) do you want?
>
> **¿Qué edad tienes?** (see **34.4**)
> What age are you?
>
> **¿En qué fecha naciste?** (see **34.5**)
> On what date were you born?
>
> **¡Qué lástima!**
> What a pity!
>
> **¿Sabes qué** (also **lo que**, see **2.7**) **hizo después?**
> Do you know what he/she did then?

NOTE   In an exclamation, when the noun is accompanied by an adjective, Spanish uses **más** or **tan** in front of the adjective, which *follows* the noun:

> **¡Qué chico más/tan listo!**
> What a clever boy!

(a) Standard Spanish cannot express the difference between English 'which'/'what book do you mean?' without using different constructions:

> **¿Qué libro quieres decir?**
> Which/what book do you mean?
>
> **¿Qué llaves?** (see **31.5**)
> Which keys?
>
> **¿Cuál de los libros compraste?**
> Which book (= which of the books) did you buy?

(b) As pronouns, **cuál** and **qué** are not distinguished in quite the same way as English 'which' and 'what'. **Cuál** tends to correspond to English 'what' in a number of cases where a selection is implied, whereas **qué** again has a less specific meaning; though this is not a hard and fast rule:

> **¿Cuál es su nombre?** (see **34.1**)
> What is your name?
>
> **¿Cuál fue la razón?** (see **43.1**)
> What was the reason?

but:

¿Qué haces esta noche?	What are you doing tonight?
¿En qué consiste la verdad?	What does truth consist of?

12.3 ¿Cuándo?

¿Cuándo nació usted?	When were you born?
No sé cuándo salió.	I don't know when he/she left.

12.4 ¿Cuánto?/¡Cuánto!

Cuánto is used both as a pronoun and as an adjective:

¿Cuánto vale?
How much does it cost?

¿Cuántos años tienes?
How old are you?

¡Cuánto lo siento!
I'm so sorry!

¡Cuántas horas llevo esperando!
What a long time I've been waiting!

Pregúntale cuántos quiere.
Ask him/her how many he/she wants.

12.5 ¿Dónde?/¿Adónde?

Adónde (a + dónde) is used when the meaning is 'where to' ('whither'). **Dónde** also combines with certain other prepositions.

¿Dónde estabais? (see 39.1)	Where were you?
¿Adónde vas?	Where are you going (to)?
¿Por dónde pasó?	Where did it go through?

12.6 ¿Para qué?/¿Por qué?

Por qué (note that this is written as *two* words) and **para qué** both correspond to English 'why': their use follows that of **por** and **para** (see 25.1.22–25.1.23), **por qué** enquiring about cause and **para qué** enquiring about purpose:

¿Por qué tardastes tanto en llegar?
Why (= for what reason) did you take so long to get here?

¿Para qué sirve este aparato?
What is this gadget for (= what is its purpose)?

> **No sé por qué vino.**
> I don't know why he/she came.

▶ **43.1** (p. 253)

12.7 *¿Qué tal?*

Qué tal is an alternative to **cómo**, used predominantly in speech:

> **¿Qué tal es tu piso?** (see **36.2**)
> What is your flat like?

> **¿Qué tal tus vacaciones?** (see **36.2**)
> What were your holidays like?

▶ **36.2** (p. 214)

12.8 *¿Quién (es)?*

> **¿Quién habla?** (see **29.8, 35.1**)
> Who's speaking?

> **¿Con quiénes estaba?**
> Who (pl.) was he/she with?

NOTE | **Quién** agrees in number with the noun it implies.

▶ **35.1** (p. 210); **40.4** (p. 240)

12.9 *¿Verdad?, ¿no?*

¿Verdad? and **¿no?** are added to the end of a sentence to form tag questions in Spanish, corresponding to a host of English expressions related to the main verb of the sentence: 'doesn't it?', 'wasn't she?', 'won't he?', etc.

> **Fernando no escuchaba, ¿verdad?**
> Fernando wasn't listening, was he?

> **Mañana hay que madrugar, ¿no?**
> Tomorrow we must get up early, mustn't we?

▶ **30.4.5** (p. 174); **31.1.3** (p. 186)

13

Indefinite and negative pronouns and adjectives

Indefinite pronouns and adjectives denote very general, unspecific concepts, like 'someone', 'something'. Many of them have negative counterparts, like 'nobody', 'nothing'.

13.1 *Alguno* and *ninguno*

(a) **Alguno** as an adjective has the meaning 'some', and agrees with its noun in the normal way (see **2** and **3**). It is shortened to **algún** before a masculine singular noun (see **5.1**). **Ninguno** 'no', its negative counterpart, behaves similarly, although **ninguno** is nowadays rarely used in the plural.

> **algunas flores** 'some flowers'
> **algún libro** 'some book'
> **ninguna manzana** 'no apple(s)'

(b) **alguno** may be used *after* a singular noun with a negative meaning (the equivalent of **ninguno**):

> **No tengo libro alguno.**
> I haven't got a single book.

(c) **Alguno** and **ninguno** (the latter again only in the singular) are also used as pronouns:

> **Alguna de ellas intentó contestar.**
> One of them tried to answer.
>
> **Algunos murmuraron contra el presidente.**
> Some grumbled about the president.
>
> **Ninguno de mis amigos estaba dispuesto a ayudarme.**
> None of my friends was prepared to help me.

13.2 *Alguien* and *nadie*

Alguien has the meaning 'someone', 'somebody': It is invariable. **Nadie** 'no one', 'nobody', is its negative counterpart.

Alguien ha mentido.
Someone has lied.

Vi a alguien en el jardín.
I saw somebody in the garden.

Nadie lo sabe.
No one knows.

No vino nadie.
Nobody came.

13.3 *Uno*

(a) **Uno** means '(any)one' (see also **7.1**):

una de las mujeres 'one of the women'

(b) **Uno** is an alternative to **alguno** (see also **4.4** and **4.6**):

¿Tienes algún problema?
Do you have a problem?

unos amigos franceses
some French friends

(c) **Uno** as an indefinite pronoun also corresponds to English 'one', 'people', and similarly often includes reference to the first person. If the indefinite reference is exclusively to females, or if the speaker is female, then the feminine form **una** is used.

Uno no sabe qué hacer.
One doesn't know what to do.

Una se siente muy amenazada andando por las calles.
A girl feels very threatened walking through the streets.

13.4 *Algo* and *nada*

Tengo algo que decirte.	I have something to tell you.
No vi nada de interés.	I saw nothing of interest.

13.5 *Cualquiera*

(a) **Cualquiera** 'any' (pl. **cualesquiera**, relatively rarely used) as an adjective is shortened to **cualquier** *before* a noun or other adjective:

cualquier día 'any day'
cualquier otro sitio 'anywhere else'
cualquier cosa 'anything'

(b) It may also *follow* the noun in the sense of 'whatever', in which case the full form is used:

> **un libro cualquiera** 'any book at all', 'a book like any other'

(c) As a pronoun the full form is always used:

> **cualquiera de ustedes** 'any of you'

▶ **18.2.5** (p. 90)

13.6 *Quienquiera*

The pronoun **quienquiera** (pl. **quienesquiera,** rarely used) corresponds to English 'whoever':

> **quienquiera que lo sepa** 'whoever knows'

▶ **18.2.5** (p. 90)

13.7 *Todo*

Todo as an adjective, in addition to its meaning as 'all', 'every', may also correspond to the notion 'any':

> **Toda persona que no haya pagado el impuesto debe hacerlo inmediatamente.**
> Any person who has not paid the tax must do so immediately.

▶ **18.2.5** (p. 90)

14
Adverbs

Formation of adverbs in *-mente*

Many adverbs are formed from the *feminine* form of an adjective by adding the ending -**mente**. Any written accent on the adjective is retained (see **1.5.4**):

Adjective	Adverb
lenta	**lentamente** 'slowly'
económica	**económicamente** 'economically'
fácil	**fácilmente** 'easily'

If two or more adverbs occur in sequence, -**mente** is attached only to the last one:

> **lenta y fácilmente** 'slowly and easily'

In the spoken language, and in some set phrases, certain adjectives function as adverbs in their own right:

> **Va muy rápido.**
> It's going very quickly.

> **¡Habla más alto!**
> Speak more loudly!

> **Trabajamos duro.**
> We're working hard.

> **No estás jugando limpio.**
> You're not playing fair.

> **Me salió fatal.**
> It turned out dreadfully for me.

> **¡Tirar fuerte!**
> Pull hard!

> **Se venden muy barato.**
> They're being sold very cheaply.

Adverbs in -**mente** are often considered clumsy in Spanish, and alternative ways of saying the same thing are sought. An adjective pertaining to the subject of the sentence may convey the adverbial idea:

Volvió penitente.	He/she came back penitently.
Triste, cerró la puerta.	He/she closed the door sadly.

Paraphrases such as **de forma** + (f.) adjective, **de manera** + (f.) adjective, **de modo** + (m.) adjective, **de carácter** + (m.) adjective are also extensively used:

Lo criticó de forma muy dura.
He/she criticized it very harshly.

¿No lo puedes arreglar de modo más informal?
Can't you arrange it more informally?

14.2 Other adverbs

There are a large number of adverbs in Spanish which do not have the ending -**mente**, and which indeed are not obviously related to adjectives at all.

Examples are:

(a) Adverbs of manner

así 'thus'
bien 'well'
deprisa 'quickly'
despacio 'slowly'
mal 'badly'

(b) Adverbs of place (see **39.3**)

acá 'here'
(a)dentro 'inside'
(a)fuera 'outside'
ahí 'there'
allá 'yonder'
allí 'there'
aquí 'here'

(c) Adverbs of time

ahora 'now'
antes 'before'
después 'then', 'after(wards)'
entonces 'then'
todavía 'still'
ya 'already', 'now'

15
Negation

▶ **32** (p. 191)

15.1 *No*

No is the most widely-used Spanish negative:

> **No sé cuántos tienen.**
> I don't know how many they've got.

> **No todos vinieron.**
> Not all of them came.

> **Entonces vino a visitarme no Juan sino Miguel.**
> Then there came to visit me not Juan but Miguel.

NOTE **Acabar de** + infinitive and **dejar de** + infinitive have a different meaning when used with **no** (see **32.2**).

15.2 Negative element following the verb

When a negative element *follows* the verb, **no** or another negative must be used in addition *before* the verb (see also **45.1**).

> **No conozco a nadie.**
> I know no one/I don't know anyone.

> **Este pobrecito no tiene ningún amigo.**
> This poor little chap has got no friends/hasn't got a friend.

> **No vino nadie.** (or, less commonly, **Nadie vino**)
> No one came.

> **Nunca dice nada.**
> He/she never says anything.

> **Juan no bebe ni té ni café.**
> Juan drinks neither tea nor coffee/doesn't drink tea or coffee.

Notice that a positive element (e.g. 'anything', 'anyone') is often used in the corresponding English constructions.

Expressions requiring a negative

A number of other expressions require a negative element to follow them.

sin + infinitive, **sin que** + clause:

> **Salí sin despedirme de nadie.**
> I left without saying goodbye to anybody.

Comparatives:

> **Sabe cocinar mejor que nadie.**
> He/she can cook better than anyone.

Negative element included as a prefix in a word, e.g. **in-, des-:**

> **Es casi imposible conocer a nadie.**
> It's almost impossible to get to know anyone.

No . . . sino . . .

No . . . sino . . . expresses a contrast or correction. The two ideas linked by **no** and **sino** are mutually exclusive. **No sólo . . . sino también . . .** is a frequent pattern (**también** 'also' corrects **sólo** 'only'). Before a clause, **sino que** is used.

> **No fue tu madre quien me lo dijo, sino tu hermana.**
> It wasn't your mother who told me, but your sister.

> **Me robó no sólo la cartera sino también la chaqueta.**
> He/she stole not only my wallet, but also my jacket.

> **No sólo era estúpido, sino que también era travieso.**
> He was not only stupid but he was also naughty.

Negation of adjectives

There are a number of ways of negating adjectives in Spanish, all of which have slightly different connotations (see **32**).

Negative questions

A negative question may expect the answer 'yes', or have a more polite overtone:

> **¿No tienes miedo?**
> Aren't you afraid?

> **¿No me podrías dejar cien pesos?**
> Couldn't you lend me a hundred pesos?

▶ **31.4** (p. 188); **18.1.5** (p. 85)

16
Verb forms

Section **16.1** gives an overall picture of Spanish verb forms. See the verb table in the Appendix to check on the forms of individual common irregular verbs.

The order of forms, unless otherwise stated, is: 1st person singular, 2nd person singular, 3rd person singular, 1st person plural, 2nd person plural, 3rd person plural. Remember that **usted** takes a 3rd person singular verb and **ustedes** a 3rd person plural verb, despite their 2nd person meaning. The **voseo** form of the 2nd person singular most common in the Río de la Plata area is given in brackets where it is different from the **tú** form of the 2nd person singular.

16.1 The overall pattern

16.1.1 Regular verbs

16.1.1.1 *Infinitive*

cant*ar* 'to sing'   **com*er*** 'to eat'   **part*ir*** 'to break'; 'to leave'

16.1.1.2 *The indicative tenses*
The present stem is the *infinitive* minus -**ar, -er** or -**ir**:

cant-   com-   part-

NOTE The present, imperfect and preterite tenses are formed by adding the endings printed in italics to the *present stem*.

(a) Present

NOTE The -**er** and -**ir** conjugations are different only in the 1st and 2nd persons plural.

---

cant*o*	com*o*	part*o*
cant*as* (cant*ás*)	com*es* (com*és*)	part*es* (part*ís*)
cant*a*	com*e*	part*e*
cant*amos*	com*emos*	part*imos*
cant*áis*	com*éis*	part*ís*
cant*an*	com*en*	part*en*

(b) Imperfect

| NOTE | The -**er** and -**ir** conjugations are identical. |

cant*aba*	com*ía*	part*ía*
cant*abas*	com*ías*	part*ías*
cant*aba*	com*ía*	part*ía*
cant*ábamos*	com*íamos*	part*íamos*
cant*abais*	com*íais*	part*íais*
cant*aban*	com*ían*	part*ían*

(c) Preterite

| NOTE | The -**er** and -**ir** conjugations are identical. |

cant*é*	com*í*	part*í*
cant*aste*	com*iste*	part*iste*
cant*ó*	com*ió*	part*ió*
cant*amos*	com*imos*	part*imos*
cant*asteis*	com*isteis*	part*isteis*
cant*aron*	com*ieron*	part*ieron*

The future stem is the infinitive:

| cantar- | comer- | partir- |

| NOTE | The future and conditional tenses are formed by adding the endings printed in italics to the *future stem*. The endings are the same for all verbs, whether regular or not. |

(d) Future

cantar*é*	comer*é*	partir*é*
cantar*ás*	comer*ás*	partir*ás*
cantar*á*	comer*á*	partir*á*
cantar*emos*	comer*emos*	partir*emos*
cantar*éis*	comer*éis*	partir*éis*
cantar*án*	comer*án*	partir*án*

(e) Conditional

cantar*ía*	comer*ía*	partir*ía*
cantar*ías*	comer*ías*	partir*ías*
cantar*ía*	comer*ía*	partir*ía*
cantar*íamos*	comer*íamos*	partir*íamos*
cantar*íais*	comer*íais*	partir*íais*
cantar*ían*	comer*ían*	partir*ían*

16.1.1.3 **The subjunctive tenses**

(a) Present subjunctive

NOTE | The present subjunctive is formed from the *first person singular* of the *present indicative*. For -**ar** verbs change the **o** or **a** of the present indicative ending to **e**. For -**er** and -**ir** verbs, change the **o** or **e** of the present indicative ending to **a**.

cant*e*	com*a*	part*a*
cant*es* (cant*és*)	com*as* (com*ás*)	part*as* (part*ás*)
cant*e*	com*a*	part*a*
cant*emos*	com*amos*	part*amos*
cant*éis*	com*áis*	part*áis*
cant*en*	com*an*	part*an*

(b) Past (imperfect) subjunctive

There are *two* forms of the past subjunctive in Spanish. They are used more or less interchangeably in the Peninsula (with a slight preference, especially in Andalusia, for the -*ra* forms in speech); in Latin America the -**ra** form is strongly preferred in speech. Both are used universally in the written language.

NOTE | For both regular and irregular verbs, the past subjunctive is formed from the *third person plural* of the *preterite*, changing -**ron** to either -**ra**, etc., or -**se**, etc.

The -**ra** forms:

cant*ara*	com*iera*	part*iera*
cant*aras*	com*ieras*	part*ieras*
cant*ara*	com*iera*	part*iera*
cant*áramos*	com*iéramos*	part*iéramos*
cant*arais*	com*ierais*	part*ierais*
cant*aran*	com*ieran*	part*ieran*

The -**se** forms:

cant*ase*	com*iese*	part*iese*
cant*ases*	com*ieses*	part*ieses*
cant*ase*	com*iese*	part*iese*
cant*ásemos*	com*iésemos*	part*iésemos*
cant*áseis*	com*ieseis*	part*ieseis*
cant*asen*	com*iesen*	part*iesen*

16.1.1.4 *Past participle*

NOTE | The past participle is formed by adding the endings in italics to the *present stem*. The -**er** and -**ir** conjugations are identical.

cant*ado*	com*ido*	part*ido*

16.1.1.5 *Gerund*

NOTE The gerund is formed by adding the endings in italics to the *present stem*. The -**er** and -**ir** conjugations are identical.

cant*ando*	com*iendo*	part*iendo*

16.1.1.6 *Imperative*

NOTE The **tú** form imperative is identical to the 3rd person singular of the present indicative; the **vosotros/as** form is formed by changing the final -**r** of the infinitive to -**d**. The **usted** and **ustedes** forms are the same as the 3rd person singular and plural respectively of the present subjunctive. The negative imperatives are all formed from the present subjunctive.

(a) Positive

(tú)	cant*a*	com*e*	part*e*
(vos)	cant*á*	com*é*	part*í*
(vosotros/as)	cant*ad*	com*ed*	part*id*
(usted)	cant*e*	com*a*	part*a*
(ustedes)	cant*en*	com*an*	part*an*

(b) Negative

(tú)	no cantes	no comas	no partas
(vos)	no cantés	no comás	no partás
(vosotros/as)	no cantéis	no comáis	no partáis
(usted)	no cante	no coma	no parta
(ustedes)	no canten	no coman	no partan

16.1.1.7 *The compound tenses*

NOTE The compound tenses for all verbs are formed from the *auxiliary verb* **haber** followed by the *past participle*.

The forms for **haber** are given below, together with one full set of specimen compound forms for **cantar**.

Present of **haber**	Perfect of **cantar**
he	he cantado
has	has cantado
ha	ha cantado

hemos	hemos cantado
habéis	habéis cantado
han	han cantado

Imperfect of **haber**	Pluperfect of **cantar**
había	había cantado
habías	habías cantado
había	había cantado
habíamos	habíamos cantado
habíais	habíais cantado
habían	habían cantado

Preterite of **haber**	Past anterior of **cantar**
hube	hube cantado
hubiste	hubiste cantado
hubo	hubo cantado
hubimos	hubimos cantado
hubisteis	hubisteis cantado
hubieron	hubieron cantado

Future of **haber**	Future perfect of **cantar**
habré	habré cantado
habrás	habrás cantado
habrá	habrá cantado
habremos	habremos cantado
habréis	habréis cantado
habrán	habrán cantado

Conditional of **haber**	Conditional perfect of **cantar**
habría	habría cantado
habrías	habrías cantado
habría	habría cantado
habríamos	habríamos cantado
habríais	habríais cantado
habrían	habrían cantado

Present subjunctive of **haber**	Perfect subjunctive of **cantar**
haya	haya cantado
hayas	hayas cantado
haya	haya cantado
hayamos	hayamos cantado
hayáis	hayáis cantado
hayan	hayan cantado

Past (imperfect) subjunctive of **haber**	Pluperfect subjunctive of **cantar**
-ra forms:	
hubiera	hubiera cantado
hubieras	hubieras cantado
hubiera	hubiera cantado
hubiéramos	hubiéramos cantado
hubierais	hubierais cantado
hubieran	hubieran cantado
-se forms:	
hubiese	hubiese cantado
hubieses	hubieses cantado
hubiese	hubiese cantado
hubiésemos	hubiésemos cantado
hubieseis	hubieseis cantado
hubiesen	hubiesen cantado
Infinitive of **haber**	Perfect infinitive of **cantar**
haber	haber cantado

NOTE The compound tenses of **haber** are formed in the same way as the compound tenses of all other verbs: its past participle is **habido**. The gerund of **haber** is **habiendo**.

The forms of **haber** in its existential meaning 'there is', 'there are' and in the expression **haber que** + infinitive 'to be necessary to' (see **21.7**) are identical to the 3rd person singular forms given above, *except* that in the present **hay** is used.

16.1.2 Irregular verbs

Spanish has a large number of irregular verbs, though there are recurrent patterns discernible.

16.1.2.1 *Radical-changing verbs*
Many verbs are radical-changing. This means that their present stem is changed when the stem is stressed: **e** changes to **ie** and **o** to **ue**. Examples are:

CERRAR (ie) 'to close' e changes to **ie**	**RECORDAR (ue)** 'to remember' o changes to **ue**

(a) Present

c*ie*rro	rec*ue*rdo
c*ie*rras (cerrás)	rec*ue*rdas (recordás)
c*ie*rra	rec*ue*rda

cerramos	recordamos
cerráis	recordáis
cierran	recuerdan

(b) Present subjunctive

cierre	recuerde
cierres (cerrés)	recuerdes (recordés)
cierre	recuerde
cerremos	recordemos
cerréis	recordéis
cierren	recuerden

A number of radical-changing -**ir** verbs not only make the above changes, but also change **e** to **i** and **o** to **u** in the *unstressed* stem forms of the present subjunctive (i.e. the 1st and 2nd persons plural).

There are also some -**ir** verbs which change **e** to **i** instead of to **ie** in the present stem; these verbs have **i** *throughout* the present subjunctive.

All these -**ir** verbs change **e** to **i** or **o** to **u** in the 3rd person singular and plural of the preterite and in the gerund. Examples are:

SENTIR (ie/i) 'to feel'; 'to regret'	**DORMIR** (ue/u) 'to sleep'	**PEDIR** (i) 'to ask for'
Present	Present	Present
siento	duermo	pido
sientes (sentís)	duermes (dormís)	pides (pedís)
siente	duerme	pide
sentimos	dormimos	pedimos
sentís	dormís	pedís
sienten	duermen	piden
Present subjunctive	Present subjunctive	Present subjunctive
sienta	duerma	pida
sientas (sentás)	duermas (dormás)	pidas (pidás)
sienta	duerma	pida
sintamos	durmamos	pidamos
sintáis	durmáis	pidáis
sientan	duerman	pidan
Preterite	Preterite	Preterite
sentí	dormí	pedí
sentiste	dormiste	pediste
sintió	durmió	pidió
sentimos	dormimos	pedimos
sentisteis	dormisteis	pedisteis
sintieron	durmieron	pidieron

Gerund	Gerund	Gerund
*si*ntiendo	*du*rmiendo	*pi*diendo

See also **adquirir** 'to acquire' and **jugar** 'to play' in the verb table in the Appendix.

16.1.2.2 | *Orthographic-changing verbs*

Some verbs, whilst not irregular to the ear, need changes in the *written form* of their stem:

- z in the stem of an -**ar** verb is written as **c** before **e** (**comenzar** 'to begin', but **comience**).
- c in the stem of an -**er** verb is written as **z** before **a** or **o** (**vencer** 'to conquer', but **venza, venzo**).
- c in the stem of an -**ar** verb is written **qu** before **e** (**atacar** 'to attack', but **ataquemos**).
- g in the stem of an -**ar** verb is written **gu** before **e** (**rogar** 'to ask', but **ruegue**).
- gu in the stem of an -**ar** verb is written **gü** before **e** (**averiguar** 'to verify', but **averigüe**).
- g in the stem of an -**er** verb is written **j** before **a** or **o** (**coger** 'to pick up', but **coja, cojo**).
- ie at the beginning of a word is written **ye** (**yerro** 'I stray', from **errar** 'to stray'). But a radical-changing verb which has **he-** in the infinitive spells this sound **hie-** in the radical-changed forms (**hiela** 'it freezes', from **helar** 'to freeze').
- ue at the beginning of a word is written **hue** (**oler** 'to smell', but **huele**).
- gu in the stem of an -**ir** verb is written **g** before **a** or **o** (**distinguir** 'to distinguish', but **distinga, distingo**).
- qu in the stem of an -**ir** verb is written **c** before **a** or **o** (**delinquir** 'to commit an offence', but **delinca, delinco**).
- ñ which would regularly be followed by a 'weak' **i** (see **1.2**) is written simply as **ñ** (**tañó**, not *****tañio**, from **tañer** 'to strum').
- ll which would regularly be followed by a 'weak' **i** is written simply as **ll** (**bulló**, not *****bullió**, from **bullir** 'to boil').
- An unstressed **i** between two vowels is written **y** (**leí**, but **leyó, leyendo** from **leer** 'to read'; **caí**, but **cayó, cayendo** from **caer** 'to fall').

16.1.2.3 | *Irregular first person singular of the present indicative*

A substantial number of verbs have a first person singular form of the present indicative which is irregular. The present subjunctive, which is formed from the first person singular of the present indicative, is correspondingly irregular. An example is:

PONER (**pongo**) 'to put', 'place'

Present indicative	Present subjunctive
po*n*go	po*n*ga
pones (ponés)	po*n*gas (po*n*gás)
pone	po*n*ga
ponemos	po*n*gamos
ponéis	po*n*gáis
ponen	po*n*gan

Some verbs ending in **-iar** and **-uar** form their present tenses with an unstressed -io, -uo ending and are essentially regular (examples are **cambiar** and **evacuar**). Others have stressed -ío, -úo endings in the singular and in the third person plural, as well as in the corresponding forms of the subjunctive. Examples of the latter are:

ENVIAR (-ío) 'to send'

Present indicative	Present subjunctive
envío	**envíe**
envías (enviás)	**envíes (enviés)**
envía	**envíe**
enviamos	**enviemos**
enviáis	**enviéis**
envían	**envíen**

CONTINUAR (-úo) 'to continue'

Present indicative	Present subjunctive
contin*ú*o	**contin*ú*e**
contin*ú*as (continuás)	**contin*ú*es (continués)**
contin*ú*a	**contin*ú*e**
continuamos	**continuemos**
continuáis	**continuéis**
contin*ú*an	**contin*ú*en**

16.1.2.4 | *Other irregular presents*

Verbs ending in -**ecer** form their first person singular in -**ezco**. Verbs ending in -**ucir** form their first person singular in -**uzco**. Examples are:

MERECER (**merezco**) 'to deserve'

Present indicative	Present subjunctive
merez*co*	**merez*ca***
mereces (merecés)	**merez*cas* (merez*cás*)**
merece	**merez*ca***
merecemos	**merez*camos***
merecéis	**merez*cáis***
merecen	**merez*can***

REDUCIR (**reduzco**) 'to reduce'

Present indicative	Present subjunctive
reduz*co*	**reduz*ca***
reduces (reducís)	**reduz*cas* (reduz*cás*)**
reduce	**reduz*ca***
reducimos	**reduz*camos***
reducís	**reduz*cáis***
reducen	**reduz*can***

A number of common verbs have irregular present indicative first person forms which also form the basis of the present subjunctive:

Infinitive	1st pers. sg. present indicative	Present subjunctive
Caber 'to be contained'	**quepo**	**quepa**, etc.
Caer 'to fall'	**caigo**	**caiga**, etc.
Decir 'to say', 'tell'	**digo**	**diga**, etc.
Hacer 'to do', 'make'	**hago**	**haga**, etc.
Oír 'to hear'	**oigo**	**oiga**, etc.
Poner 'to put', 'place'	**pongo**	**ponga**, etc.
Salir 'to go out'	**salgo**	**salga**, etc.
Traer 'to bring'	**traigo**	**traiga**, etc.
Valer 'to be worth'	**valgo**	**valga**, etc.
Venir 'to come'	**vengo**	**venga**, etc.

The following verbs are rather more irregular:

Infinitive	Present indicative	Present subjunctive
Dar 'to give'	**doy, das, da**, etc.	**dé, des, dé, demos, deis, den**
Estar 'to be'	**estoy, estás, está**, etc.	**esté, estés, esté, estemos, estéis, estén**
Ir 'to go'	see **16.1.2.9**	**vaya**, etc.
Saber 'to know'	**sé, sabes (sabés), sabe**, etc.	**sepa**, etc.
Ser 'to be'	see **16.1.2.9**	**sea**, etc.

16.1.2.5 | *Irregular preterites*

A number of verbs have irregular preterite forms: not only is their stem irregular, but the endings of such verbs are often slightly different from those of regular verbs.

Infinitive	Preterite
Andar 'to go'	**anduve, anduviste, anduvo, anduvimos, anduvisteis, anduvieron**
Caber 'to be contained'	**cupe, cupiste, cupo, cupimos, cupisteis, cupieron**
Dar 'to give'	**di, diste, dio, dimos, disteis, dieron**
Decir 'to say', 'tell' (and its compounds, e.g. **desdecir** 'to deny')	**dije, dijiste, dijo, dijimos, dijisteis, dijeron**
Estar 'to be'	**estuve, estuviste, estuvo, estuvimos, estuvisteis, estuvieron**
Haber auxiliary	**hube, hubiste, hubo, hubimos, hubisteis, hubieron**
Hacer 'to do', 'make' (and its compounds, e.g. **deshacer** 'to undo')	**hice, hiciste, hizo, hicimos, hicisteis, hicieron**
Ir 'to go'	**fui, fuiste, fue, fuimos, fuisteis, fueron**
Poder 'to be able'	**pude, pudiste, pudo, pudimos, pudisteis, pudieron**

Poner 'to put', 'place' (and its compounds, e.g. **componer** 'to compose')	**puse, pusiste, puso, pusimos, pusisteis, pusieron**
Querer 'to want', 'wish'	**quise, quisiste, quiso, quisimos, quisisteis, quisieron**
Reír 'to laugh' (and **sonreír** 'to smile')	**reí, reíste, rió, reímos, reísteis, rieron**
Saber 'to know'	**supe, supiste, supo, supimos, supisteis, supieron**
Ser 'to be'	**fui, fuiste, fue, fuimos, fuisteis, fueron**
Tener 'to have' (and its compounds, e.g. **contener** 'to contain')	**tuve, tuviste, tuvo, tuvimos, tuvisteis, tuvieron**
Traer 'to bring' (and its compounds, e.g. **atraer** 'to attract')	**traje, trajiste, trajo, trajimos, trajisteis, trajeron**
Venir 'to come' (and its compounds, e.g. **subvenir** 'to subsidize')	**vine, viniste, vino, vinimos, vinisteis, vinieron**
Ver 'to see' (and its compounds, e.g. entrever 'to catch a glimpse of')	**vi, viste, vio, vimos, visteis, vieron**
Verbs in -**ucir** (e.g. **conducir** 'to drive', 'lead')	**conduje, condujiste, condujo, condujimos, condujisteis, condujeron**

Note that in the majority of these verbs the first and third person singular endings are not stressed. In all cases, the past subjunctive is formed from the third person plural of the preterite: e.g. **supiera** or **supiese** from **supieron** (saber).

16.1.2.6 *Irregular futures and conditionals*

Infinitive	Future	Conditional
Caber 'to be contained'	**cabré**, etc.	**cabría**, etc.
Decir 'to say', 'tell' (and its compounds)	**diré**, etc.	**diría**, etc.
Haber auxiliary	**habré**, etc.	**habría**, etc.
Hacer 'to do'; 'to make' (and its compounds)	**haré**, etc.	**haría**, etc.
Poder 'to be able'	**podré**, etc.	**podría**, etc.
Poner 'to put', 'place' (and its compounds)	**pondré**, etc.	**pondría**, etc.
Querer 'to want'	**querré**, etc.	**querría**, etc.
Saber 'to know'	**sabré**, etc.	**sabría**, etc.
Salir 'to go out'	**saldré**, etc.	**saldría**, etc.
Tener 'to have' (and its compounds)	**tendré**, etc.	**tendría**, etc.
Valer 'to be worth'	**valdré**, etc.	**valdría**, etc.
Venir 'to come' (and its compounds)	**vendré**, etc.	**vendría**, etc.

16.1.2.7 *Irregular past participles*

Infinitive	Past participle
Decir 'to say', 'tell' (and its compounds)	**dicho**
Hacer 'to do'; 'to make' (and its compounds)	**hecho**
Poner 'to put', 'place' (and its compounds)	**puesto**
Ver 'to see' (and its compounds)	**visto**
Volver 'to return' (and its compounds)	**vuelto**

| 16.1.2.8 | *Irregular imperatives* |

Infinitive	2nd person singular imperative
Hacer 'to do', 'to make' (and its compounds)	**haz**
Ir 'to go'	**ve**
Poner 'to put', 'to place' (and its compounds)	**pon**
Salir 'to go out'	**sal** (**salí**)
Ser 'to be'	**sé**
Venir 'to come' (and its compounds)	**ven**

| 16.1.2.9 | ***Ser* and *ir*** |

Ser and *ir* are so irregular that they must be given special attention.

Ser 'to be'	**Ir** 'to go'

(a) Present

soy	**voy**
eres (**sos**)	**vas**
es	**va**
somos	**vamos**
sois	**vais**
son	**van**

(b) Imperfect

era	**iba**
eras	**ibas**
era	**iba**
éramos	**íbamos**
erais	**ibais**
eran	**iban**

(c) Preterite see **16.1.2.5**

NOTE | **Ser** and **ir** have the same forms in the preterite.

(d) Future and conditional

Regular (**seré**, etc.; **sería**, etc.)	Regular (**iré**, etc.; **iría**, etc.)

(e) Present subjunctive

sea	**vaya**
seas (**seás**)	**vayas** (**vayás**)
sea	**vaya**
seamos	**vayamos**
seáis	**vayáis**
sean	**vayan**

(f) Past (imperfect) subjunctive

Regular (**fuera**, etc; **fuese**, etc.)	Regular (**fuera**, etc; **fuese**, etc.)

Ser and **ir** have the same forms in the past subjunctive.

(g) Gerund

siendo	**yendo**

(h) Past participle

sido	**ido**

(i) 2nd person singular
imperative

sé (regular plural: **sed**)	**ve** (regular plural: **id**)

17
Use of the verb forms

17.1 **Present**

► 71 (p. 399)

17.1.1   Reference to present time

(a) States of affairs in or including the present:

Hace frío. (see **71.1**)	It's cold.
¿En qué piensas? (see **71.5**)	What are you thinking of?
Me gusta Segovia. (see **71.4**)	I like Segovia.

(b) Habitual actions in the present:

¿Qué haces los fines de semana? (see **71.6**)
What do you do at weekends?

(c) General truths:

La mayoría de los españoles son católicos. (see **71.2**)
The majority of Spaniards are Catholics.

(d) Ability (with appropriate verbs):

¿Lo oyes? (see **53.1**)
Can you hear it?

Teresa lee el chino y el ruso.
Teresa can read Chinese and Russian.

► 53 (p. 311)

(e) With 'since' expressions, referring to a period of time that continues up until the present:

Vive en Chile desde hace cinco años. (see **71.7**)/**Hace cinco años que vive en Chile.**
He has been living in Chile for five years. (i.e. from five years ago (up until now))

Espero desde hace mucho rato. (see **71.7**)/**Hace mucho rato que espero.**
I've been waiting for a long time.

► 71.7 (p. 403)

17.2

Reference to future time

 72 (p. 408)

A fixed event, something which has been pre-arranged (especially with verbs of motion) or which is intended:

> **El viernes 8 es festivo.**
> Friday the 8th is a holiday.

> **Los exámenes empiezan pasado mañana.**
> The exams begin the day after tomorrow.

> **Salimos mañana temprano.** (see 72.2)
> We (are due to, intend to) leave early tomorrow.

17.1.3

Reference to past time

 73 (p. 415)

(a) In formal style, usually as an alternative to the preterite:

> **En 1978 se aprueba** (= se aprobó) **la nueva Constitución.** (see 73.4)
> The new Constitution was approved in 1978.

(b) In colloquial use, as an alternative to either the preterite or the imperfect, to create an impression of greater vividness. Although this possibility exists in English, the usage is more common in Spanish.

> **Estoy en la calle, cuando se me acerca un hombre y me dice . . .**
> I was in the street, when a man came up to me and said . . .

17.1.4

As an imperative

 69 (p. 385)

> **Primero levantas el auricular y luego metes la moneda.** (see 42.1)
> First you lift up the receiver and then you insert the coin.

> **Sigue usted todo recto hasta el primer semáforo y luego tuerce a la derecha.** (see 69)
> Go straight on as far as the first traffic-light and then turn right.

17.2 Perfect

 73.1–73.2 (pp. 415–416)

(a) Referring to events taking place over a period of time including the present:

> **Todavía/aún no hemos terminado.** (see 73.1.4)
> We have not finished yet.

> **Los he visto dos veces.** (see 73.1.4)
> I've seen them twice.

(b) Referring to past events related to the present (the Spanish perfect corresponds almost exactly to the English perfect); there is some regional variation.

> **Ha bebido demasiado.** (see **73.1**) (in Latin America, **Bebió demasiado** is more usual.)
> He/she's drunk too much. (implying that he/she is now drunk)

▶ | **73.3** (p. 417)

(c) Referring to the recent past (again, variable according to region: the preterite is preferred in a number of areas):

> **He hablado con Carlos esta mañana.** (see **73.1.3**) (in Latin America, **Hablé con Carlos esta mañana** is more usual.)
> I spoke to Carlos this morning.

▶ | **20.4** (p. 98); **73.3** (p. 417)

17.3 Imperfect

17.3.1 Reference to past time

▶ | **73.8–73.11** (pp. 420–423)

(a) An ongoing state or action in the past taking place over an unspecified period of time:

> **Estaba enfermo.** (see **73.8**)   I/he was ill.

(b) Referring to past actions which were in progress when something else happened:

> **Sole tocaba el piano cuando su hermana entró en el salón.**
> Sole was playing the piano when her sister came into the living room.

(c) Referring to past habitual actions:

> **Nos veíamos todas las semanas.** (see **73.9**)
> We used to see each other every week.

17.3.2 Reference to the immediate future in the past

▶ | **72.1** (p. 408); **72.2** (p. 411)

> **Ese día por la tarde yo me iba a Santiago.** (see **72.2**)
> That day in the afternoon I was going to Santiago.

17.3.3 'Modal' uses

(a) In colloquial use, expressing the consequence of a conditional sentence (instead of the conditional).

▶ | **51.1** (p. 299)

> **Si no fuera por Miguel, no tenías (= tendrías) tantos amigos.**
> If it weren't for Miguel, you wouldn't have so many friends.

> **Yo que tú lo hacía.** (see **67.1**)
> If I were you I'd do it.

(b) Saying politeness.

> **Mire, quería decirle algo.** (see **30.2**)
> Look, I want(ed) to tell you something.

17.4 Preterite

▶ **73.4–73.8** (pp. 418–420)

(a) Referring to the beginning of a past action or state:

> **Se gustaron desde el primer momento.**
> They liked each other from the start.

> **Entonces supe la verdad.**
> Then I found out the truth.

> **Nos conocimos en México.**
> We met in Mexico.

(b) Complete events in the past, or events or a series of events lasting over a definite period in the past:

> **Ayer vi a Isabel.** (see **73.4**)
> I saw Isabel yesterday.

> **¿Y no tuviste miedo? No, en ese momento no tuve miedo.** (see **65**)
> And didn't you get frightened? No, at that moment I wasn't afraid.

> **Hubo un ruido.**
> There was a noise. (implies that the noise started at a certain point or was momentary)

> **Vivimos en Barcelona durante cinco meses.** (see **73.6**)
> We lived in Barcelona for five months.

> **Aquel año fui muchas veces a visitarla.**
> That year I went to see her often.

(c) A past event completed before another past event, as part of a sequence of events, or during an ongoing state of affairs:

> **Luego que terminó la carta, se sentó a leer.** (see **73.7**)
> After he/she had finished the letter, he/she sat down to read.

> **Luego de eso se vino abajo.**
> After that it all fell through.

> **Leía cuando llegó.**
> I was reading when he/she arrived.

It is extremely important to distinguish between the imperfect and the preterite in Spanish, since there is *always* a difference in meaning between the two. Contrast the following sentences:

> **Estábamos en España durante las elecciones.**
> We were in Spain during the elections.
> (the elections happened while we were in Spain; our stay in Spain was of unspecified duration)

> **Estuvimos un año en España.**
> We were in Spain for a year.
> (we were in Spain for a specified length of time)

> **Quería entrar.**
> He/she wanted to get in.
> (efforts over an unspecified length of time)

> **Quiso entrar.**
> He/she wanted to get in.
> (refers to a particular occasion when he/she tried to get in)

> **El siglo XVIII fue el Siglo de las Luces.**
> The eighteenth century was the Age of Enlightenment.
> (considered as part of a historical sequence)

> **En el siglo XVIII el viajar era muy peligroso.**
> In the eighteenth century travelling was very dangerous.
> (describes a state of affairs at the time)

17.5 Future

17.5.1 Reference to future time

▶ 72 (p. 408)

> **¿Cree usted que venderán el piso?** (see **49.1**)
> Do you think they'll sell the flat?

> **El presidente intentará poner fin a la crisis.**
> The president will try to put an end to the crisis.

NOTE The future is rarely used in informal spoken language with simple future meaning, the present (see **17.1.2**) or the **ir a** + infinitive forms (see **20**) being preferred.

17.5.2 'Modal' uses

(a) Saying uncertainty with regard to future plans:

> **Supongo que el jefe vendrá a la reunión.**
> I suppose the boss will come to the meeting.

(b) Saying intention:

> **¿Vendrás conmigo?** (see **70.3**)
> Will you (would you like to) come with me?

(c) Saying promises:

> **Se lo traeré mañana sin falta.** (see **72.4**)
> I'll bring it for you tomorrow without fail.

(d) Expressing probability with regard to something in the present:

▶ **48** (p. 282); **50** (p. 296)

> **Estará con alguien.** (see **48.1**)
> He/she must be with someone.

> **¿Estará en casa?** (see **48.2**)
> Can he/she be at home?

17.6 Future perfect

17.6.1 Reference to future time

(a) Saying that something will happen before a moment in the future:

> **¿Lo habrás terminado para las cinco?**
> Will you have finished by five o'clock?

(b) Saying probability (corresponding to the perfect).

▶ **48** (p. 282)

> **Ya se habrán enterado.** (see **48.1**)
> They must have found out already.

> **¿Habrá salido el avión?** (see **48.2**)
> Do you think the plane will have left?

17.7 Conditional

(a) Expressing a present or future hypothesis (the consequence of a conditional sentence, see **18.2.4**).

> **Si tuviéramos menos trabajo, tendríamos más tiempo libre.**
> If we had less work, we would have more spare time.

> **Yo que tú no iría.** (see **67.1**)
> If I were you I wouldn't go

> **¿Qué harías tú en mi lugar?** (see **67.3**)
> What would you do in my position?

(b) In reported speech as the past equivalent of the future.

▶ **33** (p. 196)

> **Me dijo Alicia que llegaría a las once.**
> Alicia told me she would arrive at eleven.

> **Pensábamos que nos encontrarían.**
> We thought they would find us.

(c) Polite use:

▶ **29.8** (p. 161); **30.4** (p. 173); **31.3** (p. 187); **68** (p. 381)

> **Por favor, ¿podría decirme a qué hora sale el próximo vuelo para Barcelona?**
> Could you please tell me what time the next flight for Barcelona is leaving?

> **¿Le importaría esperarme un momento?** (see **68**)
> Would you mind waiting for me a moment?

(d) With modal verbs (see **21**):

> **No deberías beber tanto.** (see **61.2**)
> You shouldn't drink so much.

> **¿Podría suceder?** (see **48.2**)
> Could it happen?

(e) Saying probability with regard to something in the past:

▶ **48.1** (p. 282); **50** (p. 296)

> **En aquel tiempo yo tendría unos doce años.** (see **48.1**)
> At that time I must have been about twelve.

17.8 Conditional perfect

(a) In the consequence of a past conditional sentence:

> **Si lo hubiéramos sabido antes, no habríamos dicho nada.**
> If we had known before, we would not have said anything.

(b) In reported speech, as the past equivalent of the future perfect:

> **Le dijimos que nos habríamos marchado antes del anochecer.**
> We told him/her that we would have gone before nightfall.

17.9 Pluperfect

▶ **73.11** (p. 423)

Past events which occurred before another past event or situation:

> **La reunión había terminado cuando llegó.** (see **73.11**)
> The meeting had finished when he/she arrived.

(1) If the sequence of events is obvious, the preterite is often used instead of the pluperfect:

> **Cuando salió a la calle, encontró que estaba lloviendo.**
> When he/she went out into the street, he/she found that it was raining.

(2) In the written language in Latin America, and in journalistic style in the Peninsula, the **-ra** form of the past subjunctive is sometimes used instead of the pluperfect:

> **El que fuera niño prodigio de la canción y el cine español de los años cincuenta cayó en la trampa que le preparó la policía valenciana.**
> The man who had been a child prodigy of Spanish song and cinema in the fifties fell into the trap the Valencia police prepared for him.

▶ 18.2.2 (p. 88)

17.10 Past anterior

▶ 73.7 (p. 420)

Past events which occurred before another past event or situation:

> **Luego que hubo terminado la carta, se sentó a leer.** (see **73.7**)
> After he/she had finished the letter, he/she sat down to read.

NOTE This verb form is not used in speech; it belongs to formal written register. It may be substituted by the **-ra** form of the past subjunctive in certain styles of Spanish in the same way as the pluperfect (see **17.9**).

17.11 Infinitive

The infinitive is used:

(a) As the complement of many verbs:

> **Prometió escuchar atentamente.**
> He/she promised to listen intently.

> **¿Te atreves a pedir más?**
> Do you dare to ask for more?

> **No sabe nadar.**
> He/she can't swim.

▶ 26 (p. 131)

(b) As a noun:

> **Trabajar es sano.**   Working is healthy.

An article may be used with the infinitive in such cases:

> **el gorjear de los pájaros** 'the chirping of the birds'
> **un murmurar constante** 'a constant murmuring'

NOTE English uses the '-ing' form, which looks like the Spanish gerund, in such circumstances. However, the Spanish gerund can *never* be used in this way.

(c) After many prepositions:

> **Lo hice sin pensar.**
> I did it without thinking.

> **Por no tener dinero, no fuimos a Madrid.**
> Because we didn't have any money, we didn't go to Madrid.

Two special constructions use the infinitive: **al** + infinitive indicates an adverbial clause, usually of *time*, and **de** + infinitive indicates a *condition*:

> **Al comprobar el precio Montse se negó a comprarlo.**
> When Montse found out the price she refused to buy it.

> **De no haber ido, no habríamos visto a la Reina.**
> If we hadn't gone, we wouldn't have seen the Queen.

(d) As an imperative:

▶ **69** (p. 385)

> **Seguir por la Ml hasta llegar a San Alfonso.** (see **69.1**)
> Go along the Ml until you get to San Alfonso.

> **No exponer el aparato a temperaturas extremas.** (see **69.2**)
> Do not expose the product to extreme temperatures.

17.12 Gerund

(a) The gerund is used as the complement of **seguir** and **continuar**, and sometimes of verbs of perception instead of the infinitive.

> **Marta siguió cantando.**
> Marta carried on singing.

> **Vi a los niños jugando en el parque./Vi jugar a los niños en el parque.**
> I saw the children playing in the park.

▶ **26.3 and 26.2.2.1** (pp. 140 and 134)

(b) The gerund is normally used as the equivalent of an adverbial clause, expressing manner, cause, time, condition, concession, etc.

▶ **51.3** (p. 302)

> **Salió corriendo.**
> He ran out. (= 'came out running')

> **Nos divertimos bailando.**
> We enjoyed ourselves (by) dancing.

> **Estando en Madrid, fui a saludar a mis primos.**
> While I was in Madrid, I went to say hello to my cousins.

Subiendo por esta calle llegarás al parque. (see 51.3)
If you go up this street you will get to the park.

Aun teniendo en cuenta lo que acabas de decir, no puedo darte más dinero.
Even taking into account what you've just said, I can't give you any more money.

NOTE

The Spanish gerund is *not* used:

● to translate English adjectives ending in '-ing':

'an interesting book'   **un libro interesante**
'a boring lesson'   **una clase aburrida**

● as a verbal noun (see **17.11**):

I like drawing.   **me gusta dibujar.**

17.13 Imperative

The imperative is used to give *commands* and *instructions*. It is generally rather brusque, and it is more polite to use an alternative form. The **vosotros** plural form (which is not used in Latin America) is often replaced by the infinitive, which has the additional advantage of not specifying a person, and so being neutral between polite and familiar address. The first peson plural imperative (**nosotros** form) is most frequently replaced by **vamos a** + infinitive in speech (see **20.2**), and the first person plural imperative of **ir** itself is usually **vamos**.

▶ **67–69** (pp. 375–385)

Dale un besito a papá.
Give daddy a kiss.

Déselo a él.
Give it to him.

¡Escuchad!
Listen!

¡Vengan todos!
All of you come!

Traducir al español . . .
Translate into Spanish . . .

Comencemos por preguntar . . .
Let's begin by asking . . .

Vamos a empezar con el capítulo 20.
Let's begin at Chapter 20.

¡Vámonos!
Let's go!

The imperative may be used as the equivalent of a si-clause:

> **Hazlo y te arrepentirás.** (see **51.3**)
> If you do it you'll regret it.

▶ **18.2.4** (p. 89); **51** (p. 299)

18
Use of the subjunctive

Sometimes the subjunctive is automatically required by another element in the sentence, such as a verb or a conjunction. Sometimes there is a choice between subjunctive and indicative, in which case there is always a difference in meaning between the two.

The subjunctive is not 'avoided' in Spanish, and is not in any way old-fashioned or unusual; however, in a number of cases there is an alternative construction with the infinitive which is normally preferred, especially in speech, because it is shorter and simpler. An *infinitive* is the rule when the subject of the main clause and the subject of the subordinate clause are the same:

> **Preferiríamos hacerlo más tarde.**
> We would prefer to do it later. (= *We* would prefer that *we* do it later.)

contrast:

> **Preferiríamos que lo hiciesen más tarde.**
> We would prefer them to do it later. (= *We* would prefer that *they* do it later.)

> **Llamaré a Antonia para invitarla a la fiesta.** (see **43.5**)
> I'll call Antonia in order to invite her to the party. (= *I'*ll call Antonia so that *I* can invite her . . .)

contrast:

> **Llamaré a Antonia para que no se moleste en contestar.**
> I'll call Antonia so that *she* won't have to bother replying.

The infinitive is also used in the complement of an impersonal verb to denote an indefinite subject:

▶ **26.2** (p. 132)

> **No importa tener dinero.**
> Having money doesn't matter.

18.1 The subjunctive in complements of verbs and verbal expressions

The subjunctive is used with a large number of verbs and verbal expressions.

18.1

18.1.1   Expressions denoting the influence of someone or something on someone or something else: ordering, permission, necessity, etc.

(a) Indirect commands:

> **Le rogamos que acepte nuestra oferta.** (see **70.1**)
> We ask you to accept our offer.

> **Le agradecería (que) me respondiera a la mayor brevedad posible.** (see **29.9**)
> I would be grateful if you would reply as soon as possible.

> **Prefiero que vengas mañana.** (see **57.4**)
> I'd rather you came tomorrow.

▶ **33.4** (p. 200); **57** (p. 333); **67** (p. 375); **68** (p. 381)

(b) Permission:

> **Permítame que le diga algo.** (see **54.1**)
> Allow me to tell you something.

NOTE   Several verbs of permission admit infinitive complements as an *alternative* to the subjunctive:

> **Por favor, permítanos quedarnos aquí.** (see **54.1**)
> Please allow us to stay here.

Other common verbs taking an infinitive as well as a subjunctive complement are **hacer** 'to make' and **dejar** 'to allow'.

▶ **54** (p. 314)

(c) Necessity:

> **Es necesario que vuelvas pronto.** (see **47.3**)
> You need to come back soon.

▶ **45** (p. 266)

18.1.2   Expressions of supposing and imagining

> **Imagínate que te pida dinero. ¿Se lo prestarás?** (see **50**)
> Suppose he/she asks you for money. Will you lend it to him/her?

The indicative is used after **suponer, imaginarse** and **figurarse** when they are verbs of thinking (see **50**), unless they are *negated* (see **18.1.5**):

> **Me imagino que vendrá a la reunión.**
> I imagine he/she'll come to the meeting.

but:

> **No me imagino que venga a la reunión.**
> I don't imagine he/she'll come to the meeting.

If these verbs can be used parenthetically without their meaning changing, then the indicative is used:

> **Vendrá a la reunión, me imagino.**
> He/she'll come to the meeting, I imagine.

▶ **50** (p. 296)

18.1.3 Expressions of hoping

> **¡Espero que tengas suerte!** (see **62.2**)
> I hope you are lucky!

> **Espero que no haya pasado nada.** (see **62.2**)
> I hope nothing has happened.

> **Yo esperaba que llegaras más temprano.** (see **62.2**)
> I was hoping you would arrive earlier.

▶ **62** (p. 355)

18.1.4 Verbs and expressions denoting an emotional response or a value judgement

> **Me alegro de que hayas tenido éxito.**
> I'm glad you were successful.

> **Me gustaría mucho que vinieras a mi boda.** (see **70.1**)
> I'd very much like you to come to my wedding.

> **Ella tenía miedo de que la vieran conmigo.** (see **65**)
> She was afraid/worried that they might see her with me.

> **Perdone que lo moleste.** (see **64.1**)
> I'm sorry to bother you.

> **Es mejor que se lo digan.**
> It's better that they tell him/her.

> **¡Qué bueno que hayas venido!** (see **30.8**)
> What a good thing (= I'm glad) you've come!

> **¡Qué raro que no estén aquí!** (see **59**)
> How strange that they are not here!

▶ **58** (p. 340); **59** (p. 346); **63** (p. 358)

18.1.5 Expressions of thinking

The indicative is normally used with expressions of thinking, but the subjunctive is sometimes used to dissociate the speaker from what is being thought:

> **¿Crees tú que él es la persona indicada?** (see **55.1**)
> Neutral: Do you think he's the right person?

> **¿Crees tú que él sea la persona indicada?** (see **55.1**)
> Speaker does not agree with the addressee: Do you (really) think he's the right person? (I don't.)

The subjunctive is normally used with *negated* expressions of thinking or saying:

> **No recuerdo que él estuviera aquí.** (see **45.1**)
> I don't remember his being here.

> **No estoy seguro de que sea así.** (see **49.1**)
> I'm not sure it's like that.

> **No me parecía que pudiera resolverse.** (see **55.2**)
> I didn't think it could be solved.

> **No creo que sea importante.** (see **55.2**)
> I don't think it's important.

> **No pensaba que fuera tan impulsivo.** (see **55.2**)
> I didn't think he was so impulsive.

> **¡Es increíble que se haya comportado de esa manera!** (see **59**)
> It's incredible that he/she has behaved like that!

> **¡Parece mentira que haya ganado la lotería!** (see **59**)
> It hardly seems possible that he/she has won the lottery!

Compare also:

> **No porque sea barato lo voy a comprar.** (see **32**)
> The fact that it is cheap doesn't mean I'm going to buy it.

NOTE The *polite negation* of a question (**15.6**) does not trigger the use of the subjunctive with such verbs:

> **¿No le parece a usted que es mejor aplazarlo?** (see **56.3**)
> Don't you think it's better to postpone it?

▶ **55** (p. 319); **49** (p. 291); **56** (p. 327)

18.1.6 **Expressions of possibility, impossibility, probability and improbability**

> **Es posible que no haya entendido.**
> It's possible he/she hasn't understood.

> **Era probable que no tuvieran una mayoría absoluta.**
> It was probable that they would not have an absolute majority.

> **¡No puede ser que haya dicho eso!** (see **59**)
> I can't believe that he/she has said that!

▶ **18.3.3** (p. 92); **48** (p. 282)

18.2 **The subjunctive after conjunctions**

18.2.1 **Expressing purpose**

▶ **43.5** (p. 258)

(a) **para que:**

> **Fuimos a Sevilla para que Pepe conociera a su abuela.** (see **43.5**)
> We went to Seville so that Pepe could meet his grandmother.

(b) **de modo/manera/forma que:**

> **Lo discutiremos, de manera/modo/forma que lleguemos a una conclusión lo antes posible.** (see **43.5**)
> We'll discuss it, so that we may reach a conclusion as soon as possible.

Similar to the above are **a/con el fin de que, con el objeto de que** and **con el propósito de que** (see **43.5**).

When **de manera/modo/forma que** express *consequence* and not purpose, the *indicative* is used:

> **Le hablé muy despacio, de manera/modo/forma que me entendió.** (see **43.5**)
> I spoke to him/her very slowly, so that (= and the consequence was that) he/she understood me.

18.2.2 With conjunctions of time when they relate to a future situation

> **En cuanto llegue, te llamo por teléfono.**
> As soon as I get there, I'll call you.

> **Sólo puedes ir cuando sepamos la verdad.**
> You can only go when we know the truth.

> **Manuel dijo que iba a leer hasta que llegara su amigo.**
> Manuel said that he was going to read until his friend came.

> **¡Empieza cuando quieras!**
> Begin when(ever) you like.

Other conjunctions which relate to a hypothetical future situation also take the subjunctive:

> **A pesar de que me critiquen, no desistiré.** (see **52**)
> In spite of the fact that they may criticize me, I won't give up.

> **Por mucho que protesten no voy a abandonar la empresa.** (see also **18.2.3**)
> However much they (may) protest, I'm not going to abandon the enterprise.

Contrast the following examples, in which the conjunction relates to a past situation, or to a general situation:

> **En cuanto llegué, te llamé por teléfono.**
> As soon as I got there, I called you.

> **Sólo pude ir cuando supimos la verdad.**
> I could only go when we knew the truth.

> **Manuel dijo que siempre leía hasta que llegaba su amigo.**
> Manuel said that he always read until his friend came.

A pesar de que Elena tiene tiempo, no nos visita. (see 52)
In spite of the fact that Elena has time, she doesn't visit us.

The only conjunction of time that *always* takes a subjunctive is **antes de que** 'before':

Antes de que te cases, mira lo que haces.
Before you marry, look what you're doing. (the Spanish equivalent of
'Look before you leap'.)

María se había ido antes de que lo supiera Pablo.
María had left before Pablo knew.

There is an increasing tendency in some written styles of Spanish, especially
journalistic style, to use the -**ra** past subjunctive verb form in place of the preterite or
past anterior (see **17.9** and **17.10**) with conjunctions of time, especially with **después
(de) que** and **luego que** 'after', and **desde que** 'since':

**La paz se firmó después de que/luego que todos los ministros se
pusieran de acuerdo.**
The peace was signed after all the ministers had come to an agreement.

Ha habido paz desde que se detuviera a los guerrilleros.
There has been peace since the guerrillas were arrested.

18.2.3   **Conjunctions expressing a hypothesis**

▶ **50** (p. 296); **51** (p. 299); **52** (p. 306)

(a) Conditions

En caso de que necesites ayuda, hablaré con él.
If you need help, I'll speak to him.

Como se lo digas te pego. (see 51.3)
If you tell him/her I'll beat you up.

Siempre que no te quejes, te saco de paseo.
Provided you don't complain, I'll take you out for a walk.

Conjunctions with similar meaning are **con tal (de) que, siempre y cuando, a
condición de que, con la condición de que.**

(b) Negative conditions

Lo terminaremos este sábado, a menos que ocurra algo. (see 51.3)
We'll finish it this Saturday, unless anything unforeseen happens.

Conjunctions with similar meaning are **no sea que, no vaya a ser que, a no ser que,
salvo que.**

(c) Concession

Así me echen del trabajo exigiré un aumento de sueldo. (see 52)
Even if they fire me I'll insist on a salary increase.

Lo voy a comprar, aunque me cueste mucho dinero.
I'm going to buy it even though it may cost me a lot of money.

A conjunction with similar meaning is **aun cuando.**

There are a number of other ways of expressing concession in Spanish:

> **por mucho que** + verb + subjunctive
> **por más** + noun (pl.) + **que** + subjunctive
> **por muy** + adjective + **que** + subjunctive

> **Por mucho que insistas, no voy a comprarte un helado.**
> However much you insist, I won't buy you an ice cream.

> **Por más libros que lea, no aprobará en matemáticas.**
> However many books he/she reads, he/she won't pass mathematics.

> **Por muy tonto que sea, debe comprender que no hay que comportarse de tal manera.**
> However stupid he is, he must understand that one shouldn't behave like that.

Subjunctive + **lo que** + subjunctive:

> **Cueste lo que cueste, lo voy a comprar.**
> I'll buy it, whatever it costs.

> **Sea como sea, no te quiero decir más.**
> Be that as it may, I'm telling you no more.

Subjunctive + **o no** (+ subjunctive)

> **Tenga dinero o no (tenga dinero), lo va a comprar.**
> Whether he has any money or whether he doesn't, he's going to buy it.

See also **si bien**, which takes the same verb forms as **si** (**18.2.4**).

Some conjunctions with a concessional meaning can be used to introduce the statement of a fact; when they do, the *indicative* is used:

> **Aunque llovía, salimos.**
> Even though it was raining we went out. (fact)

> **Por mucho que insistía, no le compré un helado.**
> However much he/she insisted (= even though he/she insisted a lot), I didn't buy him/her an ice cream. (fact)

Aunque can also introduce an unreal condition, in which case it has the same verb forms as **si** (see **18.2.4**):

> **Aunque estuviera aquí, no le hablaría.**
> Even if he/she were here, I wouldn't talk to him/her. (he/she *isn't* here)

18.2.4

The subjunctive and indicative with *si*

 50 (p. 296); 51 (p. 299)

Si has a special syntax. It is used:

- with the pluperfect subjunctive for unreal conditions (i.e. envisaging something which was not the case) in the past.

● with the imperfect subjunctive for unreal conditions in the present and for unlikely conditions in the future.

NOTE The present subjunctive is *never* used with **si.**

Si me lo hubieras/hubieses pedido te habría/hubiera ayudado.
(see **51.2**)
If you had asked me I would have helped you.

Si estuviera seguro lo haría.
If I were certain I would do it.

Si te invitaran, ¿aceptarías? (see 50)
If they invited you, would you accept?

If **si** expresses an open condition (i.e. envisaging something which might or equally might not be the case), or if it introduces a fact, then the indicative is used:

Si te invitan, ¿aceptarás? (see 50)
If they invite you, will you accept?

Si no llegas a las seis empezamos sin ti. (see **51.1**)
If you don't arrive at six we'll start without you.

Si le duele tanto es/será mejor llamar a un médico. (see **51.1**)
If it hurts him/her so much we'd better call a doctor.

Si ha llegado hablaré con él. (see **51.1**)
If he has arrived I will speak to him.

Si Miguel iba a volver tarde, avisaba a sus padres.
If Miguel was going to come home late, he told his parents.

Like **si** is **si bien** 'even if'/'though', which is often used to make contrasts between facts (and hence in these circumstances used with the indicative):

Si bien la casa es grande, el alquiler es muy caro. (see 52)
Even though the house is big, the rent is very high./The house may be big, but the rent is very high.

18.2.5 **The subjunctive in relative clauses**

The subjunctive is used in relative clauses which have a negative or an indefinite antecedent (i.e. the noun or pronoun to which the relative clause relates and which stands immediately in front of the relative pronoun).

▶ **11** (p. 45); **13** (p. 52)

No conozco a nadie que tenga tanta paciencia.
I don't know anyone who has such patience.

Allí no hay fábricas que contaminen el medio ambiente.
There are no factories there to pollute the environment.

Los estudiantes que no tengan libros deben hacer cola en el pasillo.
Those students who haven't got books should form a queue in the
corridor. (it is not known which students have no books)

Necesito una secretaria que hable portugués.
I need a secretary who can speak Portuguese. (I don't know who that
will be)

Toma los que quieras.
Take whichever you want.

Recognizing an indefinite antecedent is difficult for English speakers, since
indefiniteness is not marked grammatically in English in the same way as in Spanish.
There is in Spanish a substantial difference in meaning between the use of the
indicative and the subjunctive in relative clauses which sometimes cannot easily be
rendered in English:

Busco un libro que tenga 200 páginas.
I'm looking for a book that has 200 pages.
*(I don't know which it will be, but I need one that has 200 pages, perhaps to get
an idea of how thick such a book would be)*

Busco un libro que tiene 200 páginas.
I'm looking for a book that has 200 pages.
*(This must be a specific book I know about already: perhaps I've lost the book
and I can remember that one of its characteristics was that it had 200 pages)*

When the antecedent is a *person*, this difference is often also marked by the use of the
personal **a** (see **25.1.1.1**):

Necesitamos una señora que cuide a los niños.
We need a lady to look after the children.
(The lady is not yet identified)

Busco a una niña que lleva una falda amarilla.
I'm looking for a little girl who is wearing a yellow skirt.
(I know who she is already; the yellow skirt will identify her)

A special group of such antecedents are forms ending in -**quiera**, which correspond to
English forms ending in '-ever':

quienquiera que sea 'whoever it is'/'may be'
cualquiera que te guste 'whichever you like'
dondequiera que busques 'wherever you look'

▶ **13.5** (p. 53); **13.6** (p. 54)

18.3 The subjunctive in main clauses

18.3.1 Imperatives

The subjunctive forms all imperatives (see **16.1.1.6**) except for those corresponding to
tú (**vos**) and **vosotros/as**, and all negative imperatives.

¡Salga de aquí! (usted)
Get out of here!

> **Pongamos por ejemplo el caso de . . .** (see **30.10**) **(nosotros/as)**
> Let's take as an example the case of . . .
>
> **Por favor, no se lo digas. (tú)**
> Please don't tell him/her.

Que may introduce a positive imperative, especially when an imperative is repeated:

> **Que no tardes mucho.** (see **30.3**)
> Don't take too long.

18.3.2 Wishes

 62.2 (p. 355)

Que or **ojalá (que)** + subjunctive may express a wish:

> **Adiós Carmen, que tengas buen viaje.** (see **29.5**)
> Goodbye, Carmen, I hope you have a good trip.
>
> **¡Ojalá (que) hayan ganado!** (see **62.2**)
> I hope they've won!

Ojalá may also be used with the imperfect or pluperfect subjunctive to express a wish that has not been or cannot be fulfilled:

> **¡Ojalá lo hubiera sabido antes!**   I wish I had known before!
> **¡Ojalá tuviéramos más dinero!**   I wish we had more money!

18.3.3 Possibility

 48 (p. 282); **49** (p. 291)

Quizá(s), **tal vez** and **posiblemente** can be used with the subjunctive or the indicative. The following considerations are relevant to the choice of mood:

- The indicative indicates a higher degree of possibility than the subjunctive.
- Reference to a hypothetical future situation favours the subjunctive (see **18.2.2**).
- The indicative is used when these words are added parenthetically after the verb (see **18.1.2**).

Acaso always takes the subjunctive, but **a lo mejor, igual** and **lo mismo** take the *indicative* (**48.1, 49.1**).

See **48, 49.1, 71.8, 72.5** and **73.12** for examples.

19
Sequence of tense

Spanish verb forms fall into two major groups from the point of view of sequence of tense:

	Group 1: Related to the present	Group 2: Related to the past
Indicative	present perfect future perfect	imperfect pluperfect conditional perfect preterite
Subjunctive	present perfect	past (imperfect) pluperfect

Unless there are good reasons to the contrary, verb-forms from different groups should not be mixed in reported speech constructions and in constructions involving the subjunctive.

19.1 In reported (indirect) speech

▶ 33 (p. 196)

NOTE Indirect statements and questions use the *indicative*; indirect commands use the *subjunctive*.

Direct speech	Reported speech related to Present	Reported speech related to Past
Future: «**Lo haré**». 'I'll do it'.	Present/future: **Pepe *dice* que lo *hará*.** Pepe says he'll do it.	Preterite/conditional: **Pepe *dijo* que lo *haría*.** Pepe said he'd do it.
Future: «***Volveremos***». 'We will come back'.	Perfect/future: **Nos *han prometido* que *volverán*.** They've promised us that they will come back.	Pluperfect/conditional: **Nos *habían prometido* que *volverían*.** They had promised us that they would come back.

93

Direct speech	Reported speech related to Present	Reported speech related to Past
Present: «*Comemos* a mediodía». 'We eat at midday'.	Present/present: *Dicen que comen* a mediodía. They say that they eat at midday.	Imperfect/imperfect: *Decían* que *comían* a mediodía. They were saying that they ate at midday.
Perfect: «*¿Han terminado?*» 'Have they finished?'	Present/perfect: *Preguntamos si han terminado.* We ask if they've finished.	Pluperfect/pluperfect: *Habíamos preguntado* si *habían terminado.* We had asked if they had finished.
Present subjunctive (imperative): «*Vuelva* usted el lunes por la tarde» (see 33.4) 'Come back on Monday afternoon'.	Present/present subjunctive (imperative): Le *dices* que *vuelva* el lunes por la tarde. You ask him/her to come back on Monday afternoon.	Preterite/past subjunctive: Le *dijiste* que *volviera/ volviese* el lunes por la tarde. You asked him/her to come back on Monday afternoon.

But sometimes the sense may clearly require the breaking of such sequences:

Preterite: «Lo *hicimos* ayer». 'We did it yesterday.'	Present/preterite: *Dicen* que lo *hicieron* ayer. They say they did it yesterday.	Preterite/preterite: *Dijeron* que lo *hicieron* el día anterior. They said they did it the day before.
Future: «*¿Irán* mañana?» 'Will they go tomorrow?'	Present/future: *Pregunto* si *irán* mañana. I ask if they will go tomorrow.	Preterite/future: *Pregunté* si *irán* mañana. I asked if they will go tomorrow. *Contrast:* Preterite/ conditional: *Pregunté* si *irían* al día siguiente. I asked if they would go the following day (not necessarily 'tomorrow')

19.2 Constructions involving the subjunctive

Related to present	Related to past
Future/present subjunctive: *Será* **imposible que nos *entiendan*.** It will be impossible for them to understand us.	Conditional/past subjunctive: *Sería* **imposible que nos *entendieran*.** (see **48.1**) It would be impossible for you/them to understand us.
Present/future/present subjunctive: **Le *digo* a usted que *hablaré* con él siempre y cuando usted me *apoye*.** I tell you that I will speak to him providing you support me.	Preterite/conditional/past subjunctive: **Le *dije* a usted que *hablaría* con él siempre y cuando usted me *apoyara*.** (see **51.3**) I told you that I would speak to him providing you supported me.
Future/present subjunctive: **To lo *diré* a condición de que *guardes* el secreto.** I'll tell you on condition that you keep the secret.	Conditional/past subjunctive: **Te lo *diría* a condición de que *guardaras* el secreto.** (see **51.3**) I would tell you on condition that you kept the secret.

Again the rule can be broken if the sense demands:

Preterite/present subjunctive: **Ayer *llevé* el coche al garaje para que lo *reparen*.** (see **43.5**)
Yesterday I took the car to the garage so that they can repair it. (it has not been repaired yet)

Present/past subjunctive: **Me *extraña* que nunca lo *hiciera*.**
I'm surprised he/she never did it.

20
Other forms of the verb and their uses

Spanish sometimes uses more than one word to express a verb form, for example **ir a** + infinitive. Such forms are often referred to as *periphrastic* verb forms. The following are those most commonly used.

20.1 *Estar* + gerund

(a) Denoting ongoing action:

> **Estaba hablando con . . . , pero se ha cortado la comunicación.** (see **29.8**)
> I was speaking to . . . , but I got cut off.

> **Ahora está preparando la cena.** (see **71.5**)
> He/she's preparing dinner now.

> **Vivía en Madrid, pero ahora estoy viviendo en Zaragoza.** (see **71.5**)
> I used to live in Madrid, but now I'm living in Zaragoza.

The imperfect is often used to refer to actions which were taking place in the past when something else happened:

> **Ella estaba cocinando cuando él llegó.** (see **73.10**)
> She was cooking when he arrived.

The preterite denotes an ongoing action within a fixed period of time:

> **Estuve esperando en el aeropuerto más de cuatro horas.** (see 73.6)
> I was waiting at the airport for more than four hours.

▶ 73 (p. 415)

(b) Denoting prolonged action still in progress at a present moment (if used in the perfect) or at a past moment (if used in the pluperfect):

> **He estado trabajando desde las 7.00.** (see **73.2**)
> I've been working since seven o'clock.

> **Había estado trabajando desde las 7.00.**
> I had been working since seven o'clock.

(c) Expressing disapproval or surprise:

> **¡Pero qué estás haciendo!**
> But what (on earth) are you doing!

20.2 *Ir a* + infinitive

This construction is used:

(a) In the present, referring to future time. **Ir a** + infinitive is frequent in speech, and is preferred for more categoric statements:

> **Van a viajar a España.** (see **72.1**)
> They are going to travel to Spain.
>
> **Él nos va a ayudar.**
> He's going to help us. (definitely)

▶ **72** (p. 408)

(b) As the first person plural imperative:

> **Vamos a comer algo.** (see **67.2**)
> Let's eat something.

▶ **67.2** (p. 378)

(c) To express intention:

> **¿Vas a venir a mi boda?** (see **70.3**)
> Are you coming (= intending to come) to my wedding?

(d) In the imperfect, referring to future-in-the-past time:

> **Iban a hacer la compra.** (see **72.1**)
> They were going to do the shopping.

▶ **72.2** (p. 411)

20.3 *Llevar* + gerund

This has the meaning of spending time doing something.

> **Llevo mucho rato esperando/llevo esperando mucho rato.** (see **71.7**)
> I've been waiting a long time.
>
> **Llevo dos horas haciendo ejercicios.**
> I've been exercising for two hours.
>
> **Alfonso llevaba seis meses esperando a su hermano.**
> Alfonso had been waiting six months for his brother.

▶ **71.7.3** (p. 404)

20.4 *Acabar de* + infinitive

This denotes proximity to a present (in the present) or past (in the imperfect) moment and corresponds to English 'to have just'.

> **María Luisa acaba de marcharse.** (see **73.3**)
> María Luisa has just left.

> **Juan acababa de ser nombrado director cuando lo conocí.**
> Juan had just been appointed director when I met him.

20.5 *Ir* + gerund

This denotes a gradual or repeated process:

> **Va cobrando importancia.**
> It's (steadily) gaining in importance.

20.6 *Venir* + gerund

This denotes a repeated action continuing up to the present moment (with the present or perfect) or up to a past moment (with the imperfect):

> **Vengo diciendo que es imposible.**
> I've kept on saying that it's impossible.

> **Desde entonces ha venido insistiendo en su derecho al autogobierno.**
> Since that time it has (constantly) insisted on its right to self-government.

> **Venía reclamando su independencia desde el siglo XVI.**
> It had been claiming its independence since the sixteenth century.

20.7 *Tener* + past participle

This denotes completion:

> **No podías salir sin tener cumplidos los deberes.**
> You could not go out without having completed your homework.

It is frequently used with verbs like **prohibir** 'to forbid' indicating an ongoing state of affairs:

> **Me tiene prohibido criticar al jefe.**
> He/she has forbidden me to criticize the boss.

NOTE   In the **tener** + past participle construction, the past participle *agrees* with the direct object of the verb.

21
Modal auxiliary verbs and expressions

21.1 Poder

Poder is used to express:

(a) Possibility

48 (p. 282); **67** (p. 375)

> **Puede venir mañana.**
> He/she may come tomorrow.

> **Pueden haber llegado.** (see **48.1**)
> They may have arrived.

> **Podrías estudiar historia.** (see **67.1**) (advice)
> You could (= it would be possible for you to) study history.

> **¿Qué puedo hacer?** (see **67.3**)
> What can I (= is it possible for me to) do?

(b) Physical ability

53 (p. 311); **67** (p. 375)

> **No podemos alcanzarlo.**
> We can't reach it.

> **¿Podrá soportar tanto peso?**
> Will it be able to stand so much weight?

> **Pude traducirlo.**
> I was able to translate (= succeeded in translating) it.

> **Podía traducirlo.**
> I could translate it.

NOTE There is a considerable difference in meaning between the preterite and the imperfect. The imperfect denotes general ability without any implication that the action was carried out; the preterite implies that the action was in fact carried out.

17.3 (p. 74); **17.5** (p. 76); **53.1** (p. 311)

(c) Obligation

▶ **46.1** (p. 272)

> **Podríais/podíais/pudisteis habérselo explicado.** (see **46.1**)
> You might have (= ought to have) explained it to him/her.

(d) Permission

▶ **54.1** (p. 314); **70.1** (p. 390)

> **¿Puedo entrar?** (see **54.1**)
> May I come in?

> **¿Puedo cerrar la puerta?** (see **54.2**)
> May I close the door?

> **Puede usted quedarse aquí si desea.** (see **70.1**)
> You can stay if you like.

(e) With imperative force

▶ **68** (p. 381); **69.2** (p. 387)

> **¿Puedes subir un momento?** (see **68**)
> Can you come up for a moment?

> **¿Podrías poner esto allí?** (see **68**)
> Could you put this over there?

21.2 *Deber (de)*

▶ **48.1** (p. 282); **50** (p. 296)

Deber (de) is used to express:

(a) Supposition

NOTE Although strictly **deber** should be followed by **de** in this meaning, this rule is by no means always observed.

> **Deben (de) ser más de las seis.** (see **48.1, 50**)
> It must be past six o'clock.

> **Deben (de) haber regresado ya.** (see **48.1, 50**)
> They must have returned already.

> **Debían (de) ser las seis cuando empezó a llover.**
> It must have been six o'clock when it started to rain.

> **José debió (de) terminarlo ayer.**
> José must have finished it yesterday.

In referring to the past, the choice between imperfect and preterite is determined by the tense of the corresponding straightforward statement; thus

> **Debían (de) ser las seis** . . . corresponds to **Eran las seis** . . .
> **Debió (de) terminar** . . . corresponds to **Terminó** . . .

(b) Obligation

▶ **46.1** (p. 272); **61.2** (p. 353)

English 'ought' is often rendered in Spanish by the conditional (or colloquially the imperfect) form of **deber**.

> **Debo ir.**
> I must go.

> **Debería usted hacerlo de nuevo.** (see **61.2**)
> You should do it again.

> **Usted debería haber llegado más temprano.** (see **61.2**)
> You should have arrived earlier.

> **No debías habérselo dicho.** (colloquial)
> You shouldn't have said that to him/her.

21.3　*Saber*

▶ **46.2** (p. 274); **53.2** (p. 312)

Saber is used to express:

Learned ability:

> **¿Sabes tocar el piano?** (see **53.2**)
> Can you (= do you know how to) play the piano?

21.4　*Querer*

▶ **57.1** (p. 333)

(a) Wishes

A greater degree of politeness is achieved by using the imperfect or the **quisiera** form.

> **Queremos viajar a Madrid.** (see **57.1**)
> We want to travel to Madrid.

> **Quisiéramos verla.** (see **57.1**)
> We would like to see it.

> **Queríamos decirle algo.** (see **57.1**)
> We wanted (= would like) to tell you something.

(b) Invitation

▶ **70.1** (p. 390)

> **¿Quieres venir a nuestra fiesta?** (see **70.1**)
> Do you want to come to our party?

21.5 *Tener que*

(a) Obligation

▶ **46** (p. 272); **47.1** (p. 276); **69.1** (p. 385)

> **Tendrás que contestar.**
> You will have to reply.

> **Tuvimos que aplazar la reunión.**
> We had to put off the meeting.

(b) Imperative

> **Tienes que subir por esa escalera mecánica.** (see **69.1**)
> You have to go up that escalator.

21.6 *Haber de*

(a) Obligation

▶ **46.1** (p. 272); **47.3** (p. 279)

> **Hemos de separarnos.** (see **46.1**)
> We'll have to separate.

(b) Imperative

▶ **46.1** (p. 272)

> **Has de decírmelo todo.** (see **46.1**)
> You'll have to tell me everything.

21.7 *Haber que*

This is an impersonal expression, used only in the 3rd person singular (see **16.1.1.7**).

Obligation

▶ **46.3** (p. 274); **69.1** (p. 385)

> **Hay que callarlo.**   This must be kept quiet.

22
Ser and *estar*

22.1 ## *Ser*

Ser is used:

(a) With a noun or pronoun:

> **Soy arquitecto.** (see **34.6**)
> I am an architect.

> **Ayer fue un día muy frío.**
> Yesterday it was a very cold day.

> **¿Es éste su pasaporte?** (see **35.3**)
> Is this your passport?

> **¡Es algo muy insólito!** (see **36.7**)
> It's something very unusual.

▶ **34.6** (p. 208); **35** (p. 210); **36.8** (p. 217); **36.9** (p. 217)

(b) With an infinitive:

> **Eso es sufrir.**   That's suffering.

(c) With a clause:

> **La dificultad es que no tenemos dinero.**
> The difficulty is that we have no money.

Note also **es que** . . .

> **Es que se me cayó.** (see **43.2**)
> (The fact is that) I dropped it.

▶ **43.2** (p. 254)

(d) With adverbs of place when the subject is a noun denoting an event:

> **¿Dónde será la reunión?** (see **39.2**)
> Where will the meeting be?

▶ **39.2** (p. 232)

(e) With a past participle to form the passive

▶ **24.1** (p. 112)

Este libro fue escrito por un amigo mío.
This book was written by a friend of mine.

(f) With an adjective denoting membership of a class or group:

Pilar es española.   Pilar is Spanish (a Spaniard).

▶ | **34.2.1** (p. 205)

(g) With an adjective which denotes an attribute which is considered an inherent property of the subject:

La nieve es blanca. (see **36.1**)
Snow is white.

Este libro es triste.
The book is sad.

El clima de Galicia es húmedo. (see **36.9**)
The climate in Galicia is wet.

¿Cómo es tu amigo? (see **36.3.2**)
What is your friend like?

NOTE | Useful tests in English are to see whether a noun phrase can be substituted for the adjective without substantial diference in meaning resulting, e.g. **Mi tío es rico** 'My uncle is rich' = 'my uncle is a rich man', or whether the phrase 'a(n) *adjective* kind/sort of *noun*' can be substituted for the adjective, e.g. **Tu pregunta es vacía** 'Your question is an empty sort of question'.

▶ | **36** (p. 212)

(h) With an adjective when the subject noun denotes an abstract idea or a proposition:

Decir eso no sería muy prudente.
Saying that wouldn't be very wise.

Tus ideas son muy extrañas.
Your ideas are very strange.

▶ | **36** (p. 212)

(i) With a prepositional phrase (e.g. **de la ciudad**) which functions like the adjectives referred to above:

Juan es de Madrid. (see **34.2.2**)
Juan is from Madrid.

Su reloj es de oro. (see **36.5.2**)
His/her watch is made of gold.

▶ | **36** (p. 212)

(j) On its own, **ser** denotes existence or identity:

–**¿Cuántos somos?**   'How many of us are there?'
–**Somos cinco.**   'There are five of us.'

22.2 *Estar*

Estar is used:

(a) With adverbs of place (unless the adverb says where an event is to take place, when **ser** is used – see **22.1**):

> **Mi madre está en el salón.**
> My mother is in the living-room.
>
> **Aquí está correos/el correo.**
> Here is the post office.

▶ **39** (p. 230)

(b) With past participles to indicate a state of affairs consequential on an action or event:

> **La ventana está abierta.**
> The window is open. (it has been opened)
>
> **El libro está dividido en cinco capítulos.**
> The book is divided into five chapters. (the author divided it into five chapters)
>
> **La delincuencia está ligada al problema del desempleo.**
> Crime is linked to the problem of unemployment. (someone has linked crime to the problem)

With verbs which denote actions, **estar** + past participle signifies a state which is the result of the action, and is never equivalent to the corresponding active sentence: thus **la ventana está abierta** means 'the window is open' (state) while **(alguien) abre la ventana** means 'someone opens the window' (action). However, with verbs which denote states in which the subject is necessarily involved, **estar** + past participle may be equivalent to the corresponding active sentence: thus **la comisión estaba encabezada por el ministro** 'the commission was headed by the minister' (state) is equivalent to **el ministro encabezaba la comisión** 'the minister headed the commission' (also a state). Contrast also the following:

> **La habitación estaba señalada por una cifra azul.**
> The room was indicated by a blue number.
> = **Una cifra azul señalaba la habitación.**
> 'A blue number indicated the room' (state).
>
> but
> **La habitación nos fue señalada por la limpiadora.**
> The room was pointed out to us by the cleaner.
> = **La limpiadora nos señaló la habitación.**
> 'The cleaner pointed out the room to us' (action).

▶ **36.9** (p. 217)

(c) With past participles of reflexive verbs to denote the result of an action or event:

> **Estamos asombrados (asombrarse) por su audacia.**
> We are amazed by his/her audacity.

> **Mi madre estaba acostada (acostarse) cuando volvimos.**
> My mother was in bed (had gone to bed) when we returned.

(d) With adjectives denoting a state of affairs susceptible to change:

> **¿Estamos listos?**
> Are we ready?
>
> **¿Estás seguro/a?**
> Are you sure?
>
> **María está muy triste.** (see **36.3.1**)
> María is very sad.
>
> **¿Cómo está tu hermana?** (see **36.3.2**)
> How is your sister?
>
> **Ayer estuvo muy frío.** (see **36.9**)
> Yesterday was very cold.

▶ **36** (p. 212)

(e) With adjectives which do not denote an inherent property of the noun to which they relate:

> **La ciudad estaba muy sucia.** (see **36.4**)
> The city was very dirty.
>
> **La habitación estaba vacía.**
> The room was empty.
>
> **La sopa está caliente.**
> The soup is hot.
>
> **Está muy optimista.**
> He/she's taking a very optimistic attitude.

(f) With adjectives which are not used in an absolute way, but which denote a comparative notion or a particular application of the quality:

> **Estoy muy viejo para estas cosas.** (does not imply **soy viejo**)
> I'm too old for these things.
>
> **Pedro está muy orgulloso de sus hijos.** (does not imply **Pedro es orgulloso**)
> Pedro is very proud of his children.

(g) With adjectives, to denote a subjective impression:

> **Elena está muy guapa.** (see **36.3.1**)
> Elena looks very pretty. (does not imply that she is (objectively) pretty)
>
> **¡Qué alto estás!**
> How tall you've grown! (does not imply that the child is (objectively) tall)
>
> **Está muy dulce la sidra.**
> The cider tastes very sweet. (though it may not be an inherently sweet cider)

Many adjectives can be used with both **ser** and **estar**. There is always a difference in meaning: **ser listo** 'to be clever'/**estar listo** 'to be ready', **somos libres** 'we are free' (e.g. as an inherent property of human beings)/**estamos libres** 'we are (made) free' (e.g. on coming out of prison). However, the difference can be elusive to non-native speakers: **es soltero** 'he is a bachelor' (marital status)/**está soltero** 'he is a bachelor' (regarded as a state of affairs, see **34.3**); **es claro** 'it's clear' (neutral)/**está claro** 'it's been made clear, it strikes one as clear' (slightly stronger).

36 (p. 212)

(h) With a prepositional phrase which functions like the adjectives referred to above:

Estamos de vacaciones.	We're on holiday.
Juana estaba de mal humor.	Juana was in a bad mood.

(i) With **bien** and **mal**:

¿Está bien así? (see **60.3**)	Is it all right like this?
¡Eso está muy mal! (see **61.2**)	That's very bad.

(j) On its own, **estar** denotes location or a state of affairs:

Hola, ¿está José? (see **29.8**)
Hello, is José in?

Estaban todos mis amigos. (see **38.1**)
There were all my friends.

23
The reflexive

The reflexive has a large number of functions in Spanish.

NOTE	The reflexive pronoun is different from the object pronoun only in the 3rd person and the **usted/ustedes** forms, which have **se** as their unstressed reflexive pronoun and **sí** as their stressed reflexive pronoun in both the sg. and pl. (see **8.2.1**).

23.1 Literal reflexive

The reflexive pronoun refers to the subject of the verb.

> **Me defendí enérgicamente.**
> I defended myself energetically.

23.2 Reflexives with a conventionalized meaning

Some reflexives have a conventionalized meaning which is slightly different from a literal reflexive meaning.

> **Me veo en dificultades.**
> I am (not literally 'I see myself') in difficulties.

> **Se llama Dolores.**
> Her name is (not literally 'she calls herself') Dolores.

23.3 Reciprocal reflexives

In the plural, the reflexive pronoun may have a *reciprocal* meaning ('each other', 'one another').

> **Se escriben con frecuencia.**
> They frequently write to each other.

The sense is usually obvious from the context (in the above example, it is unlikely that people would write to themselves), but if necessary, the phrase **uno/a(s) a otro/a(s)** or, in formal style, an adverb such as **mutuamente** is added.

Los niños se lavaban (unos a otros).
The children were washing one another.

Los refugiados se ayudaron mutuamente.
The refugees helped one another.

23.4 Inherently reflexive verbs

Some verbs are always reflexive, although they have no literal reflexive meaning.

arrepentirse: **Se arrepintió de su falta de ánimo.**
He/she repented of his/her lack of courage.

jactarse: **Se jacta de ser muy listo.**
He boasts of being very clever.

23.5 The reflexive corresponding to an English intransitive

Many verbs in English can be used both transitively (capable of taking a direct object) and intransitively (not capable of taking a direct object); this is less common in Spanish, where intransivity is more frequently signalled by a reflexive form.

El sol secó la ropa. (transitive)
The sun dried the clothes. (transitive)
La ropa se secó al sol. (reflexive)
The clothes dried in the sun. (intransitive)

Juan cerró la puerta. (transitive)
Juan closed the door. (transitive)
La puerta se cerró. (reflexive)
The door closed. (intransitive)

Levanté la tabla. (transitive)
I raised the plank. (transitive)
Me levanté a los ocho. (reflexive)
I got up at eight. (intransitive)

23.6 Reflexive verbs with prepositional objects

Many reflexive verbs have prepositional objects:

Me alegro de tu éxito.
I'm delighted at your success.

Me asusté con su audacia.
I was frightened by his/her audacity.

¿Te olvidaste de decírmelo?
Did you forget to tell me?

23.7 The intensifying reflexive

Several non-reflexive verbs have reflexive counterparts which are similar in meaning, but which express a slightly different nuance often associated with greater intensity. Unfortunately, since each verb behaves slightly differently, no very general principle can be given. Here are some common examples:

caer 'to fall' (neutral, natural process)

caerse 'to fall' (some idea of reference to a starting point of falling, suddenness or accidental nature of fall)

La lluvia cayó.
The rain fell.
El avión cayó en el desierto.
The aeroplane crashed in the desert.

El niño se cayó de la silla.
The child fell from the chair.
La torre se cayó.
The tower fell down.
Se me cayó un libro.
I dropped a book.

comer 'to eat' (neutral)
¿Qué vamos a comer?
What shall we have to eat?

comerse 'to eat (up)'
El león se comió toda la carne.
The lion ate up all the meat.

dormir 'to sleep'
Anoche no dormí más de tres horas.
Last night I only slept for three hours.

dormirse 'to go to sleep'
Finalmente, a las ocho, María se durmió.
Finally, at eight o'clock, María went to sleep.

ir 'to go'

irse 'to go (off)', with a sense of movement away from

Esta noche voy al cine.
I'm going to the cinema tonight.

¡Vete!
Go away!
Se fue a Madrid.
He/she went (off) to Madrid.

morir 'to die' (especially as the result of accident, war, etc.)
Murieron muchos jóvenes en la Guerra Civil.
Many young men died in the Civil War.

morirse 'to die' (as a natural process; also figuratively)
Se me murió el tío hace dos años.
My uncle died two years ago.
Martín se muere por saber si ha aprobado.
Martín's dying to know if he's passed.

quedar 'to remain', though often simply 'to be'
No me queda mucho dinero.
I haven't much money left. (lit. 'not much money remains to me')
No sé si queda muy claro.
I don't know if it's very clear.

quedarse 'to stay'
Me voy a quedar dos meses.
I'm going to stay for two months.

23.8 The impersonal reflexive

The third person reflexive (**se**) has the function of denoting an impersonal or indefinite subject (i.e. corresponding to the English notion 'someone', 'people'). This reflexive can be used even with intransitive verbs which could never be literally reflexive. The verb is always in the *third person singular*.

> **Se suele decir que en España llueve poco.**
> People often say that it doesn't rain much in Spain.

> **O se es bueno, o no se es bueno.**
> Either people are good, or they're not.

It is often used as an equivalent for the English passive in this sense:

> **A continuación se leyó una poesía.**
> Straight away a poem was read. (somebody read a poem)

> **Se mató a los soldados.**
> The soldiers were killed. (somebody killed the soldiers)

23.9 The passive reflexive

Very closely associated with the impersonal reflexive (**23.8**) is the reflexive used with a *passive* value. In the third person singular, this construction is indeed often more or less indistinguishable from the impersonal reflexive; but the passive reflexive is also used in the plural.

> **El libro se publicó en 1964.**
> The book was published in 1964.

> **Se podían adquirir auténticas obras de Miró.**
> Genuine Miró works could be acquired.

> **Se cortan las verduras muy finas.** (see **42.1**)
> The vegetables are cut very finely.

Although with a plural noun both the following constructions are in theory possible:

> **Se vende naranjas.** (impersonal reflexive)
> Oranges are sold. (someone is selling oranges)

> **Se venden naranjas.** (passive reflexive)
> Oranges are sold.

there is in fact a strong tendency in such a case to use only the passive reflexive (i.e. the construction with a plural verb). The impersonal reflexive (i.e. the construction with a singular verb) is, however, still commonly found in many parts of the Spanish-speaking world.

NOTE The passive reflexive cannot always be used as an equivalent of the English passive; see **24.3**.

 24 (p. 112); **42.1** (p. 247)

24
The passive

Passive constructions have two principal functions:

● to bring a noun other than the subject of an active verb to the front of the sentence.
● to allow for the possibility of not expressing the subject of an active verb.

Both these functions are carried out by the English construction 'be' + past participle. This construction has a formal Spanish parallel in Spanish **ser** + past participle; but the latter is nowhere near so frequently used. This is partly because the **ser** + past participle construction is chiefly limited to formal written Spanish and partly because Spanish has a number of other ways of expressing the passive idea, no two of which are exactly equivalent.

24.1 *Ser* + past participle

Example:

> **Las nuevas medidas fueron adoptadas en seguida por el gobierno.**
> The new measures were adopted immediately by the government.

This construction is the most straightforward equivalent of the corresponding active construction and, like the active construction, focuses on the *action* of the verb (contrast **estar** + past participle below, which focuses on a *resultant state*).

> **Este libro fue escrito por un amigo mío.**
> This book was written by a friend of mine. (action)

Contrast:

> **El libro estaba escrito en francés.**
> The book was written in French. (state)

It cannot be used to bring anything except the *direct object* of the verb to the front of the sentence. The English sentence 'I was given a book by Pedro' cannot be rendered in Spanish by ***fui dado un libro por Pedro.**

Although the **ser** + past participle construction is infrequently used in spoken Spanish, it is not necessarily to be avoided in the formal written language.

In the present and imperfect tenses, **ser** + past participle must refer to an action actually in progress, or to a series of repeated actions which are in progress:

El delincuente es detenido por un policía armado.
The criminal is being arrested by an armed policeman.

Los libros eran apilados.
The books were being piled up.

Contrast:

El delincuente está detenido.
The criminal is under arrest. (state)

Los libros estaban apilados.
The books were piled up. (state)

▶ **42.1** (p. 247)

24.2 *Estar* + past participle

▶ **22.2** (p. 105)

Examples:

La ventana todavía no está cerrada.
The window still isn't shut.

España está dividida en varias autonomías.
Spain is divided into several autonomous regions.

This construction always denotes a *state*. An agent (i.e. whoever or whatever is responsible for the state) is expressible only if it has continuing involvement in the state.

La persiana estaba bloqueada por óxido.
The blind was blocked with rust.

La significación está determinada por el contexto.
The meaning is determined by the context.

24.3 The passive reflexive

▶ **23.9** (p. 111)

The third person reflexive is probably the commonest Spanish equivalent of the English passive. Examples are:

Se celebrarán las elecciones en marzo.
The elections will be held in March.

La nueva ley se aprobó en 1992.
The new law was approved in 1992.

Se rechazó la propuesta.
The proposal was rejected.

The passive reflexive should not in general be used when the reflexive could be interpreted literally, e.g. **los soldados se mataron**, which would mean 'the soldiers killed themselves'. (Here the impersonal reflexive could be used, **se mató a los soldados** 'the soldiers were killed' (someone killed the soldiers), or **ser** + past participle, **los soldados fueron matados** 'the soldiers were killed'.)

The passive reflexive is not used when the idea of the involvement of an agent is very strong, e.g. **este cuadro fue pintado por Picasso** 'this picture was painted by Picasso' could not normally be expressed as **este cuadro se pintó por Picasso**.

Some authorities consider that the passive reflexive should never be used with an agent, but this is an overstatement. The following Spanish sentences are perfectly acceptable:

> **Las pirámides se edificaron por esclavos.**
> The pyramids were built by slaves.

> **Este libro se va a publicar por Routledge.**
> This book will be published by Routledge.

None the less, not all such sentences are equally acceptable, and you will be best advised to avoid using an agent with the reflexive passive until you have gained a wide experience of its use.

24.4 Use of indefinite subjects

Vagueness as to the identity of the subject of a verb can be achieved by the use of a number of devices in Spanish (several of which are also available in English):

(a) An indefinite noun, such as **la gente** 'people':

> **La gente suele criticar muy duramente a los políticos.**
> People usually criticize politicians very harshly.
> (Politicians are usually very harshly criticized)

(b) Use of **uno** 'one' (see **13.3**).

> **Si uno no conoce personalmente a los niños, uno no puede enseñarles nada.**
> If one doesn't know children personally, one can't teach them anything.
> (If children aren't known personally, they can't be taught anything)

The use of **uno** is particularly favoured with a reflexive verb, since the passive and impersonal reflexive constructions are impossible with a verb that is already reflexive (see **24.3**, **23.8** and **23.9**).

> **Uno no se debe quejar del frío.**
> One shouldn't complain about the cold.

(c) Use of the verb in the third person plural:

> **Dicen que el peso va a subir.**
> They say the peso is going up.
> (The peso is said to be going up)

(d) Use of the **tú** form of the verb (especially common in speech):

Tú lees un libro determinado para divertirte.
You read a particular book to enjoy yourself.
(A book is read for enjoyment)

24.5 Bringing the object to the front of the sentence

In Spanish, an object can be brought to the beginning of an active sentence as the topic (see **28**) provided an unstressed personal pronoun (see **8.2.1, 8.3**) is also used:

La catedral la vimos desde lejos.
We saw the cathedral from a long way away.
(The cathedral was seen by us from a long way away)

A Miguel y Ana los vi jugando en el parque.
I saw Miguel and Ana playing in the park.
(Miguel and Ana were seen playing in the park by me)

25
Prepositions

Although the common prepositions of Spanish are listed alphabetically here for ease of reference, it is important to follow up the similarities and contrasts among them which are indicated by cross-references.

▶ **8.2.1** (p. 36)

8.2.1 (p. 36)

25.1 Basic use of prepositions

25.1.1 A

25.1.1.1 *Personal a*

'Personal' **a**, that is, the use of **a** before a direct object, is obligatory with proper names actually denoting people (not, for example, when standing for an inanimate notion such as a literary work or a make of car) and with pronouns denoting people.

> **Vi ayer a Juan Fernández.**
> I saw Juan Fernández yesterday.

> **¿A quién viste anoche?**
> Who did you see last night?

> **No recordamos a nadie.** (see **45.1**)
> We don't remember anybody.

But:

> **Leí todo Cervantes en un año.**
> I read the whole of Cervantes in a year.

▶ **29.4** (p. 156)

29.4 (p. 156)

Otherwise, there is some variation, in which a number of factors intervene:

	Favouring use of **a**	Not favouring use of **a**
1	Personal qualities or attribution of person-like qualities (as with a country or town or an abstract quality)	Viewing people impersonally, or as a commodity

	Favouring use of **a**	Not favouring use of **a**
2	Animals kept as pets	Animals in general, and especially those having a practical function or used for food
3	People viewed as specific individuals	Nouns referring to a class of people (especially with the indefinite article)
4	A number of verbs which denote the strong influence of the subject on the object, even when the object is not 'personal'	Verbs which express a general relation between subject and object, even when the object is 'personal'
5	To resolve potential ambiguity with verbs expressing a relation of precedence, even when the object is not 'personal'	To resolve potential ambiguity where the verb also has a 'personal' direct object and also a 'personal' indirect object

This is exemplified below:

1   **¿Conoce usted a mi colega Julio Prado?** (see 29.4)
Have you met my colleague Julio Prado?

            Criticaron muy duramente al comité.
They criticized the committee severely.

            El buen ciudadano ama a su patria.
A good citizen loves his country.

            Respetemos a la justicia.
Let us respect justice.

But:

            un coche que lleva cinco personas
a car which carries five people

2   **¡Ven a ver a mi cachorrito!**
Come and see my little puppy!

But:

            El gato cogió el gorrión.
The cat caught the sparrow.

            Comimos pollo.
We ate chicken.

3   **Busco a mi amigo.**
I'm looking for my friend.

            Conocí a tres rusos en Lisboa.
I met three Russians in Lisbon.

But:

> **Necesito un amigo.**
> I need a friend.

> **Busco tres rusos para ayudarme con un proyecto internacional.**
> I'm looking for three Russians to help me with an international project.

4   **Hay que liberar a la economía.**
     The economy must be liberated.

But:

> **Tengo dos hermanas.**
> I have two sisters.

5   **La paz siguió a la guerra.**
     Peace followed war.

But:

> **Recomendé mi amigo al jefe.**
> I recommended my friend to the boss.

Two verbs appear to change their meaning substantially according to whether they are used with or without the personal **a**, but they do follow the above principles. **Querer a una amiga** means 'to love a (girl)friend' (a specified individual) whereas **querer una amiga** means 'to want a (girl)friend' (i.e. someone unspecified to be a (girl)friend); **tener dos hijos** means 'to have two children' (a general relation between subject and object not denoting any influence of the subject on the object) whereas **tengo a mi hijo en casa** means 'I'm keeping my son at home' (a more active relationship between subject and object).

| 25.1.1.2 | ***A introducing an indirect object*** |

> **Mateo dio un beso a su madre.**
> Mateo gave his mother a kiss.

> **A Luis y Ana les gusta viajar.** (see **58.1**)
> Luis and Ana like travelling.

| 25.1.1.3 | ***A expressing direction towards*** |

> **Fuimos al cine.**   We went to the cinema.

| 25.1.1.4 | ***A expressing location*** |

The preposition most often used to express location is **en** (see **25.1.14.2**, **25.1.14.3**), but **a** is used in a number of expressions denoting a point in time or place. Examples are:

Time
a (cinco minutos) de aquí (see **39.3**) '(five minutes) from here'
a las cinco 'at five o'clock'
al mismo tiempo 'at the same time'
al día siguiente 'on the following day'

Place
a diez kilómetros de Madrid 'ten kilometres from Madrid'
al final 'at the end'

> **al aire libre** 'in the open air'
> **a la izquierda** 'on the left'
> **al otro lado** 'on the other side'
> **a la sombra** 'in the shade'

▶ **39.3** (p. 232); **39.4** (p. 235)

25.1.1.5 | *A expressing rate*

> **poco a poco** 'little by little', 'gradually'
> **a docenas** 'by the dozen'
> **a diario** 'daily'

25.1.1.6 | *A expressing manner*

> **tortilla a la española** 'omelette in the Spanish style'
> **al estilo barroco** 'in the Baroque style'

25.1.2 Ante

Ante means 'before' in the sense of 'face to face with', 'faced with'; it often has a figurative meaning. The literal notion of 'in front of' is usually rendered by **delante de**.

> **El delincuente compareció ante el tribunal.**
> The criminal appeared before the court.

> **Ante la posibilidad de morir de hambre, optaron por emigrar.**
> Faced with the possibility of starving, they decided to emigrate.

25.1.3 Antes de

Antes de means 'before' in a temporal sense.

> **Llegaron antes de las seis.**
> They arrived before six o'clock.

25.1.4 Bajo

Bajo 'under' is often used in set phrases, or with a figurative meaning. The literal notion of 'under' is also rendered by **debajo de**.

> **bajo la mesa** 'under the table'
> **bajo fianza** 'on bail'
> **España bajo los Borbones** 'Spain under the Bourbons'

▶ **39.3** (p. 232)

25.1.5 Con

Con corresponds to English 'with', and is also extensively used to form adverbial phrases of manner:

> **Voy a salir con mis amigos.**
> I'm going out with my friends.

Lo ató con una cuerda.
He/she tied it up with a piece of string.

No oigo nada con tanto ruido de fondo.
I can't hear anything with so much background noise.

Lo haré con mucho gusto.
I'll do it gladly.

25.1.6   *Contra*

Contra corresponds to English 'against'. For opinions, etc., **en contra de** is often used.

dos contra uno
two against one

Apoyó la escalera contra la pared.
He/she put the ladder against the wall.

un argumento en contra de la reforma
an argument against reform

25.1.7   *De*

De is an extremely frequent and versatile preposition in Spanish.

25.1.7.1   **De** can express a number of types of relation between one noun and another. Although it often corresponds to English 'of' (or the English genitive, 's/s'), a much wider range of prepositions are used in such cases in English.

(a) Possession or notion of belonging or association

la casa de mi abuela 'my grandmother's house'
los bares de Madrid 'the bars in Madrid'
el tren de las cinco 'the five-o'clock train'
la carretera de Sevilla 'the road to Seville'
la aldaba de la puerta principal 'the knocker on the main door'

(b) Characteristic

el hombre de los zapatos blancos 'the man in the white shoes'
una silla de ruedas 'a wheelchair' (a chair with wheels)
un niño de tres años 'a three-year-old boy'

(c) Specification

el mes de enero 'the month of January'
un libro de matemáticas 'a book about mathematics'

(d) Position

la casa de enfrente 'the house opposite'

(e) Material or manner of operation

una bolsa de plástico 'a plastic bag'
una camisa de seda 'a silk shirt'
una estufa de gas 'a gas stove'

(f) Composition or content

> **un montón de libros** 'a pile of books'
> **un paquete de caramelos** 'a packet of sweets'
> **un vaso de agua** 'a glass of water'

(g) Linking words denoting the same thing or person

> **la ciudad de Roma** 'the city of Rome'
> **el tonto de Juan** 'silly Juan'

(h) An agent or action and its object

> **los constructores de las pirámides**
> the builders of the pyramids

> **la destrucción del medio ambiente**
> the destruction of the environment

25.1.7.2 | *De expressing direction from or origin*

> **He venido del centro.**
> I've come from the centre.

> **Rosa vive a tres kilometros de aquí.**
> Rosa lives three kilometres from here.

> **Mi marido es de Argentina.**
> My husband is from Argentina.

▶ **34.2** (p. 205)

There are a number of ways of rendering English 'from . . . to . . .':

(a) **De . . . a . . .** and **desde . . . hasta . . .** are equivalent, the former being used especially with shorter nouns and in speech:

> **de Buenos Aires a Tucumán**
> from Buenos Aires to Tucumán

> **desde el siglo XV hasta el día de hoy**
> from the fifteenth century up until the present day

(b) **De . . . en . . .** is used to indicate frequency or repeated movement:

> **de vez en cuando** 'from time to time'
> **de casa en casa** 'from house to house'

25.1.7.3 | *De denoting an agent*

De is sometimes used instead of **por** to introduce an agent, especially when a state of affairs rather than a definite action is involved:

> **El campo estaba cubierto de nieve.**
> The countryside was covered in snow.

> *Yerma*, **de García Lorca**
> *Yerma*, by García Lorca

25.1.7.4 **De denoting cause**

> **Lo hizo de pura envidia.**   He/she did it out of sheer envy.

25.1.7.5 De is also used in a very wide range of adverbial phrases and idioms:

> **de vacaciones** 'on holiday'
> **de pie** 'standing up'
> **de todas formas** 'in any case'
> **de cierta manera** 'in a certain way'

25.1.8   Debajo de

Corresponds to English 'under'. See also **bajo (25.1.4)**.

> **Las llaves están debajo de la cama.** (see 39.3)
> The keys are under the bed.

▶ **39.3** (p. 232)

25.1.9   Delante de

Corresponds to English 'in front of'. See also **ante** (see **25.1.2**).

> **Delante del palacio había una plaza enorme.**
> In front of the palace there was a huge square.

▶ **39.3** (p. 232)

25.1.10   Dentro de

Dentro de corresponds to English '(with)in'.

> **Dentro de la ciudad hay muchas callecitas pintorescas.**
> (With)in the town there are many picturesque little streets.

> **dentro de lo posible**
> within the bounds of the possible

Dentro de is usually used to render temporal expressions like 'in five minutes' (time)':

> **El tren saldrá dentro de cinco minutos.**
> The train will leave in five minutes.

25.1.11   Desde

25.1.11.1 **Desde denoting direction from**
See **de (25.1.7)**, which is also often used with this meaning, especially in speech. **Desde** is more restricted in meaning than **de**, and so tends to be used if there is any possibility of ambiguity.

> **Nos llegó un rumor de voces desde abajo.**
> A sound of voices reached us from below.

> **Desde aquí se ve el mar.**
> From here you can see the sea.

> **desde distintos puntos de vista**
> from various points of view

> **desde Roma hasta Madrid**
> from Rome to Madrid

25.1.11.2 *Desde denoting time since*

> **desde los primeros días de la guerra**
> from the first days of the war

> **desde niño**
> since being a child

> **Vivimos en México desde hace muchos años.** (see **17.1.1**)
> We have lived in Mexico for many years. (lit. 'since many years ago')

> **desde las seis hasta las siete**
> from six o'clock until seven

25.1.12 *Después de*

Después de means 'after' in a temporal sense. See also **tras** (**25.1.27**).

> **después de la guerra**
> after the war

> **Después de visitar el Prado fuimos a tomar una cerveza.**
> After visiting the Prado we went to have a beer.

Después que is sometimes used instead of **después de** when what follows is the subject of a clause potentially introduced by **después (de) que**, and a personal pronoun remains in its subject form in this context:

> **Tú vas a terminar después que yo.** (= **después de que termine yo**)
> You're going to finish before me. (= 'before I finish')

25.1.13 *Detrás de*

Detrás de means 'after' in a spatial sense (the converse of **delante de**). See also **tras** (**25.1.27**).

> **Detrás de la puerta había un jardín precioso.**
> Behind the door there was a beautiful garden.

 39.4 (p. 235)

25.1.14 *En*

25.1.14.1 *En denoting position above*

See also **sobre** and **encima de** (which are more restricted in meaning than **en**). Note too that **de** may also denote position when used after a noun (**25.1.7.1**).

> **El libro está en la mesa.**   The book is on the table.

25.1.14.2 *En denoting a point in space or time or place*
Note that this use of **en** often corresponds to English 'at'.

> **en la estación** 'at the station'
> **en el jardín** 'in the garden'
> **en casa** 'at home'
> **en aquel momento** 'at that moment'

▶ **39.3** (p. 232)

25.1.14.3 *En denoting a point within a space or a period of time*
See also **dentro de** (**25.1.10**). **En** is also used in figurative expressions of this kind.

> **Ella está en la oficina.** (see **39.3**)
> She is at the office.

> **El niño se perdió en la muchedumbre.**
> The child got lost in the crowd.

> **en el siglo XV**
> in the fifteenth century

> **En mi vida he conocido a nadie tan serio.**
> I've never met anyone so serious in my life.

> **Estamos en peligro.**
> We are in danger.

▶ **39.3** (p. 232)

25.1.14.4 *En denoting movement within*
En corresponds to English 'into':

> **Entramos en la cueva.**   We went into the cave.

25.1.14.5 *En with means of transport*

> **Fuimos en bicicleta.** (*but* **a caballo, a pie**)
> We went by bicycle. ('on horseback', 'on foot')

25.1.14.6 *En with measurements*

> **Los precios subieron en un seis por ciento.**
> Prices went up by six per cent.

> **La temperatura bajó en cinco grados.**
> The temperature went down by five degrees.

25.1.15 *En contra de*

See **contra** (**25.1.6**).

25.1.16 *Encima de*

Encima de corresponds to English 'on top of', 'above', and is more specific than **en**. It is often, though not exclusively, used to denote a high position.

> **Encima de la torre había un pararrayos.**
> On top of the tower was a lightning conductor.

> **Encima de la casa se veía una nube de humo.**
> Above the house a cloud of smoke could be seen.

▶ **39.3** (p. 232)

25.1.17 *Enfrente de* (also written *en frente de*)

Enfrente de corresponds to English 'opposite': see also **frente a** (25.1.19).

> **Mi casa está enfrente de/frente a la catedral.** (see 39.3)
> My house is opposite the cathedral.

▶ **39.3** (p. 232)

25.1.18 *Entre*

Entre corresponds to English 'between', 'among'.

> **Está entre correos/el correo y el banco.** (see 39.3)
> It's between the post office and the bank.

NOTE   the use of the personal pronoun forms in the expression **entre tú y yo** 'between you and me' (see **8.2.1**).

▶ **39.3** (p. 232)

25.1.19 *Frente a*

See also **enfrente de** (**25.1.17**). **Frente a**, in the literal meaning of 'opposite', is more typical of the written language (except in L. Am.), but it is also used in the figurative sense of 'faced with': (see also **ante** (**25.1.2**)):

> **Frente a la posibilidad de perder, decidimos abandonar la empresa.**
> Faced with the possibility of losing, we decided to abandon the enterprise.

▶ **39.3** (p. 232)

25.1.20 *Hacia*

Hacia corresponds to English 'towards': in time expressions it has the meaning of 'about', 'approximately'.

> **hacia el sur** 'towards the south'
> **hacia las seis de la tarde** 'at around six in the evening'

25.1.21 *Hasta*

Hasta corresponds to English 'until' (time) and 'up to' (place).

> **Voy a trabajar hasta medianoche.**
> I'm going to work until midnight.

> **Usted sigue todo recto hasta la segunda calle a la izquierda.**
> You carry straight on as far as the second street on the left.

Desde . . . hasta . . . (see **25.1.7.2**) is an equivalent of 'from . . . to . . .':

> **Estuve esperando desde mayo hasta setiembre.**
> I was waiting from May to September.

Hasta is also used in a number of set ways of saying 'goodbye' in Spanish (see **29.5**).

> **¡Hasta mañana!**   Until tomorrow!

25.1.22 *Para*

Para and **por** both correspond to English 'for' in some of their usages, and therefore discriminating between them is difficult for English speakers.

NOTE Think of **por** as looking *backwards* to a cause or motive, or a substitution (though it has a number of other meanings too); think of **para** as looking *forward* to a destination or purpose:

> ←———————————————————— por
> para ————————————————————→

25.1.22.1 *Para denoting purpose*

> **¿Para qué me llamaste?**
> What did you call me for?

> **¿Estará listo para mañana?**
> Will it be ready for tomorrow?

> **Está estudiando mucho para aprobar en francés.**
> He/she's studying hard in order to pass in French.

▶ **43.4 (p. 257)**

25.1.22.2 *Para denoting destination*

> **He comprado estas flores para mi tía.** (see **43.5**)
> I've bought these flowers for my aunt.

> **¿Hay sitio para dos personas?**
> Is there room for two people?

> **Voy para Sevilla.**
> I'm going to Seville

Para is used with expressions denoting quantities:

> **Es demasiado fuerte para mí.**
> It's too strong for me.
>
> **Basta para satisfacer al jefe.**
> That's enough to satisfy the boss.

$\boxed{25.1.22.3}$ *Para in time expressions*

> **Hazlo para el lunes que viene.**
> Do it by next Monday.
>
> **Mi novia ha ido a España para una semana.**
> My girlfriend has gone to Spain for a week. (= in order to spend a week there)

$\boxed{\textbf{25.1.23}}$ *Por*

$\boxed{25.1.23.1}$ *Por denoting cause or motive*

> **¿Por qué te levantaste tan temprano?**
> Why did you get up so early?
>
> **Por la lluvia no pudimos venir.** (see **43.2**)
> Because of the rain we could not come.
>
> **Por razones personales no pudieron asistir.** (see **43.3**)
> For personal reasons they were not able to attend.
>
> **Por no tener dinero sólo comíamos pan.**
> Because we didn't have money we ate only bread.
>
> **Hazlo por tu madre.**
> Do it for your mother's sake.
>
> **Luchamos por la libertad.**
> We are fighting for the sake of freedom.

$\boxed{25.1.23.2}$ *Por denoting substitution*

> **Cambié el coche por una bicicleta.**
> I changed the car for a bicycle.
>
> **El ministro firmó por el presidente.**
> The minister signed on behalf of the president.

$\boxed{25.1.23.3}$ *Por denoting movement through or time during*

> **Pasamos por el centro de la ciudad.**
> We passed through the city centre.
>
> **Madrid por la N-VI.**
> Madrid by way of the N-VI (road).

Por la ventana vi las montañas.
Through the window I saw the mountains.

Entramos por la puerta trasera.
We went in via the back door.

Mi madre vendrá por una semana.
My mother will come for a week.

25.1.23.4 *Por denoting a vague place or time*

Por aquí hay muchos bares.
There are many bars around here.

Por todas partes había grupos de jóvenes.
Everywhere there were groups of youngsters.

Por agosto suele hacer mucho calor.
Round about August it is usually very hot.

25.1.23.5 *Por denoting rate*

por docena(s) 'by the dozen'
ochenta kilómetros por hora 'eighty kilometres an hour'

25.1.23.6 *Por denoting an agent*

César fue asesinado por Bruto.
Caesar was murdered by Brutus.

Se publicó por una editorial extranjera.
It was published by a foreign publisher.

25.1.23.7 *Por denoting means*

por escrito
in writing

La reconocí por las manos.
I recognized her by her hands.

Es más cómodo viajar por avión.
It is more comfortable travelling by air.

25.1.24 *Según*

Según corresponds to English 'according to', 'depending on'.

según mi madre 'according to my mother'
según las circunstancias 'depending on the circumstances'

● 55.4 (p. 325)

25.1.25 *Sin*

Sin corresponds to English 'without', and is used in a wide variety of expressions to denote a negative idea.

sin decir palabra 'without saying a word'
sin problema 'no problem'
sinvergüenza 'shameless'
una tarea sin terminar (see 32) 'an unfinished task'

25.1.26 *Sobre*

25.1.26.1 **Sobre** has the meaning of 'on' ('top of') and is an alternative to **en** in this meaning (see **25.1.14**). It is also equivalent to, but rather more frequent than, **encima de**, which is used when an idea of height is involved (see **25.1.16**). It is also used to denote superior status.

> Las llaves están sobre/en la mesa. (see 39.3)
> The keys are on the table.

> El dinero estaba sobre/encima del armario. (see 39.3)
> The money was on top of the wardrobe.

> El director de marketing está sobre el jefe de ventas. (see 39.3)
> The marketing director is above the sales manager.

25.1.26.2 **Sobre** also has the meaning of 'about', 'concerning'.

> un libro sobre Neruda
> a book about Neruda

> Sobre gustos no hay nada escrito. (idiom)
> There are no rules concerning taste.

▶ **39.3** (p. 232)

25.1.26.3 In time expressions, **sobre** means 'about', 'approximately'.

> Nos veremos sobre las cinco.
> We'll see one another round about five.

25.1.26.4 With place names, **sobre** has the meaning of 'near':

> Estaba sobre la calle de Serrano. (see 39.3)
> It was near the Calle Serrano.

▶ **39.3** (p. 232)

25.1.27 *Tras*

Tras is now used a great deal in journalistic Spanish as an alternative to **después de** (see **25.1.12**); it is otherwise used in expressions which link two nouns:

> día tras día 'day after day'

25.2 Groups of prepositions

Sequences of prepositions may be used to indicate more complex ideas, much as in English:

> **desde debajo de la silla** 'from underneath the chair'
> **de por aquí** 'from around here'

While many English prepositions indicate both position and motion, these notions are distinguished in Spanish by the use of **por** where motion is involved:

> **El gato estaba escondido debajo de la mesa.**
> The cat was hiding under the table.

But:

> **El gato corrió por debajo de la mesa.**
> The cat ran under the table.

> **Delante del ayuntamiento había una estatua de mármol.**
> In front of the town hall was a marble statue.

But:

> **La procesión pasó por delante del ayuntamiento.**
> The procession passed in front of the town hall.

26
Complementation

By complementation we mean the kind of structures which are associated with verbs and verbal expressions, and with nouns which represent a verbal idea. There are three kinds of complementation in Spanish:

- Sentence complementation. The sentence is introduced by one of two complementizers, **que** or **si**: e.g. **Pienso** *que tienes razón* 'I think you're right'; **Me pregunto** *si es tan fácil como dicen* 'I wonder if it is as easy as they say'.
- Infinitive complementation. Sometimes the infinitive is preceded by a preposition, although prepositions used in this way do not necessarily have the basic meanings given in **25.1**; e.g. **Me gusta** *nadar* 'I like swimming', **Soñaba** *con ir a la luna* 'I was dreaming of going to the moon'.
- Gerund complementation. This is much less common than the first two; e.g. **Terminé** *borrándolo todo* 'I ended up rubbing it all out'.

It is beyond the scope of this book to give a comprehensive list of the complementation patterns of verbs and verbal expressions: looking up the verb in a good dictionary will usually provide the information you need. What follows is only a representative selection of the more commonly-occurring constructions.

Rather than reading through the whole of this chapter, you may find it quicker to find out about the complementation of individual words by looking them up in the index at the end of this book to find their location in the appropriate section.

26.1   Sentence complementation

26.1.1   With *que*

Que is used for reported (indirect) speech, indirect commands, and in a large number of constructions involving the subjunctive.

(a) Reported speech

> **Dijo que no tenía la menor idea.**
> He/she said he/she hadn't the faintest idea.

(b) Indirect commands

> **Me pidió que le ayudase.**
> He/she asked me to help him/her.

(c) Subjunctive constructions

> **Quiero que me digas tu nombre.**
> I want you to tell me your name.

> **Me gusta que tengas tantos amigos.**
> I like it that you have so many friends.

Especially when it comes at the beginning of a sentence as the complementizer of a subject complement, **que** is sometimes strengthened to **el que**, which, like **el hecho de que**, means 'the fact that':

> **El (hecho de) que no tengan dinero no me extraña.**
> The fact that they have no money doesn't surprise me.

▶ **18.1** (p. 83); **20** (p. 96); **27** (p. 141); **33** (p. 196)

Sentence object complements with nouns are introduced by the preposition **de** (**de** is sometimes omitted in spoken Spanish, but such an omission is considered incorrect):

> **la idea de que tantas personas pasan hambre**
> the idea that so many people feel hungry

> **la posibilidad de que se produzca un terremoto**
> the possibility that there will be an earthquake

Sentence object complements with adjectives are introduced by various prepositions:

> **Estoy seguro de que llegará con tiempo.**
> I'm sure he/she will arrive in good time.

> **¿Estás dispuesta a ayudarme?**
> Are you prepared to help me?

NOTE   English constructions are sometimes not the same in form as their Spanish equivalents. 'I'm pleased that he is coming' is in Spanish **Me agrada que venga**, in which English 'be' + adjective corresponds to the Spanish verb **agradar**.

26.1.2   **With *si***

Si is used in indirect questions:

> **¿Me preguntas si estoy de acuerdo?**
> Are you asking me if I agree?

▶ **20** (p. 96); **33.2** (p. 196)

26.2   Infinitive complementation

26.2.1   Infinitive subject

An infinitive may be the subject complement of a verb or of **ser** + adjective (**17.11**). It usually follows the verb or **ser** + adjective in such cases. Note that English has a different construction from Spanish in such cases: study the sentences given below as examples.

> *agradar*: **Nos agrada comer al aire libre.**
> We like eating in the open air. (lit. 'Eating in the open air pleases us.')

> *apetecer*: **¿Qué te apetece tomar?**
> What would you like to drink (lit. 'Drinking what appeals to you?')

> *alegrar*: **Me alegra cantar villancicos.**
> It makes me happy singing Christmas carols. (lit. 'Singing Christmas carols makes me happy.')

> *bastar*: **Nos basta tener buena salud.**
> Having good health is enough for us.

> *complacer*: **Me complace invitarle a la cena.**
> I have pleasure in inviting you to the dinner. (lit. 'Inviting you to the dinner gives me pleasure.')

> *encantar*: **Me encanta tener tantos parientes.**
> I'm delighted to have so many relatives. (lit. 'Having so many relatives delights me.')

> *importar*: **¿Te importa cerrar la ventana?**
> Do you mind shutting the window? (lit. 'Does shutting the window matter to you?')

> *interesar*: **¿Les interesaría a Vds. saber dónde está nuestro amigo?**
> Would you be interested to know where our friend is? (lit. 'Would knowing where our friend is interest you?')

> *ser difícil*: **Es difícil decirlo con certeza.**
> It's difficult to say with certainty. (lit. 'Saying with certainty is difficult.')

> *ser fácil*: **Es fácil ir a Madrid.**
> Getting to Madrid is easy.

> *ser gracioso*: **Es gracioso ver a los chimpancés.**
> It's funny to see the chimpanzees. (lit. 'Seeing the chimpanzees is funny.')

> *ser imposible*: **Fue imposible comentarlo todo.**
> It was impossible to comment on all of it (lit. 'Commenting on all of it was impossible.')

In all the above cases, the implied subject of the infinitive complement is either indefinite or is the same as the indirect object of the main verb. Some of these verbs and expressions have the possibility of taking a sentence complement with **que** and the subjunctive when this situation does not hold, e.g.:

> **¿Te importa cerrar la ventana?**
> Lit. 'Is it important to *you* for *you* to shut the window?'

But:

> **¿Te importa que fumemos?**
> Lit: 'Is it important to *you* if *we* smoke?'

Basta tener dinero.
It's enough to have money. (indefinite subject for **tener dinero**)

Nos basta tener dinero.
It's enough for *us* that *we* have money.

But:

Basta que los escritores tengan papel.
It's enough that *writers* have paper.

Es difícil explicarlo.
It's difficult to explain it. (indefinite subject for **explicar**)

Me es difícil explicarlo.
It's difficult for *me* to explain it. (*I* must explain it.)

But:

Es difícil que el mundo cambie.
It's difficult for *the world* to change.

As in English, another kind of infinitive complement construction is possible with **ser** and adjectives meaning 'difficult', 'easy', etc. Compare:

Es difícil entender a este profesor.
It is difficult to understand this teacher.

Este profesor es difícil de entender.
This teacher is difficult to understand.

In the first sentence, **entender a este profesor** as a whole is the subject of **es difícil** and no preposition is required. In the second sentence, **este profesor** becomes the subject of **es difícil**, and **entender** requires the preposition **de** before it. It is important not to mix up these two constructions: *Es difícil de entender a este profesor is *not* acceptable.

26.2.2 Infinitive objects

26.2.2.1 *With no preposition*
Examples:

acostumbrar: **Acostumbro cenar a las nueve.**
I usually have dinner at nine o'clock.

conseguir: **¿Conseguiste ver al jefe?**
Did you manage to see the boss?

deber: **Debes decir la verdad.** (see also **21.2**)
You must tell the truth.

decidir: **Decidí no decir nada.**
I decided not to say anything.

desear: **Deseábamos saber quién se lo había dicho.**
We wanted to know who had said it.

esperar: **Espero ir a la universidad.**
I hope to go to university.

evitar: **Evitaré pagar más impuestos.**
I'll avoid paying more taxes.

intentar: **Había intentado componer una sinfonía.**
He/she had tried to compose a symphony.

lamentar: **Lamento no haber dicho nada.**
I regret not having said anything.

lograr: **¿Vas a lograr terminar el libro para las siete?**
Are you going to manage to finish the book by seven o'clock?

necesitar: **Necesito saber cuál es el mejor de todos.**
I need to know which is the best of all.

negar: **Niego haber conducido demasiado deprisa.**
I deny having driven too fast.

pedir: **Pedimos ir juntos.**
We asked to go together.

pensar: **¿Qué piensas hacer mañana?**
What do you intend to do tomorrow?

poder: **No puedo levantarme.**
I can't get up.

preferir: **Felipe prefería quedarse en casa.**
Felipe preferred to stay at home.

querer: **No quiero verla.**
I don't want to see her/it.

recordar: **Recuerdo haberlo conocido en Málaga.**
I remember meeting him in Málaga.

saber: **¿Sabes tocar el violín?**
Do you know how to play the violin?

sentir: **Siento decirle que . . .**
I regret to tell you that . . .

soler: **Suelo salir los sábados.**
I usually go out on Saturdays.

temer: **Temo no encontrar a nadie.**
I'm afraid of not finding anyone.

The subject of the main verb and the implied subject of the infinitive must be the same for the infinitive construction to be used. If this is not the case, then a sentence complement with **que** must be used, with the verb in the indicative or the subjunctive depending on the meaning (for most of the verbs given above, the subjunctive must be used).

> **Decidimos comprar dos kilos.**
> We decided to buy two kilos. (= *We* decided that *we* would buy two kilos)

But:

> **Decidimos que María nos comprara dos kilos.**
> We decided that María should buy two kilos for us. (= *We* decided that *María* should buy two kilos)

▶ 18 (p. 83)

However, verbs of ordering and verbs of perception allow infinitive object complement constructions in which the subject of the main verb and the implied subject of the infinitive are *not* the same.

(a) Verbs of ordering

> *dejar*: **Dejé salir a los niños.**
> I let the children go out. (= *I* let; *the children* went out)

> *hacer*: **Le hice callar.**
> I made him/her be quiet.

> *impedir*: **Impedimos escaparse a los delincuentes.**
> We stopped the criminals escaping.

> *mandar*: **El presidente mandó construir una nueva residencia.**
> (**construir** corresponds to the English passive 'to be built')
> The president ordered a new residence to be built.

> *permitir*: **¿Me permites salir?**
> Will you let me go out?

> *prohibir*: **Me prohibieron revelar el secreto.**
> They stopped me revealing the secret.

(b) Verbs of perception

> *ver*: **Vimos llegar a la Reina.**
> We saw the Queen arrive. (= *We* saw; *the Queen* arrived)

> *oír*: **Oímos chillar a los niños.**
> We heard the children shrieking.

NOTE | Verbs of perception also take gerund complements (see **26.3**).

26.2.2.2 | *With a*

Verbs in this category include a number of verbs of beginning and verbs of motion, as well as several reflexive verbs. Examples are:

> *apresurarse*: **Se apresuraron a terminar el trabajo.**
> They hurried to finish the work.

> *aprender*: **Los niños aprenden a bailar.**
> The children are learning to dance.

> *atreverse*: **¿Te atreverías a decírselo?**
> Would you dare to tell him/her?

bajar: **Mi madre bajó a ver lo que pasaba.**
My mother came down to see what was happening.

comenzar: **Comencé a estudiar a los dieciocho años.**
I began to study at eighteen.

decidirse: **Me decidí a salir.**
I decided to go out.

empezar: **Empezó a llover.**
It began to rain.

ir: **Fuimos a ver a mis primos.**
We went to see my cousins.

ponerse: **Se pusieron a llorar.**
They began to cry. (see **41.1.2**)

resistirse: **Se resiste a ayudarnos.**
He/she resists helping us.

salir: **¡Salga a comprar unos pasteles!**
Go out and buy some cakes!

sentarse: **Nos sentamos a discutir el asunto.**
We sat down to discuss the matter.

venir: **¿Has venido a decirme algo?**
Have you come to tell me something?

There are also a number of verbs of ordering or influence whose infinitive
object complement does *not* have the same implied subject as the main verb.
Examples are:

inducir: **Todo nos induce a pensar que no es así.**
Everything leads us to think that it's not like that. (= *Everything* leads
us . . . ; *we* think . . .)

Some verbs in this category are:

acostumbrar: **Nos han acostumbrado a acostarnos más
tarde.**
They have accustomed us to going to bed later.

convidar: **Os convido a tomar una copita conmigo.**
I invite you to have a drink with me.

enseñar: **¿Quién te enseñó a tocar el piano?**
Who taught you to play the piano?

inducir: **Todo nos induce a pensar que no es así.**
Everything leads us to think that it's not like that.

invitar: **Me invitaron a cenar.**
They invited me to dinner.

persuadir: **Trata de persuadirle a quedarse.**
Try to persuade him/her to stay.

26.2.2.3 | *With **de***

Verbs in this category often have a rather negative meaning. They include a substantial number of reflexive verbs. Examples are:

> *acabar*: **Acabamos de contestar.**
> We have just replied.
>
> *acordarse*: **Me acordé de ir a la reunión.**
> I remembered to go to the meeting.
>
> *alegrarse*: **Me alegro de saberlo.**
> I'm glad to know.
>
> *arrepentirse*: **¿Te arrepientes de hacerlo?**
> Are you sorry you did it?
>
> *avergonzarse*: **Me avergoncé de haber callado el asunto.**
> I was ashamed of having kept the matter quiet.
>
> *cansarse*: **No me canso nunca de pintar.**
> I never get tired of painting.
>
> *dejar*: **¡Deja de llorar!**
> Stop crying!
>
> *olvidarse*: **¡No te olvides de hacerlo!**
> Don't forget to do it!
>
> *terminar*: **¿Has terminado de cantar?**
> Have you finished singing?
>
> *tratar*: **Trata de recordar.**
> Try to remember.

In all the above cases, the subject of the main verb is the same as the implied subject of the infinitive complement. Some of these verbs (**alegrarse** and **avergonzarse**) also take a sentence complement with **que** and the subjunctive when the subjects are different, e.g.:

> **Me alegro de que hayas venido.**
> *I*'m pleased *you* have come.

NOTE | The **de** is preserved before the **que** in such a construction.

But there are also a small number of verbs with **de** whose infinitive complement does not have the same implied subject as that of the main verb. Two are:

> *acusar*: **Me habían acusado de no decir la verdad.**
> They had accused me of not telling the truth.
>
> *disuadir*: **No te dejes disuadir de actuar de esa manera.**
> Don't let yourself be dissuaded from acting in that way.

26.2.2.4 | *With **en***

The following are examples of verbs which take **en** with an infinitive complement:

complacerse: **Nos complacemos en recibirles.**
We take pleasure in giving you hospitality.

consentir: **Consentimos en verlos.**
We agreed to see them.

dudar: **No dudes en preguntarme.**
Don't hesitate to ask me.

insistir: **Insisto en saber.**
I insist on knowing.

tardar: **El tren tarda dos horas en llegar.**
The train takes two hours to get there.

vacilar: **Vaciló en contestar.**
He/she hesitated to reply.

In all the above cases, the subject of the main verb is the same as the implied subject of the infinitive complement. **Insistir** also takes a sentence complement with **que** and the subjunctive when the subjects are different, e.g.:

Insisto en que vengas.   *I* insist that *you* come.

NOTE

The **en** is preserved before the **que** in such a construction.

Consentir similarly also has a sentence complement construction, but the **en** is not used:

Consiento que vayas.   *I* consent to *you* going.

26.2.2.5 | *With con*

The following are examples of verbs which take **con** with an infinitive complement:

amenazar: **Amenaza con llover.**
It's threatening to rain.

soñar: **Soñé con ganar la lotería.**
I dreamed of winning the lottery.

26.2.2.6 | *With por*

The following are examples of verbs which take **por** with an infinitive complement:

acabar: **Acabó por dar un salto mortal.**
He/she finished by doing a somersault.

comenzar: **Comencemos por leer el texto.**
Let's begin by reading the text.

empezar: **Empezó por construir un modelo.**
He/she began by building a model.

esforzarse: **Me esforcé por ganar.**
I strove to win.

luchar: **Vamos a luchar por conseguir nuestros objectivos.**
We will fight to achieve our objectives.

optar: ¿Optaste por fin por estudiar empresariales?
Did you choose to do management studies in the end?

terminar: Termino por citar otro ejemplo.
I'll finish by quoting another example.

votar: Yo votaría por mantener el *status quo*.
I'd vote for maintaining the *status quo*.

In all the above cases, the subject of the main verb is the same as the implied subject of the infinitive complement. Some of these verbs (**esforzarse, luchar** and **votar**) also take a sentence complement with **que** and the subjunctive when the subjects are different, e.g.:

Nos esforzamos porque saliera bien la empresa.
We strove so that *the enterprise* turned out well.

NOTE The **por** is preserved before the **que** in such a construction. The sequence **porque** does *not* mean 'because' here.

Quedar por takes an infinitive which corresponds to a passive in English:

Dos cosas quedan por hacer.
Two things remain *to be done*.

26.3 Gerund complementation

The chief verbs which take gerund object complements are:

acabar: Acabaron peleándose.
They ended up quarrelling. (**acabar** + gerund is an alternative to **acabar por** + infinitive)

continuar: Continuó escribiendo.
He/she continued writing.

llevar: Llevo años preparando mi tesis. (see 20.3)
I've spent years preparing my thesis.

seguir: Siguieron caminando.
They carried on walking.

The gerund is also used with verbs of perception to stress the ongoing nature of the action involved:

Vimos a los diputados entrando en el palacio.
We saw the deputies going into the palace. (suggests a succession of deputies going in one after the other)

27
Conjunctions

Conjunctions are linking words which establish relations between similar items in a sentence, or between sentences.

27.1 Coordinating conjunctions

27.1.1 *Y*

Y functions very much like English 'and'. It has the form **e** before a word beginning with **i**-or **hi**- (unless **hi**- begins the diphthong **hie**-, see **1.2**).

> **mujer e hijos** 'wife and children'

But:

> **nieve y hielo** 'snow and ice'

Y . . . y . . . corresponds to 'both . . . and . . .'

27.1.2 *O*

O corresponds to English 'or'. It changes to **u** before a word beginning with **o**- or **ho**-:

> **siete u ocho** 'seven or eight'
> **albergues u hoteles** 'guest houses or hotels'

O . . . o . . . corresponds to 'either . . . or . . .' Where the alternatives are fairly far apart or dissimilar in structure, then the stronger form (**o**) . . . **o bien** . . . ('either') . . . 'or else' . . . is used:

> **O ríe o llora.**
> He/she's either laughing or crying.

> **Puede ir por París con transbordo en Irún, o bien hay un vuelo directo cada jueves y sábado.**
> You can go via Paris changing at Irún, or else there's a direct flight every Thursday and Saturday.

27.1.3 *Pero* and *sino*

Spanish distinguishes between **pero**, which corresponds to most functions of English 'but', and **sino**, which marks a mutually exclusive contrast. **No** . . . **sino** . . . 'not . . . but . . .' is described in **15.4**.

27.1.4 *Ni ... ni ...*

Ni ... ni ... corresponds to English 'neither ... nor ...':

Ni José ni Paco lo sabía. Neither José nor Paco knew.

▶ **15.2** (p. 57); **32** (p. 191)

27.1.5 *Que*

Que in written Spanish is normally a subordinating conjunction, but it is very frequently used in the spoken language to indicate a vague logical connection, often causal, between one sentence and another:

¡No lo hagas, chico, que te van a matar!
Don't do it, mate, (because) they'll kill you!

27.2 Subordinating conjunctions

27.2.1 **Complementizers**

▶ **26** (p. 131)

Que is used in reported (indirect) statements and commands (see **26.1**). In English the parallel complementizer 'that' is often omitted: 'I said (that) I was going'. Spanish **que** is *not* omitted, except in indirect commands in very formal written style:

Se ruega a los señores clientes no fumen.
Customers are requested not to smoke.

▶ **68** (p. 381)

Si is used in reported (indirect) questions (see **26.1**).

27.2.2 **Subordinating conjunctions with more specific meanings**

(a) Cause

▶ **43** (p. 253)

como 'since'
porque 'because'
pues 'so'
puesto que 'because', 'since'
ya que 'because', 'since'

For examples see **43.2** and **43.3**.

NOTE (1) These conjunctions are used with the *indicative*. However, **no porque** requires the *subjunctive* (see **18.1.5**) and **como** with the subjuntive expresses a hypothesis (see **18.2.3**).

(2) **Pues** must be used with caution as a causal conjunction, and is probaby better avoided at first. It has a relatively weak meaning, and usually introduces a cause as an afterthought.

Do *not* use **pues** at the beginning of a sentence in this sense: use one of the other conjunctions.

Pues is one of the commonest fillers in Spanish (see **30.8**).

(b) Concession

▶ **18.2.3** (p. 88); **52.1** (p. 306)

> **aunque** 'although'
> **aun cuando** 'although', 'even though'

For examples and use of the indicative and subjunctive with these conjunctions see **18.2.3**.

(c) Condition

▶ **18.2.3** (p. 88); **51.3.6** (p. 304)

> **a condición de que** 'on condition that'
> **a menos que** 'unless'
> **a no ser que** 'unless'
> **a pesar de que** 'in spite of the fact that'
> **como** 'if'
> **con tal (de) que** 'provided that'
> **si** 'if'
> **siempre que** 'provided that'

For examples and use of the indicative and subjunctive with these conjunctions see **18.2.3**.

(d) Purpose

▶ **18.2.1** (p. 86); **43.5** (p. 258)

> **para que** 'in order that'
> **de manera/modo/forma que** 'so that'

These conjunctions are used with the subjunctive: for examples see **18.2.1**.

(e) Consequence

> **conque** 'so that'
> **de manera/modo/forma que** 'so that'

These conjunctions are used with the indicative: for examples see **18.2.1**.

(f) Time

▶ **18.2.2** (p. 87)

> **antes de que** 'before'
> **apenas** 'scarcely'
> **cuando** 'when'
> **desde que** 'since'

> después de que 'after'
> en cuanto 'as soon as'
> hasta que 'until'
> mientras 'while'
> siempre que 'whenever'

NOTE

(1) **Antes de que** *always* takes the subjunctive (see **18.2.2**).

(2) **Cuando, desde que** and **después de que** are sometimes used with the -**ra** form of the past subjunctive when they relate to a past situation (see **17.9**, **17.10**, **18.2.2**).

(3) **Siempre que** takes the subjunctive when it expresses a hypothesis (see **18.2.3**).

For examples of some of these usages see **18.2.2**.

28
Word order

Statements

The order of basic elements

Spanish has more word order possibilities than English. Objects can be placed in front of the verb (see **8.3**) and the verb itself can stand in initial position. Some possible equivalents for 'the man was reading the book to the little girl' are

> **El hombre leía el libro a la niña.**
> **Leía el hombre el libro a la niña.**
> **A la niña le leía el hombre el libro.**
> **El libro lo leía el hombre a la niña.** (see **24.5**)

'New' and 'old' information

The choice among these various possibilities depends on a number of factors, and sometimes appears quite random to foreigners, but has to do with topicalization and stress. While it is inappropriate to speak of a hard and fast rule, Spanish tends to place the element which has just been a subject of interest (the topic, 'old' information) first in the sentence, and new information, or elements on which it is wished to lay some kind of stress or contrast, last. This is clearest in statements which are answers to questions asking for information. Examples are:

(a)   **–¿Quién habla?**
'Who's talking?'
–Habla Nicolás. (see **29.8**)
'*Nicolás* is talking.'

         –¿Qué hace Nicolás?
'What is Nicolás doing?'
–Nicolás *habla*.
'Nicolás is *talking*.'

(b)   **Me gusta *el helado de fresa*.**
I like *strawberry ice cream*.

         –¿No quieres un helado de fresa?
'You don't want a strawberry ice cream?'
–¡Sí, papá, que el helado de fresa *me gusta*!
'Yes, Daddy – I *like* strawberry ice cream!'

(c) **–Tu padre ¿cuándo fue capitán de artillería?**
'When was your father an artillery captain?'
–Pues fue capitán de artillería *durante la guerra*.
'Well, he was an artillery captain *during the war*.'

–¿Qué hizo tu padre durante la guerra?
'What did your father do during the war?'
–Durante la guerra fue *capitán de artillería*.
'During the war he was *an artillery captain*.'

(d) **–¿Dónde está el libro?**
'Where's the book?'
–El libro lo tengo *en casa*.
'I've got the book *at home*.'

–¿Qué has dejado en casa?
'What have you left at home?'
–En casa he dejado *el libro*.
'I've left *the book* at home.'

See also **nada** (**32.4.4**).

28.1.3 **Adverbs**

Another general difference between Spanish and English is that adverbs usually stand immediately next to the verb in Spanish:

Habla bien español.
He/she speaks Spanish well.

Salió rápidamente de la habitación.
He/she went out of the room quickly.

Saludó con entusiasmo a los hinchas.
He/she greeted the fans enthusiastically.

28.1.4 **Adjectives**

For the order of adjectives and nouns, see **5.2** and **36.1.2**.

28.2 Questions

31 (p. 185)

Questions may be indicated simply by intonation, preserving the word order of a simple statement, or the verb may be placed first:

¿Louise habla español?
Does Louise speak Spanish?

¿Ha llegado el tren?
Has the train arrived?

A topic may also be placed first, outside the scope of the question, in which case the inverted question mark appears in writing after the topicalized element (see **1.6**):

> **Y el señor Pérez ¿cómo lo reconocieron?**
> And how did they recognize Señor Pérez?

See also **¿verdad?, ¿no?** (**12.9**).

Functions

I

Social contact and communication strategies

29
Making social contacts

This chapter contains the most useful expressions used by Spanish speakers to establish social contacts, such as when greeting or introducing people, taking leave, using the phone or writing letters. Many of these are set phrases, others are constructions which vary according to context. Reference is made to register when appropriate, so that you will know for instance whether a certain expression is formal or informal, or whether it tends to be used in the spoken or written language. The expressions listed are for the most part those used by the majority of Spanish speakers, in Spain and elsewhere, but occasional mention is made too of Latin American usage.

29.1 Greeting someone

The standard most common greetings are:

Buenos días.
Good morning.

Buenas tardes.
Good afternoon (early afternoon), good evening. (before night falls)

Buenas noches.
Good evening.

¡Hola!
Hello!, Hi!

¿Qué tal?
Hi!, How are you?

¿Qué hay? (especially Spain)
Hi!, How are things?

¿Qué es de tu vida?
How's life?

Adiós.
Hello! (when passing by, esp. L. Am.)

The first three greetings are neutral, and can be used in formal and familiar address. **Hola**, 'hello', can be familiar, e.g. **¡hola!**, 'hi!', formal, e.g. **hola, ¿cómo está usted?**, 'hello, how are you?', or neutral, e.g. **hola, buenos días**, 'hello, good morning'. **¿Qué tal?** and **¿Qué hay?** (esp. Spain), 'Hi!', on their own, are familiar greetings, although they can become formal if followed by a formal greeting, for example

¿Qué tal, don Miguel, cómo está usted? Adiós, normally meaning 'goodbye', is also used as a greeting, formal or familiar, when passing by. ¿Qué es de tu vida? is a familiar greeting.

In most Latin American countries **hola** is considered an informal greeting, just like ¿qué tal? ¿Qué hay? is unknown in many Latin American countries as a form of greeting. Instead, you may hear ¿qué hubo?, how are things?, in countries like Mexico, Colombia and Chile. In Chile, this is pronounced as [kjuβo]. In the River Plate countries (Argentina and Uruguay) **buenos días** becomes **buen día**.

Note that in formal encounters people normally shake hands when greeting each other. People also do so occasionally in informal situations, especially when they have not seen each other for some time. Hand-shaking is also customary in introductions, except among the young (see **29.4**). It is also common when saying good-bye (see **29.5**), especially if you will not be seeing the other person for some time.

Friends and even acquaintances will often kiss on the cheek or both cheeks, depending on the country, when saying hello or goodbye, especially if they have not met or will not be meeting for some time. This is customary among women or among men and women, but it is rarely seen among men, particularly in Latin America, except when there is a family relationship.

29.2   Conveying greetings

29.2.1

To pass on greetings to a third person, use:

Informal/formal:

          Recuerdos/saludos a Federico.   Regards to Federico.

Informal:

          Dale recuerdos/saludos a María Luisa.
          Give María Luisa my regards.

          Dale recuerdos/saludos de mi parte.
          Give him/her my regards.

Formal:

          Dele recuerdos/saludos (de mi parte) a su marido.
          Please give your husband my regards.

▶ **16.1.1.6** (p. 62)

29.2.2

To pass on someone else's greetings, use the following:

Informal:

          Alfredo te manda/envía recuerdos/saludos.
          Alfredo sends his regards.

Formal:

> **Mi madre le manda/envía recuerdos/saludos.**
> My mother sends her regards.

Asking people how they are

To ask someone how he or she is, Spanish normally uses the following expressions:

Informal:

¿Cómo estás?
How are you?

¿Qué tal?
How are you?, How are things?

¿Qué hay? (especially Spain)
How are things?

Formal:

¿Cómo está usted?   How are you?

▶ **22** (p. 103); **12.1** (p. 48)

Alongside these expressions, especially in Latin America, you will often hear forms like **¿cómo te va?** (informal), and **¿cómo le va?** (formal), 'how are things?', 'how is it going?'

Most people will reply to the greetings above with the standard (**Muy**) **bien, gracias, ¿y tú/usted?** '(Very) well, thank you, and you?' But sometimes you may hear things like **regular**, 'so-so', or, in Spain, the very informal **tirando**, (from **tirar**, 'to get by'), 'not too bad' or 'we're getting by'. This verb is a taboo word in some Latin American countries and so it should be avoided.

To ask how someone else is, use:

Informal:

¿Cómo está tu familia?
How is your family?

¿Cómo están tus hijos?
How are your children?

Formal:

¿Cómo está su marido?   How is your husband?
¿Cómo están sus padres?   How are your parents?

29.4 Introducing yourself and others

29.4.1 Introducing yourself

Standard expressions are:

> **Soy ...**
> I am ...
>
> **Me llamo ...**
> My name is ...
>
> **Mi nombre es ...**
> My name is ...

Or formally,

> **Permitan que me presente. Me llamo ...**
> Allow me to introduce myself. My name is ...

29.4.2 Introducing others

Standard introduction forms are:

Informal/formal:

> **El señor/la señora Olmedo.**
> This is señor/señora Olmedo.
>
> **Éste/ésta es el señor/la señorita Arenas.**
> This is señor/señorita Arenas.
>
> **Éste/ésta es mi novio/a.**
> This is my boyfriend/girlfriend.

Informal:

> **¿Conoces a Fernando?**
> Have you met Fernando?
>
> **Te presento a mi padre.**
> I'd like you to meet my father *or* This is my father.
>
> **Quiero/quisiera presentarte a Elena, mi mujer.**
> I'd like to introduce you to Elena, my wife *or* This is Elena, my wife.

Formal:

> **¿Conoce usted a mi colega Julio Prado?**
> Have you met my colleague Julio Prado?
>
> **Quiero/quisiera presentarle a mi hija Cecilia.**
> I'd like to introduce you to my daughter Cecilia.
>
> **Permítame que le presente a mi marido.**
> May I introduce you to my husband?

▶ **9** (p. 40)

In the sentences with **conocer** and **presentar**, note the use of personal **a** before the name, ¿**conoce usted a** + name?, **te presento a** + name.

▶ **25.1.1.1** (p. 116)

If you have already met the person you are being introduced to, you can use the phrase **Ya nos conocemos** 'we have already met'.

The standard greetings in an introduction are:

Informal:

Hola.	Hello.
¿**Qué tal?**	Hi, how are you?

Slightly formal:

Mucho/tanto gusto.
Pleased *or* nice to meet you.

Encantado/a.
How do you do *or* Pleased to meet you.

Formal:

¿**Cómo está usted?**
How are you?

Mucho gusto en conocerlo(le)/la.
Pleased *or* nice to meet you.

El gusto es mío.
The pleasure is mine.

Encantado/a de conocerlo(le)/la.
How do you do *or* Pleased to meet you.

In introductions, younger people and equals will often use the familiar ¿**qué tal?** or ¿**hola?** instead of more formal forms like **mucho/tanto gusto** or **encantado/a.**

Latin Americans, overall, are more likely to use expressions which convey more formality or courtesy, like **mucho/tanto gusto, encantado/a de conocerlo/la.**

Note that the word **encantado/a** will change for masculine (**-o**) or feminine (**-a**), depending on whether the person saying the greeting is a male or a female. Note also that the masculine pronoun **lo** in **encantado de conocerlo** will become **le**, **encantado de conocerle**, in many parts of Spain, especially in the centre.

▶ **2.1** (p. 11); **8.2.1** (p. 36)

29.5 Taking leave

Common leave taking expressions are:

Hasta luego.
Goodbye, see you.

Adiós.
Goodbye, bye.

Hasta mañana.
See you tomorrow.

Hasta la semana que viene.
See you next week.

Hasta el lunes/martes . . .
See you on Monday/Tuesday . . .

Hasta la tarde.
See you this afternoon.

Hasta la vista.
See you, until we meet again.

Hasta pronto.
See you soon.

Hasta ahora.
See you soon, see you in a minute.

Nos vemos a las cuatro/cinco . . .
See you at four/five . . .

Buenos días.
Good morning.

Buenas tardes.
Good afternoon, good evening.

Buenas noches.
Good night.

Te veo/Nos vemos.
See you, I'll be seeing you (esp. L. Am.)

Chao/chau.
Bye, bye-bye (esp. L. Am.)

▶ 25.1.21 (p. 126)

Hasta luego and **adiós** are by far the most common expressions in all parts of the Spanish-speaking world. Generally, they can be used in both formal and informal situations. In Peninsular Spanish, people show preference for **hasta luego** if they are likely to meet again soon; otherwise they may use **adiós**. The other expressions with **hasta**, e.g. **hasta mañana/la tarde/el lunes/pronto** can be used for formal and familiar address. The exception is **hasta ahora**, which is informal.

Buenos días, buenas tardes/noches, are often used for leave-taking, usually accompanied by **adiós** or a similar expression:

Adiós señor, buenos días.
Goodbye sir, good morning (have a good day).

In some Latin American countries, for example Ecuador, the expression **hasta luego** is regarded as formal. Overall, Latin Americans show strong preference for the word **chao**, or **chau** in some places, for saying goodbye to friends or people with whom one is on familiar terms.

> **Chao Carlos, nos vemos mañana.**
> Bye-bye Carlos, see you tomorrow.

Sometimes, the more affectionate diminutives **chaíto** or **chaucito** or even **hasta lueguito** are heard:

> **Chaíto, que lo pases bien.**   Bye-bye, have a nice time.

▶ **18.3.2** (p. 92)

As in Peninsular Spanish, **adiós** is used in formal and informal situations, but its frequency varies from country to country. Many people prefer to use this word when the person leaving will be absent for a longer period of time, as when going on a journey for instance.

> **Adiós Carmen, que tengas buen viaje.**
> Goodbye Carmen, have a good trip.

29.6 Expressing wishes

Many expressions of wishing, such as the ones below, carry the construction **que** + present subjunctive (see **18**, p. 83):

29.6.1 Wishing someone a good trip

> **¡(Que tengas) buen viaje/unas felices vacaciones!**
> Have a good journey/a happy holiday!
>
> **¡Que (te) lo pases bien!**
> Have a good time!
>
> **¡Que disfrutes de las vacaciones!**
> Enjoy your holiday!
>
> **¡Que te diviertas!**
> Enjoy yourself!

29.6.2 Wishing someone luck

> **¡Que te vaya bien!**
> I hope it all goes well!
>
> **¡(Buena) suerte!**
> Good luck!
>
> **¡Que tengas suerte!**
> I hope you are lucky!
>
> **¡Ojalá tengas suerte!**
> I hope you are lucky!
>
> **Te deseo/deseamos mucha suerte.**
> I/we wish you luck.

29.6.3 **Wishing someone a good sleep or rest**

> **¡Que duermas bien!**
> I hope you sleep well!
>
> **¡Que descanses!**
> Have a good rest!

29.6.4 **Wishing someone better**

> **¡Que te mejores/recuperes pronto!**
> I hope you get better/recover soon!
>
> **¡Que te pongas bien (muy) pronto!** (Spain)
> I hope you get better (very) soon!

▶ **18.3.2** (p. 92)

29.6.5 **Drinking a toast and wishing somebody *bon appétit***

To toast somebody use the following expressions, which are common in Peninsular and Latin American Spanish, in formal and familiar situations:

> **¡Salud!**
> Cheers!, here's to you!
>
> **¡A su salud!** (formal)/**¡A tu salud!** (fam.)
> Here's to you!
>
> **¡A la salud de (los novios)!**
> The bride and groom!

▶ **10.1** (p. 42)

To wish somebody *bon appétit*, use:

> **¡Que aproveche(n)!** or **¡Buen provecho!**
> Enjoy your meal, *bon appétit*.

▶ **18.3.2** (p. 92)

29.7 ## Congratulating somebody

To congratulate somebody the following would be appropriate:

> **¡Felicidades!**
> Congratulations!; (on a special occasion) Happy birthday!, Happy Christmas!, Happy New Year!
>
> **¡Enhorabuena!**
> Congratulations!
>
> **¡Felicitaciones!** (L. Am.)
> Congratulations!
>
> Pronoun (e.g. **la/te**) + **felicito**
> Congratulations!

> **alegrarse de algo**
> to be glad or pleased about something
>
> **alegrarse de que** + subjunctive
> to be glad or pleased that . . .

¡Felicidades! is the most common and general of the expressions used in this context. **Enhorabuena** is very common in Peninsular Spanish but unknown in some Latin American countries. Expressions with **felicitar**, 'to congratulate', are used by all Spanish speakers, and will call for a change in the pronoun, depending on who we are congratulating:

> **¡Te felicito!**
> Congratulations! (fam., sg.)
>
> **¡Os felicito!**
> Congratulations! (fam., pl.)
>
> **¡Lo/s or le/s felicito!**
> Congratulations! (formal, m., sg./pl.)
>
> **¡La/s felicito!**
> Congratulations! (formal, f., sg./pl.)

Remember that in Latin American Spanish the **os** form corresponding to **vosotros** is not used in colloquial language, and therefore **los** and **las** will be appropriate in formal and familiar contexts.

▶ 8 (p. 34)

The two expressions with **alegrarse** 'to be glad or pleased', a reflexive verb, are common in all forms of Spanish. **Alegrarse de** will be followed by a noun in this context, while **alegrarse de que** will be followed by a subordinate clause containing a subjunctive.

> **Me alegro de tu éxito.**
> I'm glad *or* pleased about your success.
>
> **Me alegro de que hayas tenido éxito.**
> I'm glad *or* pleased you were successful.

Specific expressions used on special occasions are:

¡Feliz cumpleaños!	Happy birthday!
¡Feliz Navidad!	Merry *or* Happy Christmas!
¡Feliz Año Nuevo!	Happy New Year!

▶ **23.6** (p. 109); **18.1.4** (p. 85); **63.2** (p. 360)

29.8 Using the phone

29.8.1 Answering the phone

Forms used for answering the phone are not the same in all countries. Here are the most common equivalents of the English word 'Hello?'

In Spain, use:

> **¿Diga? or ¿Dígame?**
> **¿Sí (diga?)**

In Mexico:

> **¿Bueno?**

In most parts of South America:

> **¿Aló? or ¿sí?**

In the River Plate countries (Argentina, Uruguay):

> **¿Holá?**

29.8.2 Asking to speak to someone

The expressions which follow will be appropriate in any situation:

Informal:

> **Hola, ¿está José?**
> Hello, is José in?

> **Dile a Paco que se ponga.** (esp. Spain)
> Ask Paco to come to the phone/Tell Paco I want to speak to him.

Formal:

> **¿Podría hablar con el señor Medina, por favor?**
> Could I speak to señor Medina please?

> **Quisiera hablar con Raquel, por favor.**
> I would like to speak to Raquel please.

▶ 22.2 (p. 105); 18.1.1 (p. 84); 21.1 (p. 99); 21.4 (p. 101); 17.7 (p. 77)

29.8.3 Asking who is calling

To ask callers to identify themselves, use:

> **¿Quién habla?**   Who is speaking or calling?
> **¿Con quién hablo?**   Who am I speaking to?
> **¿De parte de quién?**   Who shall I say is calling?

▶ 12.8 (p. 51)

29.8.4 Identifying oneself

To say who is calling, use:

> **Soy (Álvaro).**
> This is (Álvaro).

> **Habla (Nicolás).**
> (Nicolás) speaking.

> **Con él/ella (habla).**
> Speaking.
>
> **Buenas tardes, Departamento de Ventas, González al habla.**
> Good afternoon, Sales Department, González speaking.

▶ **22.1** (p. 103)

29.8.5 Asking callers if they wish to leave a message

The expression most often heard when speaking to someone formally, for example a stranger, is:

> **¿Quiere dejar(le) algún recado?**
> Would you like to leave a message (for him/her)?

▶ **21.4** (p. 101)

In parts of Latin America you will hear:

> **¿Quiere dejar algún mensaje?** or **¿Quiere dejar algo dicho?**
> Would you like to leave a message?

If the caller is someone you know and you are using the familiar form, say:

> **¿Quieres dejar(le) algún recado/mensaje?** (L. Am.)
> Do you want to leave a message?

29.8.6 Leaving a message

To leave a message for someone, use:

> **¿Podría darle un recado/mensaje?** (L. Am.)
> Could you give him/her a message?
>
> **¿Podría decirle que . . . ?**
> Could you tell him/her that . . . ?

▶ **21.1** (p. 99); **17.7** (p. 77)

Or very formally:

> **¿Sería tan amable de darle un recado/mensaje?** (L. Am.)
> Could you possibly, or would you be so kind as to, give him/her a message?

In an informal situation, use:

¿Podrías decirle que . . . ?	Could you tell him/her that . . . ?
Por favor, ¿le dices que . . . ?	Will you please tell him/her that . . . ?
Por favor, dile que . . .	Please tell him/her that . . .

Note here the different ways of making requests: **¿podría** + infinitive?, **¿sería tan amable de** + infinitive?, present (**¿le dices que . . . ?**), imperative (**dile que . . .**).

▶ **68.1** (p. 381); **21.1** (p. 99); **17.1.4** (p. 73); **17.7** (p. 77); **17.13** (p. 81)

29.8.7 **Asking for an extension number, contact person or department**

> **Con la extensión 542 (cinco-cuatro-dos or quinientos cuarenta y dos), por favor.**
> Extension 542, please.

> **¿(Me pone con) la extensión 75 (setenta y cinco)?**
> Could you put me through to/Can I have extension 75, please?

> **¿Me puede poner con el director/el departamento de ventas, por favor?**
> Could you put me through to/Could I speak to the sales director/ department, please?

Note that the word for 'extension' in the River Plate countries (Argentina, Uruguay) is **el interno**; in Chile it is **el anexo**.

> **Con el interno/anexo 20, por favor.**
> Extension 20, please.

The use of **poner** 'to put through' in this context is not common or is unknown in many Latin American countries. The words **comunicar**, and **dar** in the River Plate and Chile, are sometimes used instead.

> **¿Me comunica con la sección de marketing?**
> Can you put me through to the marketing department?

> **¿Me da con el gerente, por favor?**
> Can I speak to the manager, please?

29.8.8 **Asking the caller to hold on**

> **Un momento/momentito, por favor.**
> Hold on please.

> **No cuelgue, por favor.**
> Hold the line please *or* Please hold. (from **colgar** 'to hang up')

> **Enseguida le pongo.**
> I'm just putting you through/connecting you.

> **Ahora/ahorita le comunico con ella.** (L. Am.)
> I'll just put you through to her.

> **Enseguida le doy con el señor Bravo.** (R. Pl. and Chile)
> I'll just put you through to Mr Bravo.

29.8.9 **Making a call through a switchboard/operator**

> **Quiero hacer una llamada de larga distancia/internacional.**
> I want to make a long distance/international call.

> **Quiero hacer una llamada personal a la señora Maricarmen Fernández . . .**
> I want to make a personal call to señora Maricarmen Fernández . . .

> **El número es el 020 8753 4210 de Londres.**
> The number is London 020 8753 4210.

Quiero hacer una llamada de/a cobro revertido al número 643 9128 de Nueva York.
I'd like a transferred charge call to New York 643 9128.

Quiero hacer una llamada por cobrar. (Mexico, Chile)
I want to make a transferred charge call.

No puedo comunicarme con el número . . .
I can't get through to number . . .

Estaba hablando con . . . , pero se ha cortado la comunicación.
I was speaking to . . . , but I got cut off.

NOTE Telephone numbers in Spanish are normally read in single figures or in pairs; for example, 741 8092 could be read as **siete-cuatro-uno-ocho-cero-nueve-dos**, or **siete**, **cuarenta y uno**, **ochenta-noventa y dos**. A brief number, such as an extension, for instance 421, can be read as above or as a single figure, **cuatrocientos veintiuno.**

29.8.10 **Arranging to meet someone**

Common expressions are:

¿Qué te/le parece si nos vemos/quedamos a las (hora) en (sitio)?
What about meeting at (time) at/in (place)?

Podríamos vernos esta tarde/mañana.
We could meet this afternoon/tomorrow.

¿Nos vemos el lunes/la próxima semana?
Shall we meet on Monday/next week?

¿Te va bien por la mañana/a las nueve? (especially Spain)
Is the morning/nine o'clock all right with you?

29.9 Writing letters

29.9.1 **Date**

This is normally preceded by the place of origin and expressed in the following way:

Barcelona, 4 de setiembre de (year)

▶ 7.3.2 (p. 32)

Note that the months are written in Spanish in lower case.

▶ 1.7 (p. 10)

29.9.2 **Salutation**

29.9.2.1 The most common forms of salutation in formal and business correspondence are:

Very formal:

Muy señor mío: or **Muy señor nuestro:**
Dear Sir

Muy señores míos: or **Muy señores nuestros:**
Dear Sirs

Distinguido señor:
Dear Sir

Distinguida señora/señorita:
Dear Madam

Distinguidos señores:
Dear Sirs

Less formal:

Estimado señor (surname):
Dear Sir/Dear Mr (surname)

Estimada señora/señorita (surname):
Dear Madam/Dear Mrs/Miss (surname)

Estimados señores:
Dear Sirs

▶ **10.2.2.2** (p. 43)

In more impersonal correspondence such as circulars you might find:

Señor:	Dear Sir
Señora:	Dear Madam
Señores:	Dear Sirs

Note that the words **señor, señora, señorita** are often written in abbreviated form:
Sr., Sra., Srta.

Note also that **señor** is sometimes followed by the word **don**, or **Dn.** in abbreviated form.

Sr. Don Pablo Rojas:
Mr Pablo Rojas, Pablo Rojas, Esq.

The feminine **señora** or **señorita** is sometimes followed by the word **Doña**, or **Dña.** in abbreviated form.

Señora Doña María Fernández:
Mrs María Fernández

In Latin American Spanish you will also encounter:

De mi (mayor) consideración:
Dear Sir/Madam

De nuestra (mayor) consideración:
Dear Sir/Madam

29.9.2.2 In informal letters to family or friends, use:

Querido Gustavo:	Dear Gustavo
Querida Cristina:	Dear Cristina

Querido tío:	Dear Uncle
Queridos primos:	Dear Cousins

When writing to people you do not know too well, use **estimado** instead of **querido**, even if you address the person with the familiar **tú**.

Estimado Alejandro:	Dear Alejandro
Estimada Alfonsina:	Dear Alfonsina

`29.9.3` Common phrases used in formal and business correspondence

`29.9.3.1` Acknowledging receipt of a letter:

Acuso/acusamos recibo de su carta de fecha 4 de octubre . . .
I/we acknowledge receipt of your letter of 4th October . . .

Obra en mi/nuestro poder su carta de fecha 17 del corriente . . .
I/we acknowledge receipt of your letter of 17th of the current month . . .

En contestación/respuesta a su (atenta) carta del 25 de marzo pasado/último . . .
In reply to your letter of 25th March . . .

`29.9.3.2` Stating purpose of letter:

El objeto de la presente es . . .
This is to . . .

Mediante/por medio de la presente quisiera informarle . . .
This is to inform you . . .

Tengo/tenemos el agrado de dirigirme/nos a usted para . . .
I/we have pleasure in writing to you to . . .

Me dirijo/Nos dirigimos a ustedes a fin de solicitarles . . .
We are writing to request . . .

▶ **43.5** (p. 258)

Note that **usted** and **ustedes** are often used in abbreviated form in writing: **Vd.**, for **usted**, and **Vds.** or **Vdes.** for **ustedes**, also found as **Ud.** and **Uds.** respectively.

`29.9.3.3` Expressing regret for something:

Siento/sentimos informarle que . . .
I am/we are sorry to inform you that . . .

Lamento/lamentamos profundamente tener que comunicarles que . . .
I am/we are very sorry to have to inform you that . . .

Note here the use of **sentir** and **lamentar** 'to be sorry', 'to regret', followed by the infinitive.

▶ **26** (p. 131); **63.1** (p. 358)

`29.9.3.4` Expressing pleasure at something:

Me/nos complace informarle que . . .
I am/we are pleased to inform you that . . .

> Tengo/tenemos mucho agrado/gusto en comunicarles que . . .
> I have/we have great pleasure in informing you that . . .

Note here the use of **complacer** 'to be pleasing' and **tener mucho agrado** or **gusto en** 'to have great pleasure in', followed by the infinitive.

 26 (p. 131)

29.9.3.5 Requesting something:

> **Le ruego que me envíe** . . .
> Please send me . . .

> **Les rogamos que se sirvan mandarnos** . . .
> Please send us . . .

> **Le agradecería (que) me respondiera con la mayor brevedad/a la brevedad posible** . . .
> I would be grateful if you would reply as soon as possible . . .

Note here the use of **ruego, rogamos**, present forms of **rogar**, literally 'to beg', followed by **que** plus a secondary verb in the present subjunctive. Note also the conditional **agradecería**, from **agradecer** 'to be grateful', followed by **que**, which is optional in letter writing, plus a subordinate clause with a verb in the imperfect subjunctive.

 16.1.2.1 (p. 64); **18.1.1** (p. 84); **19.2** (p. 95); **68.1.8** (p. 383)

29.9.4 Closing a letter

29.9.4.1 To close a formal or business letter, the following phrases are used:

Very formal:

> **Atentamente,**
> Yours sincerely

> **Muy atentamente,**
> Yours sincerely

> **Le/les saluda/saludo (muy) atentamente,**
> Yours sincerely

> **Me despido/nos despedimos de usted/ustedes atentamente,**
> Yours sincerely

> **Reciba un atento saludo de**
> Yours sincerely

Less formal:

> **Le saluda cordialmente**   Sincerely yours
> **Reciba un cordial saludo de**   Sincerely yours

Note that **le/les** stands for masculine or feminine, singular and plural, respectively. In Latin American Spanish you are more likely to find **lo/la**, or the plurals **los/las**, for masculine and feminine, respectively, in this context. The verb **saludar**, literally 'to greet', can go in the third person, **saluda** (sg.) or **saludan** (pl.), or in the first person **saludo** (sg.), **saludamos** (pl.).

🔾 **8.2.1** (p. 36)

These phrases are sometimes preceded by other formulae such as:

En espera de su respuesta, le saludamos muy atentamente,
We look forward to hearing from you. Yours sincerely,

En espera de sus gratas noticias, le saluda muy atentamente,
I look forward to hearing from you. Yours sincerely,

Sin más, quedamos a la espera de su contestación. Atentamente,
We look forward to hearing from you. Yours sincerely,

Quedo a su disposición para cualquier consulta y le saludo muy atentamente,
I am at your disposal for any questions you may have. Yours sincerely,

Sin otro particular, me despido de usted atentamente,
Yours sincerely,

29.9.4.2 To close a letter to a family member or friend, use the following:

Un (fuerte) abrazo,	Best wishes, regards, love
Un cariñoso saludo de (name)	Love
Afectuosamente	Love, kind regards
Cariños, (esp. L. Am.)	Love
Un beso/besos	Kisses

30
Basic strategies for communication

To begin and keep communication going speakers resort to a series of words and phrases which may vary not just according to the speaker's intention, for example getting someone to repeat something, but also in relation to factors which derive from the situation itself. These can be factors such as the relationship between the speakers, for example formal versus informal, or the speaker's attitude, which can be sympathetic or hostile. The sections below list and give information about the most common words and phrases used by Spanish speakers in day-to-day communication.

30.1 Attracting someone's attention and responding to a call for attention

30.1.1 The words most commonly used to attract someone's attention are:

Perdone (usted)/Perdona.	Excuse me.
¡Oiga! (usted)/¡Oye!	Excuse me!, hey!
Disculpe (usted)/Disculpa.	Excuse me.
Por favor.	Excuse me.
¡Señor!	Excuse me sir!
¡Señora!	Excuse me madam!
¡Señorita!	Excuse me madam!

Perdone and **perdona**, from **perdonar**, 'to excuse', are, together with **¡oiga!** and **¡oye!**, from **oír**, 'to listen', 'to hear', the most common forms of attracting an individual's attention. **Perdone/a** are also used as an apology. **¡Oiga!**, literally 'listen!', is considered rude in some Latin American countries, but the familiar form **¡oye!** is accepted everywhere. **Disculpe** and **disculpa**, from **disculpar**, 'to excuse', seem to be more common in Latin American than in Peninsular Spanish, but as a form of apology, **discúlpeme**, **discúlpame**, they are used more or less equally in all parts of the Spanish-speaking world.

 16.1.1.6 (p. 62); **64** (p. 362)

> **Perdone, ¿cuánto vale este libro?**
> Excuse me, how much is this book?
>
> **Perdona, ¿puedes pasarme esa carpeta?**
> Excuse me, can you pass that file?

> **¡Oiga (usted)!, sus llaves.**
> Excuse me!, your keys.

> **¡Oye, ven aquí un momento, por favor!**
> Hey, come here a moment, please.

> **Disculpe, ¿dónde están los servicios/está el baño** (L. Am)**?**
> Excuse me, where are the toilets?

> **Por favor, la carretera para el aeropuerto, ¿cuál es?**
> Excuse me, which is the road to the airport?

The words **señor, señora** and **señorita** are often used to attract someone's attention. This usage is especially common in Latin America.

> **Señor, ha olvidado su pasaporte.**
> Excuse me, you've left your passport behind.

> **Perdón señora, ¿es suya esta maleta?**
> Excuse me, is this suitcase yours?

30.1.2 The most common and neutral ways of responding to a call for attention are **¿sí?**, 'yes?', and **dígame** (formal) or **dime** (familiar), 'yes?, can I help you?', imperative forms of **decir**, 'to say', 'to tell'.

> **¡Oiga!, por favor . . .**   Excuse me, please!
> **Sí, dígame.**   Yes, can I help you?
> **¡Oye!**   Hey!
> **¿Sí?, (dime).**   Yes?

In parts of Latin America, especially in Mexico, you will hear the word **mande** as a response in this context.

> **¡Lupita! – ¿mande señora?**   Lupita! – yes señora?

▶ **30.3** (p. 172)

30.2 Starting up a conversation

The most common opening words and phrases for starting up a conversation, apart from the name of the person we want to speak to, are **mire (usted)** (formal) and **mira** (familiar), from **mirar**, to look.

> **Lola, tú y yo tenemos que hablar.**
> Lola, you and I have to speak.

> **Mire (usted), quería decirle algo.**
> Look, I wanted to tell you something.

> **Mira, quiero preguntarte una cosa.**
> Look, I want to ask you something.

▶ **21.4** (p. 101); **21.5** (p. 102)

30.3   Requesting repetition, and responding

30.3.1   To ask someone to repeat something because you haven't heard properly, use one of the following expressions:

¿Cómo?	Pardon?, sorry?
¿Cómo dice/s? (formal/fam.)	Pardon?, sorry?
¿Cómo ha(s) dicho? or **¿Cómo dijo/dijiste?** (formal/fam.)	Sorry?, what did you say?

In very informal speech you will sometimes hear the word **¿qué?**, 'what?', but this is generally considered rude, so it is better to avoid it.

> **–Hoy he visto a Ignacio.**
> 'I've seen Ignacio today.'
> **–¿Cómo (dices)?**
> 'Pardon?'

In parts of Latin America, especially in Mexico, you will hear the word **¿mande?**, 'sorry?', 'pardon?' in this context.

30.1 (p. 170)

> **–Hay una llamada para usted.**
> 'There is a phone call for you.'
> **–¿Mande?**
> 'Pardon?'

30.3.2   To answer a request for repetition, speakers will either repeat the exact words said previously or use a paraphrase. But to indicate that what is being said is a repetition of what was said earlier, speakers sometimes put other words before the words which are being repeated. Before statements, Spanish uses the following words:

> **Que** ... 'that . . .'
> **Digo que** ... 'I'm saying that . . .'
> **He dicho que** ... 'I said that . . .'
> **Decía que** ... 'I was saying that . . .'
> **–Hemos estado en casa de Isabel.**
> 'We have been in Isabel's house.'
> **–¿Cómo?**
> 'Sorry?'
> **–Que hemos estado en casa de Isabel.**
> 'We have been in Isabel's house.'
> **–Necesito más dinero.**
> 'I need more money.'
> **–Perdone, ¿cómo ha dicho/dijo?**
> 'Sorry, what did you say?'
> **–He dicho que necesito más dinero.**
> 'I said that I need more money.'

Before questions requiring a yes or no answer, use the following words:

Que si ...	I was asking you if . . .
Le/te preguntaba si ...	(formal/fam.)

> –¿Vas a ir a la universidad?
> 'Are you going to the university?'
> –¿Cómo?,
> Sorry?
> –Que si vas a ir a la universidad.
> 'Are you going to the university?'

Note that **si**, 'if', 'whether', is not used with questions beginning with interrogative words such as **¿cómo?**, 'how'?, **¿cuándo?**, 'when':

> –¿Cuándo va a volver?
> 'When is he/she going to come back?'
> –¿Cómo has dicho/dijiste?
> 'Sorry, what did you say?'
> –Que cuándo va a volver.
> 'When is he/she going to come back?'

With imperatives simply use **que**:

> –No tardes mucho.
> 'Don't take long!'
> –¿Cómo?
> 'Sorry?'
> –Que no tardes mucho.
> 'Don't take long!'

▶ 18.3.1 (p. 91)

30.4 Making sure you understand and are understood

30.4.1

If you need to apologize for your Spanish, either because you cannot understand what is being said or because you cannot express yourself properly, you can use phrases like the following, with the verbs **entender**, 'to understand', and **hablar**, 'to speak'.

> **Perdóneme (usted)/perdóname, pero no (le/te) entiendo.**
> I'm sorry, but I don't understand (you).

> **Discúlpeme (usted)/discúlpame, pero no entiendo/hablo muy bien el español.**
> I'm sorry, but I do not understand/speak Spanish very well.

Note that when reference is to language or to something being said, most speakers will use **entender** rather than **comprender**, 'to understand'.
Comprender, much less common than **entender**, is generally used with reference to more abstract things. Consider these examples:

> **No entiendo lo que dices.**
> I don't understand what you are saying.

> **¿Entiendes mi letra?**
> Do you understand my handwriting?

> **No comprendo tu actitud.**
> I don't understand your attitude.

> **Sé que tú me comprendes mejor que nadie.**
> I know you understand me better than anybody.

30.4.2 To ask people to explain the meaning of a word or a phrase simply say:

> **¿Qué significa . . . ?**
> What does . . . mean?

> **¿Qué significa esta palabra/frase?**
> What does this word/sentence mean?

> **¿Qué quiere decir esta palabra?**
> What does this word mean?

> **¿Qué quieres decir con . . . ?**
> What do you mean by . . . ?

> **¿Cuál es el significado de esta palabra/frase?**
> What is the meaning of this word/sentence?

▶ **12.2** (p. 49)

30.4.3 If you are lost for a word you can use the impersonal phrase **¿Cómo se dice . . . ?,** 'how do you say . . . ?'.

> **¿Cómo se dice** *spell* **en español?**
> How do you say *spell* in Spanish?

▶ **23.8, 23.9** (p. 111)

30.4.4 To ask people to speak more slowly or repeat what they have said, use phrases like these:

> **Por favor, ¿puede/s or podría/s hablar más despacio?**
> Could you speak more slowly please?

> **Más despacio, por favor.**
> More slowly, please.

> **Por favor, ¿podría (usted)/s repetir lo que ha/s dicho?**
> Could you please repeat what you've said?

Note that the conditional **podría/s**, 'could', from **poder**, 'can', generally expresses more politeness than the present form **puede/s**.

▶ **21.1** (p. 99); **17.7** (p. 77)

30.4.5 To check whether people have understood what you have said you can use the following sentences with **entender**, 'to understand'.

> **¿Me entiende (usted)/entiendes?**
> Can you understand me?

> **Me entiende (usted)/entiendes, ¿verdad?**
> You understand me, don't you?

▶ **12.9** (p. 51)

30.5 Signalling that one understands the speaker

Apart from the neutral word **sí**, 'yes', words which signal that one is following the speaker tend to vary according to our reaction to the speaker's words, which may be surprise, annoyance, disappointment, or some other emotion, for example **¡no!**, 'no!' (surprise), **¡uy!**, 'oh!' (annoyance), **¡ah!**, 'aw!', 'oh dear!' (disappointment). Intonation plays an important part here, and often the same word serves to signal different kinds of reactions to someone's words. The word **¡no!**, for instance, may by itself express surprise, annoyance, pity, depending on the intonation we use.

> **Ella tenía veinte años más que él, pero se casaron (¡No!). Claro que no duraron mucho.**
> She was twenty years older than him, but they got married (No!).
> Of course they didn't last long . . . (surprise)

> **Te echaron la culpa a ti de lo que pasó (¡No!), ya que tú estabas allí . . .**
> They blamed you for what happened (No!), since you were there.
> (annoyance)

30.6 Asking how to pronounce or spell a word

30.6.1

To ask someone how to pronounce a word use the impersonal phrase **¿Cómo se pronuncia?**, 'how do you pronounce?'

> **¿Cómo se pronuncia su/tu nombre/apellido?**
> How do you pronounce your name/surname?

▶ **23.8** (p. 111); **23.9** (p. 111)

30.6.2

To ask someone to spell a word you can use either the impersonal phrase **¿Cómo se escribe?**, 'how do you spell it?' or a sentence with the verb **deletrear**, 'to spell'.

> **¿Cómo se escribe su/tu nombre/apellido?**
> How do you spell your name/surname?

> **¿Podría/s deletreármelo, por favor?**
> Could you spell it for me please?

> **¿Me lo deletrea/s?**
> Will you spell it for me?

Note the use of the present, **deletrea/s**, 'you spell' (formal/fam.) in the last sentence, used commonly in requests.

▶ **68.1** (p. 381)

30.7 Interrupting a speaker

To interrupt someone during the course of a conversation use one of the following expressions with **perdonar**, 'to excuse':

> **Perdone (usted)/perdona, pero . . .** (formal/fam.)
> 'Sorry, but . . .'

Perdone (usted)/perdona un momento . . . (formal/fam.)
'Sorry, but . . .'

Perdone (usted) que lo/la interrumpa . . . (formal, m./f.)
'Sorry to interrupt you . . .'

The expression with **interrumpir** is more formal than the other two.

30.8 Using fillers

All languages use fillers, that is words which, without adding new information, serve merely to keep communication going or fill in a pause while hesitating or searching for the right word. In English, we use words like 'well', 'well then', 'you know'. Spanish uses the following words:

Pues 'well'
Bueno 'well', 'now then', 'right then'
Hombre 'well', 'I don't know', 'well!', 'hey!', 'really!'
Este 'well, er' (esp. L. Am.)
O sea 'well . . .' (lit. 'that is')
Mire/mira (formal/fam.) 'look here'
No sé 'I don't know'
¿Sabe/s? 'you know?' (esp. L. Am.)

30.8.1 **Pues** is often used as an opening, to express doubt or hesitation and in exclamations.

Pues mira, lo que tienes que hacer es esto.
Well look, what you have to do is this.

¿Qué te parece? – Pues, no lo sé.
What do you think? – Well, I don't know.

¿Te gustaría venir conmigo? – Pues, ¡claro que sí!
Would you like to come with me? – Well, of course!

In some parts of Latin America, particularly in the Andean countries, **pues** tends to be used at the end of the sentence, as a kind of reinforcement of the preceding sentence:

No ha venido, pues.
He/she hasn't come.

No es culpa mía, pues.
It's not my fault.

30.8.2 **Bueno**, like **pues**, can express doubt or hesitation, or it can be used to start or resume a conversation:

Bueno, no estoy seguro.
Well, I'm not sure.

Bueno, ¿qué me estaba diciendo usted?
Now (then)/right (then), what were you telling me?

30.8.3 The use of the word **¡hombre!** is very common in Spain, not just to express hesitation but also to convey other emotions, such as happiness, sadness.

¿Dónde viven? – Hombre, no estoy seguro.
Where do they live? Well, I'm not sure.

¡Hombre!, qué bueno que hayas venido.
Well!, I'm glad you've come.

¡Hombre!, qué lástima lo que le pasó a Mario.
Oh dear!, what a pity what happened to Mario.

18.1.4 (p. 85)

30.8.4 Este, like **pues** and **bueno**, is used for expressing doubt or hesitation and it is frequently used as a tag, especially among Latin Americans.

¿Dónde has dejado las llaves? –Este . . .
Where have you put the keys? – Well . . .

Primero estuvimos en Santiago y después . . . este . . . fuimos a Puerto Montt.
First we visited Santiago and then . . . well . . . we went to Puerto Montt.

30.8.5 O sea has a similar function as the previous words but it normally only appears in the middle of a sentence:

Pues, me llevaron a un lugar que estaba, no sé, muy lejos, o sea (que) tuvimos que andar mucho . . .
Well, they took me to a place which was, I don't know, very far, well . . . we had to walk a lot . . .

30.8.6 ¿Sabe/s?, the equivalent of the English phrase 'you know' is especially common in some Latin American countries.

Fuimos al teatro, sabes, y después pasamos a tomar una copa al bar de Pancho.
We went to the theatre, you know, and then we went to Pancho's bar for a drink.

Tendrás que venir, ¿sabes?
You'll have to come, you know.

In the last sentence, Peninsular Spanish uses the expression ¿eh? instead of ¿sabes?

30.9 Changing the subject

Common expressions are:

A propósito . . .
By the way . . .

Eso me recuerda . . .
That reminds me . . .

Cambiando de tema . . .
Changing the subject . . .

30.10 Formal development of a topic

30.10.1 Opening remarks

To present a new topic formally, in the course of a lecture, talk or a very formal discussion, there are a number of expressions that can be used as opening remarks. Amongst these, the most common are:

En primer lugar . . .
First (of all) . . .

Primeramente . . .
Firstly . . .

Para empezar . . .
First (of all) . . . , to start with . . .

Antes que nada . . .
First (of all) . . .

Quiero/quisiera referirme a . . .
I want/would like to refer to . . .

Quiero que veamos . . .
I would like us to look at . . .

Me gustaría hablar sobre/acerca de . . .
I would like to speak about . . .

▶ **21.4** (p. 101)

30.10.2 Introducing further points

To introduce further points in an argument we use expressions like these:

Además . . .
Besides . . .

También . . .
Also . . .

Ahora bien . . .
Now . . . , now then . . .

Veamos/analicemos ahora . . .
Let's look at/analyse now . . .

Pasemos ahora a tratar . . .
Now let's go on to deal with . . .

▶ **18.3.1** (p. 91)

30.10.3 Establishing a sequence

The following phrases are used to establish a sequence between various points:

En primer lugar . . .	First (of all) . . . , firstly . . .
En segundo lugar . . .	Secondly . . .

En último lugar . . .	Finally . . .
Primeramente . . .	First of all . . .
Luego . . .	Then . . . , next . . .
Después . . .	Then . . . , next . . .
Seguidamente . . .	Next . . .
A continuación . . .	Then . . . , next . . .
Más adelante veremos . . .	Further on we shall see . . .

30.10.4 Establishing references

To establish references between part of an argument or between information shared by speaker and listener with a related point we use the following phrases:

En/por lo que se refiere a . . .
In reference to . . . , with regard to . . .

En lo que respecta a . . .
With regard to . . .

Respecto de . . .
Regarding . . . , with regard to . . .

Con respecto a . . .
With regard to . . . , regarding . . .

Con relación a . . .
In connection with . . . ,

En relación con . . .
In connection with . . .

En cuanto a . . .
As for . . . , as regards . . .

En lo que concierne a . . .
With regard to . . .

The expressions listed above are also often found in formal letter writing:

Con relación a su carta de 25 de abril . . .
In connection with your letter of 25th April . . .

En lo que se refiere a su propuesta . . .
With regard to your proposal . . .

En lo que concierne a su pedido de azulejos . . .
With regard to your order for ceramic tiles . . .

30.10.5 Giving examples

To give examples and illustrate a point use the following:

Por ejemplo . . .
For example . . .

Pongamos por ejemplo (el caso de . . .)
Let's take as an example (the case of . . .)

A modo de ejemplo . . .
By way of example . . .

Así . . .
Thus . . .

Así, por ejemplo . . .
Thus, for example . . .

Como . . .
Like . . .

Tales como . . .
Such as . . .

18.3.1 (p. 91)

30.10.6   How to explain yourself

To indicate you are about to explain something again, in new terms, use the following:

Es decir . . .	That is to say . . .
En otros términos . . .	In other words . . .
Dicho de otra forma/manera . . .	In other words . . .
Me explico . . .	I'll explain myself . . .
Lo que quiero decir es . . .	What I mean is . . .

30.10.7   How to ask for and give the floor

To ask to speak in the course of a formal meeting you can use the following expressions:

Pido la palabra . . .	May I say something?
¿Me permite/puedo decir algo?	May I say something?
Quisiera decir algo.	I'd like to say something.
Tiene la palabra (nombre).	(Name) has the floor.
Doy/cedo la palabra a (nombre).	I give the floor to (name).
(Nombre) ha pedido la palabra.	(Name) has asked to speak

30.10.8   Summarizing and concluding

To summarize and abbreviate different points in an argument and to conclude a presentation, use the following expressions:

En resumen . . .	In short . . .
Resumiendo . . .	In short . . . , to sum up . . .
En una palabra . . .	In a word . . .
En pocas palabras . . .	To cut a long story short . . .
En suma . . .	In short . . .
En conclusión . . .	In short . . .
Para terminar . . .	To finish . . .
Para concluir . . ./	To conclude . . .
Como conclusión . . .	

Finalmente . . .	Finally . . .
Por último . . .	Lastly . . .
Como último punto . . .	As a final point . . .
Y concluiré diciendo . . .	And I'll finish by saying . . .
En último lugar diré . . .	Finally I'll say . . .

II

Giving and seeking factual information

31
Asking questions and responding

A basic function in any language is that of asking questions in order to seek information, and Spanish, like English, has several ways of doing so. Spanish, however, shows more flexibility than English in terms of word order for either questions or statements. There are no structures in Spanish associated specifically with interrogative sentences, although usage sometimes points in one direction instead of another, as you will see from the examples below.

▶ **28.2** (p. 146)

31.1 Questions requiring a yes or no answer

31.1.1 Verb-subject

Questions of this type, usually carry the verb in initial position, that is, before the subject, with the action expressed by the verb becoming the focus point.

> **¿Ha llegado el tren?**
> Has the train arrived?

> **¿Va a ir Álvaro a la fiesta?**
> Is Álvaro going to the party?

> **¿Ha llamado alguien?**
> Has anyone called?

> **¿No te ha escrito Amanda?**
> Hasn't Amanda written to you?

In speech, this type of question calls for a rising intonation, and it is important to bear this in mind, as a falling intonation may turn the same sentence into a statement, for example:

> **Ha llegado el tren.**
> The train has arrived.

A falling intonation, accompanied by a shift of stress from the verb to another element in the sentence, the subject for instance, may have the same effect:

> **Va a venir *Álvaro* a la fiesta.**
> *Álvaro* is coming to the party.

In writing, question marks are used at the beginning and end of the interrogative sentence.

31.1.2 **Subject-verb**

This type of question, with the subject in the first place, as in an ordinary statement, is very frequent in Spanish, much more so than in English. Speakers may or may not be certain what the answer will be, but if there is a fair degree of certainty, they are more likely to use this type of question rather than the preceding one. The intonation, again, must be rising and not falling, as it would be in a statement.

> **¿Louise habla español?**
> Does Louise speak Spanish?

> **¿Alfredo viene mañana?**
> Is Alfredo coming tomorrow?

> **¿Usted no es español?**
> You aren't Spanish?

With longer subjects, the tendency is to isolate the subject by means of a slight pause at the end of it, with the rising intonation falling on the rest of the sentence.

> **Y tus padres,** (slight pause) **¿se han enterado?**
> And have your parents found out?

> **El edificio de la calle Mayor,** (slight pause) **¿tiene ascensor?**
> Does the building on calle Mayor have a lift?

31.1.3 **Statement + *¿verdad?* or *¿no?***

Questions of this type are normally used in speech when speakers are almost certain about the response and are merely seeking confirmation of their statements. **¿Verdad?** and **¿no?** are interchangeable and they correspond in English to question tags such as 'isn't it?', 'aren't you?', 'do they?', 'did she?'. As regards intonation for these types of questions, the first element, that is, the statement, has a falling intonation, while **¿verdad?** or **¿no?** carry a rising tone.

> **Hablas inglés, ¿verdad?**
> You speak English, don't you?

> **No eres de aquí, ¿verdad?**
> You're not from here, are you?

> **Es simpático, ¿no?**
> He's nice isn't he?

> **Hace mucho calor, ¿no?**
> It's very hot, isn't it?

▶ **12.9** (p. 51)

31.2 Questions seeking partial information

31.2.1 Interrogative word – verb – subject

Questions seeking partial information such as 'Which do you prefer?', 'How much is it?' are introduced in Spanish by the appropriate interrogative word followed by the verb and the subject. The intonation of these questions will vary according to the degree of familiarity between the speakers: usually falling intonation for familiar address and rising intonation to indicate politeness. In writing, the interrogative word carries an accent.

¿Cómo se hace?	How is it done?
¿Cuál prefieres?	Which one do you prefer?
¿Cuál es su dirección?	What is your address?
¿Cuánto es?	How much is it?
¿Cuándo ocurrió?	When did it happen?
¿Dónde estabas?	Where were you?
¿Por qué lo hiciste?	Why did you do it?
¿Qué desea?	What would you like?

▶ 12 (p. 48)

31.2.2 Preposition + interrogative word

Interrogative words such as those listed above are often preceded by a preposition in questions such as the following:

¿De dónde es usted?	Where are you from?
¿Con quién hablabas?	Who were you speaking to?
¿Para qué es esto?	What is this for?
¿Hasta cuándo estaréis aquí?	Till when will you be here?

31.3 Polite and indirect questions

31.3.1 Polite questions

To make a question more polite, you can start this with the word **perdone**, 'excuse me', or/and a phrase such as **por favor**, 'please', ¿**me puede decir** or **puede decirme** . . . ?, 'can you tell me . . . ?', ¿**me podría decir** or **podría decirme** . . . ?, 'could you tell me . . . ?'

▶ 21.1 (p. 99); 17.7 (p. 77)

Perdone, ¿dónde está correos/el correo?
Excuse me, where is the post office?

Por favor, la calle de Cervantes, ¿cuál es?
Which is Cervantes street, please?

Perdone, ¿me puede decir por dónde se va al aeropuerto?
Excuse me, can you tell me how to get to the airport?

> **Por favor, ¿podría decirme a qué hora sale el próximo vuelo para Barcelona?**
> Could you please tell me what time the next flight for Barcelona is leaving?

Note that, with longer sentences, the tendency in Spanish is to place the phrase **por favor** in initial position rather than at the end of the sentence. With shorter sentences, this goes in initial or final position.

> **¿Dónde está el ayuntamiento, por favor?** or **Por favor, ¿dónde está el ayuntamiento?**
> Where is the town hall, please?

31.3.2 Indirect questions

Dígame/nos (polite) and **dime/nos** (familiar), 'tell me/us', from **decir**, 'to tell', are used in indirect questions in sentences like the following:

> **Dígame qué le pasa.**
> Tell me what's wrong with you.

> **Dime qué te dijo.**
> Tell me what he/she said to you.

> **Dinos dónde están.**
> Tell us where they are.

▶ **18.3.1** (p. 91)

Note that the interrogative word after **dígame/nos** or **dime/nos** keeps the accent.

▶ **1.5.3** (p. 8); **12** (p. 48)

31.4 Negative questions

A negative question often conveys no more than the expectancy of a negative response, as in **¿No entiende el español?** 'Doesn't he/she' or 'don't you understand Spanish?' But a speaker will sometimes use a negative question to convey surprise or annoyance, for example:

> **¿Todavía no has terminado?**
> Haven't you finished yet? (meaning you ought to have finished by now)

> **¿Aún no lo has hecho?**
> You still haven't done it? (meaning you ought to have done it by now).

▶ **15.6** (p. 58)

31.5 Responding to a question with another question

When the question being asked needs clarification, we may respond to it with another question.

–¿Dónde has dejado las llaves?
'Where have you left the keys?'
–¿Qué llaves?
'Which keys?'

The intention of the second question may be not to seek clarification but to express an emotion such as surprise or interest.

–¿Sabías que Antonia se casa con Gabriel?
'Did you know Antonia is marrying Gabriel?'
–¿Con quién (se casa)? (surprise)
'Who (is she marrying)?'
–Con Gabriel Miranda. ¿No lo sabías?
'Gabriel Miranda. Didn't you know?'
–¿De veras? (interest)
'Really?'

31.6 Responding to a yes or no question

Spanish has no equivalent of phrases such as 'Yes, I am', 'Yes, we did', 'No, they don't', when responding to a yes or no question. Instead, you must use the equivalent of words and set phrases such as 'yes', 'no', 'certainly (not)', etc. Unless you want to sound emphatic, over formal or even annoyed, it is best to avoid repetition of the words used in the question.

31.6.1 Affirmative responses

The following are the affirmative responses most frequently heard. The first one – sí, 'yes' –, the most common of all, like no in 31.6.2, is rarely used on its own, as by itself it may sound abrupt. It is often repeated two or even three times or used in combination with other expressions or followed by an additional response.

sí 'yes'
claro (que sí) 'of course'
desde luego (que sí) 'of course'
por supuesto (que sí) 'of course'
naturalmente 'of course', 'naturally'
sí, efectivamente 'yes indeed', 'yes', 'that's right'
cómo no 'certainly', 'of course'

Claro, desde luego and por supuesto are generally interchangeable and may be used in formal and informal address. When followed by the words que sí, these expressions sound more emphatic. Naturalmente and sí, efectivamente are less frequent than the previous expressions and slightly more formal. Cómo no is heard more often in Latin America, especially in formal situations, often followed by the word señor, señora or señorita.

–¿Vienes con nosotros?
'Are you coming with us?'
–Sí, claro.
'Yes, of course.'

–¿Vais a salir de vacaciones?
'Are you going on holiday?'
–Por supuesto. Vamos a ir a San Sebastián.
'Of course. We are going to San Sebastián.'

–¿No has visto a María?
Haven't you seen María?
–Sí, sí, la vi ayer.
'Yes, I saw her yesterday.'

–Vendrá usted a vernos, ¿verdad?
'You'll come and see us, won't you?'
–Naturalmente, muchas gracias.
'Naturally, thank you very much.'

31.6.2 Negative responses

The most common negative responses are:

no 'no'
claro que no 'of course not'
desde luego que no 'of course not'
por supuesto que no 'of course not'
¡qué va! 'not at all!', 'you must be joking!'

With the exception of **no**, which is neutral, the rest of the expressions are emphatic, especially ¡**qué va!**, which is restricted to informal contexts.

–¿Trabajas los sábados?
'Do you work on Saturdays?'
–No, los sábados estoy libre.
'No, I'm free on Saturdays.'

–No invitarás a Manuel, ¿verdad?
'You won't invite Manuel, will you?'
–No, no, por supuesto que no.
'No, of course not.'

–No se lo dirás, ¿verdad?
'You won't tell him/her, will you?'
–Claro que no.
'Of course not.'

31.6.2.1 *Latin American usage*

A very colloquial negative expression in Latin America is **ni modo**, 'no way', 'not a chance'. It is particularly common in Mexico and Central America, but unknown in the Southern Cone countries (Argentina, Uruguay, Chile).

–¿Conseguiste hablar con él?
'Did you manage to speak to him?'
–No, ni modo, no quiso recibirme.
'No, no way/not a chance, he didn't want to receive me.'

32
Negating

Negation in Spanish, as in English, can be expressed in a number of ways, ranging from the simple word **no**, 'no', 'not', added to the positive sentence, for example **No lo sé**, 'I do not know', to the use of prefixes such as **in-**, for instance **inapropiado**, 'inappropriate', and other devices more specific to each language. In the sections below you will find all the main constructions used by Spanish speakers to negate something.

▶ **15** (p. 57)

32.1 *No* + verb/auxiliary

Negation in Spanish is normally expressed by placing **no** before the verb or auxiliary of a positive statement or interrogative sentence.

No hablan español.	They don't speak Spanish.
No podemos hacerlo.	We can't do it.
¿No hablan español?	Don't they speak Spanish?
¿No pueden hacerlo?	Can't they do it?

If the verb or auxiliary is preceded by an object pronoun, **no** will be placed before the pronoun:

No me lo quiso decir.
He/she didn't want to tell me.

No la conozco.
I don't know her.

The negation may be the response to a 'yes' or 'no' question, in which case the negative particle is usually repeated, as it is in English:

¿Te queda dinero?	Do you have money left?
No, no me queda.	No, I don't have any left.

For emphasis, the first negation is sometimes repeated in Spanish more than once:

¿Tú tienes mi bolígrafo?
Have you got my ballpoint pen?

No no, yo no lo tengo.
No, I haven't got it.

32.2 Limiting the scope of negation

To limit the scope of the negation, place **no** before the word or phrase you want to negate.

> **No siempre llega temprano.**
> He/she doesn't always arrive early.

> **No porque sea barato lo voy a comprar.**
> The fact that it is cheap doesn't mean I'm going to buy it.

> **Ella se marchó, pero no sin antes rogarme que guardara su secreto.**
> She left, but not before asking me to keep her secret.

▶ **18.1.5** (p. 85); **15** (p. 57)

Note that the use of **no** before certain verbal expressions may change their meaning. Compare for instance:

> **Han dejado de escribirme.**
> They have stopped writing to me.

> **No dejan de escribirme todos los meses.**
> They write to me every month without fail.

> **Acabo de entenderlo.**
> I have just understood it.

> **No acabo de entenderlo.**
> I just don't understand it.

32.3 Negating adjectives and nouns

The quality or characteristic expressed by an adjective can be negated by using negative prefixes, **in-** (**im-** before **b** or **p**) or **des-**, where appropriate, or negative words such as **no, poco, nada**, where a negative prefix does not exist.

> *In-*
>
> **inadecuado** 'inadequate'
> **incapaz** 'incapable'
> **imbatible** 'unbeatable'
> **impopular** 'unpopular'
>
> *Des-*
>
> **desatento** 'discourteous'
> **desconocido** 'unknown'
> **desordenado** 'untidy'
>
> *No*
>
> **países no desarrollados** 'underdeveloped countries'
> **sueños no realizados** 'unfulfilled dreams'
> **objetos voladores no identificados** 'unidentified flying objects'

Poco

poco interesante 'not very interesting'/'uninteresting'
poco atractivo 'not very attractive'/'unattractive'

(a) **Poco** is sometimes used instead of the prefix **in-** or **des-** in order to convey a lesser degree of the quality or characteristic expressed by the adjective. Compare for instance:

algo poco apropiado 'something not very appropriate'
algo inapropiado 'something inappropriate'
un hombre poco conocido 'a not very well known man'
un hombre desconocido 'an unknown man'

(b) **Nada** conveys stronger negation than either **poco** or the prefixes **in-** and **des-**:

un problema nada fácil 'a not at all easy problem'
una persona nada inteligente 'a not at all intelligent person'

Now consider how negation varies in degree in each of these phrases, arranged here from the least strong to the strongest:

una actitud poco correcta 'a not very correct attitude'
una actitud incorrecta 'an incorrect attitude'
una actitud nada correcta 'a not at all correct attitude'

(c) The meaning expressed by a noun can be negated by placing **no** before it:

los no fumadores 'non-smokers'
la no violencia 'non-violence'
la no intervención 'non-intervention'

▶ **15** (p. 57)

32.4 Other ways of expressing negation

32.4.1 *Ni . . . ni . . .*

Ni . . . ni . . . , 'neither . . . nor', may either precede or follow the verb to which it refers. If the latter is the case, the verb must be preceded by **no**.

Ni Sofía ni Joaquín asistieron a la función.
No asistieron ni Sofía ni Joaquín a la función.
Neither Sofía nor Joaquín attended the performance.

The first construction lays more emphasis on the **ni . . . ni . . .** phrase and overall it is less frequent than the second one.

32.4.2 *Ni siquiera* + verb/*No* + verb + *siquiera*

The phrase 'not even . . .', as in 'He didn't even look at me', can be expressed in Spanish by placing the phrase **ni siquiera . . .** before the verb (or accompanying pronouns) or by using the construction **no** + verb + **siquiera**. Both constructions express strong negation, but overall the first one is more colloquial and frequent than the second one.

Ni siquiera me miró or **No me miró siquiera.**
He/she didn't even look at me.

> **Ni siquiera nos llamaron** or **No nos llamaron siquiera.**
> They didn't even call us.

Tampoco

Tampoco, 'not . . . either', 'neither . . .', 'nor . . .', the opposite of **también**, 'also', 'too', serves to add a negation to a previous negative. **Tampoco** can either precede the verb or it can follow it in a double negative construction.

> **María no estaba.**
> Maria wasn't there.

> **Guillermo tampoco estaba** or **Guillermo no estaba tampoco.**
> Guillermo wasn't there either.

Often the verb is omitted when the context makes it clear what we are negating:

Carmen no ha llegado.	Carmen hasn't arrived.
Alicia tampoco.	Nor has Alicia.
No nos parece bien.	It doesn't seem right to us.
A mí tampoco.	Nor does it to me.

Nada, nadie

Nada, 'nothing', refers to things, while **nadie**, 'nobody', 'no one', refers to people. **Nada** can be used with a verb as a negative intensifier of the meaning expressed. It normally follows the verb in a double negative construction.

No hace nada.	He/she doesn't do anything.
No sé nada.	I don't know anything.

For emphasis, it is sometimes placed in initial position, before the verb, but this use is formal and infrequent and, unless you are sure when to use it, it is best to avoid it.

> **Nada tengo que temer.**   I have nothing to fear.

Note that **nada** is sometimes used with adjectives or adverbs in order to reinforce rather than negate the characteristic expressed by the adjective or adverb. In this context it translates into English as 'not at all'.

No es nada fácil.	It is not at all easy.
No está nada mal.	It is not bad at all.

Note that by placing **nada** before the verb in these sentences you would change their meaning:

Nada es fácil.	Nothing is easy.
Nada está mal.	Nothing is wrong.

Nadie can be used with a verb to express absence or non-existence with regard to people. It can be used after the verb in a double negative construction or, for emphasis, in initial position before the verb. The first construction is much more frequent than the second, which, with certain verbs, may sound stilted or archaic.

> **No trabajó nadie aquel día** or **Nadie trabajó aquel día.**
> No one worked that day.

> **No vino nadie.**
> No one came.

32.4.5 *Nunca, jamás*

Nunca and **jamás**, 'never', are the exact opposites of **siempre**, 'always', all of which indicate frequency with regard to the action expressed by the verb. They are equally frequent in initial position, before the verb, or after the verb in a double negative construction. **Jamás** is less frequent and stronger than **nunca**.

> **Nunca/jamás nos visitan** or **No nos visitan nunca/jamás.**
> They never visit us.

> **Nunca/jamás sale** or **No sale nunca/jamás.**
> He/she never goes out.

32.4.6 *Ninguno*

Ninguno, 'nobody', 'no', 'neither', 'none', 'any', can refer to personal or non-personal nouns. It can come before a noun or it can be used as a substitute for a noun which has already been mentioned or which is understood. When used before a masculine noun, **ninguno** becomes **ningún**.

> **No hay ningún autobús esta tarde.**
> There isn't any bus this afternoon.

> **No veo ninguna solución.**
> I don't see any solution.

> **¿Conoces a alguna de ellas? No, a ninguna.**
> Do you know any of them? No, none.

> **Ninguno de los dos lo sabía** or **No lo sabía ninguno de los dos.**
> Neither of them knew it.

> **Ninguno de ellos aceptó** or **No aceptó ninguno de ellos.**
> None of them/nobody accepted.

> **Ninguno me gusta** or **No me gusta ninguno.**
> I don't like any.

Note that in the last three sentences, in which **ninguno** is part of the subject of the sentence, this can be placed before or after the verb. In initial position, the emphasis is on **ninguno**.

▶ **5.1** (p. 24); **15** (p. 57)

32.4.7 Set phrases

¡Qué va!	Of course not! (especially Spain)
¡De ningún modo/	
ninguna manera!	Certainly not!
¡Ni hablar!	Out of the question!
¡Ni pensarlo/soñarlo!	Not by any means!
¡Por nada del mundo!	Not for all the world!

33
Reporting

Direct and indirect speech

An important function in language is to report what other people have said. This may be done by reproducing the exact words expressed by the speaker or, more often, by reporting his or her words in an indirect way. Reproducing the same words said by a speaker presents no problem, as all we need is a reporting verb like **decir**, 'to say', 'to tell', plus the words we want to report, as in:

> **'No quiero volver a verte aquí', me dijo ella.**
> 'I don't want to see you here again', she said to me.

This kind of reporting is not often used in the spoken language, but it is very frequent in written narrative, especially in fiction.

33.2 ## Indirect speech

In indirect speech we need a reporting phrase like **dice que** . . . , 'he/she says (that) . . .', **dijo que** . . . , 'he/she said (that) . . .', which normally comes before the words being reported. Often, in this type of reporting, there will be changes in the original utterance, which may affect verb forms as well as other parts of speech:

(a) The time lapse between the direct statement, question, request, etc., and the reporting may call for changes in verb forms. Compare for instance:

> **Nos iremos a finales de mes.**
> We'll leave at the end of the month.
> **Dicen que se irán a finales de mes.**
> They say they will leave at the end of the month.
> **Dijeron que se irían a finales de mes.**
> They said they would leave at the end of the month.

▶ 33.3 (p. 198)

(b) Possessive adjectives and pronouns may require adjustment (e.g. **su**, 'his/her', instead of **mi**, 'my'; **suyo**, 'his/hers', instead of **mío**, 'mine').

> **Mi casa está cerca.**
> My house is near.
> **Dice que su casa está cerca.**
> He/she says his/her house is near.

La mía está muy lejos.
Mine is very far.
Dice que la suya está muy lejos.
He/she says his/hers is very far.

(c) Pronouns may need to be changed (e.g. **él**, 'he', or **ella**, 'she', instead of **yo**, 'I'; **me**, 'me', instead of **te**, you).

(Yo) no quiero volver a verte.
I don't want to see you again.
(Ella) me dijo que no quería volver a verme.
She told me she didn't want to see me again.

(d) The person of the verb may have to change (e.g. **fue**, 'he/she went', instead of **fui**, 'I went').

No fui.
I didn't go.
Dice que no fue.
He/she says he/she didn't go.

(e) Time perspective may call for the substitution of adverbs of time and other time phrases (e.g. **al día siguiente**, 'the following day', instead of **mañana**, 'tomorrow').

Me voy mañana.
I'm leaving tomorrow.
Dijo que se iba/iría al día siguiente.
He/she said he/she was leaving/would leave the following day.

(f) Space perspective may require adjustments in words and phrases related to space, including direction (e.g. **aquí**, 'here', instead of **allí**, 'there'; **traer**, 'to bring', instead of **llevar**, 'to take').

Yo mismo lo llevaré allí.
I will take it there myself.
Dijo que él mismo lo traería aquí.
He said he would bring it here himself.

Space perspective may sometimes call for changes in demonstratives (e.g. **ése**, 'that one', instead of **éste**, 'this one').

Quiero éste.
I want this one.
Ha dicho que quiere ése.
He/she said he/she wants that one.

The sections below refer more specifically to indirect speech and to the way in which we report statements, questions, requests and commands.

33.3 Reporting statements

33.3.1 Not affecting verb forms

33.3.1.1 *With reporting verb in the present or perfect*

When we report an ongoing conversation – for example with someone on the telephone – or when the time lapse between the original statement and the reporting is not significant, no change of tense is required, although other changes may be necessary. The reporting verb will normally be in the present or the perfect.

▶ **17.1** (p. 72); **17.2** (p. 73)

> **No iré a cenar esta noche. Tengo una reunión.**
> I will not come for dinner tonight. I have a meeting.
> **Andrés dice que no vendrá a cenar esta noche, pues tiene una reunión.**
> Andrés says he will not come for dinner tonight because he has a meeting.

> **Me quedaré en la oficina hasta las 6.00.**
> I will stay in the office until 6.00.
> **El jefe ha dicho que se quedará en la oficina hasta las 6.00.**
> The boss has said he will stay in the office until 6.00.

> **No pude hacerlo.**
> I couldn't do it.
> **Dice que no pudo hacerlo.**
> He/she says he/she couldn't do it.

> **Ya lo he leído.**
> I have already read it.
> **Ricardo ha dicho que ya lo ha leído.**
> Ricardo said he's already read it.

33.3.1.2 *With reporting verb in the past*

When the time lapse between the original statement and the reporting is more significant, the indirect statement is normally introduced by a verb in the past, usually the preterite. And if the idea expressed in the indirect statement is still valid, no change of verb form is necessary.

> **Me resulta difícil el español.**
> Spanish is difficult for me.
> **Ayer hablé con Karen sobre su examen. Me dijo que el español le resulta difícil.**
> I spoke to Karen about her exam yesterday. She told me Spanish is difficult for her.

> **Estaremos allí al mediodía.**
> We'll be there at midday.
> **Dijeron que estarán aquí al mediodía.**
> They said they'll be here at midday.

In the second example, if the reporting were done after midday, **estar** would need to change from the future into the conditional.

> **Dijeron que estarían aquí al mediodía,**
> They said they would be here at midday
> ('and so they were' or 'but they weren't').

▶ 33.3.2 (below)

33.3.2   **Affecting verb forms**

Most reporting is done with an introductory verb in the past, which by itself establishes a distance between the time the original statement was made and the time of the reporting. If the original statement is no longer valid, or if we are not concerned about its current validity but simply want to establish that we are merely reporting what someone else said, changes in verb forms will become necessary in most cases in this passage from direct into indirect speech. The examples below illustrate some of the main changes.

(a) Present into imperfect:

> **No tengo tiempo.**
> I haven't got time.
> **Dijo que no tenía tiempo.**
> He/she said he/she didn't have time.

(b) Present continuous into imperfect continous:

> **Estoy trabajando.**
> I'm working.
> **Dijo que estaba trabajando.**
> He/she said he/she was working.

(c) Preterite, perfect into pluperfect:

> **No pude ir.**
> I couldn't go.
> **Dijo que no había podido ir.**
> He/she said he/she hadn't been able to go.
>
> **Ya he estado allí.**
> I have already been there.
> **Dijo que ya había estado allí.**
> He/she said he/she had already been there.

(d) Future into conditional:

> **Te presentaré a mi novio.**
> I'll introduce you to my boyfriend.
> **Dijo que me presentaría a su novio.**
> She said she would introduce me to her boyfriend.

Note that a pluperfect in direct speech remains the same in indirect speech, as there is no alternative verb form to replace this.

> **Yo se lo había dicho a mi mujer.**
> I had told my wife.
> **Dijo que se lo había dicho a su mujer.**
> He said he had told his wife.

The imperfect does not change either.

> **Yo la quería mucho.**
> I loved her very much.
> **Dijo que la quería mucho.**
> He said he loved her very much.

33.3.3 | **Verbs for reporting statements**

Decir, 'to say', 'to tell', is the most common verb used when reporting statements, specially in the spoken language. In very formal speech and in writing you will encounter verbs like **afirmar**, 'to state', 'to declare', **agregar, añadir**, 'to add', **comentar**, 'to comment', **explicar**, 'to explain', **expresar**, 'to express'. Other reporting verbs may reveal the intention of the statement, for example **aconsejar**, 'to advise', **advertir**, 'to warn', **asegurar**, 'to assure', **esperar**, 'to hope', **negar**, 'to deny', **prometer**, 'to promise'.

> **Afirmó que estaría dispuesto a hacerlo.**
> He stated he would be willing to do it.

> **Agregó/añadió que no le importaba lo que dijeran.**
> He/she added that he/she didn't mind what people said.

> **Me aconsejaron que no lo comprase.**
> They advised me not to buy it.

33.4 | **Reporting questions**

The changes which may affect interrogative sentences when being reported are similar to those undergone by statements. The reporting verb, usually **preguntar**, can take the present (e.g. **pregunta**, 'he/she asks'), the perfect (e.g. **ha preguntado**, 'he/she has asked'), the imperfect (e.g. **preguntaba**, 'he/she was asking') or, more commonly, the preterite (**preguntó**, 'he/she asked'). This must be followed by **si**, 'if' or 'whether', in the case of questions which require a 'yes' or 'no' answer. **Si** is not used when reporting questions introduced by an interrogative word.

> **¿Ha llegado Amalia?**
> Has Amalia arrived?
> **El gerente pregunta si ha llegado Amalia.**
> The manager asks if Amalia has arrived.

> **¿Te gusta vivir aquí?**
> Do you like living here?
> **Me preguntabas si me gusta vivir aquí. Pues, la verdad es que no.**
> You were asking me if I like living here. Well, not really.

> **¿Recibió mamá mi carta?**
> Did mother receive my letter?

Álvaro preguntó si mamá/su madre recibió/había recibido su carta.
Álvaro asked if mother/his mother received/had received his letter.

¿Qué has hecho con el dinero que te di?
What did you do with the money I gave you?
Mi padre me ha preguntado qué he hecho con el dinero que me dio.
My father has asked me what I have done with the money he gave me.

¿Cómo lo pasasteis?
Did you have a good time?
Nos preguntó cómo lo pasamos/habíamos pasado.
He/she asked us if we'd had a good time.

¿Cuándo volverás?
When will you come back?
Marta me preguntó cuándo volvería.
Marta asked me when I would come back.

33.4.1 Reporting verbs for interrogative sentences

Next to **preguntar**, the most common verb used when reporting questions is **querer saber** (e.g. **quiere saber**, 'he/she wants to know'), which is used normally in the present or the imperfect. In more formal contexts, you may hear **desear saber** (e.g. **desea saber**, 'he/she wishes to know').

¿Vendrá Hugo a la fiesta?
Will Hugo come to the party?
Adela quiere saber si Hugo vendrá a la fiesta.
Adela wants to know if Hugo will come to the party.

¿Qué pasó?
What happened?
Él quería saber qué pasó.
He wanted to know what happened.

▶ **19.1** (p. 93)

33.5 Reporting yes and no answers

To report a yes or no answer simply use the word **que**, 'that', between the reporting verb and the word **sí** or **no**.

Él dijo que sí.	He said yes.
Dijeron que no.	They said no.

33.6 Reporting commands and requests

33.6.1 Reporting verb + *que* + subjunctive

A reporting verb – usually **decir**, 'to say', 'to tell', **pedir**, 'to ask', or **querer**, 'to want' – in the present or the perfect requires the use of a present subjunctive in the subordinate clause.

The use of a reporting verb in the present or the perfect instead of the past (see below) is determined by the proximity of the original command or request to the actual reporting.

> **Tráigame toda la documentación.**
> Bring me all the documentation.
> **Me ha dicho que le lleve toda la documentación.**
> He/she has told me to bring him/her all the documentation.

> **No se lo digáis a Enrique.**
> Don't tell Enrique.
> **Nos ha pedido que no se lo digamos a Enrique.**
> He/she has asked us not to tell Enrique.

> **Enséñame a conducir.**
> Teach me to drive.
> **Manuel quiere que le enseñe a conducir.**
> Manuel wants me to teach him to drive.

A reporting verb in the past – usually the preterite – will be used when the time lapse between the original command or request and the reporting is more significant. The use of the past for the reporting verb calls for the **-ra** or **-se** forms of the subjunctive in the subordinate clause.

▶ **16.1.1.3 (p. 61)**

> **Tráigamelo mañana mismo.**
> Bring it to me tomorrow without fail.
> **Me dijo que se lo llevara mañana mismo.**
> He/she told me to bring it to him/her tomorrow without fail.

> **Vuelva usted el lunes por la tarde.**
> Come back on Monday afternoon.
> **Me pidió que volviese el lunes por la tarde.**
> He/she asked me to come back on Monday afternoon.

> **No vuelvas a hacerlo.**
> Don't do it again.
> **Recuerda que tu padre te pidió que no volvieras a hacerlo.**
> Remember your father asked you not to do it again.

33.6.2 Reporting verbs for commands and requests

Decir is the most neutral of the verbs used when reporting commands or requests, while **pedir** and **querer** are more appropriate when reporting requests. Commands can also be reported with verbs such as **mandar, ordenar**, 'to order', **exigir**, 'to demand'.

> **Hazlo arreglar.**
> Have it repaired.
> **Me dijo que lo hiciera arreglar.**
> He/she told me to have it repaired.

> **Pasa un día por casa.**
> Drop by the house some time.

> **Me pidió que pasara un día por casa.**
> He/she asked me to drop by his/her house some time.

The words said by the original speaker may have other intentions, such as making a suggestion, giving advice or warning, etc., in which case a reporting verb may be used which reflects that intention, for example **sugerir**, 'to suggest', **aconsejar**, 'to advise', **advertir**, 'to warn'.

> **Es mejor que no se lo diga.**
> You'd better not tell him/her.
> **Me aconsejó que no se lo dijera.**
> He/she advised me not to tell him/her.
>
> **No volváis a hacerlo.**
> Don't do it again.
> **Nos advirtió que no volviéramos a hacerlo.**
> He/she warned us not to do it again.

▶ 18.1.1 (p. 84)

34
Asking and giving personal information

In this chapter you will learn different ways of asking and giving personal information such as name, nationality, place of origin, occupation, marital and professional status, religion and political affiliation. You will also learn how to say your age and when and where you were born, and to ask similar information from others.

To give personal information you will need proper names such as **Carmen**, **José**, or noun phrases such as **mi padre . . .** , 'my father', **el hermano de Ana . . .** , 'Ana's brother . . .'; you may also need the Spanish equivalent of words like 'she', 'he', 'they', instead of the actual names. These words are called *subject pronouns* and in Spanish they are not always necessary, as the ending of the verb usually indicates the person referred to. Subject pronouns are normally used for emphasis, for contrast (e.g. **Soy inglés, pero él es escocés**, 'I'm English but he is Scottish'), to add politeness in the case of **usted** or **ustedes** (**Usted no es español, ¿verdad?**, 'You aren't Spanish, are you?'), or to avoid ambiguity (e.g. **Él es de Madrid**, 'He is from Madrid', instead of **Es de Madrid**, which can mean 'He is/she is/you are from Madrid').

▶ 8.1 (p. 34)

34.1   Name

34.1.1   *Me llamo . . .*, 'my name is . . .'

Llamarse, literally 'to be called', is the verb most frequently used when saying one's name or asking someone's name. It is a **reflexive** verb, that is a verb which requires an accompanying pronoun: **me**, **te**, **se**, for the first, second and third person singular, and **nos**, **os**, **se**, for the first, second and third person plural.

▶ 23 (p. 108)

> **¿Cómo te llamas?**
> What's your name? (fam.)
>
> **¿Cómo se llama usted?**
> What's your name? (pol.)
>
> **Me llamo Rodrigo.**
> My name is Rodrigo.

> **Mi padre se llama Antonio.**
> My father is called Antonio/My father's name is Antonio.

> **El hermano de Ana se llama Pablo.**
> Ana's brother is called Pablo.

Note that ¿cómo?, like all question words, must carry an accent.

▶ 1.5 (p. 7)

34.1.2 *¿Su nombre?*, Your name?

In official situations you will often hear the phrase ¿su nombre?, 'your name?', instead of ¿cómo se llama usted? This is a short form for ¿Cuál es su nombre?, 'What is your name?', but the complete form is rarely heard in Spain. The reply is normally just the name.

> **¿Su nombre, por favor?**
> Your name, please?
> **(Jaime Solares).**

▶ 35.1 (p. 210)

34.1.3 Latin American usage

Alongside the construction with **llamarse** in **34.1.2** above, Latin Americans often use the phrase ¿Cuál es su/tu nombre?, 'What is your name?' (pol./fam.), in official and non-official situations. The reply may be simply the name or, more formally, a complete sentence such as **Mi nombre es Amanda** or **Me llamo Amanda**, 'My name is Amanda'.

34.1.4 *¿Su apellido?*, Your surname?

To ask someone's surname use the following:

> **¿Cuál/Cómo es su/tu (primer/segundo) apellido?**
> What is your (first/second) surname?

Or simply,

> **¿Su/tu (primer/segundo) apellido/apellido de soltera?**
> Your (first/second) surname/maiden name?

To say what someone else's surname is, use

> **Su apellido es** (Lagos).
> His/her surname is (Lagos).

> **Se apellida** (Lagos).
> His/her surname is (Lagos).

34.2 Nationality and place of origin

34.2.1
To state one's or someone else's nationality we use **ser** followed by the proper form of the adjective of nationality:

Soy español.	I am Spanish.
Louise es inglesa.	Louise is English.

▶ **22.1** (p. 103); **2** (p. 11)

Questions regarding nationality may carry **ser**, as in:

¿Ustedes son chilenos?	Are you Chilean?
¿Eres inglés?	Are you English?

or **tener** ('to have'), as in:

¿Qué nacionalidad tiene Vd.?
What is your nationality?

Note also

¿Cuál es su nacionalidad?
What is your nationality?

34.2.2 To say where you or others come from use **ser** followed by the preposition **de**, 'from':

Soy de Londres.	I am from London.
Paul es de Irlanda.	Paul is from Ireland.

▶ **25.1.7.2** (p. 121)

To ask where someone comes from use the construction **¿de dónde . . . ?**, literally 'from where . . . ?', followed by a form of **ser**:

¿De dónde es Vd.?	Where are you from?
¿De dónde sois?	Where are you from?

34.3 Marital status

Marital status may be expressed with **estar** or **ser**, which are to some extent interchangeable.

¿Está/es casado o soltero?	Is he married or single?
Está/es divorciada.	She is divorced.

The tendency is to use **ser** when the emphasis is on the definition of the subject as a single or married person, while **estar** is used to emphasize the present marital status of the subject, usually someone we know, for example:

¿Tu hija está casada?
Is your daughter married?

Luis (todavía) está soltero.
Luis is (still) single/unmarried.

By and large, **estar** seems to be more frequent than **ser** when referring to marital status, especially in Spain. In Latin America, you are more likely to hear **ser**.

▶ **22** (p. 103)

In official situations, you may be asked about your marital status with the following phrase:

> **¿Su estado civil, por favor?**
> Your marital status, please?

Or,

> **¿Cuál es su situación familiar?**
> What is your marital status?

You may reply to the above with a single word, for example

> **soltero/a**, single, **casado/a**, married, **divorciado/a**, divorced, **separado/a**, separated, **viudo/a**, widower/widow.

34.4 Age

To refer to someone's age Spanish uses the verb **tener**, 'to have', in sentences like the following:

> **¿Cuántos años tienes?**   How old are you? (fam.)
> **¿Cuántos años tiene usted?**   How old are you? (pol.)
> **Tengo veintiocho años.**   I'm twenty-eight years old.
> **Mi madre tiene cincuenta.**   My mother is fifty.

▶ 7.1 (p. 30)

A frequent alternative when asking someone's age is to use phrases like:

> **¿Qué edad tienes?**   What age are you?
> **¿Qué edad tiene tu hija?**   How old is your daughter?

▶ 16.1.2.3 (p. 66)

You can also ask someone's age by using **ser**, as in

> **¿Cuál es su edad?**
> What is your age?

To which you can reply

> **(Tengo) 30 años.**
> (I'm) 30 years old.
>
> **Voy a cumplir (25) en (septiembre).**
> I'll be (25) in (September).
>
> **Acabo de cumplir (42) años.**
> I've just turned (42) years old.

34.5 Date and place of birth

Reference to date and place of birth is made with the verb **nacer**, normally in the preterite.

▶ 17.4 (p. 75)

34.5.1   **Date of birth**

¿Cuándo nació/ha nacido Vd.?	(especially Spain) When were you born? (pol.)
¿Cuándo naciste/has nacido?	(especially Spain) When were you born? (fam.)
(Nací) el 23 de julio de 1970.	I was born on 23 July 1970.

A less frequent way of asking someone's date of birth is with the phrase:

¿En qué fecha naciste?	When were you born?
¿En qué fecha nació él?	When was he born?

In official situations you are more likely to hear the phrase

¿Fecha de nacimiento?	Date of birth?

34.5.2   **Place of birth**

Usually expressed in the following way:

¿Dónde naciste?	Where were you born?
Nací en Argentina.	I was born in Argentina.

In official situations you are more likely to be asked

¿Lugar de nacimiento?	Place of birth?

34.6   Occupation, status or rank, religion and political affiliation

34.6.1   To say what one's or someone else's occupation is we use **ser:**

Soy arquitecto.	I am an architect.
Elena es profesora.	Elena is a teacher.

Note that Spanish does not require the use of the indefinite article, before the word denoting occupation.

 4.5 (p. 22)

To ask what someone's occupation is, say:

¿Cuál es su/tu profesión?
What is your occupation?

¿En qué trabaja Vd./trabajas?
What work do you do?

¿A qué se dedica Vd./te dedicas?
What do you do?

¿A qué se dedica tu marido?
What does your husband do?

¿Qué hace(s)?, 'what do you do?' may be appropriate when the context makes it clear what we are referring to.

> **Yo soy enfermera. Y tú, ¿qué haces?**
> I'm a nurse. And what do *you* do?

To refer to an occupation or activity which is temporary, we use **estar**, followed by the preposition **de**:

> **¿En qué trabaja Carmen?**
> What does Carmen do?

> **Está de dependienta en una tienda.**
> She is working as a shop-assistant.

22.2 (p. 105)

To refer to an occupation or activity which is not that normally performed by the person referred to, we use **hacer de**:

> **Marta no vendrá hoy, así que tú tendrás que hacer de secretaria.**
> Marta will not come today, so you will have to act as a secretary.

> **Ella hizo de madre para mí.**
> She acted as a mother to me.

Hacer de is also used when the subject is not suited for the occupation or activity referred to:

> **Paco está haciendo de mecánico en el taller de su padre.**
> Paco is working as a mechanic in his father's garage.

> **Como no encontré trabajo como periodista, tuve que hacer de recepcionista.**
> As I could not find work as a journalist, I had to work as a receptionist.

34.6.2   To ask and give information about status or rank, religion and political affiliation use **ser**:

> **Es el gerente de la empresa.**
> He is the manager of the company.

> **Es general de ejército.**
> He is an army general.

> **Clara es católica.**
> Clara is a Catholic.

> **Miguel es socialista.**
> Miguel is a socialist.

Notice the omission of the equivalent of English 'a' in **Clara es católica, Miguel es socialista**.

4.5 (p. 22); **22.1** (p. 103)

35

Identifying people, places and things

In this chapter, which deals with identification, you will learn the Spanish equivalent of phrases such as 'I am (John)', 'this is (my brother)', 'who is he/she?', 'which is it?'. The range of phrases used to express these ideas in Spanish is very limited, and by and large constructions follow patterns which are similar to English.

35.1   Identifying oneself and others

To say who you are or who someone is we use **ser**, 'to be':

Soy Antonio Miranda.	I am Antonio Miranda.
Ella es Ana Rodríguez.	She is Ana Rodríguez.
Son mis padres.	It's my parents.

▶ **22.1** (p. 103); **16.1.2.9** (p. 70)

If the purpose of the identification is to introduce somebody, then **ser** is usually preceded by a demonstrative pronoun.

Ésta es mi mujer.	This is my wife.
Éste es mi marido.	This is my husband.
Éstos son mis hijos.	These are my children.

▶ **9.1** (p. 40); **29.4** (p. 156)

To ask who someone is, use **quién** (sg.) or **quiénes** (pl.) followed by **ser**:

¿Quién es él?	Who is he?
¿Quiénes son?	Who are they?

Note that **quién** and **quiénes**, like all question words, must carry an accent.

▶ **12.8** (p. 51); **1.5** (p. 7)

If you think you know who someone is and you simply want to corroborate this, use phrases like the following:

¿Es usted el señor Morales?	Are you señor Morales?
¿Ése es tu profesor?	That is your teacher?

35.2 Identifying places

To identify a place, Spanish often uses the verb **ser**, as in the identification of people, but to ask someone to identify a place we need to use **¿cuál?** (sg.) or **¿cuáles?** (pl.) before the appropriate form of **ser:**

¿Cuál es tu casa?
Which is your house?
(Es) ésa.
(It is) that one.

¿Cuáles eran tus habitaciones?
Which were your rooms?
(Eran) aquéllas.
(They were) those ones.

Éste es mi hotel.
This is my hotel.

▶ **12.2** (p. 49); **22.1** (p. 103); **9** (p. 40)

35.3 Identifying things

As in the identification of people and places, Spanish normally uses **ser** to identify things, while questions leading to the identification of things often carry the question words **¿cuál?** (sg.), **¿cuáles?** (pl.) or **¿qué?**.

¿Cuál es su maleta?
Which is your suitcase?
(Es) la azul.
(It is) the blue one.

¿Cuáles son sus cosas?
Which are your things?
(Son) ésas.
(They are) those ones.

¿Qué es esto?
What is this?
(Es) un plato mexicano.
(It is) a Mexican dish.

¿Es éste su pasaporte?
Is this your passport?

▶ **12.2** (p. 49); **22.1** (p. 103); **9** (p. 40)

36
Describing

In this chapter you will learn how to describe people, places and things, including the weather, and you will become familiar with the verbs and constructions associated with various forms of description.

36.1 Referring to a subject's nature or identity

36.1.1 *Ser* + adjective

To refer to a subject's nature or identity, as in 'The Earth is round', 'Ana is slim', 'This is Elena', we use **ser**, 'to be', with an adjective (words like **redondo**, 'round', **delgado**, 'slim', which tell us what a noun is like). Remember that adjectives must agree in number (singular or plural) and gender (masculine or feminine) with the noun they refer to.

La Tierra es redonda.	The Earth is round.
Ana es delgada.	Ana is slim.
Era un hombre inteligente.	He was an intelligent man.
Barcelona es grande.	Barcelona is big.
Este coche es estupendo.	This car is very good.
Ésta es Elena. Es mi hermana.	This is Elena. She's my sister.
Es una novela de aventuras.	It's an adventure novel.

▶ **2** (p. 11); **3** (p. 16); **22.1** (p. 103)

36.1.2 Position of the adjective

Descriptions, however, are often more complex than this, and one point to consider is the position of the adjective with respect to the noun to which it refers. Adjective position in Spanish is fairly flexible, and whether the adjective precedes or follows the noun depends on a number of factors, among them the following:

(a) Meaning, which in a few cases varies according to position, for example:

> **un hombre grande** 'a big man'
> **un gran hombre** 'a great man'
> **una persona pobre** 'a poor person' (without money)
> **una pobre persona** 'a poor person' (pitiful)
> **una casa nueva** 'a new house'
> **una nueva casa** 'another house'

> **una persona única** 'a unique person'
> **la única persona** 'the only person'

(b) The overtone placed on the adjective by the speaker, which may be distinctive or simply neutral, as in:

> **Es un valle fértil.**
> It is a fertile valley (fertile as opposed to barren or dry).

or affective, as in:

> **Es un fértil valle.**
> It is a fertile valley (with the adjective no longer contrasting with its opposite, and functioning as a block with the noun it qualifies).

(c) The type of adjective, which with some adjectives is essentially distinctive, and therefore is used always after the noun. Among them we find adjectives indicating nationality and place of origin, shape, substance, purpose, etc.:

> **un avión británico** 'a British aeroplane'
> **una señora catalana** 'a Catalan lady'
> **un caja cuadrada** 'a square box'
> **un cuchara plástica** 'a plastic spoon'
> **una calle peatonal** 'a pedestrian street'

Adjectives indicating colour normally follow the noun:

> **un vestido negro** 'a black dress'

But note:

> **la blanca montaña** 'the white mountain' (with the adjective acquiring a subjective and affective overtone)

(d) Style and regional differences, both beyond the scope of this book, but suffice it to say that there is a tendency in some areas of the Spanish-speaking world towards an increased use of the adjective in a preceding position with respect to the noun.

▶ 5.2 (p. 25)

36.1.3 **Other ways of describing people, places and things**

Ser is not the only verb used in descriptive language. In fact, we can use a number of constructions involving other verbs, where the aim may go beyond that of simple description. Consider for instance:

> **Desde la distancia pudo observar la figura alta y erguida de Isabel.**
> From the distance he/she was able to observe the tall and upright figure of Isabel.

▶ 21.1 (p. 99)

A verb frequently used when describing the attributes possessed by a person, a place or a thing is **tener**, 'to have', found in sentences like the following:

> **Ana tiene ojos azules.**
> Ana has blue eyes.

Él tenía mucho sentido del humor.
He had a good sense of humour.

Barcelona tiene un clima templado.
Barcelona has a temperate climate.

Este coche tiene mucha potencia.
This car has a lot of power.

36.2 Enquiring about a subject's nature or identity

To ask what someone is or was like or what a place or a thing are or were like we can use the construction **¿cómo + ser +** noun?

¿Cómo es?
What is he/she/it like?

¿Cómo es tu novia?	What is your girlfriend like?
¿Cómo eran tus padres?	What were your parents like?
¿Cómo era el hotel?	What was the hotel like?
¿Cómo son tus zapatos?	What are your shoes like?

¿Cómo? is often replaced by the more informal **¿qué tal?**:

¿Qué tal es tu jefe?	What is your boss like?
¿Qué tal es tu piso?	What is your flat like?
¿Qué tal son tus libros?	What are your books like?

In more informal language, and when the context is clear, **ser** can be omitted:

¿Qué tal el viaje?
What was the journey like?

¿Qué tal tus vacaciones?
What were your holidays like?

▶ **12.1** (p. 48); **12.7** (p. 51); **22** (p. 103); **36.9** (p. 218); **36.3.2** (p. 215)

You can also ask what someone or something is like by using questions like the following:

¿Qué aspecto tiene?
What does he/she/it look like?

¿Qué forma tiene? or **¿De qué forma es?**
What is it like? or What shape does it have?

Questions regarding identity or nature normally carry **ser**

¿Quién es?	Who is he/she?
¿Qué tipo de película es?	What sort of film is it?

36.3 Describing a state or condition

36.3.1

To refer to a state or condition of the subject noun, instead of to its properties, use **estar** rather than **ser** (see **22**).

> **Alfonso está contento.**
> Alfonso is happy.
>
> **El cine estaba lleno.**
> The cinema was full.
>
> **Tu coche está estupendo.**
> Your car is in perfect condition.

Fernando está enfermo.	Fernando is ill.
Mis padres están bien.	My parents are well.
Estaba loco.	He was mad.

Sometimes, we may wish to emphasize a particular state or condition of the subject, which is also considered as a property of this, for example

> **Elena está muy guapa.**
> Elena looks very pretty (a state or condition).
>
> **Elena es muy guapa.**
> Elena is very pretty (a physical property).

36.3.2

To ask how someone is or was we use the construction **¿cómo + estar + noun?**

¿Cómo está tu hermana?	How is your sister?
¿Cómo están tus hijos?	How are your children?
¿Cómo estaba José?	How was José?

Now consider these sentences which show the contrast between this construction and the one under **36.2** above:

> **¿Cómo es tu amigo?**
> What is your friend like?
>
> **¿Cómo está tu amigo?**
> How is your friend?
>
> **¿Cómo eran tus abuelos?**
> What were your grandparents like?
>
> **¿Cómo estaban tus abuelos?**
> How were your grandparents?

▶ **22** (p. 103); **17.3.1** (p. 74)

36.4 Descriptions involving an unspoken comparison

Descriptions of this kind, which involve some form of comparison of the subject as seen at different moments in time, require the use of **estar**:

El niño está grande.
The child is big (he is bigger than when I last saw him).

La ciudad estaba muy sucia.
The city was very dirty (it used to be clean or cleaner).

Tendrás que cambiar el coche. Está muy viejo.
You will have to change your car. It is very old (it has become old).

▶ **22** (p. 103)

36.5 Asking and saying what something is made of

36.5.1 To ask someone to describe things in terms of the material they are made of we use sentences like these:

¿De qué es la silla?	What is the chair made of?
¿De/En qué está hecho?	What is it made of?
¿Son de plata?	Are they made of silver?

NOTE **Estar** is used with the past participle **hecho** to indicate a state of affairs (see **22.2**).

▶ **22** (p. 103)

36.5.2 To describe things in relation to the material they are made of we use **ser** followed by the preposition **de**:

Su reloj es de oro.
His/her watch is made of gold.

Son de madera.
They are made of wood.

Era de cuero/piel.
It was made of leather.

▶ **22** (p. 103)

36.6 Describing events

To say what an event was like we can use either **ser** or **estar**. In this context, **ser** gives the description a more objective tone, while **estar** presents the same information in a more subjective way. First-hand experience of an event is often expressed with **estar**.

La fiesta fue/estuvo muy buena.
The party was very good.

La reunión fue/estuvo interesante.
The meeting was interesting.

Los festejos fueron/estuvieron grandiosos.
The celebrations were magnificent.

▶ **22** (p. 103)

36.7 Describing facts or information

To describe facts or information in subjective terms, as seen by the speaker, we use **ser** rather than **estar**:

> **¡Es algo muy insólito!**
> It is something very unusual!

> **Lo que me has dicho es espantoso.**
> What you have told me is dreadful.

▶ 22 (p. 103)

36.8 Describing social manners

To describe someone's social manners in general terms we use **ser**:

> **Él es una persona muy cariñosa.**
> He is a very affectionate person.

> **Ellos son muy bondadosos.**
> They are very kind.

> **Es un caballero.**
> He is a gentleman.

To describe someone's social manners at a particular point in time we can use either **ser** or **estar**:

> **Fue/estuvo muy amable conmigo.**
> He/she was very kind to me.

> **Fue/estuvo muy descortés con ellos.**
> He/she was very impolite to them.

▶ 22 (p. 103)

36.9 Describing the weather

To describe the weather, either in general terms or at a particular point in time, Spanish normally uses the verb **hacer**, literally 'to do', 'make', followed by a noun (e.g. **frío, calor, viento, sol**):

> **Aquí hace mucho calor en verano.**
> Here it is very warm in summer.

> **Hoy hace muchísimo frío.**
> It is very cold today.

> **Ayer no hizo frío.**
> It was not cold yesterday.

> **¡Ojalá haga bueno mañana!**
> I hope the weather is good tomorrow.

▶ 71.1 (p. 399)

To describe the weather at a particular point in time we can also use **estar** + adjective:

Hoy está caluroso.	Today is warm.
Ayer estuvo muy frío.	It was very cold yesterday.

Estar must be used when the adjective which describes the weather is a past participle, for example:

Hoy está nublado.	Today is cloudy.
Mañana estará despejado.	Tomorrow will be clear.

NOTE | **Estar** is used with the past participle because it indicates a state of affairs (see **22.2**).

To say what a day (**un día**) is or was like in relation to the weather, we need to use **ser**:

Ayer fue un día muy frío.
Yesterday it was a very cold day.

Mañana será un día de mucho calor.
Tomorrow it will be very warm.

NOTE | **Ser** is always used with a noun or pronoun (see **22.1**).

To describe the climate we use **ser** or **tener**:

El clima de Galicia es húmedo.
The climate in Galicia is wet.

Valencia tiene un clima templado.
Valencia has a temperate climate.

To ask what the weather or the climate is like, use phrases like the following:

¿Qué tal tiempo hace?
What is the weather like?

¿Cómo es el tiempo/clima?
What is the weather/climate like?

¿Hace/hacía (mucho) frío/calor?
Is/was it (very) cold/warm?

▶ 36.2 (p. 214)

37
Making comparisons

This chapter examines all the main constructions used by Spanish speakers to compare things. For ease of reference, these have been grouped into three main categories: comparisons of inequality, of equality, and comparisons involving more than two objects.

▶ 6 (p. 28)

37.1 Comparisons of inequality

37.1.1 *Más* + adjective + *que/Menos* + adjective + *que*

Comparisons of inequality, as in 'taller than', 'more expensive than', 'less interesting than', are expressed in Spanish with the word **más**, 'more', for superiority, and **menos**, 'less' for inferiority, followed by an adjective and **que**, 'than'.

> **Ignacio es más alto que Ricardo.**
> Ignacio is taller than Ricardo.
>
> **Mi coche es más caro que el tuyo.**
> My car is more expensive than yours.
>
> **Madrid es más grande que Valencia.**
> Madrid is larger than Valencia.
>
> **Su última película me pareció mucho menos interesante que las anteriores.**
> His/her last film seemed to me much less interesting than the previous ones.
>
> **Santiago es menos caluroso que Buenos Aires.**
> Santiago is not as warm as Buenos Aires.

▶ 5 (p. 24); 6 (p. 28)

Note that if the context makes it clear we may not express the full comparison.

> **Ignacio es más alto.**   Ignacio is taller.
> **Santiago es menos caluroso.**   Santiago is not as warm.

37.1.2 *Más* + adverb + *que/Menos* + adverb + *que*

We may also compare adverbs, that is words like **despacio**, 'slow', **fácilmente**, 'easily':

▶ **6** (p. 28); **14** (p. 55)

Juan Manuel habla más despacio que Elisa.
Juan Manuel speaks more slowly than Elisa.

Él trabajó más intensamente que ella.
He worked harder than her.

Jaime actuó menos astutamente que Raúl.
Jaime acted less cleverly than Raúl.

37.1.3 Irregular comparisons

Note that some adjectives and adverbs have irregular comparative forms. Here are the most common:

grande 'big'	**mayor** 'older'
	más grande/mayor 'bigger' (size)
pequeño 'small'	**menor** 'younger'
	más pequeño/menor 'smaller' (size)
bien 'well', **bueno** 'good'	**mejor** 'better'
mal 'badly', **mal** 'bad'	**peor** 'worse'

Él es mayor que yo.
He's older than me.

Madrid es más grande/mayor que Barcelona.
Madrid is bigger than Barcelona. (**más grande** is more common than **mayor** when reference is to size)

Elena es menor.
Elena is younger.

San Pedro de Ribes es más pequeño que Sitges.
San Pedro de Ribes is smaller than Sitges (**menor** is uncommon in this context).

Peter habla mejor que Sarah.
Peter speaks better than Sarah.

▶ **6.1** (p. 28)

37.1.4 *Más* + noun + *que/Menos* + noun + *que*

Comparisons may involve nouns, for example:

Él tiene más dinero que su padre.
He has more money than his father.

Ella sabe más inglés que yo.
She knows more English than me.

> España tiene menos inmigrantes que Inglaterra.
> Spain has fewer immigrants than England.

37.1.5 Verb + *más que*/Verb + *menos que*

Comparisons may be made between people or things in terms of an action (i.e. a verb), which is itself quantified with **más**, 'more', or **menos**, 'less'.

> Eduardo habla más que su hermano.
> Eduardo speaks more than his brother.

> España gasta menos que Inglaterra en servicios sociales.
> Spain spends less than England in social services.

37.1.6 *Más/menos* + adjective/adverb/noun + *de* + pronoun + *que*

Comparisons with an element in another clause require this structure with **de** instead of **que**, following the construction with **más/menos**. This will be followed by a pronoun plus **que: lo**, if the pronoun refers to a clause, or **el/la/los/las**, if it refers back to a noun.

> Es más rápida de lo que yo pensaba.
> She is faster than I thought.

> Tiene más aptitudes de lo que uno se imaginaba.
> He/she has more talent than was imagined (note that in this example **lo** does not refer back to **aptitudes** but to a clause: **uno se imaginaba que . . .**).

> Tiene más preparación de la que tenía cuando ingresó en la empresa.
> He/she has more training than what he/she had when he/she joined the company (**la** refers back to **la preparación**).

> Requiere más tiempo del que dispongo.
> It requires more time than I have (**el** in **del** refers back to **el tiempo**).

> Había menos personas de las que habíamos invitado.
> There were fewer people than we had invited (**las** refers back to **las personas**).

37.1.7 Verb + *más/menos* + *de* + *lo* + *que*

Here is another construction involving a comparison with a verb phrase. Compare this with **37.1.5** above.

> Trabajan más de lo que parece.
> They work more than it seems.

> Habla menos de lo que yo creía.
> He/she speaks less than I thought.

37.1.8 *Más/menos de* + numerals

In comparisons involving numerals, use **más/menos de**

> **Faltan menos de tres semanas para la Navidad.**
> There are less than three weeks left before Christmas.

> **No gana más de doscientos mil al mes.**
> He/she doesn't earn more than two hundred thousand per month
> (He/she earns about two hundred thousand per month).

Compare the last sentence with:

> **No gana más que doscientos mil al mes.**
> He/she earns only two hundred thousand per month (He/she earns
> exactly two hundred thousand per month, no more).

37.2 Comparisons of equality

37.2.1 *Tan* + adjective/adverb + *como*

Comparisons of equality involving adjectives and adverbs are expressed with the
construction **tan . . . como**, 'as . . . as'.

> **Mercedes es tan guapa como su hermana.**
> Mercedes is as pretty as her sister.

> **Barcelona es tan cara como Madrid.**
> Barcelona is as expensive as Madrid.

> **Su apartamento es tan pequeño como el mío.**
> His/her apartment is as small as mine.

> **Isabel habla tan bien como Sebastián.**
> Isabel speaks as well as Sebastián.

> **Alfonso conduce tan imprudentemente como su padre.**
> Alfonso drives as carelessly as his father.

37.2.2 *Tanto* + noun + *como*

Comparisons of equality involving a noun require this construction with **tanto . . .
como**, in which **tanto** agrees in gender (masculine or feminine) and number (singular
or plural) with the noun it refers to.

> **Él tiene tanto dinero como ella.**
> He has as much money as her.

> **Ayer había tanta gente como hoy.**
> Yesterday there were as many people as today.

> **Tengo tantos libros como tú.**
> I have as many books as you.

37.2.3 **Verb + *tanto* + *como***

If we are comparing two subjects in terms of an action (i.e. a verb), use this construction with **tanto como**, 'as much as'.

> **Hugo come tanto como su abuelo.**
> Hugo eats as much as his grandfather.

> **No trabajan tanto como yo.**
> They don't work as much as I do.

Note that **tanto**, used without **como**, means 'so much'.

> **¡Trabajan tanto!**　　　　　They work so much!

Note also **tan/tanto que**, not involving comparisons, in:

> **El examen era tan difícil que no pude responderlo.**
> The exam was so difficult that I couldn't do it.

> **Tardaron tanto que tuvimos que irnos.**
> They took so long that we had to leave.

37.2.4 **Other ways of expressing comparisons of equality**

Comparisons of equality may also be expressed with

(a) **Igual que**

> **Ella se viste igual que tú.**
> She dresses the same way as you.

(b) **Lo mismo que**

> **Ana me dijo lo mismo que tú.**
> Ana told me the same thing as you.

In the examples above **igual que**, 'the same way', and **lo mismo que**, 'the same thing', are not interchangeable. But note:

> **Me da igual** or **Me da lo mismo.**
> It makes no difference to me.

(c) **Igual a**

> **Antonio es igual a su padre.**　　　Antonio is like his father.

(d) **Igual de/igualmente**

> **El chino es igual de difícil.**
> Chinese is just as/equally difficult.

> **El japonés es igualmente difícil.**
> Japanese is just as/equally difficult.

(e) **Parecerse**

> **Carmen se parece a su abuela.**
> Carmen looks like her grandmother.

(f) Common expressions of equality

Blanco como la nieve.	As white as snow.
Negro como el carbón.	As black as coal.

37.3   Comparing more than two objects

37.3.1   Definite article + *más/menos* + adjective

To express ideas such as 'the highest', 'the most beautiful', 'the least intelligent', when comparing more than two objects, Spanish uses the definite article followed by the comparative form of the adjective.

> **Río es la ciudad más hermosa.**
> Rio is the most beautiful city.

> **El Aconcagua es el monte más alto de las Américas.**
> The Aconcagua is the tallest mountain in the Americas.

> **Éste es el mejor hotel de Zaragoza.**
> This is the best hotel in Zaragoza.

> **Es el mejor actor de todos.**
> He is the best actor of all.

> **Es el menos inteligente de todos.**
> He is the least intelligent of all.

Note the use of the preposition **de** in the examples above: **de las Américas, de Zaragoza, de todos.** When reference is to places, **de** normally translates into English as 'in'.

37.3.2   Omission of definite article

▶ 4.2 (p. 20)

There are exceptions to the use of the definite article in sentences of this type. Among these exceptions, the most common are:

(a) With adverbs

> **Cristóbal es el que se expresa mejor.**
> Cristóbal is the one who expresses himself best.

> **Fue él quien reaccionó más correctamente.**
> He was the one who reacted most correctly.

▶ 14 (p. 55)

(b) Following **estar**

> **Carlos era el que estaba más/menos enfadado.**
> Carlos was the most/least annoyed.

▶ 22.2 (p. 105)

(c) With possessive adjectives

Mi más sentido pésame.   My deepest sympathy.

▶ **10** (p. 42); **40** (p. 237); **63.1.1** (p. 358)

38

Expressing existence and availability

In this chapter dealing with existence and availability you will learn the Spanish equivalent of phrases such as 'there is/are . . .', 'there was/were . . .', 'have you got . . . ?'

38.1 Asking and answering questions regarding existence

38.1.1 *Hay, hubo, habrá . . .*

To ask and answer questions regarding existence, you will need the Spanish equivalent of phrases such as 'is/are there . . . ?', 'was/were there . . . ?', 'there is/are . . .', 'there was/were . . .', etc. In the present, Spanish uses the single word **hay**, which is a singular, impersonal, irregular form of **haber**.

> **¿Hay un hotel por aquí?**
> Is there a hotel nearby?

> **Hay dos enfrente de la estación.**
> There are two opposite the station.

> **No hay ninguno.**
> There isn't any.

Note that **hay** is used in affirmative, negative and interrogative sentences, whether we are talking about the existence of one or more than one thing. The same rule applies to the forms used in other tenses:

> **¿*Hubo* una fiesta en el pueblo?**
> Was there a party in the town?

> ***Hubo* grandes celebraciones.**
> There were great celebrations.

> ***Había* muchas personas.**
> There were many people.

> **Esta noche *habrá* un baile.**
> Tonight there will be a dance.

> ***Habrá* muchos invitados.**
> There will be many guests.

> *¿Habría* suficiente tiempo?
> Would there be enough time?
>
> **Espero que *haya tiempo*.**
> I hope there is time.
>
> **No *ha habido* problemas.**
> There haven't been any problems.

In informal and uneducated speech in general, there is a tendency among speakers to pluralize forms such as **hubo, había**, etc., when referring to the existence of more than one thing, e.g. **Hubieron/habían muchas personas**. This use seems quite prevalent in Latin America, but it is regarded as incorrect and should be avoided.

38.1.2 *¿Haber* or *estar?*

Hay, había, habrá, etc. are used to talk about the existence of something indefinite such as **un hotel**, 'a hotel', **mucha gente**, 'many people'. If we are referring to the existence or presence of something definite, already determined by the context, for example **el hotel**, 'the hotel', **mis amigos**, 'my friends', we should use **estar**, 'to be', instead of **haber**. Observe the contrast between the two verbs in these sentences:

> **¿Hay un buen hotel en la ciudad?**
> Is there a good hotel in the city?
> **Pues, está el Hotel Isla Negra, que es estupendo.**
> Well, there is the Hotel Isla Negra, which is excellent.
>
> **¿Había mucha gente en la fiesta?**
> Were there many people at the party?
> **Sí, estaban todos mis amigos.**
> Yes, there were all of my friends.

▶ 22.2 (p. 105)

38.1.3 *¿Ser* or *haber?*

Note also the use of **ser** in identification in:

¿Cuántos somos?	How many of us are there?
Somos seis.	There are six of us.

Compare this use with that of the impersonal form of **haber**, in:

¿Cuántos hay?	How many are there?
Hay seis.	There are six.

38.1.4 *Existir*

Existence can also be expressed through **existir**, 'to exist', a verb which is used in more formal contexts.

> **Existe desde hace mucho tiempo.**
> It has existed for a long time.

¿Existe Dios?
Does God exist?

25.1.11.2 (p. 123)

38.2 Describing facilities

To ask and say what facilities there are in a place we can use **haber** (see **38.1.1** above) or **tener**. In this context, **tener** seems to be much more frequent than **haber**.

Hay dos bares en el hotel.
There are two bars in the hotel.

El hotel tiene dos bares.
The hotel has two bars.

¿Tiene piscina el hotel?
Has the hotel got a swimming pool?

Hay/tiene una piscina muy grande.
There is/it has a very large swimming pool.

En todas las habitaciones hay baño.
There is a bathroom in all rooms.

¿Tiene baño la habitación?
Has the room got a bathroom?

Todas las habitaciones tienen baño.
All rooms have a bathroom.

38.3 Expressing availability

38.3.1 *Haber*

To ask and say whether something is or is not available, we can use **haber** (see **38.1** above), for example:

¿Hay alguna habitación con vista al mar?
Is there a room with a seaview?
Lo siento, no hay ninguna.
I'm sorry, there aren't any.

¿Cuánto dinero hay para nuestros gastos?
How much money is there for our expenses?
Hay trescientos euros.
There's three hundred euros.

No había nada.
There was nothing.

38.3.2 *Tener*

More often, however, availability is expressed through the verb **tener**, 'to have' (see also **38.2** above).

> ¿Tiene una habitación doble?
> Have you got a double room?
> **Sí, tenemos.**
> Yes, we have.
>
> ¿Tiene un coche disponible?
> Have you a car available?
> **En este momento no tenemos ninguno.**
> We haven't got any at the moment.

38.3.3 | *Disponer de, contar con*

Disponer de and **contar con**, 'to have', are less frequent than **haber** and **tener** and tend to be used in more formal contexts, especially in writing.

> **La empresa dispone de una gran sala de convenciones.**
> They company has a large conference room.
>
> **El estadio cuenta con todos los servicios necesarios.**
> The stadium has all the necessary facilities.

39

Expressing location and distance

This chapter examines all the various expressions used in Spanish to refer to location and distance, including verbs such as **estar**, 'to be', prepositions, and other less common forms.

39.1 Expressing location

39.1.1 *Estar*

To ask and say where something or someone is, Spanish normally uses **estar**, 'to be'. Questions are usually introduced by the interrogative word **¿dónde?** 'where'?.

> **¿Dónde está el cine?**
> Where is the cinema?
> **Está a dos manzanas de aquí.**
> It is two blocks from here.
> **Está a tres cuadras** (L. Am.) **de la catedral.**
> It's three blocks from the cathedral.
>
> **¿Dónde están los teléfonos?**
> Where are the telephones?
> **Están en la primera planta/el primer piso.**
> They are on the first floor.
>
> **¿Dónde estabais?**
> Where were you?
> **Estábamos en el jardín.**
> We were in the garden.
>
> **¿Dónde estaban las llaves?**
> Where were the keys?
> **Estaban debajo de la cama.**
> They were under the bed.

If you are asking for directions, **dónde** and **estar** can be omitted, for example:

> **¿Los lavabos/el baño?** (L. Am.), **por favor?**
> (Where are) the toilets, please?

> **Por favor, ¿la calle de Alcalá?**
> (Where is) Alcalá street, please?

39.1.2 *Encontrarse, hallarse*

These two verbs, both meaning 'to be', are found in more formal contexts, usually in writing.

> **¿Dónde se encuentra la Isla de Pascua?**
> Where is Easter Island?

> **La Isla de Pascua se encuentra en el océano Pacifico.**
> Easter Island is in the Pacific Ocean.

> **El señor Ramírez no se encuentra aquí.**
> Señor Ramírez is not here.

> **El Museo del Prado se halla en Madrid.**
> The Prado Museum is in Madrid.

> **¿Dónde se hallan las ríos Amazonas y Orinoco?**
> Where are the Amazon and Orinoco rivers?

> **Se hallan en la América del Sur.**
> They are in South America.

39.1.3 *Estar situado*

Estar situado, 'to be situated', is the least frequent of the verbs used in expressing location, and it is restricted to formal written language. The word **situado**, 'situated', functions as an adjective and therefore must agree in number (singular or plural) and gender (masculine or feminine) with the noun it refers to.

> **La ciudad está situada al pie de la montaña.**
> The city is situated at the foot of the mountain.

> **Chile está situado en la costa oeste de América del Sur.**
> Chile is situated on the west coast of South America.

> **¿Dónde está situado el monte Aconcagua?**
> Where is Mount Aconcagua?

▶ **2.1** (p. 11); **3.2** (p. 17)

39.1.4 *¿En qué parte . . . ?, ¿en qué lugar . . . ?*

To ask in which part someone or something is we use the phrase **¿en qué parte . . . ?**, or **¿en qué lugar . . . ?**, 'in which part . . . ?' 'where . . . ?', 'whereabouts?'. The first expression is more frequent and much more colloquial than the second.

> **¿En qué parte de España está tu familia?**
> In which part of/where in Spain is your family?

> **¿En qué parte de Londres está tu piso?**
> In which part of/where in London is your flat?

> **¿En qué parte estuvieron?**
> Where/whereabouts were they?
>
> **¿En qué lugar de Andalucía está Sevilla?**
> In which part of Andalusia is Seville?
>
> **¿En qué lugar está tu oficina?**
> Where is your office?

▶ **22** (p. 103)

39.1.5   *Ser* **instead of** *estar*

Colloquially, one may occasionally hear **ser** instead of **estar**, to refer to the location of places:

> **¿Dónde dijiste que era la casa de Juan?**
> Where did you say Juan's house was?
>
> **¿A que no sabes dónde es!**
> I bet you don't know where it is.

When the speaker uses **ser** instead of **estar** in this context, he seems to be referring not just to the location but also to the essence or existence of the place he is talking about. This is an infrequent occurrence of **ser**, and unless you are sure how to use it, it is best to avoid it. **Estar** will normally be correct in this context.

▶ **22** (p. 103)

39.2   **Asking and saying where an event will take or took place**

To ask and say where an event – for example a meeting, a party – will take or took place, use **ser** instead of **estar**:

> **¿Dónde será la reunión?**
> Where will the meeting be?
>
> **Será en la oficina del gerente.**
> It will be in the manager's office.
>
> **La fiesta fue en mi casa.**
> The party was in my house.

Estar is wrong in this context, as **reunión**, 'meeting', and **fiesta**, 'party', are events rather than things which can be located in space.

▶ **22** (p. 103)

39.3   **Indicating precise location**

To indicate precise location, we need the Spanish equivalent of words such as 'in', 'on', 'at', 'under', 'behind', etc. These words are called prepositions, and they sometimes combine with other words to form phrases which express location or some other notion, for example distance (see **39.4**). Here are some of the most important:

▶ **25** (p. 116)

39.3.1 **A**

▶ **25.1.1.4** (p. 118)

A is used in a number of set phrases and complex prepositions, for example:

> **a (cinco minutos) de aquí** '(five minutes) from here' (see **39.4** above)
> **a la derecha/izquierda** 'on the right/left'
> **a la vuelta (de la esquina)** 'round the corner'
> **al lado** 'near', 'nearby'
> **al otro lado** 'on the other side'
> **al final** 'at the end'
> **al fondo** 'at the bottom', 'at the end'
> **al teléfono** 'on the phone'

Note that 'at', as in 'He's at school', 'She's at the office', translates into Spanish as **en** rather than **a**: **Él está en la escuela, Ella está en la oficina.** When expressing close proximity, however, as in 'The family were sitting at the table', 'at' translates into Spanish as **a**: **La familia estaba sentada a la mesa.**

39.3.2 *Bajo, debajo de*

Bajo, 'under', is normally found in more formal registers, especially in writing, for example:

> **Viven bajo un mismo techo.**
> They live under the same roof.

▶ **25.1.4** (p. 119)

Debajo de, 'under', is used in all registers.

> **Las llaves estaban debajo de la cama.**
> The keys were under the bed.

▶ **25.1.8** (p. 122)

39.3.3 *De*

> **cerca de** 'near'
> **delante de** 'in front of'
> **detrás de** 'behind'
> **enfrente de** 'opposite'
> **al lado de** 'next to', 'near'
> **al otro lado de** 'on the other side of'
> **al final de** 'at the end of'
> **al fondo de** 'at the end/bottom of'

▶ **25.1.9** (p. 122); **25.1.13** (p. 123); **25.1.17** (p. 125); **22** (p. 103)

39.3.4 *En*

In the context of location, the single word **en** has different translations in English, for example:

Ramón está en su habitación.	Ramón is in his room.
Mi padre no está en casa.	My father is not at home.
El dinero está en la mesa.	The money is on the table.
Está en todas partes.	It is everywhere.

▶ **25.1.14** (p. 123)

39.3.5 *Encima de*

The basic meaning of this phrase is 'on', 'above', 'on top of'. It is much less frequent than **en** (see above) and **sobre** (see below), except when one is referring to a high position, for example:

Estaba encima de la montaña. It was above the mountain.

But it is an alternative to **en** in sentences like these:

Está encima de la cama.
It is on the bed.

Están encima del armario.
They are on top of the cupboard.

▶ **25.1.16** (p. 125)

39.3.6 *Enfrente de, frente a*

Both phrases have the meaning of opposite. The first is more frequent in Spain, while the second seems to be more frequent in Latin American Spanish. In Spain, **frente a** corresponds to a more formal register.

Su casa está enfrente de/frente a la catedral.
His/her house is opposite the cathedral.

▶ **25.1.17** (p. 125); **25.1.19** (p. 125)

39.3.7 *Entre*

When expressing location, **entre** translates into English as 'between' or 'among' (or 'amongst', 'in the midst of'), depending on the context.

Está entre Correos y el banco.
It is between the post office and the bank.

Estaba oculto entre la muchedumbre.
He was hidden among the crowd.

▶ **25.1.18** (p. 125)

39.3.8 | *Sobre*

The basic meaning of **sobre** is 'on top of', but it also translates into English as 'on', 'over', 'above' and 'near'. It is an alternative to **encima de**, as in:

> **El dinero estaba sobre/encima del armario.**
> The money was on top of the wardrobe.

It is also an alternative to **en**, when this has the meaning of 'on':

> **Las llaves están sobre/en la mesa.**
> The keys are on the table.

It may indicate hierarchy, as in:

> **El director de marketing está sobre el jefe de ventas.**
> The marketing director is over/above the sales manager.

It is an alternative to **cerca de**, as in:

> **Estaba sobre la calle de Serrano.**
> It was near the Calle Serrano.

▶ **25.1.26** (p. 129)

39.3.9 | Location may also be expressed with words such as **aquí**, 'here', **allí**, **allá**, 'there', which are called *adverbs*.

▶ **14.2** (p. 56)

> **Aquí está el dinero.** | Here is the money.
> **La entrada está acá.** | The entrance is here.

Acá is less precise than **aquí**. It is very frequent in Latin America, where it is used in preference to **aquí**.

> **El ascensor está allí.** | The lift is there.
> **La parada está allá.** | The stop is there.

Allá is less precise than **allí**.

▶ **22** (p. 103)

39.4 | Indicating distance

To indicate distance from something we use **estar** followed by the preposition **a** (see also **39.3.1** above) and a phrase signalling distance, for example:

> **Toledo está a (unos) 70 kilómetros de Madrid.**
> Toledo is (about) 70 km from Madrid.

> **Correos/el correo está a cinco minutos de la plaza.**
> The Post Office is five minutes from the square.

Note also

> **Está a poca/corta/gran distancia (de . . .)**
> It is a short/great distance (from . . .)

Está a la vuelta de la esquina.
It is round the corner.

The preposition **a** is not needed in phrases like the following:

Está (muy) cerca/próximo.
It is (very) near/close.

Está lejos/lejísimo.
It is far/very far.

Distance may also be expressed with **quedar, hallarse,** 'to be', **distar,** 'to be distant, to be away from'.

Queda (muy) cerca/lejos (de . . .)
It is (very) near/far away (from . . .)

Se halla a gran distancia de la ciudad.
It is a great distance from the city.

Guadalajara dista de México D.F. más de 500 kms.
Guadalajara is more than 500 km away from Mexico City.

No dista gran cosa.
It is not far off.

To ask how far a place is you can use questions like the following:

¿Está lejos/cerca?   Is it far/near?
¿A qué distancia está?   How far is it?
¿Cuánto hay de aquí a . . . ?   How far is it to . . . ?

The first question is general, while the second and third are normally used in relation to places which are more distant, for example the airport, a town:

¿A qué distancia está el aeropuerto?
How far is the airport?

¿Cuánto hay de aquí a Granada?
How far is it to Granada?

25.1.1.4 (p. 118); **22** (p. 103)

40
Expressing possessive relations

This chapter examines the forms used by Spanish speakers to express possession and to enquire about possession. The notes below explain the uses of possessive adjectives and pronouns and a range of other constructions associated with this function.

▶ **10** (p. 42)

40.1 Expressing ownership and possession

40.1.1 Using possessives

40.1.1.1 *Mi, tu, su . . .*

To express ownership and possession, when this is already established or it is understood, we use words like **mi**, 'my', **tu**, 'your' (fam.), **su**, 'your', 'his', 'her', 'its', **nuestro**, 'our', **vuestro**, 'your' (fam.), **su**, 'your', 'their'. These words are followed by a noun or a noun phrase, and they must agree in number (singular or plural) with the thing possessed; **nuestro** and **vuestro** must also agree in gender (masculine and feminine).

> **Mi llave, por favor.**
> My key, please.

> **No olvides tus gafas de sol.**
> Don't forget your sunglasses.

> **Su pasaporte, por favor.**
> Your passport, please.

> **Nuestra habitación no está mal.**
> Our room is not bad.

40.1.1.2 *Mío, tuyo, suyo . . .*

Ownership and possession may also be expressed with **mío**, 'mine', **tuyo**, 'yours' (fam.), **suyo**, 'yours', 'his', 'hers', 'its', **nuestro**, 'ours', **vuestro**, 'yours' (fam.), **suyo**, 'yours', 'theirs', which can function as adjectives or pronouns. These words follow the noun or are free standing and they all agree in number (singular or plural) and gender (masculine and feminine) with the noun they refer to, not with the possessor.

▶ **10** (p. 42)

Alicia es una gran amiga mía. (adjective)
Alicia is a good friend of mine.

Hoy llega una tía suya. (adjective)
An aunt of his/hers is arriving today.

Son tuyos. (pronoun)
They're yours.

Sí, (son) míos. (pronoun)
Yes, (they're) mine.

In certain set phrases, **mío, tuyo,** etc. translate into English as 'my', 'your', instead of 'mine', 'yours':

Eso fue idea mía.	That was my idea.
Eso es asunto suyo.	That is his/her business.

If the noun we are referring to has already been expressed or is understood, **mío, tuyo, suyo,** etc., are preceded by a definite article (**el, la, los** or **las,** 'the').

Su casa no está mal, pero la tuya es mejor.
His/her house is not bad, but yours is better.

La nuestra es un poco pequeña para una familia tan grande.
Ours is a bit small for such a large family.

Tu coche está impecable. El nuestro está hecho un asco.
Your car is impeccable. Ours is filthy.

No encuentro mis llaves. Llevaré las tuyas.
I can't find my keys. I'll take yours.

Note that in the examples above the possessive is functioning as a subject (e.g. **La tuya es mejor**) or object (e.g. **Llevaré las tuyas**) of the verb.

40.1.2 *Es de*

Possession is also frequently expressed in Spanish with the construction **es de . . . ,** which is the equivalent of ''s' in English: This is normally used when the possessor is named, as in

Es de María.	It is María's.
Son de mi hermana.	They are my sister's.

40.1.3 *De* + pronoun/noun

The preposition **de** is also found before third person personal pronouns, for example **usted, él, ella,** when one wishes to avoid ambiguity between 'your', 'his' and 'her' in such expressions as **su casa** or **la casa suya.**

La casa de él.	His house.
El padre de ella.	Her father.

Note also the use of **de** with a noun or noun phrase as in

La ventana de la cocina.
The kitchen window.

He invitado a los padres de mi novia.
I have invited my fiancée's parents.

40.1.4 *Pertenecer*

Ownership is sometimes expressed with the verb **pertenecer**, 'to belong', which corresponds to a less colloquial, more formal register.

Esta propiedad pertenece al señor Silva.
This property belongs to señor Silva.

Estos terrenos pertenecieron a mi padre.
These plots belonged to my father.

16.1.2.4 (p. 67); **10** (p. 42)

40.1.5 *Es propiedad de*

In formal written language, ownership is sometimes expressed through the phrase **Es propiedad de** . . . , 'it's the property of . . .'

Es propiedad del estado.
It is the property of the state.

Son propiedad de nuestro club.
They are property of our club.

40.2 Emphasizing possessive relations

To emphasize the idea of possession, you can either stress **mi, tu, su** . . . , or/and you can use **mío, tuyo, suyo** . . . , in sentences like the following:

Esta es *mi* colonia.
This is *my* cologne.

Este dinero es mío.
This money is mine.

Te dije que utilizaras *tu* toalla. Ésa es la mía.
I told you to use *your* towel. That one is mine.

Emphasis in expressing possessive relations can also be achieved with the adjective **propio**, 'own', which changes according to number (singular or plural) and gender (masculine or feminine). This normally precedes the noun it qualifies, except in sentences with **tener**, 'to have', where it may come before or after the noun.

Lo vi con mis propios ojos.
I saw it/him with my own eyes.

Su propia madre no sabe dónde está.
His/her own mother doesn't know where he/she is.

Tiene coche propio or tiene su propio coche.
He/she has his/her own car.

Note the omission of the possessive when **propio** follows the noun, as in **Tiene coche propio**.

▶ **10** (p. 42)

40.3 Expressing possessive relations involving parts of the body and personal effects

In sentences like 'My feet ache', 'He took off his jacket', Spanish normally uses a definite article (**el**, **la**, **los** or **las**, 'the') instead of a possessive.

Me duelen los pies.	My feet ache.
Se quitó la chaqueta.	He took off his jacket.
Le robaron la cartera.	They stole his/her wallet.

▶ **4.1** (p. 19); **10** (p. 42)

40.4 Asking whose something is

To ask whose property something is, as in 'whose is this?', Spanish normally uses the construction ¿**De quién** + **ser** + noun/noun phrase?

¿De quién es esto?
Whose is this?

¿De quién es esa agenda?
Whose is that diary?

¿De quién son estos zapatos?
Whose shoes are these?

¿De quién será aquel coche azul?
I wonder whose that blue car is.

¿De quiénes son estos pasaportes?
Whose passports are these?

▶ **12.8** (p. 51); **28.2** (p. 146); **10** (p. 42)

Questions regarding ownership are also asked through sentences like the following, which carry a possessive

¿Es éste su equipaje?
Is this your luggage?

¿Son éstas sus maletas?
Are these your suitcases?

¿Este bolso es suyo?
Is this handbag yours?

El baúl negro es tuyo, ¿verdad?
The black trunk is yours, isn't it?

Less frequently, you will hear questions with **pertenecer**, 'to belong' (see **40.1.4** above).

> **¿A quién pertenece este solar?**
> Whose is this piece of land?
>
> **¿A quién pertenecen esas tierras?**
> Whose is that land?

▶ 10 (p. 42)

40.5   Other ways of expressing possession

40.5.1   *Tener*

To ask and answer questions regarding possessions as in 'Have you got a . . . ?' 'I have one/two . . .', etc., Spanish normally uses the verb **tener**, 'to have'.

> **¿Tienes cinco euros?**
> Have you got five euros?
>
> **No tengo nada de dinero.**
> I haven't got any money.
>
> **¿Cuántos hijos tenéis?**
> How many children have you got?
>
> **Tenemos tres.**
> We have three.

40.5.2   *Poseer, disponer de, contar con*

In formal language you will sometimes hear **poseer**, 'to possess', **disponer de** and **contar con**, 'to have'.

> **Posee una gran fortuna.**
> He/she possesses a great fortune.
>
> **Dispone de un cuantioso capital.**
> He/she has a considerable capital.
>
> **¿Con cuánto dinero cuentan?**
> How much money have you got?
>
> **Contamos con muy poco.**
> We have very little.

▶ 10 (p. 42); **38.3.3** (p. 229)

NOTE   **Contar** is a *radical-changing verb* (see **16.1.2.1**).

41
Expressing changes

In English, transformations experienced by the subject are expressed in a number of ways, which are not always interchangeable. Consider, for example, the following sentences:

> She *became* very sad after she heard the news.
> He *got* furious at me.
> He *went* mad.
> The new waiter has *turned* lazy.
> She *grew* very old.
> It *started* to rain.

Spanish also uses different verbs to express ideas such as these. As in English, these verbs are not always interchangeable, as you will see from the examples below:

41.1 Talking about temporary changes

41.1.1 *Ponerse* + adjective

Changes regarded as temporary are normally expressed through the verb **ponerse**, 'to become', 'to get', followed by an adjective. The transformations expressed by **ponerse**, normally refer to changes in the subject's mood or appearance. These may be sudden, as in:

> **Ella se puso muy triste.**
> She became very sad.

> **Gonzalo se puso furioso conmigo.**
> Gonzalo got furious at me.

or gradual, as in:

> **Elena se puso muy gorda.**
> Elena became very fat.

> **Los días se están poniendo calurosos.**
> The days are getting warm.

Note that the idea expressed by **ponerse** + adjective is closely linked to the one conveyed by **estar** + adjective, with the first emphasizing the transformation itself and the second stressing the result of that transformation.

> Se puso celoso.
> Está celoso de Álvaro.

He became jealous.
He is jealous of Álvaro.

⏵ 22.2 (p. 105)

An exception to the use of **ponerse** to refer to temporary changes is **ponerse viejo**, 'to become old'.

> Mi abuela se ha puesto muy vieja.
> My grandmother has become very old.

Usually, the subject undergoing the transformation, is also the grammatical subject of the sentence. But, for emphasis, the agent causing the change may become the subject of the sentence.

Compare for instance:

> Él se puso contento con mi llegada.
> He became happy at my arrival.

Él, 'he', is the subject undergoing the transformation, and it is also the grammatical subject of the sentence.

> Mi llegada lo puso contento.   My arrival made him happy.

Here, the agent causing the change, that is, **mi llegada**, 'my arrival', has become the subject of the sentence. Note that in the second example we have used **poner** instead of the reflexive **ponerse** (see 23).

41.1.2 *Ponerse a* + infinitive

The change may involve an activity, in which case **ponerse** must be followed by the preposition **a** plus an infinitive.

> Cuando salíamos, se puso a llover.
> As we were leaving, it started to rain.

> Cuando se lo dijimos, ella se puso a llorar.
> When we told her, she started to cry.

41.2 **Talking about long-lasting changes**

41.2.1 **Involving a change in the nature of the subject**

Transformations of this kind are normally expressed in Spanish through the verb **volverse**, 'to become', 'to go', 'to turn', followed by an adjective. Usually, transformations expressed through this verb involve a gradual rather than a sudden change, often related to the subject's character, attitude, mental state, etc.

> La muerte de su hijo le causó tanto dolor que se volvió loca.
> Her son's death caused her so much pain that she went mad.

> Carlos se ha vuelto muy huraño.
> Carlos has become very unsociable.

El nuevo camarero se ha vuelto muy perezoso.
The new waiter has turned very lazy.

La ciudad se está volviendo insoportable.
The city is becoming unbearable.

41.2.2 Not involving a change in the nature of the subject

Long lasting transformations not involving the subject's character, attitude or mental state, are often expressed through the verb **hacerse**, 'to become', followed by an adjective:

Su padre se hizo rico con la compraventa de automóviles.
His/her father became rich by buying and selling cars.

Los Vega se hicieron millonarios.
The Vegas became millionaires.

Se hizo famosa en todo el mundo.
She became world-famous.

41.2.3 Voluntary changes

Transformations which are the direct result of the subject's will or of an external influence or force, and which involve a change in occupation, religion, ideology, etc., are normally expressed through the verb **hacerse**, 'to become', followed by a noun or an adjective.

A pesar de la oposición de sus padres, Lucía decidió hacerse monja.
In spite of her parents' opposition, Lucía decided to become a nun.

Pepe se hizo socialista.
Pepe became a socialist.

Para casarse con Ali, Isabel tuvo que hacerse musulmana.
To marry Ali, Isabel had to become a Muslim.

41.3 Talking about changes resulting from a natural process

Transformations of this kind are normally expressed through **hacerse**, 'to become', 'to grow', followed by an adverb or an adjective.

Pasamos la noche allí, pues se había hecho muy tarde.
We spent the night there, as it had become very late.

Mi madre se hizo muy vieja.
My mother grew very old.

41.4 Talking about the result of a process of change

The result of a slow transformation process, usually involving some kind of effort in the pursuit of a goal, is normally expressed through the phrase **llegar a ser**, 'to become', which may be followed by a noun or an adjective.

Gracias a su esfuerzo, Antonio llegó a ser director de la empresa.
Thanks to his effort, Antonio became director of the company.

Llegó a ser uno de los países más ricos del mundo.
It became one of the richest countries in the world.

Llegó a ser célebre.
He/she became famous.

▶ 42.2 (p. 250)

41.5 Talking about changes caused by an action

As in English, changes in the subject's state or condition, which are the direct result of
an action or an event, are usually expressed with **quedar**, in this context meaning 'to
look', 'to be', or **quedarse**, 'to remain', 'to turn', 'to be (left)'.

41.5.1 *Quedar*

Mi habitación quedó muy bonita. La pinté yo mismo.
My room looked very pretty. I painted it myself.

Mamá ha quedado muy bien después de su operación.
My mother is very well after her operation.

41.5.2 *Quedarse*

Cuando oyó mi respuesta, se quedó callado.
When he heard my reply, he remained silent.

Al oír la noticia, se quedó pálida.
When she heard the news, she turned pale.

In phrases such as 'to get sad', 'to turn pale', **quedarse** and **ponerse** (see **41.1** above)
are interchangeable, although **quedarse** puts more emphasis on the transformation
being due to an outside agent.

Se quedaron/pusieron tristes.	They got sad.
Se quedó/puso pálida.	She turned pale.

Transformations which imply some kind of loss or incapacity usually accept either
quedar or **quedarse**:

Quedó/se quedó inválido a consecuencia del accidente.
He was disabled as a result of the accident.

Francisco quedó/se quedó huérfano a los cinco años.
Francisco was left an orphan when he was five years old.

Quedó/se quedó viudo.
He became a widower.

Quedó/se quedó soltera.
She never married.

41.6 Other ways of expressing change

Transformations are sometimes expressed with verbs like **transformarse en**, 'to become transformed', 'to change', **convertirse en**, 'to become', 'to turn into', 'to change', **convertirse a**, 'to become', 'to convert'.

> **Este lugar se ha transformado/convertido en un basural.**
> This place has become/turned into a rubbish dump.

> **A pesar de nuestras diferencias, Dolores se ha convertido en mi mejor amiga.**
> In spite of our differences Dolores has become my best friend.

> **Se convirtió al catolicismo.**
> He/she became a Catholic.

42
Describing processes and results

In its first part, this chapter looks at the various forms used by Spanish speakers to refer to processes, including personal and impersonal expressions, while the second part is concerned with the way results are expressed.

42.1 Describing processes

Processes, defined as a way of doing things – in this sense a synonym of procedure – or as a series of actions which are carried out in order to achieve a particular result, are expressed in Spanish using either personal forms like **tienes que . . .** , 'you have to . . .', or impersonal constructions such as **hay que . . .** , 'one has to . . .'. Sections (**42.1.1**) and (**42.1.2**) below list and explain all the main constructions used by Spanish speakers to describe a process or a procedure.

42.1.1 Personal constructions

The following are the forms normally used in Spanish to explain a process in a personalized way.

(a) Present

▶ **17.1** (p. 72)

(b) Future

▶ **17.5** (p. 76)

(c) **Tener que** + infinitive

▶ **21.5** (p. 102)

These three forms are normally associated with the spoken language, especially the first two. In writing, their use is restricted to informal contexts. The present and the future are normally found in descriptions involving a series of steps, while **tener que**, 'to have to', is used more often when the explanation involves a single action. In more lengthy explanations, these expressions tend to be combined.

> **Primero levantas el auricular y después metes la moneda.**
> First you lift up the receiver and then you insert the coin.

> **Mira, primero frío la cebolla y luego agrego los champiñones.**
> Look, first I fry the onion and then I add the mushrooms.

> **Una vez que recibamos las solicitudes haremos una selección.**
> Once we receive the applications, we'll make a selection.

> **Para abrir la cuenta tiene que rellenar esta solicitud.**
> To open the account you have to fill in this form.

42.1.2 | **Impersonal expressions**

Impersonal expressions focus on the process itself, that is, on the action or actions to be carried out, directing attention away from the logical subject who performs the action. The impersonal expressions used in this context are:

(a) **Hay que** + infinitive

▶ **21.7** (p. 102)

(b) Third person plural of verb

▶ **24.4** (p. 114)

(c) **Se** + third person verb

▶ **23.8** (p. 111); **23.9** (p. 111); **24.3** (p. 113)

(d) **Ser** + past participle

▶ **24.1** (p. 112)

42.1.2.1 | *Hay que* + *infinitive/third person plural of verb*
Hay que, 'one has' or 'needs to', 'you have' or 'need to', like the third person plural of the verb, are common in colloquial, spoken language but infrequent in writing, except in a very informal style.

> **Hay que cortar la fruta en trozos pequeños.**
> You have to cut the fruit in small pieces.

> **Para conseguir un buen resultado hay que dejarlo hervir quince minutos.**
> To achieve a good result you have to let it boil for fifteen minutes.

Hay que is also found in combination with personal forms, for example the present or **tener que.**

> **Hay que poner en marcha el motor primero, y después hay que/ tienes que pisar/pisas el embrague.**
> You have to start the engine first, and then you have to press/you press the clutch.

> **Una vez que seleccionan los candidatos llaman a una entrevista.**
> Once they select the candidates they call them for an interview.

> **Recogen a los pasajeros y después los llevan a los hoteles.**
> They pick up the passengers and then they take them to the hotels.

Note that **hay que** emphasizes the precise action to be undertaken while carrying out a process, while the third person plural of the verb simply explains what is done.

42.1.2.2 **Se** + *third person verb*

 23.9 (p. 111); **24.3** (p. 113)

A very frequent way of focusing on a process or procedure when the agent performing the action is irrelevant is by using this expression with **se** followed by a verb in the third person. The verb must agree in number, singular or plural, with the noun it refers to. This construction is used in the spoken as well as the written language. In writing, it is extremely common, especially where a formal style is required, as in describing a laboratory experiment or a production process, giving a recipe, etc.

> **Se mezclan las dos sustancias en proporciones iguales en una probeta, luego se calienta la mezcla . . .**
> The two substances are mixed in equal proportions in a test tube, then the mixture is heated . . .
>
> **Se cortan las verduras muy finas.**
> The vegetables are cut very finely.
>
> **Se deja remojando toda la noche.**
> You leave it soaking all night.
>
> **Las mercancías se embalan y se trasladan en camiones hasta los puertos de embarque, y desde allí se despachan a distintos países.**
> The goods are packed and sent by lorry to the embarkation ports, and from there they are shipped to different countries.

Note that the first three sentences describe the correct way to achieve a particular result, so in this sense they are no different from a set of instructions you can follow. Here, the agent performing the action is totally irrelevant. The last example, however, is different, in as much as the process being described corresponds to a common practice rather than steps to be followed. The agent here, although not mentioned, is understood. As a general rule, you should not use this type of sentence when you need to express the agent. Note also that where the agent is understood, as in the last example, we could express the same idea more colloquially by using an impersonal sentence such as the following:

> **Embalan las mercancías y las trasladan en camiones hasta los puertos de embarque, y desde allí las despachan a distintos países.**
> They pack the goods and they send them by lorry to the embarkation ports, and from there they ship them to different countries.

If only a single action were expressed, as in 'They are sent by lorry', we would normally use the impersonal third person plural, **Las trasladan en camiones**, and not the construction with **se**.

42.1.2.3 **Ser** + *past participle*

 24.1 (p. 112)

A less frequent alternative in the expression of processes is this construction, known as passive, in which **ser**, 'to be', is followed by a past participle which agrees in number (singular/plural) and gender (masculine/feminine) with the grammatical subject. Its use in the spoken language is uncommon, except in very formal, non-spontaneous speech such as radio or television news. In writing, however, it is very common, especially in a formal style; informal written language shows preference for the forms used in ordinary speech.

With this construction, the agent performing the action is either expressed or is understood. Of the sentences with **se** above, only the last one, in which the agent is understood, accepts the construction with **ser**.

> **Las mercancías son embaladas y (son) trasladadas en camiones hasta los puertos de embarque, y desde allí son despachadas a distintos países.**
> The goods are packed and sent by lorry to the embarkation ports, and from there they are shipped to different countries.

> **Una vez que la fruta ha sido cosechada, ésta es vendida por los productores a las empresas exportadoras.**
> Once the fruit has been harvested, it is sold by the producers to export companies.

> **La madera es transportada desde los centros de producción hasta los aserraderos donde es transformada en astillas para su exportación.**
> The wood is transported from the production centres to the sawmills where it is converted into chips for export.

Note that this construction is less likely to occur where only a single action is involved. A more colloquial alternative would be preferred instead. Compare for instance:

> **La fruta es vendida por los productores a las empresas exportadoras.**
> The fruit is sold by the producers to the export companies.

> **Los productores venden la fruta a las empresas exportadoras.**
> The producers sell the fruit to the export companies.

The first sentence might be encountered in very formal writing such as in newspapers, whereas the second sentence is neutral and could be used equally in the spoken and written language. Note also the different focus or emphasis in the two sentences: in the passive sentence with **ser** the focus or emphasis is on the object, **la fruta** in this case, with the agent, **los productores**, in second place, whereas in the second sentence the emphasis falls on the agent, with the object in second place.

42.2 Describing results

42.2.1 *Estar* + past participle

To describe a state which is the result of an action or a process, as in 'This work is finished', 'The house is sold', Spanish uses **estar** followed by a past participle which, like an adjective, agrees in gender (masculine or feminine) and number (singular or plural) with the noun it refers to (see 22.2).

With a transitive verb

As in the examples above, the state referred to can be the result of an action from a transitive verb (verbs like **terminar**, 'to finish', and **vender**, 'to sell', which require an object, for instance **terminar un trabajo**, 'to finish a job', **vender una casa**, 'to sell a house').

> **El trabajo está terminado.**
> The job is finished. (it has been finished)

> **La casa está vendida.**
> The house is sold. (it has been sold)

> **La mesa estaba puesta para la cena.**
> The table was laid for dinner. (it had been laid)

> **Todas las luces estaban encendidas.**
> All the lights were on. (they had previously been turned on)

With an intransitive or a reflexive verb

The state referred to can also be the result of an action from an intransitive verb (verbs like **dormir**, 'to sleep', **morir**, 'to die', which do not require an object) or a reflexive verb (for example **acostarse**, 'to go to bed', **vestirse**, 'to get dressed').

> **El niño está dormido.**
> The child is asleep/sleeping. (he has fallen asleep)

> **Mis abuelos están muertos.**
> My grandparents are dead. (they have died)

> **Raquel estaba acostada.**
> Raquel was in bed. (she had gone to bed)

> **Aún no están vestidos.**
> They are not dressed yet. (they haven't got dressed)

Note that the construction **estar** + past participle with verbs of this kind often translates into English as 'to be' + gerund. Common examples are:

> **estar acostado** 'to be lying down'
> **estar arrodillado** 'to be kneeling'
> **estar echado** 'to be lying down'
> **estar inclinado** 'to be leaning'
> **estar sentado** 'to be sitting'
> **estar tendido** 'to be lying down'

Note also that some past participles can be used with either **ser** or **estar**, **ser** to denote an action or a process (see **42.1.2.3** above) and **estar** to indicate the result of an action or a process. This contrast is shown most clearly in the following examples:

> **Los secuestradores fueron rodeados por la policía.**
> The hijackers were surrounded by the police. (the police surrounded the hijackers)
> **Los secuestradores estaban rodeados por la policía.**
> The hijackers were surrounded by the police. (the police had surrounded the hijackers)

La casa fue decorada para la Navidad.
The house was decorated for Christmas. (they decorated the house)
La casa estaba decorada para la Navidad.
The house was decorated for Christmas. (it had previously been decorated)

43
Expressing cause, effect and purpose

As in English, there are many different ways of expressing cause, effect and purpose in Spanish. Some of the constructions are simple and not unlike those in English. Others are more complex and may require a more detailed study.

The examples given and references to certain forms in the first part of this book will help you to become confident with their use.

43.1   Enquiring about cause

To enquire about the cause or reason for something Spanish uses a number of expressions, the most common of which are

> **¿Por qué?** 'why?'
> **¿Cómo . . . ?** 'why?, how come . . . ?'
> **¿Cómo es que . . . ?** 'why is it that . . . ?, how come . . . ?'
> **¿A qué se debe?** 'what's the reason?, what is it due to?'
> **¿Por qué razón/motivo?** 'why?, what's the reason?'
> **¿Cuál es la razón/el motivo?** 'what's the reason?'

▶ 12 (p. 48)

43.1.1   **¿Por qué?** is the most common and neutral of these expressions:

> **¿Por qué dijiste eso?**
> Why did you say that?

> **¿Por qué está usted todavía aquí?**
> Why are you still here?

▶ 12.6 (p. 50)

43.1.2   **¿Cómo . . . ?** and **¿Cómo es que . . . ?** are more colloquial and used in the spoken language. Both usually convey surprise or disapproval, especially the second one. **¿Cómo . . . ?** is used in negative questions while **¿Cómo es que . . . ?** can be used in negative or positive ones.

> **¿Cómo no me lo advertiste?**
> Why/How come you didn't warn me?

> ¿Cómo es que aún no lo termina?
> Why is it he/she still hasn't finished it?

> ¿Cómo es que ha sido seleccionado?
> How come he was selected?

43.1.3 ¿A qué se debe?, from **deberse a**, 'to be due to', is less colloquial, and used in the spoken and written language.

> ¿A qué se debe, crees tú?
> What is it due to, you think?

> ¿A qué se debe tanta insistencia?
> Why all this insistence?

> ¿A qué se debió?
> What was it due to?

43.1.4 ¿Por qué razón/motivo?, ¿Cuál es la razón/el motivo?, are more formal and less commonly used.

> ¿Por qué razón/motivo se comportó así?
> Why did he/she behave like that?

> ¿Cuál fue la razón/el motivo de su alejamiento del cargo?
> What was the reason for his/her removal from the post?

43.2 Giving reasons and expressing relationships of cause and effect

To give reasons and express relationships of cause and effect, Spanish uses expressions like the following:

> **porque** 'because'
> **pues** . . . 'because . . .'
> **por** . . . 'because of . . .'
> **a causa de** . . . 'because of . . .'
> **debido a** . . . 'due to . . .', 'because of'
> **deberse a** 'to be due to'
> **como** . . . 'as', 'since'
> **ya que** . . . 'as', 'since', 'for'
> **puesto que** . . . 'as', 'since', 'for'
> **dado que**. . . 'as', 'since', 'for', 'given that'
> **es que** . . . 'the thing is . . .'

43.2.1 **Porque** is the expression most commonly used for giving reasons and for establishing links between cause and effect.

> **Porque no quiero.**
> Because I don't want to.

> **Porque sí.**
> Just because!

> **No lo compré porque no tenía suficiente dinero.**
> I didn't buy it because I didn't have enough money.

Porque is followed by a subjunctive when it is preceded by a negative.

> **Lo hago no porque me lo pidas, sino porque quiero.**
> I'm not doing it because you ask me to, but because I want to.

> **No porque sea mi jefe voy a aceptar lo que me ha hecho.**
> I'm not going to accept what he's done just because he's my boss.

▶ 18.1.5 (p. 85)

Pues is often used in colloquial speech in place of **porque**. This use is especially common in Spain.

> **No vine porque/pues me dolía la cabeza.**
> I didn't come because I had a headache.

> **Hice de intérprete porque/pues no hablaba español.**
> I acted as an interpreter because he/she didn't speak Spanish.

Porque and **pues** are not always interchangeable so, unless you are sure, you are advised to use **porque**.

43.2.2 **Por . . . , a causa de . . .** and **debido a . . .** can be used in similar contexts. The first one is more colloquial and more common in the spoken language. The other two are slightly more formal and used in the spoken as well as the written language.

> **Lo he escondido por los chicos.**
> I have hidden it because of the children.

> **Por la lluvia no pudimos venir.**
> Because of the rain we couldn't come.

> **El partido se suspendió a causa de/debido a la lluvia.**
> The game was cancelled because of/due to the rain.

43.2.3 **Se debe a . . .** , from **deberse a**, 'to be due to', is used for giving reasons or expressing relationships of cause and effect in more formal contexts, in writing as well as in the spoken language.

> **Su actitud se debe a ignorancia.**
> His/her attitude is due to ignorance.

> **El retraso se debió al mal tiempo.**
> The delay was due to bad weather.

43.2.4 **Como . . .** introduces a reason, containing information which is new or known to the listener, followed by a clause which explains the effect. **Como** is placed at the beginning of the sentence.

> **Como no viniste ayer, hoy tendrás que quedarte hasta más tarde.**
> As you didn't come yesterday, today you'll have to stay until later.

> **Como no habla español no pudieron darle el puesto.**
> As he/she doesn't speak Spanish they couldn't give him/her the job.

43.2.5 **Ya que . . .** and **puesto que . . .** introduce a reason containing information relevant to the context or to the listener. These two expressions are interchangeable and they tend to be used in more formal contexts, especially in writing. **Ya que . . .** is overall more common and colloquial than **puesto que** . . . Unlike **como** . . . , **ya que** . . . and **puesto que** . . . can be placed before or after the main sentence.

> **Ya que estás aquí, ¿por qué no me ayudas?**
> Since you are here, why don't you help me?

> **Es mejor que lo haga usted mismo, ya que la secretaria no vino.**
> You'd better do it yourself as the secretary didn't come.

> **Puesto que el diálogo se ha roto, tendrán que recurrir al arbitraje.**
> Since the talks have broken down, they will have to resort to arbitration.

Dado que . . . is used in similar constructions, but its use is restricted to very formal writing or speech.

> **Dado que necesitamos más recursos, pediremos ayuda al gobierno.**
> As we need more resources, we will ask the government for help.

> **No asistiremos a la reunión, dado que no hemos sido invitados.**
> We will not attend the meeting, since we have not been invited.

43.2.6 **Es que** . . . is a colloquial expression used in the spoken language to convey an excuse or justify something rather than give a simple reason. It is used as a reply to a question, a statement or a non-verbal context.

22.1 (p. 103)

> **¡Mira lo que has hecho! ¡Lo has roto! – Es que se me cayó.**
> Look what you've done! You've broken it! Well, I dropped it.

> **¿Por qué no lo has terminado? – Es que no he tenido tiempo.**
> Why haven't you finished it? The thing is I haven't had time.

> **¿Por qué no la invitaron? – Es que se nos olvidó.**
> Why didn't you invite her? The thing is we forgot.

43.3 Other ways of expressing relationships of cause and effect

Relationships of cause and effect can be expressed in several other ways, for example:

43.3.1 Using special verbs like **causar, ocasionar, provocar**, 'to cause', **dar lugar a**, 'to give rise to'.

> **El tabaco puede causar cáncer.**
> Smoking can cause cancer.

> **El exceso de alcohol le ocasionó la muerte.**
> Excessive drinking caused his death.

> **El exceso de velocidad fue lo que provocó el accidente.**
> Speeding was what provoked the accident.

> **La invasión dio lugar a una cruenta guerra.**
> The invasion gave rise to a bloody war.

43.3.2 Using noun phrases like the following ones: **La razón por la que** . . . 'the reason (that) . . .', **por razones/motivos** + adjective, **por razones/motivos de** + noun, 'for . . . reasons', **en razón de**, 'because of', 'on the grounds of'.

11.2 (p. 45)

> **La razón por la que no respondía fue que su teléfono no funcionaba bien.**
> The reason (that) he/she did not answer was that his/her telephone was not working properly.

> **Por razones/motivos personales no pudieron asistir.**
> For personal reasons they weren't able to attend.

> **Por razones/motivos de salud tendrá que quedarse en casa.**
> For health reasons he/she will have to stay at home.

> **En razón de su edad le harán un descuento especial.**
> On the grounds of/because of his/her age they will give him/her a special discount.

43.3.3 Using linking words and phrases such as:

> **por eso** 'that's why'
> **así que** 'so'
> **por (lo) tanto** 'therefore'
> **por consiguiente, consiguientemente** 'consequently'
> **de ahí que** 'hence'
> **de modo/manera/forma que** 'so', 'so that'
> **de tal modo/manera/forma que** 'in such a way that'

> **He estado muy ocupado, por eso no he podido venir.**
> I've been very busy, that's why I haven't been able to come.

> **Me he quedado sin dinero, así que tendré que pedir un préstamo al banco.**
> I have been left without money, so I will have to ask the bank for a loan.

> **No sabía nada, por (lo) tanto la reprobaron.**
> She didn't know anything, so she failed.

> **No hablaban nada de español, de modo que tuvieron que contratar un intérprete.**
> They didn't speak any Spanish, so they had to hire an interpreter.

> **Estaba enfermo, de ahí su larga ausencia.**
> He was ill, hence his long absence.

> **Carlos bebió de tal forma que terminó totalmente borracho.**
> Carlos drank in such a way that he ended up completely drunk.

43.4 Enquiring about purpose

Purpose is often associated in Spanish with the preposition **para**, just as cause is sometimes associated with **por**. To enquire about purpose Spanish normally uses the phrase **¿para qué** . . . ?, 'what . . . for?', 'why?'.

> **¿Para qué me llamaste?**
> What did you call me for?

> **¿Para qué le dices eso si sabes que a él no le gusta?**
> What are you telling him that for/why are you telling him that when you know he doesn't like it?

> **¿Para qué lo quiere?**
> What does he/she want it for?

▶ **25.1.22** (p. 126); **25.1.23** (p. 127)

43.5 Expressing purpose

To express purpose, Spanish uses several constructions, of which the most common are those which carry the preposition **para** (see **25.1.22**).

43.5.1 *Para que* + subjunctive

Para is followed by **que** plus a subjunctive when the subject of the main verb is different from that of the complement verb.

▶ **18.2.1** (p. 86)

> **Lo traeré para que lo veas.**
> I'll bring it so that/in order that you may see it.

> **He cerrado la puerta para que no me molesten.**
> I've closed the door so that/in order that they will not bother me.

Note sequence of tense agreement between the main verb and complement verb. A main verb in the preterite or imperfect, for instance, will be followed by a complement verb in the imperfect subjunctive, especially when the latter refers to the past.

▶ **16.1.1.3** (p. 61); **19.2** (p. 95)

> **Fuimos a Sevilla para que Pepe conociera a su abuela.**
> We went to Seville so that/in order that Pepe could meet his grandmother.

> **La traíamos todos los años para que nos acompañara en nuestras vacaciones.**
> We used to bring her every year so that/in order that she would accompany us on our holidays.

When the complement verb refers to the present or to the future, this often takes the present subjunctive, even when the main verb is in the past.

▶ **16.1.1.3** (p. 61); **19.2** (p. 95)

> **Ayer llevé el coche al garaje para que lo reparen.**
> I took the car to the garage yesterday so that/in order that they will repair it.

> **Te llamaba para que no te olvides de lo que acordamos ayer.**
> I was calling you so that/in order that you don't forget what we agreed yesterday.

43.5.2 *Para* + infinitive

Para will be followed by the infinitive when the subject of the main verb is the same as that of the complement verb.

> **Llamaré a Antonia para invitarla a la fiesta.** (see **25.1.22.1**)
> I'll call Antonia in order to invite her to the party.
>
> **Nos reunimos con el contable para revisar las cuentas.**
> We met with the accountant in order to check the accounts.

43.5.3 *Para* + noun/pronoun

When followed by a noun or pronoun **para** indicates destination.

> **He comprado estas flores para mi tía.** (see **25.1.22.2**)
> I've bought these flowers for my aunt.
>
> **Son para ella.**
> They are for her.

43.5.4 *De manera/modo/forma que* + subjunctive

After **para que**, these are the expressions most commonly heard in the expression of purpose. Like **para que**, they will be followed by the subjunctive, except when expressing consequence, in which case they will be followed by an indicative verb, and they will often translate into English as 'and so' instead of 'so that'. Unlike **para** and the expressions which follow, **de manera/modo/forma que** are not used with an infinitive.

> **Lo discutiremos, de manera/modo/forma que lleguemos a una conclusión lo antes posible.**
> We'll discuss it so that/in order that we may reach a conclusion as soon as possible.
>
> **Le hablé muy despacio de manera/modo/forma que me entendiera.**
> I spoke to him/her very slowly so that/in order that he/she might understand me.

▶ **18.2.1** (p. 86)

Compare these sentences with:

> **Lo discutimos mucho, de manera/modo/forma que llegamos a una conclusión.**
> We discussed it at length, and so we reached a conclusion.
>
> **Le hablé muy despacio de manera/modo/forma que me entendió.**
> I spoke to him/her very slowly, and so (as a result) he/she understood me.

43.5.5 *A fin/con el fin de que* + subjunctive; *con el objeto de que* + subjunctive; *con el propósito de que* + subjunctive

These expressions are used in the same way as **para que**, and have the same meaning, but are more formal than **para que** and the expressions in **43.5.4** above.

Hemos convocado una reunión a fin/con el fin de que nos informen sobre su viaje.
We have called a meeting so that/in order that they may report to us on their trip.

Después del terremoto les dieron un préstamo con el objeto de que reconstruyeran sus viviendas.
After the earthquake they gave them a loan so that/in order that they might rebuild their homes.

Traerán más policías con el propósito de que controlen a la muchedumbre durante el partido.
They will bring in more policemen so that/in order that they may control the crowd during the match.

▶ 18.2.1 (p. 86)

43.5.6 | *A fin/con el fin de* + infinitive; *con el objeto de* + infinitive; *con el propósito de* + infinitive

Like **para**, these expressions will be followed by the infinitive when the subjects of the main verb and that of the complement verb are the same.

Nos reuniremos a fin/con el fin de tomar un acuerdo.
We'll meet so as to/in order to reach an agreement.

Habrá una asamblea con el objeto de analizar la situación.
There'll be an assembly so as to/in order to analyse the situation.

Con el propósito de investigar lo que pasaba decidimos contratar un detective.
So as to/in order to investigate what was happening we decided to hire a detective.

▶ 17.11 (p. 79)

III

Putting events into a
wider context

44
Expressing knowledge

To express knowledge, Spanish uses two different verbs, **saber** and **conocer**, 'to know'. Their uses are clearly differentiated by native speakers, as you will see from the examples below.

Expressing knowledge of a fact

To express knowledge or ignorance of a fact and, generally, to say that one has or does not have information about something, Spanish uses the verb **saber**. Remember that **saber** is irregular in the first person singular of the present, **yo sé**, 'I know'.

> **¿Sabes dónde está Fernando?**
> Do you know where Fernando is?

> **No lo sé.**
> I don't know.

> **¿Sabías que se casó Laura?**
> Did you know Laura got married?

> **Sí, ya lo sabía.**
> Yes, I knew.

Ignorance of a fact can also be expressed by using verbs such as **ignorar** or **desconocer**, 'not to know', 'to be unaware of'.

> **Ignoro qué les ha pasado.**
> I don't know what has happened to them.

> **Desconozco la razón.**
> I don't know the reason.

Note also the following more colloquial expressions:

> **No tengo ni idea.**
> I haven't a clue.

> **No tengo ni la menor/ni la más mínima/remota idea.**
> I haven't the slightest idea.

> **¡Ni idea!**
> No idea!

44.2 Saying that one knows a person, a place or an object

To say that one knows or does not know a person, a place or an object, Spanish uses **conocer**, a verb which is irregular in the first person singular of the present, **yo conozco**, 'I know'.

¿Conoces a Ricardo?
Do you know Ricardo?
Lo conozco muy bien.
I know him very well.

Conocimos muchos países.
We knew several countries.

¿Conoces esta fruta?
Do you know this fruit?
No la conozco.
I do not know it.

Notice the use of the personal **a** before a direct object denoting a person: **¿Conoces a Ricardo?**

25.1.1.1 (p. 116)

44.3 Expressing knowledge of a subject or a skill

44.3.1 To say that we know or do not know a subject, for example Spanish, painting, etc., we use **saber** or **conocer**. The first, however, seems to be more colloquial and frequent in this context.

Paul no sabe nada de español.
Paul does not know any Spanish.

Ella conoce mucho de pintura.
She knows a lot about painting.

44.3.2 To express knowledge of a skill and, generally, to say that we know or do not know how to do something, we use **saber** followed by an infinitive.

Pablo no sabía conducir.
Pablo did not know how to drive.

¿Sabes nadar?
Do you know how to swim?

Sé conducir, pero no muy bien.
I know how to drive, but not very well.

21.3 (p. 101)

44.4 Getting to know, becoming acquainted with or meeting someone

These ideas are expressed in Spanish through **conocerse**.

Cuando nos conozcamos mejor.
When we get to know each other better.

Se conocieron en Nueva York.
They met in New York.

Nos conocimos hace un año.
We met a year ago.

44.5 Learning or finding out about something

To say that we learned or found out about something, we use **saber**.

¿Supiste que llegó Sara?
Did you know that Sara arrived?

Lo supe por Pepe.
I found out through Pepe.

Supimos lo que pasó.
We learned what happened.

He sabido que viene Raúl.
I have heard Raúl is coming.

In this context, **saber** is similar in meaning to **enterarse**, e.g. **Me enteré por Pepe**, 'I found out through Pepe'.

45
Remembering and forgetting

This chapter examines the use of verbs such as **acordarse de**, 'to remember', **recordar**, 'to remember', 'to remind', **olvidarse**, **olvidar**, 'to forget', and the constructions associated with them.

45.1 Saying whether one remembers something or someone

To say whether one remembers something or someone, we use either **acordarse de** or **recordar**, 'to remember'. **Acordarse de** is used to refer to the involuntary process of remembering or not remembering something or someone, e.g. **(No) me acuerdo de él**, 'I (don't) remember him'. **Recordar** can either refer to an involuntary process, in which case it has the same meaning as **acordarse de**, or to the voluntary act of causing someone to remember something or someone, in which case it translates into English as 'to remind', e.g. **Recuérdame que tengo que hacer una llamada**, 'Remind me that I have to make a telephone call'.

When reference is made to concrete things, such as 'Sorry, but I don't remember his telephone number', most speakers will use **acordarse de**, as in **Lo siento, pero no me acuerdo de su número de teléfono**. But if the idea is that of evoking something or someone, in the sense of having memories, for example 'I will always remember the day when we met', most people will use **recordar**, as in **Siempre recordaré el día que nos conocimos**. However, the difference between one meaning and the other is not always clear and the two verbs are sometimes interchangeable.

45.1.1 Acordarse de is used normally in the following constructions:

45.1.1.1 *(No) acordarse de + noun or noun phrase:*

> **No me acuerdo de su número de teléfono.**
> I don't remember his telephone number.

> **Me acuerdo de Pablo, pero no de su mujer.**
> I remember Pablo, but not his wife.

45.1.1.2 *(No) acordarse de + pronoun*
The accompanying pronoun can be a personal one (e.g. **él**, 'him', **ella**, 'her', **usted**, 'you'), a demonstrative (e.g. **eso**, 'that', **esto**, 'this'), or an indefinite pronoun (e.g. **nadie**, 'no one', 'nobody', **nada**, 'nothing').

> **Nos acordamos muy bien de él.**
> We remember him very well.

> **No me acuerdo de eso.**
> I don't remember that.

> **No me acuerdo de nadie.**
> I don't remember anyone.

45.1.2   **Recordar** is found in the following constructions:

45.1.2.1   *(No) recordar* + *noun or noun phrase*

> **Recuerdo aquel día.**
> I remember that day.

> **Recuerdo muy claramente a Carmen.**
> I remember Carmen very clearly.

> **No recuerdo su voz.**
> I don't remember his/her voice.

Notice the use of personal **a** before the name Carmen.

▶ **25.1.1.1** (p. 116)

45.1.2.2   *With object pronouns* (see 8.2)

> **Lo recuerdo como si hubiera ocurrido hoy.**
> I remember it as if it had happened today.

> **La recordamos con mucho cariño.**
> We remember her very dearly.

> **Me entristece recordarla.**
> It saddens me to remember her.

> **No quiero recordarlo. Lo pasado, pasado.**
> I don't want to remember it. What's past is past.

45.1.2.3   *(No)* + *recordar* + *pronoun*
The accompanying pronoun can be an indefinite one (e.g. **nada**, 'nothing') or a demonstrative (e.g. **aquello**, 'that').

> **No recuerdo nada.**
> I don't remember anything.

> **Recuerdo sólo algo.**
> I only remember something.

> **No recordamos a nadie.**
> We don't remember anybody.

> **Recuerdo muy bien aquello.**
> I remember that very well.

Note the use of personal **a** before **nadie**, an indefinite pronoun referring to people.

▶ **2.7** (p. 14); **9.3.1** (p. 41); **13** (p. 52); **25.1.1.1** (p. 116)

45.1.2.4 **(No) recordar que . . .**

Recuerdo que . . . , 'I remember that . . .', is followed by a clause containing an indicative verb, while **No recuerdo que . . .** , 'I don't remember that . . .', requires a verb in the subjunctive, imperfect or perfect subjunctive. The positive sentence is far more frequent than the negative one.

▶ **16.1.1.3** (p. 61); **16.1.1.7** (p. 62); **18.1.5** (p. 85)

> **Recuerdo que era un día de mucho sol.**
> I remember it was a very sunny day.

> **Recuerdo que solía venir todos los veranos.**
> I remember he/she used to come every summer.

> **No recuerdo que él estuviera aquí.**
> I don't remember him being here. (the positive equivalent being **Recuerdo (muy bien) que él estuvo aquí**, 'I remember (very well) that he was here')

> **No recuerdo que él haya estado aquí antes.**
> I don't remember him being here before. (the positive equivalent being **Recuerdo (muy bien) que él ha estado aquí antes**, 'I remember (very well) that he has been here before')

▶ **18.1.5** (p. 85)

Some speakers may use **acordarse de** instead of **recordar** in the above context, but this use seems to be less frequent. In informal language, the preposition **de** is often omitted.

> **Me acuerdo (de) que era un día de mucho sol.**
> I remember it was a very sunny day.

45.1.2.5 **(No) recordar** + past infinitive

> **Recuerdo haberlo visto antes.**
> I remember having seen him/it before.

> **No recuerdo haberlo hecho.**
> I don't remember having done it.

▶ **16.1.1.7** (p. 62); **23.6** (p. 109); **26** (p. 131)

45.2 Asking people whether they remember something or someone

To ask people whether they remember or don't remember something or someone, use **acordarse** or **recordar** in the following expressions which, by and large, are similar to the ones above.

45.2.1 *¿Se acuerda usted/te acuerdas de* + **noun or noun phrase?**

¿Te acuerdas de ese lugar?
Do you remember that place?

¿No se acuerda usted de mi amigo?
Don't you remember my friend?

45.2.2 *¿Se acuerda usted/te acuerdas de* + **pronoun?**

¿Te acuerdas de ella?
Do you remember her?

¿No te acuerdas de ellos?
Don't you remember them?

¿Se acuerda usted de eso?
Do you remember that?

¿No se acuerda usted de nadie?
Don't you remember anyone?

45.2.3 *¿Se ha acordado usted/te has acordado de* + **infinitive?**

¿Se ha acordado usted de hacerlo?
Have you remembered doing it?

¿Te has acordado de pagar la cuenta?
Have you remembered to pay the bill?

45.2.4 **Object pronoun** + *recuerda usted/recuerdas*

¿Lo recuerda usted?	Do you remember him/it?
¿La recuerdas?	Do you remember her?

45.2.5 *¿Recuerda usted/recuerdas* + **pronoun?**

¿Recuerda usted esto?
Do you remember this?

¿Recuerdas a alguien?
Do you remember anyone?

¿No recuerdas a nadie?
Don't you remember anyone?

45.2.6 *¿Recuerda usted/recuerdas que . . . ?*

¿Recuerda usted que ella trabajaba conmigo?
Do you remember she used to work with me?

¿Recuerdas que yo vivía cerca de aquí?
Do you remember that I used to live near here?

> **¿No recuerdas que fue Luis quien te lo dijo?**
> Don't you remember that it was Luis who told you?

Note that unlike negative statements with **recordar** (e.g. **No recuerdo que** . . . , 'I don't remember that . . .'), negative questions do not require the use of the subjunctive in the subordinate clause.

▶ 18.1.5 (p. 85)

45.3 Saying that one has forgotten something or someone

45.3.1 *Olvidarse, olvidar*

To say that one has forgotten something, in the sense of leaving something behind, use **olvidarse** or **olvidar**, 'to forget'. **Olvidarse**, which emphasizes the idea that the forgetting was accidental, must agree in number with the thing forgotten, and is in effect a passive reflexive.

▶ 24.3 (p. 113)

> **Se me olvidó el paraguas** or **Olvidé el paraguas.**
> I forgot my umbrella.

> **Se nos olvidaron los documentos** or **Olvidamos los documentos.**
> We forgot the documents.

45.3.2 *Dejarse, dejar*, 'to leave', 'to forget'

In Spain, you will also hear **dejarse** or **dejar** with the meaning of leaving something behind accidentally.

> **Me he dejado/he dejado el carné en casa.**
> I've left my identity card at home.

45.3.3 *Olvidar, olvidarse de*

To say that one has forgotten someone or a fact, or has forgotten to do something, use **olvidar** or **olvidarse de**, 'to forget'.

> **Lo he olvidado** or **Me he olvidado de él.**
> I have forgotten him.

> **Ya he olvidado/me he olvidado de todo lo que ocurrió.**
> I have already forgotten everything that happened.

> **Olvidaste/te olvidaste de apagar la luz.**
> You forgot to turn off the light.

The difference between **olvidar** and **olvidarse de** is that the first implies intentional forgetting, while the second denotes unintentional forgetting.

Note also the use of these verbs in the imperative:

> **No se te olvide que la reunión es a las 6.00.**
> Don't forget that the meeting is at 6.00.

> **Por favor, no se olviden de apagar las luces.** Or
> **Por favor, no olviden apagar las luces.**
> Please, don't forget to turn off the lights.

> **¡Olvídalo ya!**
> Forget it!

23.6 (p. 109); **26** (p. 131)

45.4 Enquiring whether someone has forgotten something or someone

To enquire whether someone has forgotten something or someone, use the same verbs in **45.3.1** and **45.3.3** above, that is, **olvidar, olvidarse** or **olvidarse de**.

> **¿Se te olvidó el dinero?** or **¿Olvidaste el dinero?**
> Did you forget the money?

> **¿Ya la has olvidado?** or **¿Ya te has olvidado de ella?**
> Have you forgotten her already?

46
Expressing obligation and duty

This chapter deals with the ideas of obligation and duty and the verbs and expressions associated with them.

46.1 Expressing obligation and duty with regard to oneself and others

To express obligation or duty with regard to oneself and others, Spanish uses the following verbs, all followed by infinitives:

46.1.1 *Tener que* + infinitive

Tener que, 'to have to', is by far the most frequent verb used in the expression of obligation or duty and it may be used for present, past or future reference. Its use usually carries with it the notion that the obligation involved stems from outside the speaker himself, that is, from external circumstances.

> **Tengo que salir.**
> I have to go out.

> **No tengo que hacerlo.**
> I don't have to do it.

> **Tendremos que trabajar.**
> We'll have to work.

> **Tuvimos que quedarnos en casa.**
> We had to stay at home.

> **No tenías que decírselo/habérselo dicho.**
> You should not have told him/her.

▶ 21.5 (p. 102)

46.1.2 *Deber* + infinitive

Deber, 'to have to', 'must', is used when the obligation is seen as stemming from the speaker himself, as a kind of moral obligation. In general terms, however, the construction with **deber** is much less frequent than the one with **tener que**, and it is generally seen as implying strong obligation. **Deber** is found in a range of verb forms, including the present, future, preterite, conditional, imperfect indicative and imperfect subjunctive. Of these, the present and the conditional are the tenses most frequently used.

> **Debo hacerlo.**
> I must do it.

> **Deberás repararlo.**
> You will have to repair it.

> **Debí decírselo.**
> I ought to have told him.

> **Deberíamos/debíamos/debiéramos invitarlos.**
> We should invite them.

> **Deberías/debías/debieras traerlo.**
> You should bring it.

> **Deberías/debías/debieras haberlo traído.**
> You should have brought it.

> **Debería/debía/debiera habérselo contado.**
> I should have told him/her.

▶ **21.2** (p. 100)

46.1.3 *Poder* + infinitive

In the context of obligation and duty, **poder** is used in the conditional or imperfect (e.g. **podría** or **podía**) with the meaning of 'might'. It expresses mild obligation.

> **Podrías/podías llamarla.**
> You might call her.

> **Podríamos/podíamos explicárselo.**
> We might explain it to him/her.

> **Podríais/podíais/pudisteis habérselo explicado.**
> You might have explained it to him/her.

▶ **21.1** (p. 99)

46.1.4 *Haber de* + infinitive

Mild obligation or duty is sometimes expressed through **haber de**, 'to have to', normally found in literary registers.

> **He de salir al amanecer.**
> I have to leave at dawn.

> **Hemos de separarnos.**
> We'll have to separate.

> **Han de estar aquí a las ocho.**
> You/they will have to be here at eight.

> **Has de decírmelo todo.**
> You'll have to tell me everything.

▶ **21.6** (p. 102)

46.2 Enquiring whether one is obliged to do something

To enquire whether one is obliged to do something, Spanish normally uses the construction **tener que** + infinitive (see **46.1.1** above).

> **¿Tengo que hacerlo?**
> Do I have to do it?
>
> **¿Tenemos que devolverlo hoy?**
> Do we have to return it today?
>
> **¿Tendrás que volver?**
> Will you have to come back?

46.3 Expressing obligation in an impersonal way

Obligation is sometimes expressed in an impersonal way, without reference to a specific person. The verb most frequently associated with this use is **hay que**, 'one has to', 'one must'. **Hay** is an impersonal, irregular form of the present indicative of **haber**. In other tenses, use the third person singular of **haber: había que**, 'one/we had to', **hubo que**, 'one/we had to', **habrá que**, 'one/we will have to', **habría que**, 'one/we would have to'.

▶ **16.1.1.7** (p. 62)

> **Para ir a Egipto hay que tener visado/visa** (L.Am.).
> To go to Egypt, one has to/must have a visa.
>
> **Primero hay que pasar por la aduana.**
> First one has to/must go through customs.
>
> **Hubo que pagar derechos de aduana.**
> We had to pay customs duties.
>
> **Habrá que coger/tomar un taxi.**
> We'll have to take a taxi.
>
> **Habría que alquilar un coche/carro** (L.Am.).
> We would have to hire a car.

46.4 Other ways of expressing obligation and duty

Obligation and duty are also expressed through the following constructions:

> **estar** or **verse obligado a** 'to have to', 'to be obliged to'
> **verse en la obligación de** 'to have to', 'to be forced to', 'to be obliged to'
> **tener (la) obligación de** 'to have to', 'to be under an obligation to'
>
> **Estás obligado a hacerlo.**
> You have to do it.
>
> **Me vi obligado a decírselo.**
> I had to tell him/her.

Nos vimos en la obligación de despedirla.
We were forced to dismiss her.

Tienes la obligación de cuidar de ellos.
You are under an obligation to look after them.

47
Expressing needs

This chapter deals with different ways of expressing needs. In the sections below you will learn to express needs in a personal way, through the Spanish equivalent of phrases such as 'I have to . . .', 'I need to . . .', 'we need you to . . .', 'they need it', and also in an impersonal way through expressions like 'one has to . . .', 'one needs to', 'it is necessary'.

47.1 Expressing needs with regard to oneself and others

To express needs or lack of need with regard to onself or others, Spanish normally uses **tener que**, 'to have to' or **necesitar**, 'to need', in the following constructions, all of them used in informal and formal registers, with the exception of **47.1.6** below.

47.1.1 *Tener que* + infinitive

Tener que, 'to have to', expresses strong need, almost in the sense of having no alternative but to do what is implied.

> **Se ha roto, tendré que comprar otro.**
> It has broken, I'll have to buy another one.

> **Tiene que darse prisa, o perderá el tren.**
> You'll have to hurry, or you'll miss the train.

> **Tienes que comer más, estás demasiado delgado.**
> You have to eat more, you are too thin.

▶ 21.5 (p. 102); 46.1.1 (p. 272)

47.1.2 *Necesitar* + infinitive

Necesitar, 'to need', is less frequent than **tener que** and it conveys need in a more neutral or slightly mild way.

> **Necesito hablar con Vd.**
> I need to talk to you.

> **Necesitamos mudarnos de aquí.**
> We need to move from here.

> **Necesitaban trabajar.**
> You/they needed to work.

> No necesitan volver.
> You don't need to come back.

▶ 26 (p. 131)

47.1.3 *Necesitar* + subjunctive

This construction is used when the subject of the main verb is different from that of the complement verb, as in **(Yo) necesito que (tú) me aconsejes** 'I need you to advise me'. Here are some further examples:

> Necesitamos que estéis aquí antes de la cena.
> We need you to be here before dinner.

> Necesitaba que me lo dijeras.
> I needed you to tell me that.

> Carlos necesitaba que sus padres lo supieran.
> Carlos needed his parents to know it.

> No necesito que me lo digas.
> I don't need you to tell me.

▶ 18.1.1 (p. 84)

47.1.4 *Necesitar* + noun or noun phrase

> Necesita una gran suma de dinero.
> He/she needs a large sum of money.

> Necesito mi diccionario.
> I need my dictionary.

> Dijo que no necesitaba ayuda.
> He/she said he/she didn't need help.

47.1.5 Pronoun + *necesitar/Necesitar* + pronoun

> Te necesito.
> I need you.

> No necesitamos nada.
> We don't need anything.

> Parece que tu padre necesita algo.
> It seems your father needs something.

47.1.6 *Necesitar de* + noun/pronoun

This construction is infrequent and belongs to a formal register.

> Necesita de usted.   He/she needs you.
> Necesitamos de ese préstamo.   We need that loan.

If you are not sure how and when to use this construction, it will be safer to use the more colloquial forms:

Lo/la necesita.	He/she needs you.
Necesitamos ese préstamo.	We need that loan.

47.2 Asking people about their needs

Most of the constructions under **47.1** above are also used to ask people about their needs.

47.2.1 *Necesitar* + infinitive

¿Necesita usted entrar?
Do you need to come in?

¿Necesitáis comprar algo?
Do you need to buy anything?

47.2.2 *Necesitar* + subjunctive

¿Necesitas que te ayude?
Do you need help (from me)?

¿Necesita usted que lo despierte?
Do you need to be woken up (by me)?

47.2.3 *Necesitar* + noun or noun phrase

¿Necesitan ustedes el coche/carro (L. Am.)?
Do you need the car?

¿Necesitas la maleta grande o la pequeña?
Do you need the large or the small suitcase?

47.2.4 Pronoun + *necesitar/necesitar* + pronoun

¿Me necesita Vd.?
Do you need me?

¿Necesitáis algo?
Do you need something?

Note also the use of **necesitar** with certain question words, as in:

¿Qué necesitas?
What do you need?

¿Cuál necesita?
Which one do you/does he/she need?

¿Cuánto tiempo necesita usted?
How much time do you need?

¿Cuándo lo necesitáis?
When do you need it?

¿Por qué lo necesitan?
Why do you/they need it?

47.3 Expressing needs in an impersonal way

To ask and answer questions about needs in an impersonal way, that is, without reference to a specific person, we use the following expressions.

47.3.1 *Hay que* + infinitive

Hay que, 'one needs' or 'has to' is by far the most common expression used in expressing need in an impersonal way.

¿**Hay que hacerlo de nuevo?**
Does one/do we need to do it again?

Hay que estar muy alerta.
One needs to be very alert.

Hay que trabajar para vivir.
One needs to work in order to live.

To express the need not to do something we use the same expression in a negative construction, which indicates strong need, closer to prohibition:

Aquí no hay que fumar, está prohibido.
You mustn't smoke here, it's forbidden.

▶ **16.1.1.7** (p. 62); **46.3** (p. 274)

47.3.2 *Hacer falta* + infinitive

Hacer falta, 'to be necessary', is less common than **hay que** in positive sentences but very common in negative sentences to express the idea that something is unnecessary.

¿**Hace falta comprar algo?**
Do we need to buy anything?

No hace falta traer nada.
We don't need to bring anything.

Hace falta ser muy cuidadoso.
One needs to be very careful.

No hace falta preparar más comida. Hay suficiente.
We don't need to prepare more food. There is enough.

Hacer falta is often found by itself in reply to a question or a statement, for example an offer:

¿**Quieres que te compre uno?**
Shall I buy one for you?
No hace falta, gracias.
There's no need, thank you.

Te serviré algo de comer.
I'll give you something to eat.
No hace falta, no te molestes.
It's not necessary, don't bother.

47.3.3 *Hacer falta* + subjunctive

Although **hace falta** is an impersonal construction, not referring to any specific person, the complement verb may be personal, that is, it may refer to a specific person. If this is the case, **hacer falta** must be followed by **que** and a subjunctive.

No hace falta que me lo repitas.
You don't need to repeat it to me.

No hace falta que nos lo devuelvas.
You don't need to return it to us.

¿Hace falta que yo esté aquí?
Do I need to be here?

Hace falta que vengan todos.
Everyone needs to come.

▶ 18.1.1 (p. 84)

47.3.4 *Hacer falta* + noun

Hacer falta can be followed by a noun in sentences like the following to express the need or lack of need for somebody or something.

Hace falta Luis. Él sabría qué hacer.
Luis is needed here. He would know what to do.

No hace falta ese dinero.
That money is not necessary.

Note that sometimes the expression of need through **hacer falta** is personalized through the use of an indirect object pronoun, for example:

Me hace falta concentrarme más.
I need to concentrate more.

Nos hace falta un martillo.
We need a hammer.

¿Os hace falta algo?
Do you need something?

Note also the phrase:

¿Qué te hace falta?   What do you need?

▶ 8.2 (p. 36)

47.3.5 *Ser necesario* + infinitive

Ser necesario, 'to be necessary', is less common than **hay que** + infinitive or **hacer falta** + infinitive, and much less common than the equivalent English expression 'to be necessary'. Its use overall seems more frequent in negative than in positive sentences.

> **No es necesario repetirlo.**
> It is not necessary to repeat it.

> **No es necesario insistir tanto.**
> It is not necessary to insist so much.

> **¿Es necesario pagar ahora?**
> Is it necessary to pay now?

> **Es absolutamente necesario hacerlo.**
> It is absolutely necessary to do it.

47.3.6 *Ser necesario* + subjunctive

Ser necesario may be followed by a complement verb in the subjunctive, expressing need with regard to a specific person.

> **¿Es necesario que Cristina lo sepa?**
> Does Cristina need to know it?

> **Es necesario que vuelvas pronto.**
> You need to come back soon.

> **No es necesario que seas tan descortés.**
> You needn't be so rude.

○ 18.1.1 (p. 84)

47.4 Expressing strong need

To express strong need, we use the following expressions, in constructions similar to those with **ser necesario** (see **47.3.6** above). The most common of these are **ser esencial**, 'to be essential', **ser preciso**, 'to be necessary', **ser imprescindible**, 'to be essential', **ser indispensable**, 'to be essential', **ser fundamental**, 'to be vital', 'essential'. Here are some examples:

> **Es preciso tener coche/carro** (L. Am.).
> It is necessary to have a car.

> **Es indispensable llegar a la hora.**
> It is essential to arrive on time.

> **Es imprescindible que nos reunamos.**
> It is essential that we meet.

48

Expressing possibility and probability

The concepts of possibility and probability are expressed in Spanish in a number of ways, ranging from set words and phrases to more complex constructions. In the notes below you will find references to the first part of the book which will help you revise the forms associated with this language usage.

▶ **18.1.6** (p. 86); **18.3.3** (p. 92); **19.2** (p. 95); **16.1.1.3** (p. 61)

48.1 Saying whether something is considered possible or impossible

To say whether something is considered possible or impossible, as in 'It is (not) possible', 'It is possible that he may leave', 'Perhaps he may leave', etc., Spanish, like English, uses a number of expressions, of which the most common are:

48.1.1 Set phrases

> **es posible** 'it is possible'
> **es probable** 'probably'
> **es imposible** 'it is impossible'
> **no es posible** 'it is not possible'
> **posiblemente** 'possibly', 'maybe'
> **probablemente** 'probably'
> **es (muy) poco probable** 'it is (very) unlikely'
> **puede ser** 'maybe'
> **quizá(s)** 'perhaps'
> **tal vez** 'perhaps'
> **a lo mejor** 'perhaps'

These expressions are normally used in the spoken language as a response to a question or a statement. In the expression of impossibility, **es imposible** is much more frequent than **no es posible**, and it conveys a stronger notion of impossibility. The rest of the expressions are all equally frequent.

> **¿Crees que vendrá mañana? – Es posible/probable.**
> Do you think he/she will come tomorrow? –
> It is possible./Maybe./Probably.

¿Estarán en casa en este momento? – Sí, es posible/probable.
Will they be at home now? – Yes, it is possible./Maybe./Probably.

¿Puedes hacerlo solo? – Es imposible/No es posible.
Can you do it on your own? – It is impossible./It is not possible.

Va a llover – Posiblemente/Probablemente.
It's going to rain – Maybe./Probably.

Although these expressions occur much more frequently in the present, as illustrated by the examples above, they are also used in other tenses, for example:

No fue posible.	It wasn't possible.
Será imposible.	It will be impossible.
Sería imposible.	It would be impossible.

48.1.2 | *(No) es posible* + infinitive; *es imposible* + infinitive

These impersonal constructions with an infinitive are used when the expression of possibility or impossibility does not refer to any specific person. The words **probable**, 'probable', and **improbable**, 'improbable', cannot be used with this type of sentence.

Es posible encontrar algo mejor.
It is possible to find something better.

No fue posible encontrar lo que buscábamos.
It was impossible to find what we were looking for.

Creo que será imposible terminarlo hoy.
I think it will be impossible to finish it today.

The expressions above can be personalized by placing an indirect object pronoun before them, for example:

Me es imposible aceptar.	I cannot possibly accept.
No nos es posible hacerlo.	We cannot possibly do it.

▶ 8.2 (p. 36); 17.11 (p. 79)

48.1.3 | *(No) es posible/probable que* + subjunctive; *es imposible/improbable/poco probable que* + subjunctive

If the expression of possibility or impossibility refers to a specific person, these impersonal constructions must be followed by a subjunctive. In the expression of impossibility, **es imposible/improbable/poco probable que . . .**, 'it is impossible/improbable/unlikely that . . .', are heard much more often than the negative forms **no es posible/probable que . . .**, 'it is not possible/probable that . . .'.

Es posible/probable que lleguen en el próximo vuelo.
It is possible that they may arrive on the next flight.

No es posible que haya desaparecido así como así.
It is not possible that he/she/it may have disappeared just like that. (he/she/it can't have disappeared just like that)

Es imposible que podamos reunirlos a todos.
It is impossible for us to gather them all.

Es muy improbable que lo consigamos.
It's very unlikely/improbable that we'll get it.

Es poco probable que se hayan enterado.
It's unlikely that they have found out.

These expressions are also found in tenses other than the present, as shown by the examples below. But note that the complement verb, which is in the subjunctive, must show agreement with the main verb. Thus, if the main verb is in the conditional, the complement verb must be in the imperfect and not the present subjunctive.

Será imposible que nos entiendan.
It will be impossible for you/them to understand us.

Sería imposible que nos entendieran.
It would be impossible for you/them to understand us.

To say that something is unlikely or not very likely we can also use the expression **Es poco probable que** + subjunctive:

Es poco probable que lo sepan.
It is unlikely that they may know it.

▶ **15.5** (p. 58); **18.3.3** (p. 92); **32** (p. 191)

48.1.4   *Poder* + infinitive

Poder, 'may', is often used in the expression of possibility in sentences like the following:

Puede venir mañana.
He/she may come tomorrow.

Pueden haber llegado.
They may have arrived.

The first sentence is equivalent to **Es posible que venga mañana**, 'it is possible that he/she may come tomorrow', while the second can be expressed as **Es posible que hayan llegado**, 'it is possible that they may have arrived'. Both constructions are equally frequent, but the one with **puede** is more common in the spoken language.

▶ **21.1** (p. 99)

48.1.5   *Puede (ser) que* + subjunctive

Puede (ser) que . . . , 'maybe . . .', is an impersonal expression, as **puede** here does not refer to a specific person, unlike **puede** or **pueden** in the previous construction, which stand for 'he/she may' and 'they may' respectively. This phrase is especially common in the spoken language.

Puede (ser) que hayan salido.
They may have gone out.

Puede (ser) que no nos hayan oído.
They may not have heard us.

Quizá(s)/tal vez/posiblemente/probablemente/acaso + **subjunctive or indicative;** *a lo mejor* + **indicative**

▶ **18.3.3** (p. 92); **49.1.3** (p. 293)

Quizá(s) and **tal vez**, 'perhaps', are equally common in informal as well as formal registers, in spoken and written language. General usage of them seems to indicate that they can be followed by a verb in the subjunctive or indicative, depending on the degree of possibility involved, the indicative indicating a higher degree of possibility than the subjunctive. This duality is especially true when reference is to the present, or to the past – when this bears relationship with the present – as shown in the examples below:

Quizá(s)/tal vez esté en casa.
Perhaps he/she may be at home.

Quizá(s)/tal vez está en casa.
Perhaps he/she is at home.

Quizá(s)/tal vez no nos hayan visto.
Perhaps they may not have seen us.

Quizá(s)/tal vez no nos han visto.
Perhaps they have not seen us.

When reference is to the future, most speakers seem to use the present subjunctive, although the future indicative is also sometimes heard.

Quizá(s)/tal vez se vayan/se irán mañana.
Perhaps they will leave tomorrow.

Quizá(s)/tal vez se queden/se quedarán en un hotel.
Perhaps they will stay in a hotel.

When **quizá(s)** and **tal vez** follow the verb, the indicative and not the subjunctive is used.

Va a llover, quizá(s)/tal vez.
It is going to rain, perhaps.

No vendrán a la fiesta, quizá(s)/tal vez.
They won't come to the party, perhaps.

Posiblemente, like **probablemente**, 'possibly', 'perhaps', usually occurs on its own (see **48.1.1** above), but when followed by a verb, **posiblemente** normally takes the subjunctive, while **probablemente** tends to be used with the indicative.

Posiblemente lo vea.   Perhaps I will see him.
Probablemente lo veré.   I'll probably see him.

Acaso, 'perhaps', is a special case. In statements expressing uncertainty it is followed by a subjunctive verb; it is formal in terms of register and rarely used in the spoken language.

Acaso sea él quien lo hizo.
Perhaps it was him who did it.

Acaso tengamos que recordárselo.
Perhaps we may have to remind him/her.

In questions, however, **acaso** is followed by an indicative verb, conveying sarcasm and annoyance rather than uncertainty, and used frequently in the spoken language, especially in familiar address.

¿Acaso no te dije que no lo hicieras?
Didn't I tell you not to do it?

¿Acaso no sabías que había que entregarlo hoy?
Didn't you know it had to be handed in today?

A lo mejor, 'perhaps', which takes the indicative, is very common in the spoken language.

A lo mejor se casan.
Maybe/perhaps they will get married.

A lo mejor están fuera de Madrid.
Maybe/perhaps they are away from Madrid.

A lo mejor iremos a Cuba.
Perhaps we'll go to Cuba.

48.1.7 *Seguramente*, 'probably'

Seguramente, which is found on its own or with an indicative verb, is used in preference to **probablemente** when the speaker feels that the event being referred to is more likely to happen.

¿Crees que ganarán el partido? – Seguramente.
Do you think they will win the match? – Probably.

Seguramente lloverá.
It will probably rain.

▶ **49** (p. 291)

48.1.8 *Deber (de)* + infinitive

This construction with **deber (de)**, 'must', plus infinitive, is specially common in the spoken language. Although the preposition **de** serves to differentiate this expression from **deber** + infinitive, which expresses obligation, most speakers tend to omit it, with the result that there is no difference in form between the two expressions. However, the context or the type of verb will normally establish the appropriate meaning.

▶ **21.2** (p. 100)

¿Dónde está Ignacio? – No lo sé, debe (de) estar en el patio.
Where is Ignacio? – I don't know, he must be in the patio.

Deben (de) ser más de las seis.
It must be past six o'clock.

If reference is to the past, **deber (de)** must be followed by **haber** and a past participle.

> **Deben (de) haber regresado ya.**
> They must have returned already.

> **Debe (de) haber llamado.**
> He/she must have phoned.

> **Debe (de) haberse molestado.**
> He/she must have got annoyed.

▶ **50** (p. 296)

48.1.9 *Deber (de)* + *estar* + gerund

This construction with **estar** + gerund (see **20.1**) is used when the notion of probability or supposition refers to an action in progress.

> **Debe (de) estar trabajando.**   He/she must be working.
> **Deben (de) estar peleando.**   They must be having a row.

If reference is to the past, **deber (de)** must be followed by **haber** + past participle of **estar** + a gerund.

> **Deben (de) haber estado esperando.**
> They must have been waiting.

> **Debe (de) haber estado nadando.**
> He/she must have been swimming.

▶ **50** (p. 296); **21.2** (p. 100); **20.1** (p. 96)

48.1.10 Future

Probability with regard to something in the present is sometimes expressed with the future. Compare these sentences in which the second of each pair expresses probability while the first indicates certainty:

> **Está con alguien.**
> He/she is with someone.

> **Estará con alguien.**
> He/she must be with someone.

> **Ya van camino del/al trabajo.**
> They are on their way to work already.

> **Ya irán camino del/al trabajo.**
> They must be on their way to work already.

▶ **17.5.2** (p. 76); **50** (p. 296)

48.1.11 Future perfect

Probability with regard to something in the past, but which bears some relationship with the present is expressed with the future perfect. Consider these examples:

Ya se han enterado.
They have found out already.

Ya se habrán enterado.
They must have found out already.

Has oído lo que pasó.
You've heard what happened.

Habrás oído lo que pasó.
You must have heard what happened.

The first sentence in each pair indicates certainty while the second expresses probability.

▶ **17.6** (p. 77); **50** (p. 296)

48.1.12 Conditional

Probability with regard to the past is sometimes expressed with the conditional. Compare these sentences, which illustrate the contrast between certainty and probability:

En aquel tiempo yo tenía doce años.
At that time I was twelve.

En aquel tiempo yo tendría doce años.
At that time I must have been twelve.

Eran las tres cuando se fueron de aquí.
It was three o'clock when they left here.

Serían las tres cuando se fueron de aquí.
It must have been three o'clock when they left here.

▶ **17.7** (p. 77); **50** (p. 296)

48.1.13 *Igual, lo mismo*, 'perhaps', 'maybe'

These two expressions, which can be followed by any tense which is appropriate for the context, are used in Spain to express remote possibility and both correspond to an informal, colloquial usage.

¿Has visto a José? – No, igual se ha ido al pueblo.
Have you seen José? – No, perhaps he's gone to his village.

Igual han perdido el tren.
They may have missed the train.

Lo mismo te pide que te cases con él.
Maybe he'll ask you to marry him.

Lo mismo nos habrían echado.
Maybe they would have thrown us out.

▶ **18.3.3** (p. 92)

48.1.14 **Other ways of expressing possibility and impossibility**

Possibility and impossibility can also be conveyed through expressions such as the following:

> **Hay muchas/pocas probabilidades de** + infinitive 'there is a good/little chance of . . .'
> **Hay muchas/pocas probabilidades de que** + subjunctive 'there is a good/little chance that . . .'
> **Tener mucha/poca probabilidad de** + infinitive 'to have a good/little chance of . . .'
> **(No) tener la posibilidad de** + infinitive '(not) to have a chance to . . .'
> **No tener ninguna posibilidad/posibilidad alguna de** + infinitive 'not to have any chance (at all) of . . .'
> **No tener ninguna posibilidad/posibilidad alguna de que** + subjunctive 'not to have any chance (at all) of . . .'

> **Hay pocas probabilidades de sobrevivir/de que sobrevivan.**
> There is little chance of surviving/that they may survive.

> **El equipo tiene mucha/poca probabilidad de ganar.**
> The team has a good/little chance of winning.

> **No tiene ninguna posibilidad de ser aceptado/de que lo acepten.**
> He has no chance at all of being accepted/by them.

48.2 Enquiring whether something is considered possible or impossible

The expressions most commonly used to enquire about possibility or probability are the following:

48.2.1 **¿*Se puede* + infinitive?**

This construction with **poder**, which is usually found in the present, is the one most commonly used when inquiring about possibility in an impersonal way.

> **¿Se puede llamar a Londres desde aquí?**
> Can one call London from here?

> **¿Se puede marcar directamente?**
> Can one dial directly?

It can also be preceded by question words, as in:

> **¿Cómo se puede viajar a Toledo?**
> How can one travel to Toledo?

> **¿Qué se puede hacer?**
> What can one do?

Apart from the present, the tense most commonly associated with it is the conditional:

¿**Se podría recuperar el dinero?**
Could one recover the money?

¿**Qué se podría hacer?**
What could one do?

▶ **21.1** (p. 99); **23.7** (p. 110)

48.2.2 ¿*Poder* + **infinitive?**

See **48.1.4** above.

¿**Puede ser él?**
Can it be him?/Do you think it may be him?

¿**Podría suceder?**
Might/could it happen?

▶ **21.1** (p. 99)

48.2.3 **The future or the future perfect**

¿**Estará en casa?**
Will he/she be at home?/I wonder if he/she is at home.

¿**Habrá salido el avión?**
Do you think the plane has left?/I wonder if the plane has left.

▶ **17.5.2** (p. 76); **17.6** (p. 77)

48.2.4 ¿*Es posible* + **infinitive?**

This impersonal construction, normally heard in the present, is less common and colloquial than those above.

¿**Es posible ver el mar desde allí?**
Is it possible to see the sea from there?

¿**Será posible convencerlos?**
Will it be possible to convince them?

¿**Será posible encontrar entradas?**
Will it be possible to find tickets?

▶ **17.11** (p. 79); **18.1.6** (p. 86); **18.3.3** (p. 92)

49

Expressing certainty and uncertainty

The concepts of certainty and uncertainty can be expressed in Spanish in a number of ways, ranging from set phrases to more complex constructions. The examples below should help you to understand these, but should you have difficulty with the verb forms associated with these expressions, you may need to refer to the first part of this book for a revision of them.

49.1 Saying how certain one is of something

49.1.1 Strong positive certainty

To express strong positive certainty, Spanish uses expressions like the following, arranged here from the strongest to the weakest form.

49.1.1.1 *Set phrases*

> **no cabe ninguna** *or* **la menor duda** 'there cannot be the slightest doubt'
> **sin lugar a dudas** 'without doubt'
> **por supuesto** 'of course'
> **claro** 'of course'
> **desde luego** 'of course'

49.1.1.2 *Other expressions*

> **Estar (completamente/totalmente) seguro/convencido** 'to be (absolutely) sure/certain/convinced'
> **estar seguro/convencido de que** . . . 'to be sure/certain/convinced that . . .'
> **estar seguro/convencido de** + pronoun 'to be sure/certain/convinced of . . .'
> **sin duda** . . . 'no doubt . . .'
> **indudablemente** . . . 'undoubtedly', 'unquestionably . . .'
> **por supuesto que** . . . 'of course . . .'
> **claro que** . . . 'of course . . .'
> **desde luego que** . . . 'of course . . .'

¿Estás seguro/a?
Are you sure?
Sí, estoy (completamente/totalmente) seguro/a.
Yes, I'm (absolutely) sure.

Estoy convencido/a de que lo hará.
I'm convinced that he/she will do it.

Estoy seguro/a de eso.
I'm sure of that.

Sin duda llegarán con retraso.
No doubt they will be late.

Indudablemente es lo más apropiado.
It is undoubtedly the most appropriate thing to do.

Por supuesto que ganarán.
Of course they'll win.

Claro que se venderá.
Of course it will sell.

49.1.2 Intermediate certainty and uncertainty

Intermediate certainty and uncertainty are expressed through expressions like these:

Me parece que sí/no 'I think/don't think so'
Me parece que . . . 'I think that . . .'
Supongo que sí/no 'I suppose so/not'
Creo que sí/no 'I think/don't think so'
Creo que . . . 'I think that . . .'

Delia está en casa, ¿verdad?
Delia is at home, isn't she?
Me parece que sí/no.
I think/don't think so.

Me parece que habrá problemas.
I think there will be problems.

¿Estará listo para mañana?
Will it be ready for tomorrow?
Supongo que sí.
I suppose so.

¿Han reparado el ordenador/computador/la computadora (L. Am)?
Have they repaired the computer?
Creo que no.
I don't think so.

Creo que no le darán el puesto.
I don't think they will give him/her the job.

Intermediate certainty with regard to a future event is usually expressed through the future tense.

Tendrá mucho éxito.
He/she will be very successful.

Aprobarás el examen.
You will pass the examination.

No llegarán allí a tiempo.
They won't get there on time.

49.1.3 Weak certainty and uncertainty

To express weak certainty or uncertainty, use expressions like the following:

No sé si . . . 'I don't know whether . . .'
No estoy seguro 'I'm not sure'
No estoy seguro de + pronoun 'I'm not sure of + pronoun'
No estoy seguro de que + subjunctive 'I'm not sure that . . .'
No creo que + subjunctive 'I don't think that . . .'
Me pregunto si . . . 'I wonder if . . .'
puede ser 'maybe'
a lo mejor (. . .)/**quizá(s)** (. . .)/**tal vez** (. . .) 'perhaps (. . .)'

No sé si iré.
I'm not sure whether I'll go.

¿Crees que nos llamará? – No estoy seguro/a.
Do you think he/she will call us? – I'm not sure.

No estoy seguro/a de eso.
I'm not sure of that.

Me pregunto si hablará español.
I wonder if he/she speaks Spanish.

¿Crees que me recibirá?
Do you think he/she will receive me?
Puede ser.
Maybe.

Note that the negative expressions **No estoy seguro de que** . . . , 'I'm not sure that', and **No creo que** . . . , 'I don't think that . . .' are followed by a subjunctive.

No estoy seguro/a de que sea así.
I'm not sure it's like that.

No creo que aparezca.
I don't think it will appear.

Compare these with the positive sentences:

Estoy seguro/a de que es así.
I'm sure it's like that.

Creo que aparecerá.
I think it will appear.

▶ 18.1.5 (p. 85)

Quizá(s) and **tal vez**, 'perhaps', can be followed by an indicative or subjunctive verb, with the subjunctive being used when there is a greater degree of doubt. But note that if the event or action referred to has not yet occurred, you normally use the future indicative or the present subjunctive rather than the present indicative. **A lo mejor**, 'perhaps', is always followed by an indicative verb. These three expressions can also be used on their own.

48.1.6 (p. 285); **18.3.3** (p. 92)

> **Quizá(s)/tal vez regresen la semana que viene** or **Quizá(s)/tal vez regresarán la próxima semana.**
> Perhaps they'll come back next week.
>
> **A lo mejor regresan/regresarán la próxima semana.**
> Perhaps they'll come back next week.
>
> **¿Cree usted que lo encontraremos?**
> Do you think we'll find it?
> **A lo mejor/quizá(s)/tal vez.**
> Perhaps.

49.1.4 **Negative certainty**

To express negative certainty, use the following expressions:

> **No** 'no'
> **Por supuesto que no** 'of course not'
> **Claro que no** 'of course not'
> **Desde luego que no** 'of course not'
> **No me parece** 'I don't think so'
>
> **¿Devolverán el dinero?**
> Will they return the money?
> **Por supuesto que no.**
> Of course not.
>
> **¿Crees que se casarán?**
> Do you think they'll get married?
> **Claro que no.**
> Of course not.
>
> **¿Cree usted que venderán el piso?**
> Do you think they will sell the flat?
> **No me parece.**
> I don't think so.

49.2 Enquiring about certainty or uncertainty

To enquire about certainty or uncertainty, Spanish normally uses the following expressions:

> **¿Está usted/estás (completamente) seguro/a?**
> Are you (absolutely) sure?

¿Está usted/estás (completamente) seguro/a de que . . . ?
Are you (quite) sure that . . . ?

¿Le/te parece?
Do you think so?

¿Cree usted/crees?
Do you think so?

¿Cree usted/crees que . . . ?
Do you think that . . . ?

¿Estás seguro/a?
Are you sure?

¿Está usted seguro/a de que está allí?
Are you sure it's there?

¿Crees que lo convencerás?
Do you think you'll convince him?

50
Expressing supposition

This chapter examines the concept of supposition and the verbs and phrases associated with it.

50.1 Common expressions of supposition

To express supposition, as in 'If they come . . .', 'Suppose that he asks you for money', 'Imagine that he doesn't accept', 'In case he arrives today', 'They must be there', etc., Spanish uses a range of words and expressions, of which the most common are the following.

50.1.1 *Si* + present indicative; *si* + imperfect subjunctive

When expressing supposition, these two expressions with **si**, 'if', have a similar meaning, although with the present indicative, the possibility referred to by the verb appears as more real and likely than with the imperfect subjunctive. When using the present indicative, the verb in the accompanying sentence will be in the future; when using the imperfect subjunctive, the other verb will be a conditional.

> **Si te invitan, ¿aceptarás?**
> If they invite you, will you accept?

> **Si te invitaran, ¿aceptarías?**
> If they invited you, would you accept?

> **¿Qué le dirás, si te llama?**
> What will you say to him/her if he/she calls?

> **¿Qué le dirías, si te llamara?**
> What would you say to him/her if he/she called you?

▶ 51 (p. 299); 18.2.4 (p. 89)

50.1.2 *Suponer/imaginar(se)/figurarse/poner* + *que* + subjunctive

Suponer, 'to suppose', and **imaginar** or **imaginarse**, 'to imagine', are equally common in informal and formal contexts, while **figurarse**, 'to imagine', and **poner**, 'to suppose', tend to be used in more informal contexts, especially in the spoken language.

> **Supón que te pida dinero. ¿Se lo prestarás?**
> Suppose he/she asks you for money. Will you lend it to him/her?

Supongamos que te llame. ¿Qué le dirás?
Let's suppose he/she calls you. What will you tell him/her?

Suponiendo que te escriba, ¿le contestarás?
Supposing he/she writes to you, will you reply to him/her?

In these sentences, **suponer**, 'to suppose', has the same value as **si**, 'if':

Si te pide dinero, ¿se lo prestarás?
If he/she asks you for money, will you lend it to him/her?

Si te escribe, ¿le contestarás?
If he/she writes to you, will you reply to him/her?

Imagina/imagínate que no acepte tu propuesta.
Imagine he/she doesn't accept your proposal.

Imagine/imagínese que no aparezca.
Imagine it/he/she doesn't appear.

Figúrate que se hayan ido.
Imagine they have left.

Pon que hayan tenido un accidente.
Suppose they have had an accident.

Pongamos que no respondan.
Suppose they do not reply.

Note that **suponer, imaginar** and **figurarse** can also function as verbs of thinking, in which case they are followed by the indicative instead of subjunctive, unless the main verb is negated:

Supongo/me imagino/me figuro que no vendrán.
I suppose (think) that they will not come.

No me imagino que vengan.
I can't imagine they will come.

▶ **18.1.2** (p. 84); **18.1.5** (p. 85)

50.1.3 *Deber (de)* + infinitive

To express supposition with regard to the present:

Debe (de) estar enferma.
She must be ill.

Deben (de) estar fuera de Barcelona.
They must be away from Barcelona.

To express supposition with regard to the past:

Debe (de) haber vuelto.
He/she must have come back.

Deben (de) haberse perdido.
They must have got lost.

▶ **21.2** (p. 100); **48.1.8** (p. 286)

50.1.4 *Deber (de)* + *estar* + gerund

This construction expresses supposition with regard to an action in progress.

▶ **20.1** (p. 96)

> **Tu padre debe (de) estar descansando.**
> Your father must be having a rest.

> **Deben (de) estar durmiendo.**
> They must be sleeping.

▶ **21.2** (p. 100); **48.1.9** (p. 287)

50.1.5 **The future, future perfect and conditional in the expression of probability**

Supposition or probability with regard to something in the present or the past, can be expressed with verb forms other than those most frequently associated with the present and past. Note these examples:

> **Estará en casa.**
> He/she must be at home now.

> **Habrán salido.**
> They must have gone out.

> **Sería medianoche.**
> It must have been midnight.

▶ **17.5.2** (p. 76); **17.6** (p. 77); **17.7** (p. 77); **48.1.10** (p. 287); **48.1.11** (p. 287)

51
Expressing conditions

This chapter deals with conditions and conditional sentences, normally expressed in Spanish with the word **si**, 'if'. In the following sections, you will learn to express basic conditions like 'If I have money I'll come with you', 'If I had money I would come with you', 'If I had had money I would have come with you'. You will also learn the Spanish equivalent of other conditional forms such as 'provided (that)', 'as long as', 'on condition (that)'.

▶ **18.2.4** (p. 89); **18.2.3** (p. 88)

51.1 | Open conditions

In open conditions, that is, conditions which may or may not be fulfilled, e.g. **Si podemos . . .** , 'if we can . . .', or conditions which may or may not be true, e.g. **Si es como usted dice . . .** , 'if it is as you say . . .', we use the following constructions:

51.1.1 | *Si* + present + future

Here, the verb in the **si**-clause refers to the future but its form is that of the present, e.g. **Si tengo dinero . . .** , 'If I have money . . .'. The verb in the main clause, which conveys a future action dependent on a condition, normally takes the future, e.g. **iré contigo**, 'I'll come with you'. The **si**-clause usually goes in initial position in the sentence, but for emphasis or focus the main clause may go first.

> **Si tengo dinero iré contigo.**
> If I have money I'll come with you.
>
> **Si podemos lo haremos.**
> If we can we'll do it.
>
> **Se lo diré si lo veo.**
> I'll tell him if I see him.

Occasionally, in the spoken language, the verb in the main clause can take the present instead of the future, although reference is to the future. A verb in the present rather than the future normally conveys more resoluteness on the part of the speaker.

> **Si tengo dinero voy contigo.**
> If I have money I'll come with you.

> **Si no llegas a las seis empezamos sin ti.**
> If you don't arrive at six we'll start without you.

16.1.1.2 (p. 59)

51.1.2 *Si* + present + present/future

The verb in the **si**-clause is in the present, no matter whether the action conveyed by it refers to the present, e.g. **si es como usted dice . . .** , 'if it is as you say . . .', or to the future, e.g. **si llueve mañana . . .**, 'if it rains tomorrow'. The verb in the other clause may be in any appropriate tense, usually the present or the future.

We use this construction with **si**, 'if', when we want to express uncertainty with regard to something, as in:

> **Si es como usted dice estamos cometiendo un grave error.**
> If it is as you say we are making a grave mistake.

> **Si es como usted dice cometeremos un grave error.**
> If it is as you say we'll make a grave mistake.

> **Si le duele tanto es/será mejor llamar a un médico.**
> If it hurts him/her so much we'd better call a doctor.

51.1.3 *Si* + verb in the past + present/future

To express doubt with regard to something in the past, for example, **Si ha llegado . . .**, 'if he/she has arrived . . .', we use this construction with the verb in the if-clause in the perfect, preterite or imperfect, followed by the main clause with a verb in the present or future.

> **Si ha llegado hablaré con él.**
> If he has arrived I'll speak to him.

> **Si llegó sólo ayer no lo llamaré hasta mañana.**
> If he only arrived yesterday I won't call him until tomorrow.

> **Si estaba tan cansada será mejor no molestarla.**
> If she was so tired we'd better not bother her.

51.1.4 *Si* + present + imperative

> **Si necesitas dinero pídemelo.**
> If you need money ask me.

> **Si tenéis tiempo no dejéis de ir.**
> If you have time don't fail to go.

16.1.1.6 (p. 62)

51.1.5 **_Si_ + imperfect subjunctive + conditional**

A condition which is seen as more remote or less likely to be fulfilled is expressed in Spanish with an imperfect subjunctive in the if-clause, followed by a conditional in the main clause.

▶ **16.1.1.3** (p. 61); **16.1.1.2** (p. 59)

> **Si vinieran mañana los verías.**
> If they came tomorrow you would see them.

> **Si usted se lo explicara probablemente lo entendería.**
> If you explained it to him/her he/she would probably understand it.

The two previous examples are not too different from:

> **Si vienen mañana los veras.**
> If they come tomorrow you will see them.

> **Si usted se lo explica probablemente lo entenderá.**
> If you explain it to him/her he/she will probably understand it.

With the present, the condition is seen as more likely to be fulfilled.

51.1.6 **_Si_ + imperfect subjunctive + imperfect indicative**

This construction with an imperfect indicative instead of a conditional in the main clause is a much less common variant of the construction in **51.1.5** above, and generally restricted to informal spoken language. Although generally acceptable in Peninsular Spanish, this construction may be considered substandard in some Latin American countries.

▶ **16.1.1.2** (p. 59)

> **Si volviera a pegarme lo dejaba** (for **dejaría**).
> If he beat me up again I would leave him.

> **Si me ofrecieran el puesto lo aceptaba** (for **aceptaría**).
> If they offered me the job I would take it.

51.2 Unfulfilled conditions

51.2.1 **_Si_ + imperfect subjunctive + conditional**

A condition relating to the present which cannot be fulfilled or which is contrary to fact, such as **Si fueras más alto...** 'If you were taller ...' is expressed by the imperfect subjunctive after **si** and the conditional in the main clause. See **51.1.5** above.

> **Si fueras más alto lo verías.**
> If you were taller you would see it.

> **Si tuviera buena voz la podríamos contratar.**
> If she had a good voice we could hire her.

51.2.2   *Si* + pluperfect subjunctive + conditional perfect/pluperfect subjunctive

A condition which was not fulfilled is expressed with **si**, 'if', plus a pluperfect subjunctive, e.g. **Si me hubieran/hubiesen escuchado . . .** , 'if they had listened to me . . .', followed by a conditional perfect or a pluperfect subjunctive in the main clause, e.g. **no habría sucedido** or **no hubiera sucedido**, 'it would not have happened'. Note however that whereas in the si-clause one can use either the **-ra** or **-se** form of the pluperfect subjunctive (e.g. **hubiera** or **hubiese**), the pluperfect subjunctive in the main clause normally takes the **-ra** form (e.g. **hubiera**).

▶ 16.1.1.3 (p. 61); 16.1.1.7 (p. 62)

> **Si me lo hubieras/hubieses pedido te habría/hubiera ayudado.**
> If you had asked me I would have helped you.

> **Si lo hubiera/hubiese sabido no habría/hubiera venido.**
> If I had known I wouldn't have come.

▶ 18.2.4 (p. 89)

51.3   Other conditional expressions

51.3.1   *De* + infinitive instead of *si*-clause

The **si**-clause can be replaced by **de** + infinitive, especially in unfulfilled conditions. Generally, however, this alternative is possible when the subject of the **si**-clause and that of the subordinate clause are the same. Its use is more common in the spoken language.

> **Si hubiera/hubiese tenido tiempo habría/hubiera asistido a la reunión.**
> **De haber tenido tiempo habría/hubiera asistido a la reunión.**
> If I had had time I would have attended the meeting.

> **Si hubiéramos/hubiésemos viajado en tren no habríamos/ hubiéramos llegado a tiempo a la boda.**
> **De haber viajado en tren no habríamos/hubiéramos llegado a tiempo a la boda.**
> If we had travelled by train we wouldn't have arrived on time for the wedding.

De is often used with **ser** in sentences like the following, where the subject of the **si**-clause is different from that of the main clause.

> **De ser así tendremos que volver. (Si es así . . .)**
> If it is like that we'll have to come back.

> **De ser como tú dices no queda otra alternativa. (Si es como tú dices . . .)**
> If it is as you say there is no other alternative.

Gerund instead of *si*-clause

In colloquial language, the gerund (words like **estudiando**, 'studying', **subiendo**, 'going up') can be used to express open conditions.

> **Subiendo por esta calle llegarás al parque. (Si subes . . .)**
> Going up this street you'll get to the park.

> **Estudiando inglés encontrarás un trabajo mejor. (Si estudias . . .)**
> By studying English you'll find a better job.

▶ **16.1.1.5** (p. 62); **17.12** (p. 80)

Imperative instead of *si*-clause

The imperative may acquire a conditional value in informal spoken language, especially with warnings or threats.

> **Hazlo y te arrepentirás. (Si lo haces . . .)**
> If you do it you'll regret it.

> **Vuelve a llegar tarde y te despedirán. (Si vuelves . . .)**
> If you are late again they'll fire you.

▶ **16.1.1.6** (p. 62); **17.13** (p. 81)

Como + subjunctive instead of *si*-clause

Como + subjunctive can be used with a conditional value, to express warnings or threats like the imperative in **51.3.3** above, or to express fear with regard to something. This use seems restricted to informal spoken language.

> **Como se lo digas te pego. (Si se lo dices . . .)**
> If you tell him/her I'll beat you up.

> **Como lo vea mi madre se pondrá furiosa. (Si lo ve . . .)**
> If my mother sees it she'll be furious.

The use of **como** in this context is uncommon in Latin America.

En caso de que + subjunctive, *en caso de* + infinitive

En caso de que, 'in case', 'if', is used for expressing open conditions, and is followed by a present or an imperfect subjunctive. With the imperfect subjunctive, the condition is seen as more remote.

> **En caso de que venga/viniera/viniese Gabriel, dile que volveré pronto.**
> In case Gabriel comes, tell him I'll be back soon.

> **En caso de que no puedas/pudieras/pudieses asistir, avísame.**
> In case you can't attend, let me know.

> **En caso de que haya/hubiera/hubiese problemas, no dejes de llamarme.**
> If there are problems, don't fail to call me.

▶ **16.1.1.3** (p. 61)

When the subject is understood or when the subject of the main verb and the subordinate verb are the same, we can use **en caso de** + infinitive:

> **En caso de no poder asistir avísame.**
> In case you cannot attend let me know.

> **En caso de no encontrarlo te llamaré.**
> In case I can't find it I'll call you.

51.3.6 *Con tal (de) que, siempre que, siempre y cuando, a condición de que, con la condición de que* + subjunctive

These expressions, which translate into English as 'as long as', 'provided (that)', 'providing (that)', 'on condition that', are normally used in reply to a request. They are all followed by a subjunctive: the present subjunctive when reference is to the present or the future.

> **Puedes usarlo, con tal (de) que lo cuides.**
> You can use it as long as you look after it.

> **Sí, llévalo, pero siempre que me lo devuelvas mañana.**
> Yes, take it, but provided you return it to me tomorrow.

> **Hablaré con él, siempre y cuando usted me apoye.**
> I'll speak to him providing you support me.

> **Te lo diré, a condición de que guardes el secreto.**
> I'll tell you, on condition that you keep the secret.

> **Si queréis podéis usar mi apartamento, con la condición de que lo dejéis limpio.**
> If you like you can use my apartment, on condition that you leave it clean.

When reference is to the past, the conditional clause will carry a verb in the imperfect subjunctive.

> **Te lo dije a condición de que guardaras el secreto.**
> I told you on condition that you kept the secret.

> **Le dije a usted que hablaría con él siempre y cuando usted me apoyara.**
> I told you I would speak to him providing you supported me.

The speaker may sometimes express uncertainty with regard to a request, in which case the verb in the main clause will be in the conditional and the verb in the conditional clause will be in the imperfect subjunctive.

> **Te lo diría a condición de que guardaras el secreto.**
> I would tell you on condition that you kept the secret.

51.3.7 *A menos que, a no ser que, salvo que* + subjunctive

These expressions correspond to the English 'unless' and are used to express conditions which might cause something, e.g. a plan which may not be carried out or may not be fulfilled. The verb in the conditional clause will be in the present or the imperfect subjunctive, the latter conveying a greater degree of uncertainty and being much less frequent than the former.

> **Volveré a casa a las seis, a menos que haya demasiado trabajo en la oficina.**
> I'll come back home at six, unless there is too much work at the office.

> **Lo terminaremos este sábado, a menos que ocurra algo imprevisto.**
> We'll finish it this Saturday, unless something unforseen happens.

> **Me quedaré con ella, salvo que prefiera estar sola.**
> I'll stay with her, unless she prefers to be alone.

> **A menos que pasara algo, estaré aquí a la hora acordada.**
> Unless something happened, I'll be here at the agreed time.

▶ **18.2.4** (p. 89); **18.2.3** (p. 88)

51.3.8 *Aunque* + subjunctive

Aunque followed by the subjunctive indicates that the idea introduced by this word is a condition rather than a fact.

> **Aunque me lo pidan no se lo daré.**
> Even if they ask me for it I will not give it to them.

> **Incluso aunque me lo explicaras creo que no lo entendería.**
> Even if you explained it to me I think I wouldn't understand it.

▶ **52.1.4** (p. 307): **18.2.3** (p. 89), **27.2.2** (p. 143)

52
Expressing contrast or opposition

This chapter deals with the concept of contrast and the words and expressions associated with this. Contrast between different ideas is expressed in English through the use of words like 'but', 'though', 'although', for example 'He doesn't speak the language but he gets along all right', 'Though/although they don't earn much, they manage quite well'.

52.1 Common expressions of contrast or opposition

Below you will find a list of the most common expressions used in Spanish for linking two contrasting ideas, together with an explanation of their use.

52.1.1 Pero...

Pero, 'but', is the word most commonly used for expressing contrast or opposition. The contrast, in this case, is between a new idea or information, introduced by **pero**, with previous information. Like the English word 'but', **pero** goes between the two contrasting ideas and it is normally preceded by a comma.

> **Viven lejos, pero vienen a visitarnos a menudo.**
> They live far away, but they come and visit us often.

> **Es un vago, pero es muy simpático.**
> He's lazy but he's very nice.

52.1.2 Sin embargo, pero sin embargo

Sin embargo functions in a similar way as **pero**, but is used in more formal contexts, especially in writing.

> **La inflación ha bajado, sin embargo el desempleo continúa aumentando.**
> Inflation has come down, however unemployment is still on the increase.

> **Vive en Chile desde hace cinco años, sin embargo todavía no habla español.**
> He/she has been living in Chile for five years, however he/she still doesn't speak Spanish.

Further emphasis can be placed on the contrast by using the expression **pero sin embargo**.

> **Siempre está corta de dinero, pero sin embargo no quiere trabajar.**
> She's always short of money, but she doesn't want to work.

> **Está muy gordo, pero sin embargo no para de comer.**
> He's very fat, but he doesn't stop eating.

52.1.3 *Aunque* + indicative

Aunque, 'though', 'although', 'even though', will be followed by an indicative verb when the information it introduces is a fact, usually presented as new to the listener, rather than a possibility or something hypothetical, as in **52.1.4** below. **Aunque** is used in formal and informal contexts, in spoken as well as written Spanish. It is usually placed at the beginning of the sentence, but it can also go between the two contrasting ideas. Compare its use in these examples with the constructions in **52.1.1** and **52.1.2** above.

> **Aunque viven lejos, vienen a visitarnos a menudo.**
> Although they live far away they come and visit us often.

> **Vienen a visitarnos a menudo, aunque viven lejos.**
> They come and visit us often even though they live far away.

> **Aunque la inflación ha bajado, el desempleo continúa aumentando.**
> Although inflation has come down unemployment is still on the increase.

> **El desempleo continúa aumentando, aunque la inflación ha bajado.**
> Unemployment is still on the increase even though inflation has come down.

▶ 18.2.3 (p. 88): 27.2.2 (p. 143)

52.1.4 *Aunque* + subjunctive

When the information introduced by **aunque** is not a fact but a possibility or something hypothetical, the verb following **aunque** will be in the subjunctive. In this context, the word **aunque** is equivalent to the English expression 'even if'.

> **Aunque llueva iremos.**
> Even if it rains we'll go.

> **Iremos aunque llueva.**
> We'll go even if it rains.

> **Aunque sea difícil lo haré.**
> Even if it's difficult I'll do it.

> **Lo haré aunque sea difícil.**
> I'll do it even if it is difficult.

Compare these sentences with the ones below in which **aunque** introduces a fact rather than a hypothetical situation, and is therefore followed by an indicative verb.

> **Aunque llueve iremos.** (see 52.1.3)
> Even though it's raining we'll go.

> **Aunque es difícil lo haré.** (see 52.1.3)
> Even though it's difficult I'll do it.

Aunque may introduce a sentence which is an answer to an objection, in which case the verb which follows will be in the subjunctive, even when the information introduced by **aunque** is a fact.

> **Aunque no te gusten las lentejas tendrás que comértelas.**
> Even if you don't like lentils you'll have to eat them.

> **Irás al dentista, aunque no quieras.**
> You'll go to the dentist, even if you don't want to.

▶ 18.2.3 (p. 88); 27.2.2 (p. 143); 51.3.8 (p. 305)

52.1.5   *A pesar de* + noun/pronoun/infinitive, *a pesar de que* + indicative/subjunctive, *pese a (que)*

A pesar de, 'despite', 'in spite of', can be placed at the beginning of the sentence or between the two contrasting ideas. Unlike **aunque, a pesar de** can be followed by a noun, a pronoun or an infinitive.

> **A pesar del frío saldremos.**
> Despite the cold we'll go out.

> **La quiero a pesar de eso.**
> I love her in spite of that.

> **A pesar de no tener mucho dinero cooperó con nuestra causa.**
> Despite not having much money he/she cooperated with our cause.

Note that the infinitive can be used when the subjects of the verbs in the contrasting sentences are identical.

A pesar de que, 'despite the fact that', 'in spite of the fact that', functions like **aunque**, but places more emphasis on the contrast between the two ideas. Like **aunque**, it will be followed by an indicative verb when the information it introduces is a fact, and by a subjunctive when this relates to the future or is hypothetical (see 52.1.4).

(a) With an indicative verb:

> **A pesar de que tiene tiempo, no nos visita.**
> Despite the fact that he/she has time, he/she doesn't visit us.

> **No han llamado, a pesar de que ahora tienen teléfono.**
> They haven't called, in spite of the fact that they now have a telephone.

(b) With a subjunctive verb:

> **No se lo aceptaré, a pesar de que me lo ofrezca.**
> I won't accept it, despite the fact that he/she may offer it to me.

> A pesar de que me critiquen, no desistiré.
> Despite the fact that they may criticize me, I won't give up.

18.2.2 (p. 87)

Pese a, and **pese a que**, function like **a pesar de** and **a pesar de que**, respectively, and have similar meanings, but are less colloquial.

> **Pese a todo, estoy seguro de que no nos defraudará.**
> Despite/in spite of everything, I'm sure he/she will not disappoint us.

> **Pese a la ausencia de mi madre, nos arreglamos muy bien.**
> In spite of my mother's absence, we managed very well.

> **Pese a no tener más de siete años, tocaba la guitarra perfectamente.**
> Despite the fact that he/she was only seven, he/she played the guitar perfectly well.

> **Pese a que le rogaron que aceptara el puesto, lo rechazó.**
> Despite the fact that they begged him/her to accept the job, he/she rejected it.

> **Pese a que me amenacen, no se los diré.**
> Despite the fact that they may threaten me, I will not tell them.

52.1.6 *No obstante*

No obstante, 'nevertheless', 'despite', 'in spite of', is the most formal of the words used in expressing contrast, and is found more often in written Spanish. It may function like **sin embargo** (see **52.1.2** above), in sentences like the following:

> **El país dispone de pocos recursos, no obstante (sin embargo) el gasto público ha aumentado.**
> The country has few resources, nevertheless public expenditure has increased.

> **Insistimos mucho, no obstante (sin embargo) se negó a aceptar.**
> We insisted very much, nevertheless he/she refused to accept.

No obstante is also a more formal substitute for **a pesar de** and **pese a** (see **52.1.5** above).

> **No obstante (a pesar de/pese a) la escasez de dinero ella logró educar a sus hijos.**
> Despite/in spite of the shortage of money she managed to bring up her children.

> **No obstante (a pesar de/pese a) nuestras excusas rehusaron perdonarnos.**
> Despite/in spite of our excuses they refused to forgive us.

52.1.7 Other ways of expressing contrast or opposition

Other less common but more colloquial words and phrases used for expressing contrast are the following, some of which can be replaced by the more common word **aunque**:

aun cuando 'even though', 'although', 'even if'
si bien 'even though', 'although'
así 'even if'
aun así 'still'
así y todo 'all the same'
por el contrario 'while', 'on the contrary'
mientras que 'while'
en cambio 'while', 'on the other hand'
al contrario de lo que . . . 'contrary to what . . .'

Aun cuando/aunque estaba enferma, decidió viajar.
Even though/although she was ill, she decided to travel.

Aun cuando/aunque lo supiera no te lo diría.
Even if I knew it I wouldn't tell you.

Si bien/aunque la casa es grande, el alquiler es muy caro.
The house may be big, but the rent is very high.

Así/aunque me echen del trabajo exigiré un aumento de sueldo.
Even if they fire me I will insist on a salary increase.

No me siento bien; aun así iré a la oficina.
I'm not feeling well; still I'll go to the office.

No tienen mucho; así y todo nos ofrecieron su ayuda.
They haven't got much; all the same they offered us their help.

Carmen es muy tranquila. Luis, por el contrario, es muy inquieto.
Carmen is very quiet. Luis, on the other hand, is very restless.

A él le costó mucho, mientras que a ella le resultó fácil.
He had great difficulty, while she found it easy.

Antonio adora el fútbol, en cambio su mujer lo detesta.
Antonio loves football, while his wife hates it.

Al contrario de lo que pensábamos, terminaron a tiempo.
Contrary to what we thought, they finished on time.

53
Expressing capability and incapability

This chapter examines the ways in which the concepts of capability and incapability are expressed in Spanish, and it considers also learned abilities.

53.1 Enquiring and making statements about capability or incapability

53.1.1 *Poder* + infinitive

To enquire and make statements about capability, or incapability, as in 'Can you do it?'/'Are you able to do it?', 'I cannot do it'/'I am unable to do it', Spanish normally uses a construction with **poder**, 'to be able to', 'can', plus infinitive. In the examples below, **poder** indicates physical or mental ability, but the same construction is used to express other functions, for example possibility, permission, requests.

▶ **21.1** (p. 99); **48** (p. 282); **54** (p. 314); **68.1.4** (p. 382)

> **¿Puedes hacerlo?**
> Can you do it?
>
> **Claro que puedo hacerlo.**
> Of course I can do it.
>
> **¿Podéis alcanzar aquella rama?**
> Can you reach that branch?
>
> **No podemos alcanzarla.**
> We cannot reach it.
>
> **No puedo imaginármelo.**
> I can't imagine it.
>
> **¿Podrías traducirlo?**
> Could you (would you be able to) translate it?

Note that in positive sentences, the preterite of **poder** expresses the idea of 'managing to'.

> **Después de muchos intentos, pude arreglarlo.**
> After many attempts, I managed to repair it.

In the imperfect, **poder** indicates capability with regard to something in the past but not necessarily fulfilment of the action referred to.

> **Fernando podía arreglarlo.**
> Fernando was capable of repairing it. (but may not have actually done so)

▶ **17.4** (p. 75); **17.3** (p. 74)

17.4 (p. 75); **17.3** (p. 74)

53.1.2 **Using a single verb to express capability or incapability**

Capability or incapability are sometimes expressed, not by **poder** + infinitive but by a single verb, for example:

> **¿Entiendes?**
> Can you understand?

> **No entiendo nada.**
> I can't understand anything.

> **¿Lo oyes?**
> Can you hear it?

> **No oigo bien.**
> I can't hear well.

> **Desde aquí veo todo.**
> I can see everything from here.

> **No siento nada.**
> I can't feel anything.

▶ **17.1.1** (p. 72)

53.1.3 *(No) ser capaz de* + infinitive

Ser capaz de, 'to be able to', is much less common than **poder**, and it indicates stronger capability or incapability.

> **¿Eres capaz de saltar esa reja?**
> Are you able to jump over that fence?

> **No es capaz de hacerlo.**
> He/she is not able to do it.

> **¿Seríais capaz de escalar esa montaña?**
> Would you be able to climb that mountain?

> **Por supuesto que seríamos capaces.**
> Of course we would be able to.

53.2 # Enquiring and making statements about learned abilities

53.2.1 *Saber* + infinitive

To enquire and make statements about learned abilities, as in 'Can you play the piano?', 'She can swim quite well', Spanish uses the construction **saber**, literally 'to know', plus infinitive, not **poder**.

¿Sabes tocar el piano?
Can you play the piano?
Sí, sé tocar muy bien.
Yes, I can play very well.

Ella sabe nadar, ¿verdad?
She can swim, can't she?
Sabe nadar bastante bien.
She can swim quite well.

▶ **21.3** (p. 101)

53.2.2 **Present**

Learned abilities are sometimes expressed with the present:

Nada muy bien.
He/she swims very well.

El profesor habla inglés y francés.
The teacher speaks English and French.

▶ **17.1.1** (p. 72)

54
Seeking and giving permission

This chapter considers the ways in which Spanish expresses the concept of permission, in formal as well as in informal situations, both orally and in writing.

54.1 Seeking permission

To seek permission, as in 'May/can I can come in?', 'Let me come in', 'Do you mind if I come in?', Spanish, like English, uses a number of verbs and expressions. Of these, the most common are the following:

54.1.1 *Poder* + infinitive

To seek or request permission to do something we normally use **poder**, 'may', 'can', followed by an infinitive.

> **¿Puedo entrar?**
> May/can I come in?

> **¿Puedo dejar mi maleta aquí?**
> May/can I leave my suitcase here?

> **¿Podemos pasar?**
> May/can we come in?

> **¿Podemos esperar allí?**
> May/can we wait over there?

▶ 21.1 (p. 99)

54.1.2 *¿Se puede* + infinitive?

This impersonal construction, used when asking whether something is allowed, corresponds in meaning to English phrases such as 'can you . . . ?', 'can one . . . ?', 'are you allowed to . . . ?'.

▶ 42.1.2 (p. 248)

> **¿Se puede acampar en la playa?**
> Can one/you camp on the beach? (Are you allowed to camp on the beach?)

> **¿Se puede fumar?**
> Can one/you smoke? (Is smoking allowed?)

54.1.3 ¿Se puede?

On its own, the expression **¿Se puede?** is used when seeking permission to enter a room, as in 'May I (come in)?'

> **¿Se puede? – Sí, pase.**
> May I/we (come in)? – Yes, come in!

> **¿Se puede? – ¡Adelante!**
> May I/we (come in)? – Come in!

54.1.4 Dejar + infinitive

This expression with **dejar**, 'to let', is also very frequent when seeking permission to do something, especially in an informal context, with a verb in the familiar form, but it is also heard in formal situations. There are two alternative ways of using this construction:

54.1.4.1 Imperative form of **dejar**, with an object pronoun attached to it:

> **Déjame usar tu bicicleta.**
> Let me use your bicycle.

> **Por favor, déjeme llamar a casa.**
> Please, let me call home.

> **Dejadnos pasar.**
> Let us go through.

▶ 16.1.1.6 (p. 62); 8.2 (p. 36)

54.1.4.2 Present of **dejar** with an object pronoun preceding the verb, normally in an interrogative sentence with a rising intonation. This construction is as common as the preceding one, but it is regarded as more polite than the first. Compare these sentences with the ones above, and note the way in which they translate in English.

> **¿Me dejas usar tu bicicleta?**
> Will you let me use your bicycle?

> **Por favor, ¿me deja llamar a casa?**
> Will you let me call home please?

> **¿Nos dejáis pasar?**
> Will you let us go through?

54.1.5 Importar/molestar que + subjunctive

This construction with **importar/molestar**, 'to mind', is less common than the previous ones, and it tends to be used more in formal than in informal contexts. In this context, **importar** and **molestar** are used in the third person singular (i.e. **importa/molesta**), normally in the present, and they must be preceded by an object pronoun, signalling the person one is seeking permission from. The sentence is interrogative, as it corresponds to a request.

▶ 68.1.6 (p. 383)

¿Le importa/molesta que fume?
Do you mind if I smoke?

¿Les importa/molesta que abra la ventana?
Do you mind if I open the window?

¿Te importa/molesta que cierre la puerta?
Do you mind if I close the door?

54.1.6 *Permitir que* + subjunctive

In this construction, which is generally infrequent and normally used in formal contexts, **permitir**, 'to allow', 'to let', must be in the imperative form, with an object pronoun (e.g. **me, te, le**) attached to the verb.

Permítame que le diga algo.
Allow me to tell you something.

Por favor, permítanos que dejemos nuestras cosas aquí.
Please let us leave our things here.

Por favor, permítale que asista a su clase.
Please allow him/her to attend your class.

54.1.7 *Permitir* + infinitive

As with **dejar** (see **54.1.4** above), there are two ways of using this construction, both generally infrequent but more common in formal contexts:

54.1.7.1 Imperative form of **permitir**, with an object pronoun attached to it.

Por favor, permítanos quedarnos aquí.
Please allow us to stay here.

Por favor, permítame usar su teléfono.
Please allow me to use your telephone.

54.1.7.2 Present of **permitir**, in an interrogative sentence, with the object pronoun preceding the verb.

The intonation of this sentence should be rising. Compare the following examples with those in **54.1.7.1** above.

¿Nos permite quedarnos aquí?
Will you allow us to stay here?

¿Me permite usar su teléfono?
Will you allow me to use your telephone?

Note that the expressions **¡Permítame!** and **¡Me permite!**, 'allow me!', on their own, are used to offer help, for example to carry or lift something. They also have the meaning of 'Excuse me!', in the sense of seeking permission rather than apologizing.

Rogar que + subjunctive

Rogar, literally 'to beg', 'to request', is normally used to request something formally, for example permission, preferably in writing, but sometimes also orally. It is very common in formal letter writing, such as business correspondence. Note that **rogar** is a *radical-changing verb* (e.g. **ruego**).

▶ **16.1.2.1** (p. 64); **18.1.1** (p. 84); **29.9.3.5** (p. 168)

> **Le ruego que me autorice para utilizar sus instalaciones.**
> Please/kindly allow me to use your facilities.

> **Le rogamos que nos permita asistir a la reunión de la junta directiva.**
> Please/kindly allow us to attend the board of directors' meeting.

> **Les rogamos que nos dejen pasar.**
> Please let us go in.

54.2 # Giving permission

The expressions most commonly used when giving permission are the following:

> **sí** 'yes'
> **desde luego** 'certainly', 'of course'
> **por supuesto** 'certainly', 'of course'
> **claro (que sí)** 'certainly', 'of course'
> **¡no faltaba más!** 'certainly', 'of course'
> **muy bien** 'very well'
> **está bien** 'it's all right'
> **de acuerdo** 'OK!', 'agreed', 'right'
> **vale** 'OK'
> **poder** + infinitive (see **54.1.1** above) 'may'

These expressions are often preceded by the word **sí**. Furthermore, speakers normally show that they really have no objection to what is being requested by repeating the word **sí** and/or the one that follows.

> **¿Puedo cerrar la puerta? – Sí, sí, ciérrala.**
> May I close the door? – Yes, close it.

> **¿Puedo aparcar aquí? – Sí, sí, puede aparcar, no hay problema.**
> Can I park here? – Yes, you can park, there's no problem.

> **¿Se puede usar la piscina? – Sí, sí, se puede.**
> Can one/you use the swimming pool? – Yes, one/you can.

> **¿Te importa que deje esto aquí? – ¡Vale, vale!, déjalo.**
> Do you mind if I leave this here? – OK, OK, leave it.

> **¿Me dejas usar tu teléfono? – Sí, sí, desde luego.**
> May I use your phone? – Yes, of course.

> **¿Me permite pasar al lavabo/baño (L. Am.), por favor? – Sí, pase, pase.**
> May I use the toilet please? – Yes, come in, come in.

54.3 | **Stating that permission is withheld**

To withhold permission, use expressions like the following:

> **no** 'no'
> **perdone(a)/lo siento, pero . . .** 'I'm sorry, but . . .'
> **no poder** + infinitive 'cannot'/'may not'
> **prohibir** + infinitive 'to forbid'
> **está prohibido** 'it's forbidden/prohibited'
> **no está permitido** 'it's not allowed/permitted'

> **¿Te importa que fume? – Lo siento/perdona, pero me molesta el humo.**
> Do you mind if I smoke? – I'm sorry, but smoke bothers me.

> **Se prohibe fumar.**
> No smoking.

> **Perdone señor, pero aquí no puede entrar.**
> I'm sorry sir, but you can't go in here.

> **¿Se puede aparcar en la plaza? – No, no se puede, está prohibido.**
> Can you park in the square? – No, you can't, it's forbidden.

Signs normally use the word **prohibido**, followed by an infinitive, signalling that which is forbidden, for example:

> **Prohibido aparcar.** Parking not allowed.
> **Prohibido fumar.** Smoking not allowed.

55
Asking and giving opinions

This chapter examines the different ways in which Spanish speakers ask and give opinions, and it also looks at the expressions used for reporting on other people's opinions.

55.1 Asking someone's opinion

To ask people their opinion, Spanish uses several verbs and constructions, the most common of which are:

55.1.1 *Parecer*

Parecer, 'to seem', is the most frequent verb in this context. It functions like **gustar**, that is, with an indirect object pronoun (i.e. **me, te, le, nos, os, les**) preceding the verb, e.g. **me parece**, literally 'it seems to me'. The constructions in which this verb normally appears are the following:

> **¿Qué te/le parece?** 'What do you think?' (fam./pol.)
> **¿Qué os parece . . . ?** 'What do you think of . . . ?'
> **¿Qué les parece si** + present indicative? 'What do you think if . . . ?'/
> 'How about . . . ?'

> **¡Vamos al cine! ¿Qué te parece?**
> Let's go to the cinema. What do you think?

> **¿Qué te pareció la película?**
> What did you think of the film?

> **¿Qué le parece si empezamos ahora?**
> What do you think if we start now?/How about starting now?

> **¿Qué os parece si cenamos fuera?**
> What do you think if we eat out?/How about eating out?

► 8.2 (p. 36)

55.1.2 *Creer*

Creer, 'to think', is found in expressions like these:

> **¿Qué cree usted/crees tú?** 'What do you think?'
> **¿Qué cree usted/crees tú que** + indicative? 'What do you think . . . ?'

> **¿Cree usted/crees tú que** + subjunctive or indicative? 'Do you think . . . ?'

The choice between present subjunctive and present indicative after **¿Cree usted/crees tú que . . . ?** depends on the degree of doubt involved. By and large, however, the present subjunctive is more common than the indicative.

▶ **18.1.5 (p. 85)**

> **No sé si llevar el rojo o el azul. ¿Qué crees tú?**
> I don't know whether to take the red or the blue one. What do you think?

> **¿Qué cree usted que podemos hacer?**
> What do you think we can do?

> **¿Crees tú que él sea/es la persona indicada?**
> Do you think he's the right person?

55.1.3 *Opinar, pensar*

Opinar and **pensar**, 'to think', are normally found in the following constructions:

> **¿Qué opina/piensa usted?** 'What do you think?'
> **¿Qué opinas/piensas tú de/sobre . . . ?** 'What do you think of/ about . . . ?'

> **No sé si decírselo o no. ¿Qué opinas/piensas tú?**
> I don't know whether to tell him/her or not. What do you think?

> **¿Qué opina/piensa usted de ella?**
> What do you think of her?

55.1.4 *¿Cuál es su/tu opinión?*

This phrase, similar in meaning to the English phrase 'What's your opinion?', is much less frequent than the equivalent English expression, and it tends to be used in more formal contexts. When asking for an opinion, most Spanish speakers will use one of the expressions above, especially the ones with **parecer** and **creer**.

> **¿Cuál es su opinión al respecto?**
> What is your opinion of this?

> **¿Cuál es su opinión sobre este proyecto?**
> What is your opinion about this project?

▶ **12.2 (p. 49)**

55.1.5 *Me/nos gustaría or quisiera/quisiéramos conocer su opinión . . .*

Like the phrase in **55.1.4** above, these expressions with **gustar** and **querer**, meaning 'I/ we would like to know your opinion', are less common than the ones which actually carry verbs of thinking like **parecer** or **creer**, and they tend to be restricted to more formal contexts.

> Me gustaría conocer su opinión sobre este problema.
> I'd like to know your opinion about this problem.
>
> Quisiéramos conocer su opinión acerca de esta materia.
> We'd like to know your opinion about this matter.

● 58.1 (p. 340)

55.1.6 Other ways of asking someone's opinion

The following expressions are fairly common and can be used in either formal or informal situations:

> ¿Cuál es su/tu parecer (sobre . . .)? 'What's your opinion (about . . .)?'
> ¿Qué opinión le/te merece (. . .)? 'What's your opinion (about..)?'
> En su/tu opinión . . . 'In your opinion . . .'
> Y Vd./tú, ¿cómo lo ve/s? 'How do you see it?'
> ¿Está/s de acuerdo conmigo? 'Do you agree with me?'
> ¿No le/te parece? 'Don't you think so?'

55.2 Expressing opinions

Personal opinions are normally conveyed by asserting an idea directly, using an indicative verb:

> El clima de Andalucía es muy agradable.
> The climate in Andalusia is very pleasant.
>
> Sevilla es una ciudad bonita.
> Seville is a beautiful city.
>
> Los españoles son muy sociables.
> Spaniards are very sociable.

In addition, there are certain verbs and expressions which are associated more specifically with opinions, the most common of which are:

55.2.1 *Parecer*

Parecer, 'to seem', is found in set phrases like:

> Me/nos parece que sí 'I/we think so'
> Me/nos parece que no 'I/we don't think so'
>
> ¿Vendrá Pepe a la reunión?
> Will Pepe come to the meeting?
> Me parece que sí/no.
> I think/don't think so.

It also occurs in constructions like the following ones:

> Me/nos parece que + indicative 'I/we think that . . .'
> No me/nos parece que + subjunctive 'I/we don't think that . . .'

> **Nos parece que no hay otra alternativa.**
> We think there's no other alternative.

> **No nos parece que haya necesidad.**
> We don't think there is any need.

Notice that when **parecer** is negated, as in the last example, the verb in the subordinate clause must be a subjunctive.

18.1.5 (p. 85)

Note also that the verb in the main clause, in this instance **parecer**, may be in a tense other than the present, in which case the complement verb must show appropriate agreement with it.

> **Me parecía que podía resolverse.**
> I thought it could be solved.

> **No me parecía que pudiera resolverse.**
> I didn't think it could be solved.

Parecer may be followed by an adjective or an adverb in constructions like the following ones:

> **Me/nos parece** + adjective/adverb
> **Me/nos parece** + adjective/adverb + **que** + subjunctive.
> 'I/we think . . .'

In the second construction, the complement verb is in the subjunctive, even when **parecer** is in the affirmative.

> **Me parece muy raro.**
> He/it seems very strange to me.

> **Nos parece muy bien.**
> It seems all right to us.

> **Me parece raro que él no esté aquí.**
> It seems strange to me that he is not here.

> **Nos parece mal que hayan dicho eso.**
> We think it's wrong that they have said that.

55.2.2   *Creer*

Creer, 'to think', is found in set phrases like:

> **Creo/creemos que sí** 'I/we think so'
> **Creo/creemos que no** 'I/we don't think so'

> **Es estupendo, ¿no crees?**
> It's great, don't you think so?

> **Sí, creo que sí.**
> Yes, I think so.

It is also very common in the following constructions:

> Creo/creemos que + indicative 'I/we think that . . .'
> No creo/creemos que + subjunctive 'I/we don't think that . . .'

Observe that when the main clause with **creer** is negative, the verb that follows must be in the subjunctive and not the indicative.

> **Creemos que es importante.**
> We think it's important.

> **No creo que sea importante.**
> I don't think it's important.

▶ **18.1.5** (p. 85)

Note also tense agreement between the main verb and the complement verb when **creer** is in a tense other than the present.

> **Creía que era más responsable.**
> I thought/used to think he/she was more responsible.

> **Creí que era más responsable.**
> I thought he/she was more responsible.

> **No creí que fuera/fuese tan irresponsable.**
> I didn't think he/she was so irresponsible.

▶ **19.2** (p. 95)

Creer, like **parecer**, can be followed by an adjective, but such a construction is uncommon.

> **La creo capaz de todo.**
> I think she is capable of anything.

> **No lo creo necesario.**
> I don't think it is necessary.

55.2.3 *Pensar*

Pensar, 'to think', is used in constructions similar to those with **creer**, except that overall it is used less commonly.

> **Pienso que es mejor que no vayas.**
> I think you'd better not go.

> **Pensamos que tiene un gran potencial.**
> We think he/she has great potential.

> **No pensaba que fuera tan impulsivo.**
> I didn't think he was so impulsive.

55.2.4 *Opinar, considerar*

In the expression of opinions, **opinar**, 'to think', and **considerar**, 'to think', 'to consider', are much less common than **parecer** and **creer**, and they tend to be used in more formal contexts, especially **considerar**. Although used infrequently, **opinar** can be found in set phrases like

Opino que sí 'I think so'
Opino que no 'I don't think so'

These two verbs are found in a construction with **que** plus indicative verb:

Considero que su trabajo es excelente.
I think his/her work is excellent.

Yo también opino que sí.
I also think so.

Opino que tenemos que cambiar la ley.
I think we must change the law.

Consideramos que se debe convocar una nueva reunión.
We consider a new meeting must be summoned.

Note also tense agreement between the main verb and the complement verb when **opinar** and **considerar** are used in tenses other than the present.

Considerábamos que era una persona honrada.
We thought he/she was an honest person.

Ellos opinaban que había que vender.
They thought it was necessary to sell.

▶ 19.1 (p. 93)

55.2.5   *Soy de la opinión de que . . . , mi opinión es que . . . , a mi parecer, a mi juicio, en mi opinión, a mi modo de ver, desde mi punto de vista, a mi entender*

An alternative way of giving your opinion is to use phrases like the ones above. Overall, they seem to be less frequent than the constructions seen previously, with verbs such as **creer, pensar** and **opinar**.

Soy de la opinión de que hay que hacerlo de nuevo.
I'm of the opinion that it has to be done again.

Mi opinión es que es mejor que no se lo digas a nadie.
My opinion is that you'd better not tell anyone.

A mi parecer/juicio/modo de ver, deberíamos llamarlos a declarar.
In my opinion, we should summon them to give evidence.

En mi opinión, éste es un asunto delicado.
In my opinion, this is a delicate matter.

Desde mi punto de vista, es una tontería.
From my point of view, it's nonsense.

A mi entender, no es eso lo que deberíamos hacer.
To my mind, that's not what we should do.

55.3   Enquiring about other people's opinions

The verbs most commonly used when inquiring about other people's opinions are **parecer, opinar** and **pensar**.

▶ **55.1** (p. 319)

> **¿Qué le parece a tu padre?**
> What does your father think?

> **¿Qué opinan/piensan ellos?**
> What do they think?

▶ **8.3** (p. 39)

55.4   Reporting on other people's opinions

55.4.1

To report other people's opinions, use **decir, parecer, creer, pensar, opinar** or **considerar**, followed by **que** and a clause containing the assertion. Of these, **decir, pensar** and **creer** are the most common.

▶ **33** (p. 196)

> **José dijo que la fiesta fue un éxito.**
> José said that the party was a success.

> **Ellos piensan/creen que el conflicto tiene solución.**
> They think the conflict has a solution.

> **Ella opina/considera que no es correcto.**
> She thinks it is not correct.

> **A él le parece que no debemos ceder.**
> He thinks we must not give up.

In addition, we can also report someone's opinion by using one of the following words and expressions:

55.4.2   *Según . . . ,* 'according to . . .'

This is by far the most common word used when referring to someone's opinion in both formal and informal contexts.

> **Según el señor García, deberíamos despedirlo.**
> According to señor García, we should sack him.

> **Según el gerente, la huelga es innecesaria.**
> According to the manager, the strike is unnecessary.

▶ **25.1.24** (p. 128)

55.4.3   *Según el parecer de . . . ,* 'according to . . .'

This is less common and more formal than the single word **según**.

Según el parecer de nuestros socios, hay que comprar más acciones.
According to our partners' opinion, we ought to buy more shares.

Según el parecer de los miembros, el club debería cerrar.
According to the members, the club should close.

55.4.4   *Ser del parecer que . . .*

This way of referring to someone's opinion is generally infrequent and formal.

Los trabajadores son del parecer que la huelga debe continuar.
The workers think the strike must continue.

El ministro es del parecer que se prohiba la manifestación.
The minister thinks the demonstration should be banned.

▶ 33 (p. 196)

56

Expressing agreement, disagreement and indifference

This chapter explains and illustrates the ways in which Spanish speakers normally express agreement, disagreement and indifference and how they ask others whether they agree or disagree. As you will see from the examples below, the expressions associated with these concepts vary greatly depending on the degree of formality of the situation.

56.1 Expressing agreement

Most of the expressions used to express agreement are set words and phrases. Below is a list of the most common.

> **sí** 'yes'
> **de acuerdo** 'OK', 'right', 'all right'
> **vale** 'OK', 'all right'
> **bien** 'very well', 'all right', 'OK'
> **bueno** 'very well', 'all right', 'OK'
> **conforme** 'OK', 'all right'
> **tener razón** 'to be right'
> **eso es** 'that's right'
> **efectivamente** 'indeed', 'exactly'
> **cierto** 'of course', 'certainly'
> **desde luego** 'of course', 'certainly'
> **seguro** 'sure'
> **claro** 'of course', 'obviously'
> **estar de acuerdo** 'to agree', 'to be in agreement'

Most of these words and expressions can be used in informal and formal contexts. The exceptions are ¡**vale**!, which most people would regard as informal, and ¡**efectivamente**!, which is rather formal. Apart from **sí**, the most common expressions seem to be **de acuerdo**, **vale** (used especially in Spain), **bien**, **bueno**, **conforme**, **desde luego**. Others are used less often. The word ¡**claro**! seems to be much more frequent among Latin Americans, while the phrases **tener razón** and **estar de acuerdo** tend to be used when one wants to be more emphatic. Note also that in these two phrases the verbs **tener** and **estar** will change for person and tense, e.g. **Tienes razón**, 'you're right'.

The kind of agreement expressed by these words and phrases is not the same for all of them. Some, like **de acuerdo**, **vale**, **bien**, **bueno**, **conforme**, are used to agree and accept a proposal or an invitation to do something, while others, like **cierto, eso es, efectivamente, desde luego, tener razón, estar de acuerdo**, are normally used to express agreement with a statement, for example an opinion, made by someone else.

> **¿Qué te parece si vamos al cine? – De acuerdo/vale/bien/bueno.**
> What about going to the cinema? – All right/OK.
>
> **Lo terminaremos mañana. – De acuerdo/vale/conforme/bien.**
> We'll finish it tomorrow. – All right/OK.
>
> **Es un coche estupendo, ¿no te parece? – Sí/desde luego/cierto.**
> It's a great car, don't you think so? – Yes/certainly.
>
> **Es una chica alta y delgada, ¿verdad? – Eso es/efectivamente.**
> She's a tall, thin girl, isn't she? – That's it/exactly.
>
> **No deberíamos haberlo hecho. – Tienes razón/estoy de acuerdo.**
> We shouldn't have done it. – You are right/I agree.
>
> **Tiene usted toda la razón.**
> You're absolutely right.
>
> **Estoy completamente de acuerdo.**
> I agree entirely.

56.2 Expressing disagreement

The words and phrases most commonly used in the expression of disagreement are the following:

> **no** 'no'
> **no sé** 'I don't know'
> **no estar seguro** 'not to be sure'
> **de ninguna manera/ningún modo** 'certainly not', 'by no means'
> **¿tú crees?** 'you think so?'
> **no creo** 'I don't think so'
> **no es cierto/verdad** 'that's not true'
> **no estar de acuerdo** 'not to agree'
> **estar equivocado** 'to be wrong'
> **¡qué va!** 'nonsense', 'rubbish'
> **¡cómo que . . . !** 'what do you mean . . .'

Apart from **no**, which is frequent in most contexts, on its own or preceding one of the expressions above, expressions like **no sé, no estoy seguro(a)**, are used to express mild disagreement with a proposal or invitation to do something, in contrast with **de ninguna manera/ningún modo**, which convey strong disagreement.

Phrases like **¿tú crees?, no creo**, express mild disagreement with a statement, such as an opinion. In the same context, **no es cierto/verdad, no estar de acuerdo, estar equivocado**, are slightly stronger, although less categoric than **¡qué va!** The strongest form of disagreement in this context is conveyed by the phrase **¡cómo que . . . !**, followed by a statement similar to that made by the person we disagree with.

Supongo que vendrás a París conmigo. – No/No sé/No estoy seguro.
I suppose you'll come to Paris with me. – No/I don't know/I'm not sure.

Me pondré tu camisa nueva. – ¡De ninguna manera!
I'll wear your new shirt. – Certainly not!

Es un poco extraña. – ¿Tú crees?/No creo.
She's a bit strange. – You think so?/I don't think so.

Estoy seguro de que ha sido él. – No es cierto/verdad.
I'm sure it was him. – That's not true.

El fracaso se debe a él. – No estoy de acuerdo/Estás equivocado.
The failure is due to him. – I don't agree/you're wrong.

Terminarán divorciándose. – ¡Qué va!
They'll end up getting divorced. – Nonsense!/rubbish!

No hiciste lo que te pedí. – ¡Cómo que no lo hice!
You didn't do what I asked you to. – What do you mean I didn't do it!

56.3 Asking about agreement and disagreement

To ask people whether they agree or disagree with something, we use expressions like the following:

¿está usted/estás de acuerdo? 'do you agree?'
¿está usted/estás de acuerdo con . . . ? 'do you agree with . . . ?'
¿(no) le/te parece? 'don't you think so?'
si le/te parece 'if it's all right with you'
si le/te parece bien 'if it's all right with you'
si le/te parece mal 'if you disagree'
¿(no) cree usted/crees? 'don't you think so?', 'you think so?'

Estás de acuerdo conmigo, ¿no?
You agree with me, don't you?

¿No está usted de acuerdo con nosotros?
Don't you agree with us?

¿No le parece a usted que es mejor aplazarlo?
Don't you think it's better to postpone it?

⏵ 18.1.5 (p. 85)

Si les parece bien, podemos hacerlo ahora mismo.
If it's all right with you, we can do it right now.

Si os parece mal, es mejor que se lo digáis.
If you disagree, you'd better tell him/her.

¿No cree usted que es una estupenda idea?
Don't you think it's a great idea?

56.4 ## Expressing indifference

To express indifference with regard to something, use expressions like the following:

Me da (exactamente) igual/lo mismo 'I don't care', 'It makes no difference to me'
Me es igual 'It makes no difference to me'
Me tiene/trae sin cuidado 'I don't care', 'I couldn't care less'
No me importa/interesa 'I don't care'
A mí ni me va ni me viene 'It makes no difference to me', 'I don't care'
Y (a mí) ¿qué? 'So what?'

¿Qué tal si la invitamos? – Me da igual/lo mismo.
What about inviting her? – I don't care.

A él no le gustará nada, ¿no crees? – Me tiene/trae sin cuidado.
He won't like it at all, will he? – I couldn't care less.

Se lo diré al jefe. – Y a mí ¿qué?
I'll tell the boss. – So what?

¿No crees que se molestaría? – A mí eso ni me va ni me viene.
Don't you think he/she might get annoyed? – I don't care.

IV

Expressing emotional attitudes

57
Expressing desires and preferences

This chapter covers the language associated with the concepts of desires and preferences. As you will see from the examples below, some of the expressions used in this context are similar to those in English, while others involve more complex constructions which may require reference to Part A of this book.

57.1 Expressing desires

To express desires, Spanish normally uses the following verbs and expressions:

> **querer** 'to want'
> **gustar** 'to like'
> **apetecer** 'to be appealing to', 'to fancy', 'to feel like'
> **tener ganas de** 'to feel like'
> **hacer ilusión** 'to feel like'
> **desear** 'to wish'

57.1.1 Querer

Querer, 'to want', a *radical-changing verb* (**e/ie**), is probably the most frequent verb used in the expression of desires, either present or past. It may be followed by a noun or noun phrase (e.g. **un café con leche**, 'a white coffee'), an infinitive (e.g. **viajar**, 'to travel'), a demonstrative pronoun (e.g. **éste**, 'this one'), or it may be preceded by an object pronoun (e.g. **lo**, 'it'). To say what you want now, you can use:

(a) The present tense, for example:

Por favor, quiero un café.	I want a coffee, please.
Lo quiero con leche.	I want it with milk.
Queremos viajar a Madrid.	We want to travel to Madrid.

▶ 21.4 (p. 101); 16.1.2.1 (p. 64); 17.1 (p. 72)

(b) **Quisiera**

Sometimes, depending on the context, **quiero**, 'I want', or **queremos**, 'we want', may sound a little abrupt, unless they are followed by the phrase **por favor**, with the proper intonation of a request. To avoid sounding rude, you can use the more polite and formal forms **quisiera**, 'I'd like', or **quisiéramos**, 'we'd like', for example:

> **Quisiera una habitación doble.**
> I'd like a double room.

> **Quisiéramos verla.**
> We'd like to see it.

(c) The imperfect, i.e. **quería**, 'I wanted', is very common when requesting something in a shop, restaurant, etc.

Quería otra cerveza.	I want another beer.
Quería un kilo de tomates.	I want a kilo of tomatoes.
Quería éste.	I want this one.

Quería, 'I wanted', softens the expression of wanting, therefore it is sometimes used to address people you don't know well or people in authority.

> **Perdone, quería hablar con usted.**
> Excuse me, I wanted to speak to you.

> **Queríamos decirle algo.**
> We wanted to tell you something.

Desires with regard to something in the past are normally expressed with the imperfect:

> **Queríamos pasar las vacaciones en Londres, pero no pudimos.**
> We wanted to spend our holidays in London, but we couldn't.

> **Quería hablar con Pamela, pero no estaba.**
> I wanted to speak to Pamela, but she wasn't in.

57.1.2 *Gustar*

The conditional form of **gustar**, 'to like', is frequently used for expressing desires in sentences like the following:

Me gustaría ir a Egipto.	I'd like to go to Egypt.
Nos gustaría alquilar un coche.	We'd like to hire a car.
Les gustaría tener un hijo.	They'd like to have a child.

Note that **gustar**, which is in the third person singular, and followed by an infinitive, is preceded by an indirect *object pronoun*.

▶ 58 (p. 340)

57.1.3 *Apetecer, tener ganas de, hacer ilusión*

These expressions are all very colloquial and common, especially the first two.

57.1.3.1 **Apetecer**, 'to be appealing to', 'to feel like', 'to fancy', is used in a construction similar to that with **gustar**, that is, preceded by an indirect *object pronoun* (e.g. **me**, **te**, **le**) and agreeing in number with the thing wanted (third person singular or plural). It may be followed by a noun or noun phrase, an infinitive or a demonstrative pronoun. This verb is normally found in the present tense indicative, but sometimes also in the conditional or, less frequently, in the imperfect, which softens the expression of want. **Apetecer** is uncommon in Latin America.

▶ **58** (p. 340); **8.2** (p. 36)

> **Me apetece un jerez.**
> I fancy a sherry.

> **No me apetecen.**
> I don't want them/They don't appeal to me.

> **No nos apetece jugar al tenis.**
> We don't feel like playing tennis.

> **Me apetecería tomar un chocolate.**
> I'd like to have a chocolate.

> **Le apetecía comer algo.**
> He/she wanted to eat something.

> **Me apetece éste.**
> They want this one.

| 57.1.3.2 | **Tener ganas de**, 'to feel like', is used with an infinitive, not with a noun. It is usually found in the present tense, but also in the imperfect indicative when reference is to past desires.

> **Tengo ganas de salir.**
> I feel like going out.

> **No tengo ganas de trabajar.**
> I don't feel like working.

> **Tienen ganas de quedarse.**
> They feel like staying.

> **Tenía muchas ganas de verte.**
> I very much wanted to see you.

This expression is sometimes used on its own, without the preposition **de**:

> **Gracias, no tengo ganas.** Thank you, I don't feel like it.

| 57.1.3.3 | **Hacer ilusión**, 'to look forward', is used in a construction similar to that with **apetecer** or **gustar**, and it is normally followed by an infinitive. Its use is more common in positive sentences, either in the present tense, or the imperfect when reference is to past desires. This expression is generally unknown in Latin America.

> **Me hace mucha ilusión ir a Marbella.**
> I'd very much like to go to Marbella *or* I'm so looking forward to going to Marbella.

> **Nos hace ilusión verlo de nuevo.**
> We'd like to see him again *or* We're looking forward to seeing him again.

> **Me hacía mucha ilusión visitar Nueva York otra vez.**
> I very much wanted to visit New York again./I was looking forward to visiting New York again.

57.1.4 *Desear*

Desear, 'to wish', is rarely found in spoken informal language. Its use seems to be restricted to formal contexts, but it is also especially common in certain sub-registers, for example advertising, shop-assistants' or waiters' jargon (see **57.2** below), etc. It is normally found in constructions similar to those with **querer** (see **57.1.1** above).

> **Si usted lo desea, podemos reunirnos en nuestra oficina.**
> If you wish, we can meet in our office.

> **Deseo expresar a usted mi más profundo pesar.**
> I want to express to you my deepest sympathy.

57.2 Enquiring about desires

To enquire about desires, we normally use the same verbs as above, except **hacer ilusión**, which is unusual in interrogative sentences.

Informal

¿Qué quieres hacer?	What do you want to do?
¿Qué te gustaría comer?	What would you like to eat?
¿Qué quieres beber?	What do you want to drink?
¿Qué te apetece hacer?	What do you feel like doing?
¿Tenéis ganas de salir?	Do you feel like going out?

Formal

> **¿Cómo quiere la carne?**
> How do you want the meat?

> **¿A qué restaurante le gustaría ir?**
> What restaurant would you like to go to?

> **¿Qué desea hacer usted?**
> What would you like to do?

> **¿Qué quería usted?**
> Can I help you? (e.g. in a shop)

> **¿Qué desea/deseaba usted?**
> Can I help you? (e.g. in a shop)

> **¿Qué desean tomar?**
> What would you like to have?

57.3 Expressing preferences and enquiring about preferences

57.3.1 *Preferir*

The verb most commonly associated with preferences, in positive as well as interrogative sentences is **preferir**, 'to prefer', a *radical-changing verb*, like **querer** (e/ie). It is normally found in the present tense indicative, but also sometimes in the conditional, as a way of softening the expression of preference. Like **querer**, it is normally followed by a noun or noun phrase, an infinitive, a demonstrative pronoun, or it may be preceded by an object pronoun (e.g. **lo**, 'it').

> **¿Prefieres el cine o el teatro?**
> Do you prefer cinema or theatre?
>
> **Prefiero el cine.**
> I prefer cinema.
>
> **¿Qué prefiere hacer usted?**
> What do you prefer to do?
>
> **Prefiero salir a tomar una copa.**
> I prefer to go out for a drink.
>
> **¿Prefieres éste o ése?**
> Do you prefer this one or that one?
>
> **Prefiero éste.**
> I prefer this one.
>
> **¿Cómo la prefiere usted?**
> How do you prefer it?
>
> **La prefiero muy hecha.**
> I prefer it well done.

Note also the use of **preferir** with the preposition **a** in:

> **Prefiero el ballet a la ópera.**   I prefer ballet to opera.
> **Prefiero la cerveza al vino.**   I prefer beer to wine.
> **Prefiero Carmen a María.**   I prefer Carmen to María.

▶ 16.1.2.1 (p. 64)

57.3.2   *Me gustaría más, me parece mejor*

Me gustaría más, 'I would prefer', 'I like . . . best', and **me parece mejor**, 'I prefer', 'I like . . . best' (literally 'it seems better to me'), are two alternative ways of expressing preferences, normally used in the spoken language. Remember that in this construction **gustar** and **parecer** must be preceded by an indirect *object pronoun* (e.g. **me, te, le**).

> **¿Cuál te gustaría más?**
> Which one would you prefer/like best?
>
> **Me gustaría más el azul.**
> I would prefer/like the blue one best.
>
> **¿Cuál les parece mejor?**
> Which one do you prefer/like best?
>
> **Nos parece mejor aquél.**
> We prefer that one/We like that one best.

▶ 58.1 (p. 340)

57.4 Expressing desires and preferences involving others

57.4.1 *Querer/preferir que* + subjunctive

Desires and preferences involving others, for example 'I want/wanted you to help me', 'I'd rather you came tomorrow', are expressed in Spanish with a construction carrying a subjunctive verb in the subordinate clause. Consider the following examples:

▶ **18.1** (p. 83); **19.2** (p. 95)

> **Quiero que me ayudes.**
> I want you to help me.
>
> **Quería que me ayudaras/ayudases.**
> I wanted you to help me.
>
> **Prefiero que vengas mañana.**
> I'd rather you came tomorrow.
>
> **Preferiría que vinieras mañana.**
> I'd rather you came tomorrow.
>
> **Prefiero que no lo hagas.**
> I'd rather you didn't do it.
>
> **Preferiría que no lo hicieras.**
> I'd rather you didn't do it.

57.4.2 *Me parece mejor que* + subjunctive, *me gustaría que* + subjunctive

Preferences involving other people are sometimes expressed with **parecer** and **gustar** (see **57.3.2** above), in a construction with **que**, followed by a clause containing a subjunctive verb, in the following sequence of tenses:

Main clause	Subordinate clause
Present	Present subjunctive
Conditional	Imperfect subjunctive

▶ **19.2** (p. 95)

> **Me parece mejor que lo termines hoy.**
> I think it's best if you finish it today/I'd rather you finished it today.
>
> **Me gustaría que lo terminaras hoy.**
> I'd rather you finished it today.

▶ **18.1.4** (p. 85); **70.1.8** (p. 392)

57.4.3 *Es mejor que* + present subjunctive, *sería mejor que* + imperfect subjunctive

The first construction, used normally with the present subjunctive, is similar in meaning to **me parece mejor que . . .** , as seen in **57.4.2**. The second, usually found with the imperfect subjunctive, may be used in the same context as **me gustaría que . . .** Both expressions are common in the spoken and the written language.

> **Es mejor que lo haga usted mismo/a.**
> I'd rather you did it yourself/You'd better do it yourself.
>
> **Sería mejor que vinieras tú conmigo.**
> I'd rather you came with me.

57.4.4 *Es preferible que* + present subjunctive, *sería preferible que* + imperfect subjunctive

These two expressions may be used for indicating preferences with regard to oneself or others.

> **Es preferible que yo/Vd. se lo diga.**
> I'd rather tell him/her myself/I'd rather you tell him/her.
>
> **Sería preferible que no viajaras.**
> I'd rather you didn't travel.

58
Expressing likes and dislikes

This chapter looks at the ways in which Spanish expresses the concept of likes and dislikes. It considers the verbs associated with them and the way in which these function, as well as a range of other colloquial expressions.

58.1 How to say you like or dislike someone or something

Gustar, 'to please', is the verb most commonly associated with likes and dislikes. Spanish **me gusta el fútbol** corresponds to English 'I like football'; it is important to realize, however, that the Spanish sentence literally means 'football pleases me'. Thus **gustar** is normally preceded by an indirect *object pronoun* (**me, te, le, nos, os**, or **les**), which signals the person to whom something is pleasing, while the verb itself takes the third person ending, agreeing with its subject, the thing which is pleasing, which, however, normally follows this verb. So, instead of saying 'I like something', as you would in English, Spanish speakers would say literally 'Something pleases me' (e.g. **me gusta el español**, 'I like Spanish').

▶ **8.2** (p. 36); **28.1** (p. 145)

58.1.1 Using *gustar* with a noun or pronoun

Gustar may be followed by a noun or a pronoun, in which case the verb will agree in number (third person singular or plural) with the noun or pronoun (e.g. a personal, demonstrative or possessive pronoun).

> **Me gusta.**
> I like it.
>
> **No me gustan.**
> I don't like them.
>
> **Me gusta mucho el tenis.**
> I like tennis very much.
>
> **Me gustan los deportes.**
> I like sports.
>
> **Nos gusta ella.**
> We like her.
>
> **No nos gustan ellos.**
> We don't like them.

> **Creo que le gustará éste.**
> I think he/she will like this one.

> **No les gustó mucho el tuyo.**
> They didn't like yours much.

> **Les gustaron los míos.**
> They liked mine.

In order to focus attention on the thing liked, the noun or pronoun is sometimes placed in initial position, before the object pronoun.

> **El fútbol no me gusta.**
> I don't like football.

> **España me gustó mucho.**
> I liked Spain very much.

> **Las playas también nos gustaron.**
> We also liked the beaches.

58.1.2 Using *gustar* with an infinitive

To say whether one or others like or liked doing something, use an infinitive after the appropriate form of **gustar**.

> **Me gusta jugar al tenis.**
> I like playing tennis.

> **Le gusta hacer deportes.**
> You like *or* he/she likes playing sports.

58.1.3 Use of *a* + pronoun to avoid ambiguity in the third person

To avoid ambiguity in the third person singular and plural, as in **le gusta**, 'you like' 'he/she likes', **les gusta**, 'you/they like', the object pronoun (in this case **le/les**), is preceded by the preposition **a** followed by the corresponding pronoun, **usted, él, ella, ustedes, ellos**, or **ellas**. Often however, this is not necessary, as the context makes it clear to whom one is referring.

▶ 25.1.1.2 (p. 118); **8.2.1** (p. 36); **8.3** (p. 39)

> **A él le gusta el vino.**
> He likes wine.

> **A ella no le gusta Bilbao.**
> She doesn't like Bilbao.

> **A ustedes les gusta el hotel, ¿no?**
> You like the hotel, don't you?

> **A ellos no les gustan los deportes.**
> They don't like sports.

58.1.4   **A + proper name**

The preposition **a** is also required before a proper name

> **A Carlos le gustó mucho Granada.**
> Carlos liked Granada very much.

> **A Luis y Ana les gusta viajar.**
> Luis y Ana like travelling.

58.1.5   **A + pronoun, to show focus or emphasis**

The construction **a** + pronoun is also used for emphasis, contrast or in short forms, and not just with the third person singular or plural. For the first and second person singular (**yo**, 'I', **tú**, 'you'), the pronouns which follow the preposition **a** are **mí** and **ti** respectively.

> **A mí me gusta el español.**   I like Spanish.
> **A ti te gusta el francés.**   You like French.

Note also the short positive and negative forms:

> **A mí también (me gusta).**   So do I.
> **A ti tampoco (te gusta).**   Neither do you.

For all other persons, use subject pronouns (**usted, él, ella, nosotros/as, vosotros/as, ustedes, ellos, ellas**).

> **A nosotros nos gusta el campo.**
> We like the country.

> **A ellos no les gusta la playa.**
> They don't like the beach.

Note that even when **me, te, le**, etc. become 'redundant' in this construction, they cannot be omitted.

 8.3 (p. 39)

58.2   **Enquiring about likes and dislikes**

To ask people about their likes and dislikes, you can use the same constructions as those for statements but with the proper intonation, as for a question.

> **¿Te gusta leer?**
> Do you like reading?

> **¿Te gustó la novela?**
> Did you like the novel?

> **¿A usted le gustan** (or **¿Le gustan a usted . . . ?**) **los escritores latinoamericanos?**
> Do you like Latin American writers?

> **¿La música cubana, te gusta?**
> Do you like Cuban music?

>   ¿No te gusta el jazz?
>   Don't you like jazz?

Note also the short forms:

>   **¿A él también (le gustan)?**
>   Does he (like them) too?

>   **¿Y a él?**
>   And what about him? (Does he like them?)

To ask people what or which they like/d, how they like/d something, etc., simply place the appropriate question word, **¿qué?**, **¿cómo?**, etc. at the start of the sentence.

>   **¿Qué te gusta hacer durante las vacaciones?**
>   What do you like doing during the holidays?

>   **¿Cuál le gustó a Carmen?**
>   Which one did Carmen like?

>   **¿Cómo les gusta la carne?**
>   How do you/they like the meat?

▶ 12.2 (p. 49)

58.3   Other ways of expressing likes and dislikes

58.3.1   *Encantar, fascinar, adorar, agradar*

Encantar and **fascinar**, 'to like very much', 'to love', and **adorar**, 'to adore' are normally used in positive sentences to express a stronger feeling of liking than that expressed by **gustar**. **Agradar**, 'to like', is used in positive and negative sentences (see **58.3.2** below) in more formal contexts. With the exception of **adorar**, these verbs function grammatically in the same way as **gustar**.

Me encanta ese traje.	I love that suit.
Me encantan tus zapatos.	I love your shows.
Te encantará.	You will love it/him/her.
Me fascina su forma de hablar.	I love his way of speaking.
Me fascina venir aquí.	I love coming here.
Adoro las flores.	I just love flowers.
Antonio adora el mar.	Antonio loves the sea.
El lugar nos agradó muchísimo.	We liked the place very much.

58.3.2   *No agradar, desagradar, disgustar*, not to like, to dislike, *molestar*, to bother

These verbs are used for expressing disliking, and in this context they normally function like **gustar**. **Desagradar**, **disgustar** and **molestar** indicate a stronger feeling of disliking than **no agradar** and **no gustar**.

>   **Esa persona no me agrada en absoluto.**
>   I don't like that person at all.

Me desagrada su actitud.
I don't like his/her attitude.

Eso nos desagradó muchísimo.
We didn't like that at all.

Le disgustó mi comportamiento.
He/she didn't like/disliked my behaviour.

Lo que dijeron de mí me disgustó enormemente.
I very much disliked what they said of me.

Me molestó mucho lo que hiciste.
What you did bothered me very much.

▶ 58.1 (p. 340)

Miscellaneous expressions

A range of other colloquial expressions can be used to express likes and dislikes. The following are the most common.

¡Es estupendo/fantástico!
It's great/fantastic!

¡Es horrible!
It's horrible!

Es (muy) bonito/feo.
It's (very) pretty/ugly.

Es (muy) agradable/desagradable.
It's (very) pleasant/unpleasant.

Es (muy) simpático/a.
He/she is (very) nice.

Es insoportable.
He/she is unbearable.

No lo soporto.
I can't stand him/it.

Detesto . . .
I detest . . .

Odio . . . /Aborrezco . . .
I hate . . .

Detestar, odiar and **aborrecer** express strong dislike.

Verbs of liking and disliking followed by *que*

Verbs such as **gustar, encantar, fascinar, agradar, molestar, soportar, odiar,** are also used in sentences which carry a subordinate clause introduced by **que**, with a verb in the subjunctive.

Me molesta que me trates así.
I don't like you to treat me like this.

Me gusta que me regalen flores.
I like to be given flowers.

Le encanta/fascina que le digan eso.
He/she loves to be told that.

No le agradaba/gustaba que le pidiera/pidiese dinero.
He/she didn't like being asked for money.

Nos agradó mucho que nos visitaran/visitasen.
We were very pleased that they visited us.

No soporto que me den órdenes.
I hate to be ordered around.

Odio que te comportes de esa manera.
I hate it when you behave like that.

18.1.4 (p. 85)

59
Expressing surprise

This chapter considers the concept of surprise and examines the ways in which Spanish speakers normally express this idea.

To express surprise, Spanish, like English, uses a range of expressions. Some of these are fixed words or phrases, others are complete sentences which vary according to context.

59.1 | Set expressions

¿Sí?
Oh yes?

¿De veras?
Really?

¿Verdad?
Really?

¡Fíjate (fam.)/ **fíjese** (pol.)!
Imagine!, just think!

¡Qué bien!
Oh, good!, great!

¡No me diga/s!
You don't say!

¡Hombre!
Good heavens! I never!

¡Vaya sorpresa!
What a surprise!

¡No!
No!

¡No puede ser!
It/that is impossible!

¡Qué raro/extraño!
How strange!

¡Es increíble!
It/that's incredible!

¡Parece mentira!
It's unbelievable! It hardly seems possible!

¡Dios mío! or **¡Dios santo!**
God! Good God!

¡No lo puedo creer!
I just can't believe it!

Some of these expressions convey mild surprise, and almost indifference, for example ¿sí?, ¿de veras?, ¿verdad?, ¡fíjate/fíjese!, ¡qué bien!. Others, like ¡no me digas!, ¡hombre!, ¡vaya sorpresa!, convey a slightly stronger sense of surprise, while ¡no!, ¡no puede ser!, ¡qué raro/extraño!, ¡es increíble!, ¡Dios mío! or ¡Dios santo!, ¡no lo puedo creer! . . . express strong surprise.

59.1.1   **Latin American usage**

Apart from the expressions listed above, which are common in most Spanish-speaking countries, there are others which are restricted to certain regions, like ¡Híjole! (Mexico) 'wow!'.

59.2   **Expressing surprise with regard to someone or something**

To express ideas such as 'How strange that they are not here!', 'I'm surprised you say that', Spanish normally uses a construction in which the expression of surprise is followed by **que** and a verb in the subjunctive. The tense of the subjunctive verb will depend on the time reference: present subjunctive for present or future reference, and perfect or imperfect subjunctive for past reference.

▶ **18.1.4** (p. 85)

¡Qué raro que no estén aquí!
How strange that they're not here!

Me sorprende que digas eso.
I'm surprised you say that.

Me extraña que no nos escriba.
I'm surprised he/she hasn't written to us.

Me asombra que estés aquí.
I'm surprised to see you here.

¡Qué extraño que no estuviera allí!
How strange that he/she wasn't there!

¡No puede ser que haya dicho eso!
I can't believe he/she has said that!

¡Es increíble que se haya comportado de esa manera!
It's incredible that he/she has behaved like that!

¡Parece mentira que haya ganado la lotería!
It hardly seems possible that he/she has won the lottery!

Note that in this context the verbs **sorprender, extrañar,** and **asombrar** behave like **gustar**, 'to like', so they must go in the third person singular, with an object pronoun preceding the verb: **Me sorprende/extraña/asombra que** . . . 'It surprises me that . . .' (lit.), **Nos sorprende/extraña/asombra que** . . . 'It surprises us that . . .' (lit.).

▶ **58.1** (p. 340); **8.2** (p. 36)

60
Expressing satisfaction and dissatisfaction

This chapter deals with the concepts of satisfaction and dissatisfaction and examines the ways in which Spanish normally expresses them.

60.1 Expressing satisfaction

60.1.1 Set phrases

To express satisfaction, Spanish uses a range of expressions, of which the most common are

¡Eso es!	That's it!
¡Estupendo!	Great!
¡Es estupendo/a!	It's great!
Esto/eso está bien.	This/that is fine.
Me gusta/n.	I like it/them.
Es justamente lo que	It's just what
quiero/quería	I want(ed).
busco/buscaba	I am/was looking for.
necesito/necesitaba.	I need(ed).
Me parece bien.	I think it's fine.
No está mal.	It's not bad.
Estoy satisfecho/a de . . .	I'm satisfied with . . .
Me satisface plenamente.	I'm completely satisfied.
Siento una gran satisfacción.	I feel great satisfaction.

With the exception of ¡eso es!, 'that's it' and ¡estupendo! 'great!', these are not fixed expressions, but they may vary according to the context or the degree of satisfaction that we wish to express. Thus, we may shorten them, or expand them, using noun phrases or intensifiers (i.e. words like **muy**, 'very' **bastante**, 'quite') for example, or we can substitute words with others of similar meaning, or even combine two or more expressions so as to express a greater degree of satisfaction. Here are some examples:

> **Me gusta mucho. Es exactamente lo que me hacía falta.**
> I like it very much. It's exactly what I needed.

> **¡Eso es! Es justo lo que busco. ¡Estupendo!**
> That's it! That's just what I'm looking for. Great!

> **¡Me encanta lo que has hecho! Me parece muy bien.**
> I love what you've done. I think it's great.
>
> **No está nada mal.**
> It's not bad at all.

Note that **parecer**, 'to seem', behaves in the same way as **gustar**, 'to like', that is, with an indirect *object pronoun* (**me, te, le, nos, os**, or **les**), preceding the verb.

▶ **8.2** (p. 36)

> **Me parece excelente.**   I think it's excellent.
> **Nos parece muy bien.**   We think it's fine.

▶ **61.1** (p. 352); **58** (p. 340)

60.1.2 **Latin American usage**

There are a few expressions which are characteristic of certain Latin American countries or certain regions, for example:

> **¡Qué chévere!** (L. Am., except Southern Cone)
> That's great!
>
> **¡Macanudo!** (Southern Cone)
> Great!
>
> **¡Regio!** (Southern Cone, Colombia)
> Great!

60.2 Expressing dissatisfaction

Dissatisfaction is commonly expressed through expressions like the following:

No me gusta.	I don't like it.
Así no me gusta.	I don't like it like this.
No me convence.	I'm not sure/convinced.
Esto/eso no está bien.	This/that is not right.
No me parece bien.	It doesn't seem right to me.
Esto/eso está mal.	This/that is wrong.
Esto/eso no es lo que	This/that is not what
quiero/quería	I want(ed)
busco/buscaba	I am/was looking for
necesito/necesitaba.	I need(ed).
No estoy satisfecho/a	
(en absoluto).	I'm not (at all) satisfied.
No nos satisface.	We're not satisfied.
Deja mucho que desear.	It leaves much to be desired.

As above, these expressions can be adapted to fit different contexts.

> **Esto no me convence mucho. Me parece que no está bien.**
> I'm not quite sure about this. I don't think it's right.
>
> **No me gusta nada.**
> I don't like it at all.

No es lo que yo quería.
It's not what I wanted.

▶ **61.2** (p. 353); **58** (p. 340)

61.2 (p. 353); **58** (p. 340)

60.3 **Enquiring about satisfaction or dissatisfaction**

Among the expressions used to enquire about satisfaction or dissatisfaction we find the following ones

¿Está bien (ahora)?	Is it all right (now)?
¿Está bien así?	Is it all right like this?
¿Le/te gusta (así)?	Do you like it (like this)?
¿Qué le/te parece?	What do you think?
¿Está/s conforme?	Are you satisfied?
¿Es esto/eso lo que	Is this/that what
quiere(s)/quería(s)?	you want(ed)?
busca(s)/buscaba(s)?	you are/were looking for?
necesita(s)/necesitaba(s)?	you need(ed)?
¿Está/s satisfecho/a (ahora)?	Are you satisfied (now)?
¿Está/s conforme?	Are you satisfied?

The examples below illustrate some of the variations that these expressions can undergo.

¿Está bien de esta manera?
Is it all right this way?

¿Qué te parece? ¿Estás conforme?
What do you think? Are you satisfied?

Esto es lo que usted necesitaba, ¿verdad?
This is what you needed, isn't it?

▶ **61.3** (p. 353)

61.3 (p. 353)

61
Expressing approval and disapproval

The concepts of approval and disapproval discussed in this chapter are usually expressed through set phrases, but there is also a small number of expressions linked to certain verbs, which are considered below.

61.1 Expressing approval

61.1.1 Set phrases

Approval is normally expressed in Spanish with the following expressions, all of which are very common.

¡(Muy) bien!	Good!/Very well!
¡Qué bien!	Good!, great!
¡Perfectamente!	Right!
¡Estupendo!	Great!
¡Fantástico!	Great!, fantastic!
¡Excelente!	Excellent!
¡Perfecto!	Perfect!
¡Eso es!	That's it!
Está bastante/muy bien.	It's quite/very good.
Está perfecto/excelente/ estupendo/fenomenal.	It's perfect/excellent great/wonderful.
No está (nada) mal.	It's not bad (at all).

61.1.2 *Parecer*

Approval is often expressed with **parecer**, 'to seem', a verb which behaves in the same way as **gustar**, 'to like', that is, with an indirect *object pronoun* (**me, te, le, nos, os, les**) preceding the verb.

Me parece (muy) bien.	I think it's fine.
Nos parece fantástico.	We think it's fantastic.

▶ **8.2** (p. 36); **60** (p. 349)

61.2 Expressing disapproval

61.2.1 Set phrases

(Eso) no está bien.	That's not right.
¡(Eso) está (muy) mal!	That's (very) bad!
Deja mucho que desear.	It leaves much to be desired.

61.2.2 *(No) debería* + infinitive

To say things like 'You should (not) do this or that', use this construction with a conditional form of **deber**, e.g. **debería** (pol.), **deberías** (fam.), 'you should', followed by an infinitive.

> **Eso no está bien. Debería usted hacerlo de nuevo.**
> That's not right. You should do it again.

> **No deberías beber tanto.**
> You shouldn't drink so much.

> **No deberías salir con esta lluvia.**
> You shouldn't go out in this rain.

▶ 21.2 (p. 100); 17.7 (p. 77)

61.2.3 *(No) debería* + *haber* + past participle

To say things like 'You should (not) have done this or that', use this construction with a conditional form of **deber**, followed by **haber** and a past participle.

▶ 16.1.1.7 (p. 62)

> **Usted debería haber llegado más temprano.**
> You should have arrived earlier.

> **No deberías haber dicho eso.**
> You shouldn't have said that.

> **Ustedes no deberían haber aceptado.**
> You shouldn't have accepted.

Note that in speech **debería** is sometimes replaced by the imperfect, **debía**.

> **No debías habérselo dicho.**
> You shouldn't have told him/her.

61.3 Enquiring about approval or disapproval

To enquire about approval or disapproval, use expressions like the following:

> **¿Está bien esto?**
> Is this all right?

¿Cree usted que esto está bien?
Do you think this is all right?

¿Le parece bien?
Does it seem all right to you? (pol.)

Si te parece, . . .
'If it's all right with you . . .' (fam.)

¿Qué te parece?
What do you think? (fam.)

Note that **parecer**, 'to seem', like **gustar**, has to be preceded by an indirect *object pronoun* (**le** or **les**, 'to you', for polite address, and **te** or **os**, 'to you', for familiar address).

▶ **8.2** (p. 36)

¿Está bien ese informe?
Is that report all right?

¿Crees tú que este trabajo está bien?
Do you think this job is all right?

Si le parece, puedo traérselo mañana.
If it's all right with you, I can bring it tomorrow.

¿Qué os parece?
What do you think?

62
Expressing hope

This chapter considers the concept of hope, in relation to the speaker himself as well as to others.

62.1 Saying what one hopes or others hope to do

To express this idea, Spanish normally uses the verb **esperar**, 'to hope', followed by an infinitive

> **Este año espero ir a Berlín.**
> This year I hope to go to Berlin.

> **Francisco espera aprobar el examen.**
> Francisco hopes to pass the exam.

> **Esperamos recibir el dinero mañana.**
> We hope to receive the money tomorrow.

▶ **26.2.2.1** (p. 134)

62.2 Expressing hope with regard to others

When the expression of hope involves a subject other than that of the main verb, as in 'I hope you are lucky!', we use the following expressions.

62.2.1 *Esperar* + *que* + subjunctive

This construction with **esperar** is by far the most frequent form of expressing hope involving others, and it is used in all registers. When hope refers to the present or the future, the main verb, that is **esperar**, must be in the present indicative, while the verb in the subordinate clause must be in the present subjunctive.

▶ **16.1.1.3** (p. 61)

> **¡Espero que tengas suerte!**
> I hope you are lucky!

> **Elena espera que tú la ayudes.**
> Elena hopes you can help her.

> **Mis padres esperan que yo estudie medicina.**
> My parents hope I will study medicine.

Hope with regard to something in the past is expressed with the present of **esperar** followed by a verb in the perfect subjunctive in the secondary clause.

▶ **16.1.1.7** (p. 62)

> **Espero que no haya pasado nada.**
> I hope nothing has happened.

> **Espero que no se hayan perdido.**
> I hope they haven't got lost.

> **Espero que lo hayas encontrado.**
> I hope you have found it.

To say what you or others *hoped* or *were hoping* other people to do, we use the same construction as above, with **esperar** in the imperfect indicative and the verb in the subordinate clause in the imperfect subjunctive.

▶ **16.1.1.2** (p. 59); **16.1.1.3** (p. 61); **19.2** (p. 95)

> **Yo esperaba que llegaras más temprano.**
> I was hoping you would arrive earlier.

> **Él esperaba que yo no dijera nada.**
> He hoped/was hoping I wouldn't say anything.

> **Ellos esperaban que guardáramos el secreto.**
> They hoped/were hoping we would keep the secret.

Note in all the examples above that the word **que**, 'that', which links the two clauses, cannot be omitted as 'that' can be in English.

▶ **18.1.3** (p. 85)

62.2.2 | *Ojalá (que)* + subjunctive

This alternative construction for expressing hope with regard to others or something outside ourselves, is also very common. In informal, colloquial language, the word **que**, 'that', is usually omitted. Like the previous construction with **esperar**, this one with **ojalá** (see also **62.3** below) can be used to express hope with regard to the present, the future or the past.

> **¡Ojalá (que) Juan Pablo esté aquí!**
> I hope Juan Pablo is here!

> **¡Ojalá (que) todo salga bien!**
> Let's hope everything turns out all right.

> **¡Ojalá (que) hayan ganado!**
> I hope they have won.

▶ **18.3.2** (p. 92)

62.3 **Expressing hope in reply to a question or a statement**

To say one hopes so or hopes not in answer to someone's question or as a reaction to a statement, the following set expressions are used

Espero que sí 'I hope so'
Espero que no 'I hope not'
Eso espero 'I hope so'
¡Ojalá! 'I hope so!'

(¿Vendrás mañana?) – Espero que sí.
(Will you come tomorrow?) – I hope so.

(¿Te pagarán hoy?) – Eso espero.
(Will they pay you today?) – I hope so.

(¿No crees que puede haber tenido un accidente?) – Espero que no.
(Don't you think he/she may have had an accident?) – I hope not.

(Seguro que consigues la beca) – ¡Ojalá!
(I'm sure you'll get the scholarship) – I hope so!

(No te molestarán más) – ¡Ojalá!
(They will not bother you again) – I hope so!

63
Expressing sympathy

To tell people we are sorry or glad about something which has happened to them, for example, the loss of a job or a promotion, we can do so by using one of several set phrases without referring to the event as such, as one would in English, with set phrases such as 'I'm so sorry', 'I'm glad'. Alternatively, we can refer to the event for which we are expressing sympathy, in which case we need a construction where some of the elements will vary according to the context, as in 'I'm very sorry you lost your job' or 'I'm glad you got that promotion'. This chapter considers both types of expressions.

63.1 Saying one is sorry about something

▶ 18.1.4 (p. 85)

63.1.1 Set phrases

¡Lástima!
What a pity!, what a shame!

¡Qué pena!
What a pity!, what a shame!

¡Qué lástima!
What a pity!, what a shame!

¡Es una pena/lástima!
It's a pity!

¡Lo siento (mucho)!
I'm (very) sorry!

¡Qué pena tan grande!
What a great pity!

¡Lo siento tanto!
I'm so sorry!

¡Cuánto lo siento!
I'm so sorry!

Lo siento en el alma.
I'm terribly sorry, I'm so sorry.

For formal condolences, use the set phrases:

Mi más sentido pésame.	My deepest sympathies.
Or **Lo(le)/la acompaño**	
en el sentimiento.	I share your grief.

¡Qué pena/lástima que + **subjunctive!**

This is the most common way of saying one is sorry about something while at the same time referring to the event which brings forth that sympathy. This may be some present or future state or event, in which case the verb in the subordinate clause normally takes the present subjunctive; but it may be something in the past, in which case we would use the perfect or imperfect subjunctive.

▶ **16.1.1.3** (p. 61); **16.1.1.7** (p. 62); **18.1.4** (p. 85)

¡Qué lástima/pena que no te sientas bien!
What a pity you are not feeling well!

¡Qué lástima/pena que deba usted marcharse mañana!
What a pity you'll have to leave tomorrow.

¡Qué lástima/pena que Vd. no haya venido a nuestra fiesta!
What a pity you didn't come to our party!

¡Qué lástima/pena que perdierais el partido!
What a pity you lost the game!

Lástima is sometimes used without the preceding **qué**, to convey sympathy in a more colloquial and informal way:

¡Lástima que no lo hayas podido comprar!
I'm sorry you weren't able to buy it.

A slightly less frequent alternative to this construction with ¡Qué lástima/pena que . . . ! is ¡Es/fue una lástima/pena que . . . !, 'It is/was a pity that . . . !'

¡Es una lástima/pena que no hayas conseguido ese puesto!
It's a pity you didn't get that job!

¡Fue una lástima/pena que les pasara eso!
It was a pity what happened to them.

Siento/sentimos mucho + **noun phrase**

Sentir, 'to regret', a *radical-changing verb* (**e/ie**), is the verb most commonly used when we want to say that we are sorry about something. Note that the **lo** of the set phrase ¡**Lo siento!**, 'I'm sorry!' (about it), literally 'I regret it', is not required in this case.

Siento mucho la muerte de tu tía.
I'm so sorry about your aunt's death.

Sentimos mucho tu accidente.
We're (so) sorry about your accident.

> **Siento mucho lo sucedido.**
> I'm sorry about what happened.

🔘 **16.1.2.1** (p. 64)

An alternative to the last sentence is to use a construction with **lo que** + verb phrase:

> **Siento mucho lo que sucedió.**
> I'm sorry about what happened.

To say one was sorry to hear about something, use the preterite of **sentir**.

> **Sentí mucho su muerte.**
> I was very sorry to hear about his/her death.

> **Sentimos mucho tu separación de Luis.**
> We were sorry to hear about your separation from Luis.

63.1.4 | *Siento/sentimos mucho que* + **subjunctive**

As in **63.1.2** above, the verb in the subordinate clause may be in the present, perfect or imperfect subjunctive, depending on whether we want to express sympathy about a current or future state or event, or about something in the past.

> **Siento mucho que estés enfermo.**
> I'm sorry you are ill.

> **Siento mucho que tengan que operarte.**
> I'm sorry you'll have to have an operation.

> **Siento mucho que lo haya perdido.**
> I'm (so) sorry you lost it.

> **Siento mucho que os hayan robado el coche.**
> I'm (so) sorry they stole your car.

To say that you were sorry that something happened use the preterite of **sentir** (e.g. **sentí**, 'I was sorry'); the verb in the **que** clause must be in the imperfect subjunctive.

> **Sentí mucho que muriera.**
> I was (so) sorry he/she died.

> **Sentimos mucho que se divorciaran.**
> We were (so) sorry they got divorced.

🔘 **18.1.4** (p. 85)

63.2 | Saying one is glad about something

63.2.1 | Set phrases

> **¡Me alegro (mucho)!** I'm (so) glad!
> **¡Me alegro (tanto)!** I'm so glad!
> **¡Cuánto me alegro!** I'm so glad!

63.2.2 *Me alegro/nos alegramos de que* + subjunctive

Alegrarse, 'to be glad', is a reflexive verb, so you will need to use a *reflexive pronoun* with it (i.e. **me, te, se, nos, os,** or **se**). In this construction, a verb of emotion, **alegrarse**, is followed by a clause introduced by **que**, which requires a subjunctive: present subjunctive if we are expressing sympathy with a current or future state or event, and perfect or imperfect subjunctive if reference is to the past.

23.6 (p. 109)

> **Me alegro de que estés bien otra vez.**
> I'm glad you are well again.

> **Me alegro de que se case.**
> I'm glad you are getting married.

> **Me alegro de que hayáis conseguido lo que queríais.**
> I'm glad you got what you wanted.

> **Me alegro mucho de que hayas conseguido trabajo.**
> I'm very glad you got a job.

To say one was glad about something, use the preterite of **alegrarse** (e.g. **me alegré**, 'I was glad'); the verb in the **que** clause must be in the imperfect subjunctive.

> **Me alegré mucho de que te ascendieran.**
> I was glad you were promoted.

> **Nos alegramos mucho de que la nombraran directora.**
> We were glad she was appointed director.

19.2 (p. 95); **18.1.4** (p. 85)

Note: Although strictly **alegrarse** should be followed by **de** in this construction, this rule is by no means always observed.

64
Apologizing and expressing forgiveness

By and large, apologies are much less common in Spanish than in English, just as **por favor**, 'please', and **gracias**, 'thank you', are much less common. Bumping into someone accidentally in the street, for instance, does not always meet with an apology in Spanish, as it would in English, and this is not necessarily regarded as rude. Likewise, expressions for granting forgiveness also seem to be used less frequently in Spanish. When apologizing, set phrases, the equivalent of English expressions such as 'Sorry!', 'I'm so sorry!', are much more common than more complex constructions which actually specify the reason for the apology. This chapter examines set phrases first, and then expressions which vary depending on the situation.

64.1 Apologizing

64.1.1 Set phrases

> **Perdón.**
> Sorry.
>
> **Perdone usted/perdona.**
> I'm sorry. (pol./fam.)
>
> **Perdóneme usted/perdóname.**
> I'm sorry. (pol./fam.)
>
> **Disculpe usted/disculpa.**
> I'm sorry. (pol./fam.)
>
> **Lo siento/lamento (mucho).**
> I'm (very) sorry.
>
> **Lo siento/lamento muchísimo.**
> I'm extremely sorry.

▶ 16.1.1.6 (p. 62)

64.1.2 Set phrase + excuse/reason for the apology

These set phrases are often found followed by a sentence expressing an excuse or giving the actual reason for the apology. This sentence is often introduced by the word **pero**, 'but'.

Perdone usted, (pero) no me di cuenta de que estaba ocupado.
I'm sorry, but I didn't realize you were busy.

Disculpa, (pero) no tuve tiempo de terminarlo.
I'm sorry, I didn't have time to finish it.

Perdona, (pero) no podré venir mañana.
I'm sorry but I won't be able to come tomorrow.

Lo siento (mucho), (pero) perdí el tren.
I'm (very) sorry, but I missed the train.

64.1.3 *Perdone usted/perdona que* + subjunctive

Sentences such as 'I'm sorry to bother you', 'I'm sorry to have bothered you', may be expressed in Spanish in two ways. The most common way is by using the verb **perdonar** or **disculpar**, 'to be sorry', followed by **que** and a subjunctive: present subjunctive, when reference is to the present or the future, and normally perfect subjunctive when reference is to the past. An alternative and less frequent way, is to use the construction in **64.1.4** below, with the verb **sentir** followed by an infinitive. Here are some examples with the first construction.

▶ **16.1.1.3** (p. 61); **16.1.1.7** (p. 62)

Perdone/disculpe que lo moleste.
I'm sorry to bother you.

Perdone/disculpe que lo haya molestado.
I'm sorry to have bothered you.

Perdona/disculpa que no pueda ayudarte.
I'm sorry I can't help you.

Perdona/disculpa que no te haya ayudado.
I'm sorry I didn't help you.

▶ **18.1.4** (p. 85)

64.1.4 *Siento/sentí mucho* + infinitive

An apology related to the present or the future, as in 'I'm sorry I can't lend you the money', is expressed with the present of **sentir, siento**, followed by the infinitive, usually preceded by **poder**, 'to be able to', 'can'.

Siento (mucho) no poder prestarte el dinero.
I'm sorry I can't lend you the money.

Siento (mucho) no poder acompañarlo mañana.
I'm sorry I can't accompany you tomorrow.

Sentimos (mucho) no estar allí contigo.
We're sorry not to be there with you.

To apologize about something related to the past, as in 'I was sorry not to be able to call you', use the preterite of **sentir, sentí**, 'I was sorry', **sentimos**, 'we were sorry', followed by the infinitive. Usage calls for the addition of **mucho** in this case.

Sentí mucho no poder llamarlo.
I was sorry not to be able to call you.

Sentí mucho decepcionarte.
I was sorry to disappoint you.

Sometimes, an apology related to a past event carries the verb **sentir** in the preterite, as above, followed by **haber** + past participle.

Sentimos mucho no haber asistido a tu fiesta de cumpleaños.
We were sorry not to attend your birthday party.

▶ **63.1** (p. 358)

64.2 Expressing forgiveness

To grant forgiveness, use expressions like the following, all of them equally common:

No importa.
It doesn't matter.

Nada, nada.
It's all right.

Está bien.
It's all right.

No tiene importancia.
That's all right.

No se preocupe/no te preocupes.
Don't worry! (pol./fam.)

▶ **16.1.1.6** (p. 62)

65
Expressing fear or worry

This chapter considers the concepts of fear and worry and the expressions normally associated with them. Some of these are set phrases while others vary depending on the situation.

65.1 Common expressions of fear

The idea of being or getting frightened or worried is normally expressed in Spanish with the following expressions

> **tener miedo** 'to be scared/afraid/frightened'
> **temer** 'to be afraid/frightened', 'to fear'
> **estar asustado(a)** 'to be scared/afraid/frightened'
> **asustarse** 'to get frightened'
> **estar preocupado(a)** 'to be worried'
> **preocuparse** 'to worry'

● 22.2 (p. 105)

Listed below are the main constructions in which some of these expressions can occur.

65.1.1 (No) tener miedo

This is the most common way of saying that one is or others are or are not afraid and of asking people if they are afraid. Note that here 'to be', as in 'to be afraid', translates in Spanish as **tener**, 'to have', literally 'to have fear'.

Tengo (mucho) miedo.	I'm (very) afraid.
¿Tienes miedo?	Are you afraid?
No tengo miedo.	I'm not afraid.
No tengas miedo.	Don't be afraid.

To say that one was or was not afraid, use the imperfect of **tener**:

Tenía mucho miedo.	I was afraid.
No tenía nada de miedo.	I was not afraid at all.

To say that one got frightened or was afraid with regard to something at some definite point in the past, use the preterite.

> **¿Y no tuviste miedo?**
> And didn't you get frightened?

No, en ese momento no tuve miedo.
No, at that moment I wasn't afraid.

▶ **17.4** (p. 75)

65.1.2 *(No) tener miedo a* + **noun/pronoun**

Note that in this expression Spanish uses the preposition **a**, whereas English uses 'of', 'to be afraid of'.

¿Le tienes miedo a la muerte?
Are you afraid of death?

El chico le tiene miedo a la oscuridad.
The boy is scared of the dark.

No le tengo miedo a nada.
I'm not afraid of anything.

Le tenía miedo a la gente.
He/she was scared of people.

65.1.3 *(No) tener miedo de* + **infinitive**

Observe that here the expression **tener miedo** takes the preposition **de** followed by the infinitive, while English uses only the infinitive, 'to be afraid to . . .'

Tengo miedo de decírselo.
I'm afraid to tell him/her.

Tiene miedo de perderlo.
He/she is afraid to lose it/him.

¿No tienes miedo de caerte?
Aren't you afraid to fall?

65.1.4 *(No) tener miedo de que* + **subjunctive**

This construction is used when the subject of the main verb is different from that of the complement verb. As in **65.1.3** above the Spanish expression carries the preposition **de**, this time followed by **que** and a subjunctive. This will be the present subjunctive or the imperfect subjunctive, depending on whether **tener** is in the present (e.g. **tengo miedo de que . . .**, 'I'm afraid that . . .') or the imperfect (**teníamos miedo de que . . .**, 'we were afraid that . . .').

▶ **18** (p. 83); **19** (p. 93)

Tengo miedo de que él se enfade.
I'm afraid he will get annoyed/I'm worried he might get annoyed.

¿No tienes miedo de que te oigan?
Aren't you afraid/worried they might hear you?

Ella tenía miedo de que la vieran conmigo.
She was afraid/worried they might see her with me.

▶ **18.1.4** (p. 85)

65.1.5 *(No)* + (pronoun) *temer* + (*a* + noun/pronoun)

Temer, 'to be afraid', 'to fear', is less common and less strong than **tener miedo** and it tends to be used in more formal contexts.

> **¡No temas!**
> Don't be afraid!

> **No le teme.**
> He/she is not frightened of him/her.

> **Todos le temían.**
> Everyone was afraid of him/her.

> **¿Es verdad que le temes al mar?**
> Is it true you are afraid of the sea?

> **No le temen a nadie.**
> They are not afraid of anyone.

In the last two examples note the redundant pronoun **le**, a common feature in Spanish. Here are two more examples with different verbs:

> **Le dije a Carlos.**
> I told Carlos.

> **Les hice un regalo a mis padres.**
> I gave my parents a present.

 8.3 (p. 39)

65.1.6 *(No) temer* + infinitive

> **Temo molestarlo.**
> I'm afraid of bothering him.

> **No temas hacerlo.**
> Don't be afraid of doing it.

> **Temían llegar atrasados.**
> They were afraid of being late.

65.1.7 *(No) temer* + *que* + subjunctive

We use this construction with a subjunctive when the subject of the main verb and that of the complement verb are different. If the main verb, in this case **temer**, is in the present (e.g. **temo que . . .** , 'I'm afraid that . . .'), the second verb will take the present subjunctive; but if we use **temer** in the preterite (e.g. **temí que . . .** , 'I was afraid that . . .') or the imperfect (**temíamos que . . .** , 'we were afraid that . . .'), we will need to use the imperfect subjunctive in the second clause.

> **Temo que me deje.**
> I'm afraid he/she may leave me.

> **Temo que vuelva a hacerlo.**
> I'm afraid he/she may do it again.

Temían que la policía los descubriera.
They were afraid the police might track them down.

▶ **18.1.4** (p. 85); **19** (p. 93)

65.1.8 *Estar asustado(a), asustarse*

Estar asustado(a) is less frequent than the two previous verbs and it can be found in sentences such as these:

Estoy (muy) asustado(a).	I'm (very) scared.
Estábamos asustados(as).	We were scared.
Estás asustado(a), ¿verdad?	You are scared, aren't you?

▶ **22.2** (p. 105)

Asustarse, a reflexive verb, conveys the idea of getting frightened rather than of being afraid, and it normally occurs in sentences like the following:

Me asusté.	I got frightened/worried.
Nos asustamos mucho.	We got very scared/worried.
¡No se asuste!	Don't be (get) frightened!

▶ **23.6** (p. 109)

65.1.9 *Estar preocupado(a)*

This is the only one of the expressions listed above which translates literally as 'to be worried', although the other verbs can in certain contexts express this idea as well. This expression is frequent and it can be found in sentences such as these:

Estoy (muy) preocupado(a).
I'm very worried.

Estamos preocupados por su salud.
We are worried about his/her health.

Mi madre estaba preocupada.
My mother was worried.

▶ **22.2** (p. 105)

65.1.10 *Preocuparse*

Preocuparse, a reflexive verb, can be used on its own or followed by the preposition **por**, in sentences like the following:

No se preocupe usted.
Don't worry.

No se preocupan por sus hijos.
They don't worry about their children.

No te preocupes por mí.
Don't worry about me.

▶ **23.6** (p. 109)

65.2 Other ways of expressing fear

The following expressions are highly colloquial and very common in contexts such as the present one.

> **Tengo verdadero pánico.**
> I'm really afraid.

> **¡Qué miedo/susto pasamos!**
> We were so frightened.

> **Estábamos temblando de miedo.**
> We were trembling with fear.

> **Estoy muerto/a de miedo/del susto.**
> I'm really scared.

> **Casi me muero de miedo.**
> I am almost dying of fright.

> **Me da (mucho) miedo entrar allí.**
> I'm (very) afraid to go in there.

> **Me llevé un susto de padre y señor mío.**
> I got the fright of my life.

> **Se llevó un susto de muerte.**
> He/she had the fright of his/her life.

> **Después del accidente le cogí/agarré miedo al coche.**
> After the accident I became scared of the car.

Note that the word **coger**, in other contexts meaning 'to take', 'to catch' (e.g. **coger un autobús**, 'to catch a bus') is a taboo word in some Latin American countries, for example Mexico, Argentina, and it should be avoided there.

66
Expressing gratitude

This chapter deals with the concept of gratitude. Generally speaking, expressions of gratitude, including the word **gracias**, 'thank you', tend to be used much less frequently in Spanish than in English. This is specially true among equals and, generally, in any informal situation.

66.1 Expressing gratitude

Gratitude is expressed in Spanish with the following expressions. Several of these are set phrases, but others vary according to the context. Those at the top of each list tend to be more informal and common than the rest.

66.1.1 Set phrases

The expressions listed here are the ones most Spanish speakers would use to express gratitude. Other less frequent phrases have not been included.

> **Gracias.**
> Thank you.
>
> **Muchas gracias.**
> Thank you very much.
>
> **Muchísimas gracias.**
> Thanks a lot.
>
> **Un millón de/mil gracias.**
> Thank you very much.
>
> **Es usted muy amable/eres muy amable.**
> That's very kind of you.
>
> **Se/te lo agradezco (mucho/muchísimo).**
> I'm (very) grateful to you.
>
> **Se/te lo agradezco sinceramente/de todo corazón/en el alma.**
> I'm extremely grateful to you.
>
> **Le estoy muy/sumamente agradecido/a.**
> I'm very grateful to you.
>
> **No sabe cuánto/cómo se lo agradezco.**
> You don't know how grateful I am.

66.1.2 *Gracias por* + **infinitive/noun**

Gracias por . . . , 'thank you for . . .', is the most frequent of the more specific expressions and it is common in the spoken language, both formal and informal.

> **Gracias por venir.**
> Thank you for coming.

> **Muchas gracias por tu consejo.**
> Thank you very much/many thanks for your advice.

▶ **25.1.23.1** (p. 127)

66.1.3 *Le/te agradezco (mucho)* (+ **noun**)

Le agradezco . . . , 'I'm grateful to you . . .', from **agradecer**, 'to be grateful', 'to thank', conveys more force and it is more formal than the expression above; it is found in the spoken as well as in the written language.

> **Le agradezco (mucho) la información.**
> I'm (very) grateful for the information.

> **Te agradezco (mucho) tu regalo. Es precioso.**
> Thank you (very much) for your present. It's beautiful.

66.1.4 *Le/te agradezco (mucho)* + *el haber* + **past participle**

This expression, which in English is expressed as 'I'm very grateful to you for' + gerund, goes one step further in the expression of gratitude and is more likely to be found in formal contexts, both in the spoken and the written language. Note that the reference here is to the past, that is, the speaker is thanking someone for having done something. Hence the use of **haber** + past participle in Spanish.

▶ **16.1.1.7** (p. 62)

> **Le agradezco mucho el haberme ayudado.**
> I'm very grateful to you for helping me.

> **Te agradezco mucho el habérselo dicho.**
> I'm very grateful to you for telling him/her.

66.1.5 *Le/te agradezco (mucho)* + *que* + **perfect subjunctive**

This construction conveys the same degree of gratitude as the one in **66.1.4** above, and, as you can see from the examples below, they are interchangeable. As with the previous expression, reference here is to the past. Notice how Spanish and English differ here in terms of structure: . . . **que** + perfect subjunctive expresses '. . . for' + gerund.

▶ **16.1.1.7** (p. 62)

> **Le agradezco mucho que me haya ayudado.**
> I'm very grateful to you for helping me.

> **Te agradezco mucho que se lo hayas dicho.**
> I'm very grateful to you for telling him/her.

66.2 Responding to an expression of gratitude

The way you respond to an expression of gratitude will vary according to the situation. British people, unlike Americans, tend not to respond to a word such as 'thank you', although people in service in Britain (e.g. shop assistants) seem to be using the phrase 'you're welcome' more often. Spanish speakers usually say something, however brief. The expressions used by most Spanish speakers are: **¡De nada!, ¡No hay de qué!, ¡No es nada!,** 'You're welcome'. More purposeful and formal responses are **No me lo agradezca, por favor. No es nada.** 'Please don't thank me. It's all right'. **No tiene nada que agradecerme.** 'You don't have to thank me'. **No tiene por qué agradecérmelo.** 'You don't have to thank me'.

V

The language of persuasion

67
Giving advice and making suggestions

In the sections below you will find the most commonly used expressions to give advice and make suggestions.

67.1 Giving advice and making suggestions not involving the speaker

67.1.1 *Yo que tú/usted* + conditional

Yo que tú/usted, 'if I were you', is one of the most common expressions for giving advice and making suggestions not involving the speaker, in the spoken language. Unlike English, this does not carry a verb, but like English it is followed by a clause containing a conditional.

▶ 16.1.1.2 (p. 59)

> **Yo que tú no iría.**
> If I were you I wouldn't go.
>
> **Yo que tú se lo daría.**
> If I were you I would give it to him/her.
>
> **Yo que usted la contrataría.**
> If I were you I would hire her.

In spontaneous speech, especially in the Peninsula, the conditional is sometimes replaced by the imperfect.

> **Yo que tú lo hacía** (for **haría**).
> If I were you I would do it.
>
> **Yo que usted me quedaba** (for **quedaría**).
> If I were you I would stay.

Alternative expressions with similar meaning are:

> **Yo, en tu lugar, . . .** or
> **Si estuviera en tu lugar, . . .**
> If I were you/in your place . . .

> **Yo, en tu lugar, me quejaría a la gerencia.**
> If I were you, I'd complain to the management.
>
> **Si estuviera en tu lugar, no la perdonaría.**
> If I were in your place, I wouldn't forgive her.

▶ **18.2.4** (p. 89); **51.2** (p. 301)

67.1.2   *¿Por qué no?* + **present**

¿Por qué no . . . ?, 'Why don't you . . . ?', is another common phrase for giving advice or suggesting a course of action not involving the speaker. It is especially frequent in informal spoken language, but it is also heard in formal address.

> **¿Por qué no lo compras?**
> Why don't you buy it?
>
> **¿Por qué no preparas una sopa?**
> Why don't you prepare a soup?
>
> **¿Por qué no se lo decís?**
> Why don't you tell him/her?
>
> **¿Por qué no la entrevista?**
> Why don't you interview her?

67.1.3   **Imperative**

Advice and suggestions not involving the speaker are also made with the imperative. This is common in informal language, both spoken and written. In formal language other forms are preferred.

▶ **16.1.1.6** (p. 62); **17.13** (p. 81)

> **¡Cómpraselo! Está barato.**
> Buy it! It's cheap.
>
> **¡Explícale lo que pasó! No se enfadará.**
> Explain to him/her what happened. He/she won't get annoyed.
>
> **Si vas a Sevilla, llama a María.**
> If you go to Seville, call María.

67.1.4   *Podría(s)* + **infinitive**

This construction with **podría(s)**, 'you could', a conditional form of **poder**, 'can', 'to be able to', is used in informal and formal address, in spoken as well as in written language.

> **Podrías estudiar historia.**
> You could study history.
>
> **Podrían comprar un apartamento en este barrio.**
> You could buy an apartment in this area.
>
> **Vd. podría pasar por mi oficina el lunes, si le parece bien.**
> You could come round to my office on Monday, if that's all right with you.

▶ **21.1** (p. 99)

67.1.5 *Debería(s)/tendría(s) que/haría(s) bien en* + infinitive

Like the previous construction, these expressions are common in all forms of language, particularly in the spoken one.

> **Deberías intentarlo de nuevo.**
> You should try again.

> **Tendría Vd. que pensarlo muy bien.**
> You would have to think it over.

> **Harías bien en no contárselo a Pedro.**
> You'd better not tell Pedro.

67.1.6 *Es mejor que* + present subjunctive, *sería mejor que* + imperfect subjunctive

These two expressions with the subjunctive are generally interchangeable but slightly more forceful than the previous ones.

> **Es mejor que renuncies. No puedes seguir así.**
> You'd better resign. You can't carry on like this.

> **Sería mejor que siguieras estudiando.**
> It would be better if you continued studying.

67.1.7 *Aconsejar/sugerir que* + subjunctive

In direct address, these two verbs are usually found in the present tense, with the verb in the subordinate clause in the present subjunctive.

> **Te aconsejo que estés preparado.**
> I would advise you to be prepared.

> **Le sugiero que compre esas acciones.**
> I suggest you buy those shares.

Less frequently, the verb in the main clause may be in the conditional, in which case the verb in the subordinate clause normally takes the imperfect subjunctive.

> **Te aconsejaría que no fueras.**
> I would advise you not to go.

> **Te sugeriría que lo leyeses cuidadosamente.**
> I would suggest you read it carefully.

67.1.8 *Aconsejar/sugerir* + infinitive

Aconsejar and **sugerir** are also found with the infinitive, but this use appears to be less common than that with **que** and the subjunctive.

> **Le aconsejo volver (que vuelva) mañana.**
> I would advise you to return tomorrow.

> **Te sugiero dejarlo (que lo dejes) para otra oportunidad.**
> I suggest you leave it for another opportunity.

▶ 18.1.1 (p. 84)

67.2 Suggesting a course of action involving the speaker

67.2.1 *Vamos a* + infinitive

Vamos a . . . , 'Let's go and . . .', corresponds mainly to an informal, spoken register, and it is the most frequent way of suggesting a course of action involving the speaker. It is more forceful than other expressions, leaving little ground for dissent.

Vamos a tomar una copa.	Let's go and have a drink.
Vamos a comer algo.	Let's go and eat something.
Vamos a descansar.	Let's go and rest.

With a rising intonation, this expression will seem less peremptory, more like the English construction 'Shall we . . . ?'

¿Vamos a nadar?
Shall we go and swim?

¿Vamos a buscar a Martín?
Shall we go and fetch Martín?

▶ 20.2 (p. 97)

67.2.2 *Podríamos* + infinitive

This construction, which is similar to **67.1.4** above, occurs frequently in spoken registers.

Podríamos pasar la noche aquí.
We could spend the night here.

Podríamos reservar una habitación.
We could reserve a room.

Podríamos ir en el coche.
We could go in the car.

▶ 21.1 (p. 99)

67.2.3 *Deberíamos/tendríamos que/haríamos bien en* + infinitive

Deberíamos entrevistarlos, ¿no crees tú?
We should interview them, don't you think?

A mí me parece que tendríamos que insistir.
I think we should insist.

Haríamos bien en no demostrar ninguna sospecha.
We would do well not to show any suspicion.

▶ 67.1.5 (p. 377)

67.2.4 *¿Qué le/te parece si* + present?

This expression is equivalent in meaning to the English expression 'What about' + gerund, and it is probably just as frequent as the one in **67.2.2** above. It is, though, a less forceful form of suggestion than that with **podríamos**, leaving more ground for dissent, and it can be used in informal and formal address.

> **¿Qué te parece si vemos esta película?**
> What about seeing this film?

> **¿Qué os parece si invitamos a Raúl?**
> What about inviting Raúl?

> **¿Qué les parece si empezamos ahora mismo?**
> What about starting right now?

67.2.5 | *¿Y si . . .* + indicative/imperfect subjunctive*?*

A more colloquial alternative to the construction in **67.2.3** above is this expression introduced by **¿Y si . . . ?**, and which can be used with the present indicative or the imperfect subjunctive.

> **¿Y si lo ponemos/pusiéramos aquí?**
> What if we put it here?

> **¿Y si vamos/fuéramos a París?**
> What about going to Paris?

67.2.6 | *Es mejor que* + present subjunctive/*sería mejor que* + imperfect subjunctive

Suggestions involving the speaker can also be expressed with these constructions carrying a subjunctive in the subordinate clause.

> **Es mejor que sigamos.**
> We'd better carry on.

> **Es mejor que le ocultemos la verdad.**
> We'd better hide the truth from him/her.

> **Sería mejor que hiciéramos las reservas ahora mismo, ¿no crees tú?**
> It would be better if we made the reservations right now, don't you think so?

▶ **67.1.6** (p. 377)

67.3 | **Asking for advice and suggestions**

67.3.1 | Question word + present

This is the most commonly used expression to ask for advice or suggestions, and it is equivalent in meaning to the English construction: question word + 'shall I . . . ?' It is especially frequent in the spoken language.

¿Qué hago?	What shall I do?
¿Qué les digo?	What shall I tell them?
¿Dónde lo pongo?	Where shall I put it?

▶ **12** (p. 48)

67.3.2 Question word + *poder* + infinitive

Like the construction above, this expression with **poder** is commonly used in the spoken language.

¿Qué puedo hacer?	What can I do?
¿Qué puedo decirles?	What can I tell them?
¿Dónde puedo ponerlo?	Where can I put it?

▶ **21.1** (p. 99)

67.3.3 Question word + conditional

This construction is similar to that in **67.3.1** above but slightly less common.

¿Cómo lo harías tú?
How would you do it?

¿Cuál comprarías tú?
Which one would you buy?

¿Qué le respondería usted?
What would you answer to him/her?

▶ **16.1.1.2** (p. 59); **17.7** (p. 77)

67.3.4 *¿Qué harías tú/haría usted en mi lugar?*

This is another colloquial and common way of asking for advice and suggestions, and apart from the use of the familiar or polite form, there are no other variations within this construction.

No sé qué hacer. ¿Qué harías tú en mi lugar?
I don't know what to do. What would you do in my position?

Es una situación muy difícil. ¿Qué haría usted en mi lugar?
It is a very difficult situation. What would you do in my position?

67.3.5 *Aconsejar/sugerir* (+ *que* + subjunctive)

Aconsejar and **sugerir** may be used in independent sentences or as part of a main clause followed by a subordinate clause containing a subjunctive. Their use is equally common in the spoken and the written language.

¿Qué me aconsejas?
What would you advise?

¿Qué (nos) sugieres?
What do you suggest?

¿Qué me aconsejas que haga?
What would you advise me to do?

¿Qué (nos) sugieres que le digamos?
What do you suggest we should tell him/her?

▶ **18.1.1** (p. 84); **12** (p. 48)

68
Making requests

In this chapter you will learn how to request others to do something and to say things like 'Could you help me, please?', 'Would you mind closing the window?' Spanish, like English, expresses these ideas in a number of ways, some more colloquial than others.

68.1 Common expressions of request

68.1.1 *Por favor* + present

This construction with the present, perhaps the most common one when requesting others to do something, is an alternative to the one with the imperative in **68.1.2** below, but, unlike the imperative, it leaves the person addressed with no doubt that what he has heard is a request and not a command. This is closer in meaning to the English expression 'Will you (do this)?' than the one below, and it is especially common in formal address.

> **Por favor, ¿me pasa la sal?**
> Will you pass the salt please?

> **Por favor, ¿le dice a mi marido que se ponga al teléfono?**
> Will you tell my husband to come to the telephone please?

> **Por favor, ¿subes tú el equipaje?**
> Will you bring up the luggage please?

68.1.2 *(Por favor)* + imperative

This is the most peremptory way of requesting others to do something, and it is common in the spoken language in informal contexts. It is also often heard in exchanges between strangers in situations where a service is being requested, in a shop or restaurant for example, or in exchanges between someone in authority and a subordinate. The intonation is important here, a rising intonation being more appropriate for a polite request – especially in formal address – than a falling intonation, which can make this sound like an order or command. In either case, the word **por favor**, placed at the beginning or at the end of the imperative form should establish that this is a request.

▶ 16.1.1.6 (p. 62); 17.13 (p. 81)

> **Por favor cierra la puerta.**
> Please close the door.

> **Por favor, no se lo digas.**
> Please don't tell him/her.

> **Por favor tráigame un sándwich de jamón y una cerveza.**
> Please bring me a ham sandwich and a beer.

> **Isabel, páseme la carpeta azul, por favor.**
> Isabel, please give me the blue file.

68.1.3 | *Haga/haz el favor de . . . /¿Haría el favor de . . . ?*+ infinitive

These constructions are heard much less often than those in **68.1.1** and **68.1.2** above, but like the others, they belong more to the spoken than to the written language.

> **Haga el favor de no fumar.**
> Would you mind not smoking, please?

> **Hagan el favor de entrar.**
> Would you mind coming in, please?

> **Haz el favor de decirle que venga.**
> Would you tell him/her to come, please?

> **¿Haría Vd. el favor de apagar la televisión?**
> Would you turn the television off, please?

68.1.4 | *¿Puedes(s)?* + infinitive

This construction with **¿puede(s)?**, 'can you?' is a more neutral form in terms of register, as in spoken language it is equally common in familiar and formal address. In writing, however, it falls into the informal register.

> **Por favor, ¿puedes echarme una mano?**
> Can you give me a hand, please?

> **¿Puede usted hacerme un favor?**
> Can you do me a favour?

> **¿Puedes subir un momento?**
> Can you come up for a moment?

> **¿Puedes llamarme la semana que viene?**
> Can you call me next week?

▶ 21.1 (p. 99)

68.1.5 | *¿Podría(s)?* + infinitive

The use of the conditional form of **poder**, **¿podría(s)?**, 'could you?' lends more formality and force to a spoken request. But like the previous form, it is used in formal as well as informal address. In writing, however, one is more likely to find it in an informal register, although in a formal note or message it would be quite appropriate.

> **¿Podrías poner esto allí?**
> Could you put this over there?

> ¿Podrías decirle a tu madre que me escriba?
> Could you tell your mother to write to me?
>
> ¿Podría usted explicármelo?
> Could you explain it to me?

▶ **21.1** (p. 99)

68.1.6 *¿Le/te importaría?* + infinitive

This expression which carries the conditional of the verb **importar**, literally 'to matter', is similar in meaning to the English phrase 'Would you mind' + gerund and, as a form of request, it is used in contexts similar to this. Note that **importar** is similar to **gustar** (e.g. ¿**le gustaría?**, 'would you like?'), that is, with the third person ending of the verb, and preceded by an indirect *object pronoun*.

▶ **17.7** (p. 77); **58.1** (p. 340)

> ¿Le importaría esperarme un momento?
> Would you mind waiting for me a moment?
>
> ¿Te importaría llevar mi maleta?
> Would you mind carrying my suitcase?

68.1.7 *¿Sería tan amable de . . . ?/¿Tendría la amabilidad de . . . ?/Tenga la bondad de . . .* + infinitive

These expressions correspond to a formal, spoken register.

> ¿Sería tan amable de ayudarme a bajar esa maleta?
> Would you be kind enough to help me get that suitcase down?
>
> ¿Tendría la amabilidad de cambiármelo?
> Would you be kind enough to change it for me?
>
> Tenga la bondad de explicármelo de nuevo.
> Please be kind enough to explain it to me again.

68.1.8 *Le(s) ruego/rogamos (que)* + present subjunctive

This construction with **rogar**, literally 'to beg', is a typical form of request found in formal letter writing, especially in business letters. Note that **que** can be omitted in this case.

▶ **16.1.1.3** (p. 61); **18.1.1** (p. 84)

> Le ruego (que) me envíe más información.
> Please send me more information.
>
> Les ruego (que) me reserven una habitación.
> Please reserve me a room.
>
> Les rogamos (que) nos contesten a la brevedad posible.
> Please answer us as soon as possible.

68.1.9 | *Le(s) agradecería/agradeceríamos (que)* + **imperfect subjunctive**

This expression with **agradecer**, 'to be grateful', is, after the expression in **68.1.8** above, the second most common form for requesting something formally in writing. Note that **que** can also be omitted in this expression.

▶ **16.1.1.3** (p. 61); **18.1.1** (p. 84)

> **Les agradecería (que) lo enviaran por avión.**
> I would be grateful/I would appreciate it if you would send it by plane.

> **Le agradecería (que) me llamara cuando llegue a Madrid.**
> I would be grateful/I would appreciate it if you would call me when you get to Madrid.

> **Le agradeceríamos (que) nos acusara recibo de nuestra carta.**
> I would be grateful/I would appreciate it if you would acknowledge receipt of our letter.

▶ **19.2** (p. 95)

69

Giving directions, instructions and orders

This chapter covers the language of directions, instructions and orders, from basic forms such as the present tense and the imperative, to others which are less frequent or more specialized.

69.1 Giving directions

69.1.1 The present tense

In the spoken language, directions are commonly given with the present tense, which is also found in personalized writing such as letters and messages. In the Peninsula, this seems to be more frequent than the imperative form.

▶ **16.1.1.2** (p. 59); **17.1.4** (p. 73); **39** (p. 230)

> **Sigue usted todo recto hasta el primer semáforo y luego tuerce a la derecha.**
> Go straight on as far as the first traffic light and then turn right.
>
> **Se baja usted en la próxima estación.**
> Get off at the next station.
>
> **Subes por esta calle.**
> Go up along this street.
>
> **Cruzas aquel puente.**
> Cross that bridge.

69.1.2 The imperative

Directions are also given with the imperative form, especially in the spoken language. In Spanish, the imperative has different forms for familiar and formal address, so whichever form one uses will depend on one's relationship with the person with whom one is speaking. In formal address, there is a tendency to use the pronoun **usted**, for further politeness.

▶ **16.1.1.6** (p. 62); **17.13** (p. 81)

> **Siga (usted) todo recto hasta el primer semáforo y luego tuerza a la derecha.**
> Go straight on as far as the first traffic light and then turn right.

> **Bájese (usted) en la próxima estación.**
> Get off at the next station.
>
> **Sube por esta calle.** (fam.)
> Go up along this street.
>
> **Cruza aquel puente.** (fam.)
> Cross that bridge.

69.1.3 *Tener que* + infinitive, *hay que* + infinitive

Spoken directions may sometimes include sentences with **tener que**, 'to have to', or the impersonal form **hay que**, both followed by the infinitive.

▶ **21.5** (p. 102); **21.7** (p. 102)

> **Tiene que subir por esa escalera mecánica.**
> You have to go up that escalator.
>
> **Tienes que cambiar de andén.**
> You have to change platforms.
>
> **Hay que cambiar de trenes en Calatayud.**
> You have to change trains in Calatayud.

69.1.4 The infinitive

The infinitive is used mainly in formal, impersonal written language, with the same value as the imperative form.

> **Seguir por la M1 hasta llegar a San Alfonso. En San Alfonso, buscar la calle Mayor y continuar por esa calle hasta la plaza de Santa Julia. Doblar allí a la izquierda y seguir todo recto hasta Santa Eulalia.**
> Go along the M1 until you get to San Alfonso. In San Alfonso look for calle Mayor and continue along that street as far as Santa Julia square. Turn left there and go straight on as far as Santa Eulalia.

▶ **17.11** (p. 79)

69.1.5 Latin American usage

Directions in Latin America are given in much the same way as above, except that the actual phrases used may differ from country to country. Instead of **siga todo recto**, 'go straight on', you may hear **siga (todo) derecho** in some countries. Instead of **tuerza a la derecha/izquierda**, 'turn right/left', you may hear **doble a la derecha/izquierda**; instead of **coja este tren/esta calle**, 'take this train/this road', you will hear **tome este tren/esta calle. Coger** is a taboo word in some Latin American countries, for example Argentina and Mexico (see **65**), so if you are addressing Spanish American speakers it is better to avoid it.

69.2 ## Giving instructions

Instructions are given in much the same way as directions, except that to soften the command one often hears forms with **poder** + infinitive, like those used with requests. The examples below illustrate all the various uses.

▶ **68** (p. 381)

69.2.1 ### *Poder* + infinitive

Por favor Isabel, ¿puede pasar al banco e ingresar/depositar (L. Am.) estos cheques?
Isabel, can you go to the bank and deposit these cheques please?

Esteban, ¿podría traerme la carpeta del señor Rivera?
Esteban, could you bring señor Rivera's file?

▶ **21.1** (p. 99)

69.2.2 ### The present tense

This may appear on its own or combined with other forms, for example the imperative.

▶ **17.1.4** (p. 73); **17.13** (p. 81)

Primero vas a correos y echas estas cartas, luego me compras unas aspirinas en la farmacia.
First go to the post office and post these letters, then buy some aspirins for me at the chemist's.

Por favor, vaya a la papelería y me trae una docena de sobres.
Please go to the stationer's and bring me a dozen envelopes.

69.2.3 ### The imperative

The imperative, like the infinitive below, is particularly common in written instructions, such as those found in manuals.

▶ **17.13** (p. 81)

Procure abrir el menor número de veces la puerta de su frigorífico y no la deje abierta después de retirar o colocar alimentos.
Try to open the door of your refrigerator as little as possible and don't leave it open after putting in or taking out food.

Limpie su frigorífico antes de usarlo por primera vez y repita esta operación en forma periódica, por lo menos cada 15 días.
Clean your refrigerator before using it for the first time and repeat this operation regularly, at least every 15 days.

69.2.4 **The infinitive**

> **Antes de usar este aparato, leer detenidamente las instrucciones de este manual.**
> Before using this appliance, please read the instructions in this manual carefully.

> **Dejar siempre suficiente espacio alrededor del aparato para que se ventile.**
> Always leave sufficient space around the appliance for ventilation.

> **No exponer el aparato a temperaturas extremas.**
> Do not expose product to extreme temperatures.

The infinitive is often used in road signs and public notices and warnings, for example

No adelantar.	Do not overtake.
No aparcar.	Do not park.
No fumar.	Do not smoke.

▶ 17.11 (p. 79)

69.3 Giving orders

69.3.1 **The imperative, the present tense or the infinitive**

As with directions and instructions, direct orders or commands are normally given with the imperative, the present indicative or the infinitive. The use of the infinitive in this context is generally uncommon in Latin America.

> **Sal de aquí.**
> Get out of here.

> **¡Cállate!**
> Be quiet!

> **Te vas de aquí inmediatamente.**
> You get out of here immediately.

> **¡No hacerlo nunca más!**
> Don't ever do it again!

69.3.2 ***A* + infinitive**

This construction is a very colloquial and peremptory way of ordering someone to do something. It is used normally by adults addressing young children.

> **¡A dormir! Es muy tarde.**
> Go to sleep! It's very late.

> **¡A hacer los deberes/las tareas!**
> Go and do your homework.

69.3.3 | **The future tense**

The use of the future tense instead of the present tense lends more force to the command.

> **No hablarás más con él. ¿Me has oído?**
> You won't speak to him any more. Did you hear that?

> **Lo harás ahora mismo.**
> You'll do it right now.

69.3.4 | *Te ordeno/mando que* + **present subjunctive,** *te ordeno/mando* + **infinitive**

These constructions are uncommon, except as a reiteration of an order already given.

> **Te ordeno/mando que lo hagas. No discutas.**
> I'm ordering you to do it. Don't argue with me.

> **Te ordeno/mando pedirle perdón.**
> I order you to apologize to him/her.

70
Making an offer or invitation and accepting or declining

This chapter considers the main expressions used by Spanish speakers to make offers or invitations and to accept or decline them.

70.1 Making an offer or invitation

To make an offer or invitation, Spanish, like English, uses a range of constructions, depending on the type of offer or invitation and the degree of formality involved. Below you will find a list of the most common, including formal and informal forms.

70.1.1 *Te invito . . .*

Invitations, especially informal ones, may be made with the verb **invitar**.

> **Te invito a tomar un café.**
> Let me invite/buy you a coffee.

> **Vamos a comer algo. Invito yo.**
> Let's go and have something to eat. My treat.

> **¿Os apetece beber una cerveza? Os invito.** (Spain)
> Would you like to have a beer? I'll treat you.

70.1.2 Imperative

Remember that the imperative has polite and familiar forms, so you will need to use the appropriate form according to the situation. The imperative is usually associated with informal invitations, so you will normally need to use the familiar form. But a word like **por favor**, or an additional polite phrase can make the imperative perfectly suitable for a formal invitation.

> **Ven a cenar con nosotros mañana.**
> Come and have dinner with us tomorrow. (fam.)

> **Me gustaría mucho que conociera a mi familia. Venga a cenar con nosotros mañana.**
> I'd very much like you to meet my family. Come and have dinner with us tomorrow. (pol.)

Vamos a tomar una copa.
Let's go and have a drink.

▶ **16.1.1.6** (p. 62); **17.13** (p. 81)

70.1.3   *¿Por qué no* + present?

¿Por qué no . . . ?, 'Why don't you . . . ?', followed by a verb in the present, can be used to make formal as well as informal invitations.

¿Por qué no se queda a cenar con nosotros?
Why don't you stay and have dinner with us?

¿Por qué no pasas por casa esta noche?
Why don't you come round to our house tonight?

70.1.4   Present of *querer* + infinitive/noun

The use of **querer**, 'to want', in the present to make an invitation or to offer something to somebody is regarded as informal. In a formal situation **querer** may sound a little abrupt. For a formal equivalent expression see **70.1.5** below.

¿Quieres venir a nuestra fiesta?
Do you want to come to our party?

¿Quieres un café?
Do you want a coffee?

▶ **21.4** (p. 101)

70.1.5   *Desear* + infinitive/noun

Desear, 'to want', 'to wish', a verb which is much less common than **querer**, is regarded as more formal than this, and therefore suitable for making formal invitations or offers.

¿Desea usted comer algo?
Would you like to eat something?

¿Desea usted un aperitivo?
Would you like an apéritif?

▶ **26.2.2.1** (p. 134)

70.1.6   *Querer que* + subjunctive

This construction with a subjunctive is used with both formal and informal invitations and offers.

¿Quiere usted/quieres que le/te ayude?
Do you want me to help you?

¿Quieres que te acompañe a casa?
Do you want me to accompany you home?

> **Quiero que vengas a mi fiesta de cumpleaños.**
> I want you to come to my birthday party.

▶ **18.1.1** (p. 84)

70.1.7 *Poder* + infinitive

Like the expression in **70.1.5** above, **poder**, 'can', with an infinitive, can be used when making formal or informal invitations or offers.

> **Puede usted quedarse aquí si desea.**
> You can stay here if you like.

> **¿Puedes venir a comer con nosotros?**
> Can you come and have lunch with us?

> **Podemos llevarte en el coche si quieres.**
> We can take you in the car if you like.

▶ **21.1** (p. 99)

70.1.8 *Me/nos gustaría que* + subjunctive

This expression with **me gustaría**, 'I would like', or **nos gustaría**, 'we would like', can be used to make formal or informal invitations or offers. However, the use of **me gustaría/nos gustaría que** . . . in informal address conveys a certain degree of formality and earnestness on the part of the person who is making the invitation, as if wanting to commit the person being invited to an acceptance. In formal address it may simply convey politeness.

> **Me gustaría mucho que vinieras a mi boda.**
> I'd very much like you to come to my wedding.

> **Me gustaría que viniera a nuestra reunión.**
> I would like you to come to our meeting.

> **Nos gustaría que estuviera con nosotros en esta ocasión.**
> We would like you to be with us on this occasion.

▶ **57.4.2** (p. 338); **18.1.4** (p. 85); **19.2** (p. 95)

70.1.9 *Quisiera/quisiéramos* + infinitive

A very formal way of making an invitation or offering something to someone is by using **quisiera**, 'I would like', or **quisiéramos**, 'we would like', plus an infinitive. Remember that **quisiera** is a form of **querer**, 'to want', which is also used when expressing desires (see **57**).

> **Quisiera invitarle/la a nuestra celebración.**
> I would like to invite you to our celebration.

> **Quisiéramos ofrecerle nuestra casa.**
> We would like to offer you our house.

70.1.10 *Me/nos gustaría* + infinitive

Also very formal is this construction with **me gustaría** or **nos gustaría**, followed by an infinitive.

> **Me gustaría invitarlo/la a mi boda.**
> I would like to invite you to my wedding.

> **Nos gustaría ofrecerle nuestros servicios.**
> We would like to offer you our services.

▶ **57.1.2** (p. 334)

70.1.11 *Le ruego/rogamos que* + subjunctive

This construction with **rogar**, literally 'to beg', 'to request', corresponds to a formal, written register. In business correspondence it is extremely common.

> **Le ruego que acepte nuestra invitación.**
> Please accept our invitation.

> **Le rogamos que acepte nuestra oferta.**
> Please accept our offer.

▶ **18.1.1** (p. 84); **29.9.3.5** (p. 168)

70.1.12 *Tengo/tenemos el agrado de* + infinitive

Also restricted to very formal, written language is this expression with **tener el agrado de**, 'to have the pleasure of', used with an infinitive.

> **Tengo el agrado de invitar a usted a la inauguración de nuestra nueva sucursal.**
> I have pleasure in inviting you to the inauguration of our new branch.

> **Tenemos el agrado de ofrecer a usted dos entradas liberadas para la Exposición Universal.**
> We have pleasure in offering you two free tickets for the World Fair.

70.1.13 *Tendría/tendríamos mucho gusto en que . . .* + imperfect subjunctive/*tendría/tendríamos mucho gusto en . . .* + infinitive

These constructions correspond to a very formal register, and they may be used in the spoken language as well as in writing.

> **Tendría mucho gusto en que pasara unos días con nosotros.**
> We would be very pleased if you spent a few days with us.

> **Tendríamos mucho gusto en ayudarle.**
> We would be very glad to help you/him.

70.2 Accepting or declining an offer or invitation

70.2.1 The expressions normally used when accepting an offer or invitation are the following:

> **(Muchas) gracias.** (formal/informal)
> Thank you (very much).
>
> **¡Vale, gracias!** (very informal, esp. Spain)
> OK, thank you.
>
> **¡Bueno, gracias!** (informal)
> All right, thank you.
>
> **Me gustaría mucho.** (formal/informal)
> I'd like to very much.
>
> **Con mucho gusto.** (formal)
> With great pleasure.
>
> **Encantado/a.** (formal)
> With great pleasure/delighted.
>
> **Muy amable.** (formal)
> That's very kind.

70.2.2 To decline an offer or invitation, Spanish uses expressions like the following:

> **No hace falta, gracias.** (formal/informal)
> It's not necessary, thank you.
>
> **No se moleste.** (formal)
> Don't worry.
>
> **No, muchas gracias.** (formal/informal)
> No, thank you very much.
>
> **Lo siento, pero (no puedo).** (formal/informal)
> I'm sorry, but (I can't).
>
> **Desgraciadamente/desafortunadamente no puedo.** (formal/informal)
> Unfortunately I can't.
>
> **Me gustaría, pero (tengo otro compromiso).** (formal/informal)
> I'd like to, but (I have another engagement/date).
>
> **Lo siento mucho, pero me es imposible/no me es posible.**
> I'm very sorry, but it's impossible/not possible.

70.3 Enquiring whether an invitation is accepted or declined

To enquire whether an invitation is accepted or declined, use either a construction with **ir a** + infinitive or the future tense, in sentences like the following:

> **¿Va usted a venir a la fiesta?**
> Are you coming to the party?

¿Vas a venir a mi boda?
Are you coming to my wedding?

¿Vendrá usted a nuestra fiesta de aniversario?
Will you come to our anniversary party.

¿Vendrás conmigo?
Will you come with me?

▶ **20.2** (p. 97); **17.5.2** (p. 76)

VI

Expressing temporal relations

71
Talking about the present

Statements and questions regarding present states and events are expressed in English in more than one way. Think, for example, of sentences such as 'He is at work', 'He is working', 'He usually works until late', 'He has been working since 10.00', all involving some form of reference to the present. Spanish also expresses such ideas with different constructions, as you will see from the examples below.

In the sections which follow you will find information on how to refer to states, facts, events and actions which bear a relationship with the present.

71.1 Describing present states or conditions

To describe or enquire about present states or conditions, for example 'Is it warm?', 'It's cold', 'He's tired', we use the present tense.

▶ 17.1.1 (p. 72)

¿Hace calor?	Is it warm?
Hace frío.	It's cold.
Está muy cansado.	He's very tired.
Están muy contentos.	They're very happy.

71.2 Giving information about facts which are generally true or true in the present

To inform about facts which are generally true or true in the present, e.g. 'Most Spaniards are Catholic', 'He's the chairman of the committee', we use the present tense.

La mayoría de los españoles son católicos.
Most Spaniards are Catholic.

España es mucho más grande que Holanda.
Spain is much bigger than Holland.

Él es el presidente del comité.
He's the chairman of the committee.

71.3 Referring to events which are in the present but not in progress

In sentences such as 'Your father's calling you', 'Someone's knocking at the door', we are referring to events which are in the present, but not necessarily in progress at the moment of speaking. To talk about these we use the present tense.

> **Tu padre te llama.**
> Your father's calling you.
>
> **Alguien llama a la puerta.**
> Someone's knocking at the door.
>
> **Ahora voy.**
> I'm coming right away.

In the first two examples the action itself may have already taken place, while in the third this has not yet started.

71.4 Expressing timeless ideas or emotions

Ideas or emotions such as 'Segovia is nice', 'I like Segovia', 'It's an excellent idea', may be considered as timeless, in so far as they are not linked to any specific time. In fact, they may be a reaction to a present, past or even a future event or situation. In Spanish, as in English, these ideas or emotions are normally expressed with the present tense.

Segovia es bonita.	Segovia is nice.
Me gusta Segovia.	I like Segovia.
Es una excelente idea.	It's an excellent idea.

71.5 Referring to events taking place in the present

71.5.1 *Estar* + gerund

In sentences such as 'I'm writing a letter', 'The child is sleeping', the action is taking place at the moment of speaking. To refer to such events, Spanish usually uses **estar**, 'to be', followed by a gerund (i.e. words like **mirando**, 'looking', **comiendo**, 'eating'). Sometimes, this construction may be accompanied by an expression of time signalling the present moment, for example **ahora** 'now', **en este momento** 'at this moment'.

▶ 20.1 (p. 96)

> **Ahora está preparando la cena.**
> He/she is preparing dinner now.
>
> **Estoy mirando la televisión.**
> I'm watching television.
>
> **Están comiendo.**
> They're eating.

Present tense

With verbs denoting actions which can have duration, like 'speak', 'sleep', 'play', etc., actions in progress at the moment of speaking can be expressed with the present tense. The present tense of **hacer** is often used to refer to such actions.

> **¿Qué haces?**
> What are you doing?
>
> **No hagáis ruido, que el niño duerme.**
> Don't make noise, the child is sleeping.
>
> **¿En qué piensas?**
> What are you thinking of?

In these examples, the construction with **estar** + gerund and the one with the present tense are interchangeable. Compare the previous sentences with these:

> **¿Qué estás haciendo?**
> What are you doing?
>
> **No hagáis ruido, que el niño está durmiendo.**
> Don't make noise, the child is sleeping.
>
> **¿En qué estás pensando?**
> What are you thinking of?

By and large, the tendency is to use the construction with **estar** + gerund for actions in progress, as this is more specific. With the present tense, only the context makes it clear that we are referring to an action in progress. This ambiguity does not arise with the construction with **estar**, which actually stresses the continuity of the action.

Estar + gerund is also used in preference to the present when we want to emphasize some kind of change in the action in relation with the past or the fact that the action is somewhat unexpected. In the first case, a time expression such as **ahora** 'now', **actualmente** 'at present', usually accompanies this construction.

> **Vivía en Madrid, pero ahora estoy viviendo en Zaragoza.**
> I used to live in Madrid, but now I'm living in Zaragoza.
>
> **Es profesora, pero está trabajando de camarera.**
> She's a teacher, but she's working as a waitress.

71.6 Talking about permanent and habitual actions

To ask and give information about a permanent state of affairs, Spanish, like English, uses the present tense.

> **¿Dónde vives?**
> Where do you live?
> **Vivo en Granada.**
> I live in Granada.
>
> **¿A qué te dedicas?**
> What do you do for a living?

> **Trabajo en un banco.**
> I work in a bank.

To ask and give information about actions which occur often or regularly, for example 'What do you do at weekends?', 'I usually stay at home', use the following forms:

71.6.1 Present tense

This is by far the most common way of talking about actions which occur regularly. To say how often one performs or others perform such actions and to ask similar information of other people one will need words like **normalmente** 'normally', **generalmente, por lo general** 'generally', 'usually', **nunca** 'never', **siempre** 'always', **a veces** 'sometimes', **cada día, todos los días** 'every day', etc. To relate a series of habitual actions, as in 'First I read the paper, then I have dinner', one needs to use words such as **primero** 'first', **después, luego** 'then', 'afterwards'. These words are called *adverbs*.

▶ **14** (p. 55)

> **¿Qué haces los fines de semana?**
> What do you do at weekends?

> **Por lo general me quedo en casa.**
> I usually stay at home.

> **¿Qué haces después de llegar a casa?**
> What do you do after you get home?

> **Primero leo el periódico, después ceno.**
> First I read the newspaper, then I have dinner.

To ask and state the exact time at which certain habitual actions are performed one needs the Spanish equivalent of phrases such as 'What time do you (normally) leave?', 'I (always) leave at 9.00'.

> **¿A qué hora sales normalmente?**
> What time do you normally leave?

> **Siempre salgo a las nueve.**
> I always leave at nine.

> **¿A qué hora te acuestas generalmente?**
> What time do you usually go to bed?

> **Nunca me acuesto antes de las 12.00.**
> I never go to bed before 12.00.

▶ **17.1.1** (p. 72).

71.6.2 Present tense of *soler* + infinitive

Soler, 'to usually (do, etc.)', 'to be in the habit of', is a *radical-changing verb* (o/ue), which in the present tense can be used to ask and give information about actions which occur regularly. Although less common than the previous form, it is used in both formal and informal contexts.

▶ **16.1.2.1** (p. 64); **26.2.2.1** (p. 135)

> ¿Qué sueles hacer los sábados por la noche?
> What do you usually do on Saturday nights?
>
> Suelo ir al cine.
> I usually go to the cinema.
>
> ¿Qué soléis hacer los domingos?
> What do you usually do on Sundays?
>
> Solemos visitar a nuestros padres.
> We usually visit our parents.

71.6.3 Present tense of *acostumbrar* + infinitive

Acostumbrar, 'to usually (do, etc.)', 'to be in the habit of', a regular verb, functions here in the same way as **soler**, but it is less frequent and it tends to be used in more formal contexts.

> No acostumbro levantarme tarde.
> I don't usually get up late.
>
> Acostumbramos hacer mucho ejercicio.
> We usually do a lot of exercise.
>
> ¿A qué hora acostumbra levantarse usted?
> What time do you usually get up?
>
> Acostumbro levantarme a las 7.00.
> I usually get up at 7.00.

⊙ **26.2.2.1** (p. 134)

In parts of Latin America **acostumbrar** takes the preposition **a**.

> Acostumbra a tomar un café a eso de las 11.00.
> He/she usually has coffee about 11.00.

71.7 Saying how long one has been doing something

71.7.1 *Hace* + time phrase + *que* + present tense

Sentences like 'I've been waiting for a long time', 'He's been like that for an hour', express a continuous action or state which began at some moment in the past and which is still in progress. To express such ideas, Spanish uses the present tense in a construction with **hace** followed by an expression of time (e.g. **mucho tiempo**, 'a long time'), plus **que** and a verb in the present.

> Hace mucho rato que espero.
> I've been waiting for a long time.
>
> Hace una hora que está así.
> He/she's been like that for an hour.
>
> Hace dos años que vivo aquí.
> I've been living here for two years.

Questions to elicit information like the one above carry the same word order as in a statement but with the rising intonation, or else are introduced by a phrase such as **¿Cuánto tiempo hace que . . . ?**, 'How long have you/has he/she . . . ?'.

> **¿Hace mucho rato que esperas?**
> Have you been waiting long?

> **¿Cuánto tiempo hace que está así?** (or, **¿Hace cuánto tiempo que . . .?**)
> How long has he/she been like this?

When the period of time refers to an action which has not yet taken place, we may use either the present or the perfect tense.

> **Hace muchísimo tiempo que no nos llaman/han llamado.**
> They haven't called us for a very long time.

> **Hace casi seis meses que no me escribe/ha escrito.**
> He/she hasn't written for almost six months.

▶ **17.1.1** (p. 72)

71.7.2 | **Present tense + *desde* + *hace* + time phrase**

This construction, which starts with the verb phrase, is an alternative to the one in **71.7.1** above. Here, the emphasis is on the action or the state, while in the previous example the stress is on the period of time during which the action or state has been in progress.

> **Espero desde hace mucho rato.**
> I've been waiting for a long time.

> **Está así desde hace una hora.**
> He/she's been like that for an hour.

> **Vivo aquí desde hace dos años.**
> I've been living here for two years.

▶ **17.1.1** (p. 72); **25.1.11.2** (p. 123)

71.7.3 | ***Llevar* + time phrase + gerund/*llevar* + gerund + time phrase**

These constructions with **llevar**, which are interchangeable, are used specifically with actions, not with states, and they stress the fact that the action has been in progress for some time. The construction with **hace** is also valid in this context.

> **Llevo mucho rato esperando. (Hace mucho rato que espero.)**
> **Llevo esperando mucho rato.**
> I've been waiting for a long time.

> **Llevo dos años viviendo aquí. (Hace dos años que vivo aquí.)**
> **Llevo viviendo aquí dos años.**
> I've been living here for two years.

▶ **20.3** (p. 97); **26.3** (p. 140); **71.7.1** (p. 403)

For the use of **llevar** + time phrase to refer to states see **71.7.5** below.

71.7.4 Omission of the gerund with certain verbs

The gerund is sometimes omitted with verbs like **vivir**, 'to live', and **trabajar**, 'to work', when the context makes it clear that we mean living and working.

> **Llevan tres años en España.**
> They've been (living) in Spain for three years.

> **Lleva dos meses en esta empresa.**
> He's been (working) in this company for two months.

Note also the absence of the gerund in sentences carrying a prepositional phrase in which no specific action or no action is implied (see also **71.7.5**).

> **Mi madre lleva una hora en la cocina.**
> My mother has been in the kitchen for an hour.

> **Gonzalo lleva dos días en cama.**
> Gonzalo has been in bed for two days.

71.7.5 *Llevar* + time phrase to refer to states

When reference is to a state rather than an action, no verb other than **llevar** is usually necessary.

> **Lleva una hora así.**
> He/she's been like that for an hour.

> **Lleva una semana enferma.**
> She's been ill for a week.

71.7.6 *Llevar* + time phrase + *sin* + infinitive

You can use this expression to say how long it is since an action has *not* taken place. This is an alternative to the construction with **hace** in **71.7.1**.

> **Llevamos dos meses sin hablarnos. (Hace dos meses que no nos hablamos.)**
> We have not spoken to each other for two months.

> **Llevan mucho tiempo sin verse. (Hace mucho tiempo que no se ven.)**
> They have not seen each other for a long time.

71.7.7 *Llevar* + time phrase (+ gerund) in interrogative sentences

Questions with **llevar** for enquiring about a continuous action follow the same word order as in a statement but with a rising intonation or are introduced by a phrase such as ¿**Cuánto tiempo lleva usted/llevas . . . ?** 'How long have you . . . ?'

> ¿**Llevas mucho rato esperando?**
> Have you been waiting long?

> ¿**Cuánto tiempo lleva usted viviendo aquí?**
> How long have you been living here?

> **¿Cuánto tiempo lleva en esta empresa?**
> How long has he/she been in this company?

71.7.8 *Seguir/continuar* + gerund

This construction with the gerund signals a present and continuous action which began at some moment in the past. Here, the length of time the action has been in progress is not normally specified.

> **Sigue lloviendo.**
> It's still raining.

> **Continúa hablando.**
> He/she's still talking.

▶ **17.12** (p. 80)

71.7.9 *Seguir sin* + infinitive

Negative continuity may be expressed with this construction carrying the preposition **sin** and the infinitive.

> **Siguen sin enterarse.**
> They still haven't found out.

> **Sigo sin saber una palabra de él.**
> I still haven't heard a word from him.

71.8 Expressing possibility, probability or uncertainty with regard to something in the present

Possibility, probability and uncertainty in relation to present actions or states may be expressed with the following constructions (see also **48**):

71.8.1 Present indicative

> **A lo mejor tiene fiebre.**
> Perhaps he/she is running a fever.

> **A lo mejor está cansada.**
> Perhaps she is tired.

A lo mejor, 'perhaps' is always used with the indicative.

▶ **48.1.6** (p. 285); **49.1.3** (p. 293)

71.8.2 Present subjunctive or present indicative

> **Quizá(s)/tal vez se encuentren/encuentran en casa.**
> Perhaps they are at home.

> **Posiblemente no esté/está enterado.**
> Perhaps he doesn't know.

> **Probablemente no sabe quién soy.**
> He/she probably doesn't know who I am.

Both the present subjunctive and the present indicative are correct with these expressions, but **quizá(s)**, **tal vez** and **posiblemente** are usually found with the subjunctive, while **probablemente** is normally followed by the indicative. By and large however, the use of the indicative seems to be spreading, even among educated speakers.

▶ **18.3.3** (p. 92); **48.1.6** (p. 285); **49.1.3** (p. 293)

71.8.3 **Present subjunctive**

> **Es probable que Juan lo sepa.**
> Juan probably knows about it.

> **Puede (ser) que estén durmiendo.**
> They are probably sleeping.

Constructions such as the above are always used with a subjunctive verb.

▶ **48.1.3** (p. 283); **48.1.5** (p. 284)

71.8.4 **Future tense**

> **¿Dónde estará Juan Carlos ahora?**
> I wonder where Juan Carlos is now.

> **A esta hora ya estarán en Los Angeles.**
> At this time they must be in Los Angeles.

▶ **17.5.2** (p. 76); **48.1.10** (p. 287)

72
Talking about the future

In English you can talk about the future in a number of ways. You can use the future, as in 'I will travel to Spain', or a construction such as 'to be going to' followed by an infinitive, for example 'I am going to stay with friends'. Alternatively, and especially with verbs which indicate movement, you could use the present, as in 'I leave early tomorrow'. Spanish has similar constructions and, as in English, these are not always interchangeable. The sections which follow will teach you how to express the idea of future in Spanish, in relation to intentions, the immediate future and events, covering all the main constructions, starting with the most common and leading into less frequent forms. You will also learn how to convey promises, and to express possibility, probability and uncertainty in relation with the future.

72.1 Expressing plans and intentions

Plans and intentions are normally expressed in Spanish with the following constructions:

72.1.1 Present of *ir* + *a* + infinitive

If we refer to future plans and intentions in relation to the present moment, we need to use the present of **ir**, followed by **a** + infinitive, which has an equivalent in the English expression 'to be going to' + infinitive. This construction is very common in Spanish, especially in informal spoken language, where it has virtually replaced the future (see **72.1.5** below). Compared with other expressions, such as **pensar** + infinitive, 'to be thinking of' + gerund (see **72.1.3** below) and **tener la intención de** + infinitive, 'to intend to' + infinitive (see **72.1.4** below), the construction with **ir a**, expresses more resoluteness than the others.

▶ 20.2 (p. 97)

> **¿Qué vas a hacer?**
> What are you going to do?
>
> **Voy a ir al cine.**
> I'm going to the cinema.
>
> **Vamos a trabajar.**
> We're going to work.
>
> **¿Dónde van a pasar las vacaciones?**
> Where are they going to spend their holidays?

> Van a viajar a España.
> They're going to travel to Spain.

72.1.2 **Imperfect of *ir* + *a* + infinitive**

If we refer to future plans and intentions in relation to some moment in the past, we need to use the imperfect of **ir**.

▶ **20.2** (p. 97); **17.3.2** (p. 74); **17.3** (p. 74)

> Mi padre iba a escribir una carta cuando Julio llamó.
> My father was going to write a letter when Julio called.

> Íbamos a ver una obra de teatro.
> We were going to see a play.

> Iban a hacer la compra.
> They were going to do the shopping.

To show hesitancy with regard to future plans, or willingness to alter them, we also use the imperfect.

> ¿Qué vas a hacer?
> What are you going to do?

> Iba a ver la televisión.
> I was going to watch television.

> Iba a dormir la siesta.
> I was going to have a nap.

72.1.3 **Present/imperfect of *pensar* + infinitive**

Pensar + infinitive, 'to be thinking of' + gerund (i.e. words like 'speaking', 'eating') is also normally used in the present or the imperfect, depending on whether we are referring to future plans or intentions in relation to the present or the past.

▶ **17.3.2** (p. 74)

> ¿Qué piensas hacer?
> What do you intend to do?

> Pienso escribir un libro.
> I intend to write a book./I'm thinking of writing a book.

> Pensamos mudarnos de casa.
> We intend to move house./We're thinking of moving house.

> ¿Piensas ir a alguna parte?
> Do you mean to go somewhere?

> Pensaba ver una película.
> I was planning to watch/thinking of watching a film.

> Pensábamos cenar aquí.
> We were planning to have/thinking of having dinner here.

72.1.4 Present/imperfect of *tener (la) intención de* + infinitive

Tener (la) intención de, 'to intend to', is much less common and more formal than the two expressions above, but like the others it is also used in the present or the imperfect, depending on whether reference is to the present or to the past.

> **Tengo (la) intención de cambiarme de trabajo.**
> I intend to change jobs.

> **Tienen (la) intención de casarse.**
> They intend to get married.

> **Tenían (la) intención de hacerlo.**
> They intended to do it.

> **Teníamos (la) intención de vernos otra vez.**
> We intended to see each other again.

72.1.5 The future

The future is rarely used in informal spoken language with reference to plans or intentions, except when these involve a promise (see **72.4** below). In writing, however, this is used frequently, in both formal and informal registers.

▶ **17.5 (p. 76)**

> **Ricardo: Pasaré por ti sobre las 6.00. Te llamaré antes de salir de casa. Alfonso.**
> Ricardo: I'll pick you up about 6.00. I'll call you before I leave home. Alfonso.

> **El presidente intentará poner fin a la crisis.**
> The president will try to put an end to the crisis.

72.1.6 Other ways of expressing plans and intentions

Plans and intentions can also be expressed by using the following phrases, all equally common, especially in the spoken language.

> **tener pensado/previsto/planeado** 'to be planning', 'to intend'
> **proponerse** 'to propose'
> **estar decidido(a)/resuelto(a) a** 'to be determined/resolved'

> **Tengo pensado/previsto/planeado ir a Turquía.**
> I'm planning to go to Turkey.

> **Nos proponemos salir al amanecer.**
> We propose to leave at dawn.

> **Está decidido/resuelto a hacerlo.**
> He's determined/resolved to do it.

72.2 Referring to the immediate future

72.2.1 Present for future reference

To refer to the immediate future in relation to the present, especially to something which has been pre-arranged, we normally use the present instead of the future. This is particularly common with verbs of movement such as **ir** 'to go', **salir** 'to leave', **llegar** 'to arrive', etc. Time phrases such as **mañana** 'tomorrow', **esta noche** 'tonight', **hoy** 'today', etc., will make it clear that the time reference is the future and not the present.

▶ 17.1.2 (p. 73)

¿Qué hacen esta tarde?
What are you doing this afternoon?

Esta tarde vamos a la playa.
We'll be going to the beach this afternoon.

¿Cuándo salís?
When are you leaving?

Salimos mañana a las seis.
We leave tomorrow at six.

¿Cuándo llegan?
When are they arriving?

Llegan hoy por la noche.
They'll be arriving tonight.

Te veo luego.
I'll see you later.

Esta noche habla el presidente.
The president will be speaking tonight.

72.2.2 The future

In certain formal registers, for example in radio or TV news bulletins and newspapers, the future is very common. It is also frequently found in informal written language, for example notes and letters.

▶ 17.5.1 (p. 76)

Los reyes saldrán hoy para Mallorca.
The king and queen will leave for Mallorca today.

Saldremos de Madrid el lunes y llegaremos a Lima el martes.
We'll leave Madrid on Monday and we'll arrive in Lima on Tuesday.

72.2.3 Imperfect for future reference

When reference is to the immediate future or some pre-arranged plan in relation to some moment in the past, we use the imperfect.

Aquella misma noche llegaban nuestros invitados de Londres.
Our guests from London were arriving that same night.

Ese día por la tarde yo me iba a Santiago.
That day in the afternoon I was going to Santiago.

▶ **17.3.2** (p. 74)

72.3 Referring to future events

72.3.1 Present/imperfect of *ir* + *a* + infinitive

In informal, spoken language, future events such as 'England will play Spain', 'The game will start at 6.00', are usually referred to with the construction **ir** + **a** + infinitive. If reference is to the future with relation to some moment in the present, we use the present of **ir** (see **72.1.1**):

Inglaterra va a jugar con España.
England will play Spain.

El partido va a empezar a las 6.00.
The game will start at 6.00.

If reference is to the future with relation to some moment in the past, we use the imperfect of **ir** (see **72.1.2**):

Iban a jugar en Madrid.
They were going to play in Madrid.

Iba a empezar a las 6.00.
It was going to start at 6.00.

▶ **20.2** (p. 97)

72.3.2 *Ir* + *a* + infinitive or future

Educated speakers will often alternate between the construction with **ir** and the future when referring to future events, thus making them almost interchangeable.

La función va a ser/será mañana por la noche.
The performance will be tomorrow night.

Va a terminar/terminará a las 10.00.
It will end at 10.00.

Generally, in writing, reference to future events is usually made using the future. In the press, for example, future events are normally reported in that tense.

El sábado 23 se inaugurará la X Feria del Libro de Valladolid.
The X Valladolid Book Fair will open on Saturday 23rd . . .

Las celebraciones se iniciarán a las 10 de la mañana.
Celebrations will start at 10.00 a.m.

72.3.3 Present tense for fixed future events

To refer to future events which are fixed, such as a national holiday, someone's anniversary or birthday, etc. we use the present.

El viernes 8 es festivo.
Friday the 8th is a holiday.

Nuestro aniversario es el próximo mes.
Our anniversary is next month.

¿Cuándo es el cumpleaños de mamá?
When is mother's birthday?

Es el miércoles que viene.
It's this coming Wednesday.

▶ 17.1.2 (p. 73)

72.4 Expressing promises

Promises are normally expressed using the future tense.

▶ 17.5.2 (p. 77)

¿Me prometes que lo harás?
Do you promise me you'll do it?

Te prometo que lo haré.
I promise I will do it.

Se lo traeré mañana sin falta.
I will bring it to you tomorrow without fail.

No lo volveremos a hacer.
We will not do it again.

72.5 Expressing possibility, probability or uncertainty with regard to something in the future

Possibility, probability or uncertainty in relation to future actions or states may be expressed with the following constructions (see also **48**).

72.5.1 Present or future indicative

A lo mejor vamos/iremos a Cuba.
Perhaps we'll go to Cuba.

A lo mejor te arrepientes/arrepentirás.
Perhaps you'll regret it.

▶ 17.1.2 (p. 73); **48.1.6** (p.285)

72.5.2   **Present subjunctive or future indicative**

Both tenses are correct in this context, but the tendency is to use **quizá(s)**, **tal vez** and **posiblemente** with the present subjunctive, and **probablemente** with the future indicative.

> **Quizá(s)/tal vez/posiblemente alquilemos/alquilaremos un apartamento.**
> Perhaps we'll rent an apartment.

> **Probablemente celebraremos/celebremos nuestro aniversario en casa.**
> We'll probably celebrate our anniversary at home.

▶ **18.3.3** (p. 92); **48.1.6** (p. 285); **49.1.3** (p. 293)

72.5.3   **Present subjunctive**

> **Es probable que se divorcien.**
> They'll probably get divorced.

> **Puede (ser) que nos llamen mañana.**
> Perhaps they'll call us tomorrow.

▶ **18.3.3** (p. 92); **48.1.3** (p. 283); **48.1.5** (p. 284)

72.5.4   **Future tense**

> **Supongo que vendrá a la reunión.**
> I suppose he/she will come to the meeting.

> **Creo que nos quedaremos en casa.**
> I think we'll stay at home.

▶ **17.5.2** (p. 76); **50.1.2** (p. 296)

72.5.5   **Conditional**

Uncertainty about the future in relation to some moment in the past is usually expressed with the conditional.

> **Creía que me llamarías.**
> I thought you would call me.

> **Pensábamos que nos encontrarían.**
> We thought they would find us.

73
Talking about the past

This chapter covers all the main forms used in Spanish to refer to the past. You will learn to refer to past states and events related to the present as well as the recent, immediate and more distant past. Through coverage of these and other uses you will become familiar with the Spanish equivalent of constructions such as 'I have/had done it', 'I did it', and a range of other forms related to the past.

73.1 Talking about past events related to the present or the recent past

73.1.1 Past events related to the present

Past events which are related to the present, for example 'He's not feeling well because he's drunk too much', are normally expressed in Peninsular Spanish with the perfect.

▶ 17.2 (p. 73)

Ha bebido demasiado.	He/she has drunk too much.
¡Lo has quebrado!	You've broken it.
¿Qué ha dicho usted?	What have you said?
¿Qué te ha pasado?	What has happened to you?

Note that in these examples, there is a relation between an action which has taken place and a context or situation which is still valid. In the second example, ¡Lo has quebrado!, 'You've broken it', that context might be said to be something like **Era el único que tenía**, 'It was the only one I had'.

73.1.2 Regional variations

In Galicia and Asturias as in Latin America, the preterite is common in this context, and it is often used instead of the perfect. But among indigenous people, in countries like Bolivia and Peru, the perfect seems much more common, even in contexts where most Spanish speakers would use the preterite.

▶ 17.4 (p. 75)

Bebió demasiado.
He/she's drunk/drank too much.

¡Lo quebraste!
You've broken/broke it.

> **¿Qué dijiste?**
> What have you said/did you say?

73.1.3   The recent past

To refer to recent past events in general, Peninsular Spanish normally uses the perfect, while English tends to use the simple past.

> **He hablado con Carlos esta mañana.**
> I spoke to Carlos this morning.

> **Ha llamado María.**
> Maria phoned.

> **Han llegado con diez minutos de retraso.**
> They arrived ten minutes late.

In this context, Latin Americans tend to use the preterite rather than the perfect tense.

▶ 17.2 (p. 73)

73.1.4   Events which have taken place over a period of time, including the present

Sentences such as 'We still haven't finished', 'I've seen them twice this week', in which reference is made to events which have occurred over a period of time, including the present, are normally expressed in Spanish with the perfect. This use also extends to most forms of Latin American Spanish.

▶ 17.2 (p. 73)

> **Los he visto dos veces esta semana.**
> I've seen them twice this week.

> **Todavía/aún no hemos terminado.**
> We still haven't finished.

> **Ha estado en casa toda la mañana.**
> He/she has been at home the whole morning.

The relation with the present, which is a prevalent feature of the perfect, is clear in these examples. Furthermore, the first example denotes an unfinished action: **Los he visto dos veces.** 'I have seen them twice' (and I may see them again).

73.2   Referring to a prolonged action which began in the past and is still in progress

In a sentence such as 'He has been sleeping the whole morning', the emphasis is not so much on the action itself, but on the fact that this has been in progress for some time. To express such an idea, Spanish uses the perfect of **estar** (e.g. **he estado**, 'I have been') + gerund (e.g. **trabajando**, 'working').

▶ 20.1 (p. 96); 17.2 (p. 73)

> **Ha estado durmiendo toda la mañana.**
> He/she has been sleeping the whole morning.

He estado trabajando desde las 7.00.
I have been working since 7.00.

Han estado bailando desde que se abrió la discoteca.
They have been dancing since the disco opened.

Compare the first example with the following sentence: **Ha dormido toda la mañana**, 'He slept/has slept the whole morning.' In this sentence, which also denotes a prolonged action which began in the past, it is unclear whether this action is still in progress.

73.3 Referring to the immediate past

73.3.1 *Acabar de* + infinitive, to have just + past participle

This construction with **acabar** is very frequent in spoken Spanish, and it denotes closer proximity to the past than the one with the perfect. If the reference point is the present, as in 'He has just left', then we must use **acabar** in the present.

María Luisa acaba de irse.
María Luisa has just left.

Acaba de salir.
He/she has just gone out.

Acabamos de llegar.
We have just arrived.

Acaban de desayunar.
They have just had breakfast.

If we wish to refer to the immediate past in relation to some other moment in the past, as in 'He had just come in' (when it happened), we use the imperfect of **acabar** instead of the present.

Acababa de entrar.
He/she had just come in.

Acabábamos de sentarnos a la mesa.
We had just sat at the table.

Acababan de cenar.
They had just had dinner.

The use of **acabar de** + infinitive in these sentences instead of the perfect lays the stress on the immediacy of the past. Compare for instance the first example above, **María Luisa acaba de marcharse**, 'María Luisa has just left', with **María Luisa se ha marchado**, 'María Luisa has left'. The first sentence tells us that María Luisa left a moment ago, while the second one indicates that she left recently, today or this morning for instance.

73.3.2 **Latin American usage**

Latin American Spanish also uses the construction with **acabar**, but there is also a parallel construction which is common in some countries, and which carries the word **recién**, literally 'recently', followed by a verb in the preterite.

> **Recién llegó.**
> He/she has (only) just arrived.

> **Recién lo vi.**
> I've (only) just seen it/him.

73.3.3 *En este mismo momento . . .*

Another common way of referring to the immediate past is with this expression, used especially in the spoken language.

> **En este mismo momento ha salido con su padre. (Acaba de salir . . .)**
> He/she has gone out with his/her father just now.

> **En este mismo momento se han ido. (Acaban de irse.)**
> They have left just now.

73.4 Referring to events which are past and complete

73.4.1 **The preterite**

To refer to events which took place in the past and ended in the past, Spanish normally uses the preterite. The verb will sometimes be accompanied by a time expression such as **ayer** 'yesterday', **anteayer** 'the day before yesterday', **la semana pasada** 'last week', **el mes/año pasado** 'last month/year', **el martes pasado** 'last Tuesday', **hace dos días** 'two days ago', etc.

▶ 17.4 (p. 75)

> **Fui al cine con Raúl.**
> I went to the cinema with Raúl.

> **Ayer vi a Isabel.**
> I saw Isabel yesterday.

> **Llegaron hace dos días.**
> They arrived two days ago.

In Madrid, and generally in central Spain, the perfect often replaces the preterite in this context.

> **Ayer ha llegado mi madre.**
> My mother arrived yesterday.

> **El sábado por la noche he salido con Laura.**
> I went out with Laura on Saturday night.

The present or historic present

In narrative contexts, completed past events are sometimes expressed with the present. This usage of the present, usually known as the historic present, is much more common in Spanish than it is in English.

▶ **17.1.3** (p. 73)

> **La guerra civil comienza en 1936 y termina en 1939.**
> The civil war began in 1936 and ended in 1939.

> **En 1978 se aprueba la nueva Constitución.**
> The new Constitution was approved in 1978.

> **Me llama a su despacho y me dice que estoy despedido.**
> He calls/called me to his office and tells/told me that I'm/was fired.

The use of the present instead of the preterite in this context lends more force and dramatic quality to the events which are being recounted.

73.5 Saying how long ago something happened

The use of **hace** with a time phrase and a verb in the preterite serves to indicate how long ago something happened.

▶ **17.4** (p. 75)

> **Regresaron hace un cuarto de hora./Hace un cuarto de hora que regresaron.**
> They came back a quarter of an hour ago.

> **Se fue hace tres días./Hace tres días que se fue.**
> He/she left three days ago.

▶ **71.7** (p. 403)

73.6 Talking about long-lasting past events

The preterite

In a sentence like 'We lived in Barcelona for five months', we are referring to a past event, 'we lived', which lasted over a certain period of time, 'for five months'. To express an idea such as this, Spanish uses the preterite.

▶ **17.4** (p. 75)

> **Vivimos en Barcelona durante cinco meses.**
> We lived in Barcelona for five months.

> **Trabajó aquí durante cinco años.**
> He/she worked here for five years.

> **Esperó en el aeropuerto más de cuatro horas.**
> He/she waited at the airport for more than four hours.

73.6.2 **Preterite of *estar* + gerund**

With certain verbs, emphasis on the continuity of the past action is expressed with the preterite of **estar** (e.g. **estuve**, 'I was'), followed by a gerund (e.g. **esperando**, 'waiting'). Compare the last example above with the following:

> **Estuvo esperando en el aeropuerto más de cuatro horas.**
> He/she was waiting at the airport for more than four hours.

▶ **20.1** (p. 96)

Note that, as with the use of the preterite in **73.6.1** above, this construction denotes a past state of affairs which is viewed as a single episode, that is, as a completed action. Overall, however, this form is uncommon, and unless you are certain of its usage, it is best to avoid it.

73.7 Talking about actions which were completed before another past event took place

73.7.1 **The preterite**

A sentence such as 'When they had finished their dinner, they went into the sitting room', is usually expressed in spoken Spanish with the preterite, **Cuando terminaron de cenar, pasaron al salón**. Here are some further examples:

> **En cuanto salimos, se puso a llover.**
> As soon as we had gone out, it started to rain.

> **Luego que terminó la carta, se sentó a leer.**
> After he/she had finished the letter, he/she sat down to read.

▶ **17.4** (p. 75)

73.7.2 **The past anterior**

In formal written language, especially in literary style, the first of the two actions is expressed with the past anterior, that is, the preterite of **haber** (e.g. **hube**, 'I had') followed by a past participle (e.g. **terminado**, 'finished'). Compare the last example above with the one below.

> **Luego que hubo terminado la carta, se sentó a leer.**
> After he had finished the letter, he sat down to read.

▶ **17.10** (p. 79)

73.8 Describing past states or actions in progress over an unspecified period of time

In sentences such as 'I was tired', 'I used to live there', the beginning or the end of the state and the action are not specified. To describe states or actions in progress in an open period of time, as above, Spanish uses the imperfect. In this context, the imperfect is sometimes accompanied by a time phrase such as **entonces** 'then', **en aquel tiempo** 'at that time', **en aquella época** 'at that time', etc.

17.3 (p. 74)

> **Recuerdo que aquel día hacía muchísimo frío.**
> I remember it was very cold that day.

> **Javier estaba enfermo.**
> Javier was ill.

> **En aquella época ella estaba en Granada.**
> At that time she was in Granada.

> **Yo vivía allí entonces.**
> I lived/used to live there then.

> **Elena trabajaba en un hospital.**
> Elena worked/used to work in a hospital.

In contrast with the preterite, the imperfect cannot refer to states or actions which took place in a closed period of time, even when these may have been prolonged or repeated. Compare the examples above with the following ones, which carry the preterite.

> **Hizo muchísimo frío todo el día.**
> It was very cold the whole day.

> **Estuvo enfermo toda la semana.**
> He/she was ill the whole week.

> **Estuvo en Granada varias veces.**
> He/she was in Granada several times.

> **Viví allí cinco años.**
> I lived there for five years.

> **Elena trabajó allí desde 1990 a 1994.**
> Elena worked there from 1990 till 1994.

17.4 (p. 75)

73.9 Talking about past habitual actions

73.9.1 The imperfect

To ask and give information about actions which occurred regularly in the past, over an unspecified period, we use the imperfect. This will sometimes be accompanied by a time phrase indicating frequency, for example **todos los días** 'everyday', **a menudo** 'often', **nunca** 'never', **casi nunca** 'almost never', **siempre** 'always', **de vez en cuando** 'from time to time', etc.

> **Él venía aquí todos los días.**
> He used to come here everyday.

> **Nos veíamos todas las semanas.**
> We used to see each other every week.

Nos visitaban muy a menudo.
They used to visit us very often.

▶ **17.3.1** (p. 74)

73.9.2   **Imperfect of *soler* + infinitive**

Past habits can also be referred to with this construction carrying the imperfect of **soler** (e.g. **solía**, 'I used to'), which is less frequent and less colloquial than the one above. Its occurrence seems to be more common in writing, especially in a narrative context.

Ella solía llegar muy tarde.
She used to arrive very late.

Solíamos levantarnos a las 6.00.
We used to get up at 6.00.

Solía cerrar con llave todas las puertas.
I/he/she used to lock all the doors.

▶ **71.6.2** (p. 402)

73.9.3   **Imperfect of *acostumbrar* + infinitive**

This construction with the imperfect of **acostumbrar** (e.g. **acostumbraba**, 'I/you/he/she/it used to') is less frequent than the one with **soler**, and it is rarely heard in the spoken language. Like **soler**, it occurs more often in writing, especially in narrative contexts.

Yo acostumbraba leer hasta muy tarde.
I used to read until very late.

Acostumbraban dormir la siesta.
They used to have a siesta.

Acostumbrábamos ir a la costa todos los veranos.
We used to go to the coast every summer.

In parts of Latin America, **acostumbrar** carries the preposition **a**.

Acostumbraba a dar un paseo por las tardes.
He/she used to go for a walk in the evenings.

▶ **71.6.3** (p. 403)

73.10   Talking about actions which were taking place when something else happened

73.10.1   **Imperfect of *estar* + gerund + preterite**

To refer to an action which was in progress before some other past event, e.g. 'We were sleeping when the burglars broke in', we use the imperfect of **estar** (e.g. **estaba**, 'I/you/he/she/it was') followed by a gerund (e.g. **haciendo**, 'doing'). The second event is expressed with the preterite.

> **Estábamos durmiendo cuando entraron los ladrones.**
> We were sleeping when the burglars broke in.
>
> **Ella estaba cocinando cuando él llegó.**
> She was cooking when he arrived.
>
> **¿Qué estabas haciendo cuando te llamé?**
> What were you doing when I called you?

> ▶ 17.3 (p. 74); 17.4 (p. 75); 20.1 (p. 96)

73.10.2 Imperfect

A less frequent alternative for expressing the above is to use the imperfect instead of the construction with **estar**. A few verbs, like **hacer, decir, hablar**, are very common in this context in spoken Spanish, but other verbs occur less frequently, except in literary style. Here are some examples:

> **¿Qué hacías?**
> What were you doing?
>
> **Me decías que habías visto a Pedro.**
> You were telling me that you had seen Pedro.
>
> **¿Con quién hablabas?**
> Who were you speaking to?

The tendency, even with these verbs, is to use the construction with the imperfect of **estar** + gerund when the speaker wants to put the emphasis on the action in progress.

73.11 Describing past events which occurred before another past event or situation

In a sentence like 'The meeting had finished when he arrived', the first event 'had finished' occurred before a subsequent event 'he arrived'. This first event is expressed in Spanish with the pluperfect (e.g. **había terminado**, 'it had finished'), while for the subsequent event or situation we normally use the preterite. Often, the second event is not expressed at all, but is understood from the context.

> **La reunión había terminado cuando él llegó.**
> The meeting had finished when he arrived.
>
> **El avión ya había salido.**
> The plane had already left.

> ▶ 17.9 (p. 78)

73.12 Expressing possibility, probability or uncertainty with regard to something in the past

Possibility, probability or uncertainty in relation to past actions or states may be expressed with the following constructions (see also **48**):

Subjunctive or indicative

Quizá(s)/tal vez haya/ha sido Pablo quien lo quebró.
Perhaps it was Pablo who broke it.

Quizá(s)/tal vez estuviese/estaba molesto contigo.
Perhaps he was annoyed with you.

Posiblemente haya/ha sufrido un accidente.
Perhaps he/she has had an accident.

Probablemente no nos han visto/vieron.
They haven't seen/didn't see us probably.

Both the subjunctive and the indicative are correct in this context, but the tendency amongst most speakers is to use **quizá(s)**, **tal vez** and **posiblemente** with the subjunctive, and **probablemente** with the indicative. The alternative form **a lo mejor** requires the indicative.

A lo mejor han salido/salieron.
Perhaps they've gone/went out.

▶ **18.1.6** (p. 86); **48.1.6** (p. 285)

Subjunctive

Es posible/puede (ser) que hayan perdido el avión.
Perhaps they have missed the plane.

Era probable que no tuvieran suficiente dinero.
It was probable that they would not have enough money.

▶ **18.1.6** (p. 86); **48.1.3** (p. 283); **48.1.5** (p. 284); **48.1.6** (p. 285)

Future perfect

Probability or uncertainty with regard to an action in the past which bears a relationship with the present may be expressed with the future perfect.

Carlos no está en su habitación. ¿Adónde habrá ido?
Carlos is not in his room. I wonder where he's gone.

Habrá salido con Carmen.
Perhaps he's gone out with Carmen.

▶ **17.6** (p. 77); **48.1.11** (p. 287)

Conditional and conditional perfect

Probability or uncertainty with regard to a state or action in the past which is unrelated to the present may be expressed with the conditional. In the first two examples below, the conditional tense conveys the idea of approximation.

Tendría veinte años cuando la conocí.
She must have been twenty when I met her.

> **Serían las seis cuando salieron.**
> It must have been six o'clock when they left.

▶ **17.7** (p. 77); **48.1.12** (p. 288)

With the conditional perfect, the speaker expresses probability in relation to something in the past which is previous to another past situation.

> **Estaban muy callados. Seguramente habrían estado discutiendo.**
> They were very quiet. They had (very) probably been arguing.

> **El día que llegué estaba llorando. Habría tenido una mala noticia, quizá(s).**
> The day I arrived he/she was crying. Perhaps he/she'd had some bad news.

Appendix

Table of common irregular verbs

This table should be used in conjunction with 16.1. Where a column has nothing in it, the form is regular. For convenience, however, all 1st person singular present indicative and 3rd person present subjunctive forms are given.

Verb (including compound forms)	Meaning	Radical-changing	Orthographic-changing	1sg. Present	3sg. Pres. Subj.	1sg. Future	1sg. Imperfect	3sg. Preterite	2sg. Imperative	Past participle	Gerund
ABRIR	'to open'			abro	abra					abierto	
ABSOLVER	'to absolve'	ue		absuelvo	absuelva					absuelto	
ACENTUAR	'to accentuate'			acentúo	acentúe						
ACERTAR	'to hit'; 'to get right'	ie		acierto	acierte						
ACONTECER	'to happen'			(acontezco)	acontezca						
ACORDAR	'to agree'; 'to remind'	ue		acuerdo	acuerde						
ACOSTAR	'to put to bed'	ue		acuesto	acueste						
ACTUAR	'to act'			actúo	actúe						
ADHERIR	'to adhere'	ie/i		adhiero	adhiera			adhirió			adhiriendo
ADQUIRIR	'to acquire'	ie		adquiero (but adquirimos)	adquiera			adquirió			adquiriendo
ADVERTIR	'to warn'	ie/i		advierto	advierta			advirtió			advirtiendo
AGRADECER	'to thank'			agradezco	agradezca						
ALMORZAR	'to have lunch'	ue	z becomes c before e	almuerzo	almuerce						
AMANECER	'to dawn'			(amanezco)	amanezca						
AMPLIAR	'to enlarge'			amplío	amplíe						
ANDAR	'to go', 'walk'			ando	ande			anduvo			
ANOCHECER	'to get dark'			(anochezco)	anochezca						
APARECER	'to appear'			aparezco	aparezca						
APETECER	'to appeal'			apetezco	apetezca						
APOSTAR	'to bet'	ue		apuesto	apueste						
APRETAR	'to squeeze'	ie		aprieto	apriete						
ARREPENTIRSE	'to repent'	ie/i		arrepiento	arrepienta			arrepintió			arrepintiendo

Verb	Meaning	Stem change	Spelling note	Present indicative	Present subjunctive	Future	Command	Preterite	Past participle	Gerund
ATENDER	'to attend to'	ie		atiendo	atienda					
ATRAVESAR	'to cross'	ie		atravieso	atraviese					
CABER	'to be contained'			quepo	quepa	cabré		cupo		
CAER	'to fall'			caigo	caiga			cayó		cayendo
CALENTAR	'to heat'	ie		caliento	caliente					
CARECER	'to lack'			carezco	carezca					
CEGAR	'to blind'	ie	g becomes gu before e	ciego	ciegue					
CERRAR	'to close'	ie		cierro	cierre					
COCER	'to cook'	ue	c becomes z before a or o	cuezo	cueza					
COLGAR	'to hang'	ue	g becomes gu before e	cuelgo	cuelgue					
COMENZAR	'to begin'	ie	z becomes c before e	comienzo	comience					
COMPADECER	'to pity'			compadezco	compadezca					
COMPETIR	'to compete'	i/i		compito	compita			compitió		compitiendo
CONCEBIR	'to conceive'	i/i		concibo	conciba			concibió		concibiendo
CONCERNIR	'to concern'	ie/i		concierno	concierna			concirnió		concirniendo
CONDUCIR	'to drive'			conduzco	conduzca			condujo		
CONFESAR	'to confess'	ie		confieso	confiese					
CONFIAR	'to entrust'			confío	confíe					
CONOCER	'to know'			conozco	conozca					
CONTAR	'to count'; 'to tell'	ue		cuento	cuente					
CONTINUAR	'to continue'			continúo	continúe					
CONVERTIR	'to convert'	ie/i		convierto	convierta			convirtió		convirtiendo
CORREGIR	'to correct'	i/i	g becomes j before a or o	corrijo	corrija			corrigió		corrigiendo
COSTAR	'to cost'	ue		cuesto	cueste					
CRIAR	'to rear'			crío	críe					
CUBRIR	'to cover'			cubro	cubra				cubierto	
DAR	'to give'			doy	dé			dio		
DECIR	'to say'			digo	diga	diré	di	dijo	dicho	diciendo
DEFENDER	'to defend'	ie		defiendo	defienda					
DESAFIAR	'to challenge'			desafío	desafíe					
DESCENDER	'to descend'	ie		desciendo	descienda					
DESCONFIAR	'to distrust'			desconfío	desconfíe					
DESPEDIR	'to dismiss'	i/i		despido	despida			despidió		despidiendo
DESPERTAR	'to wake'	ie		despierto	despierte					
DESVIAR	'to divert'			desvío	desvíe					
DIGERIR	'to digest'	ie/i		digiero	digiera			digirió		digiriendo

Verb (including compound forms)	Meaning	Radical-changing	Orthographic-changing	1sg. Present	3sg. Pres. Subj.	1sg. Future	1sg. Imperfect	3sg. Preterite	2sg. Imperative	Past participle	Gerund
DISOLVER	'to dissolve'	ue		disuelvo	disuelva						
DIVERTIR	'to divert'	ie/i		divierto	divierta			divirtió			divirtiendo
DOLER	'to hurt'	ue		duelo	duela						
DORMIR	'to sleep'	ue/u		duermo	duerma			durmió			durmiendo
EFECTUAR	'to effect'			efectúo	efectúe						
ELEGIR	'to choose'	i/i	g becomes j before a or o	elijo	elija			eligió			eligiendo
EMPEZAR	'to begin'	ie		empiezo	empiece						
ENCENDER	'to switch on', 'light'	ie		enciendo	encienda						
ENCONTRAR	'to find'	ue		encuentro	encuentre						
ENFRIAR	'to cool'			enfrío	enfríe						
ENTENDER	'to understand'	ie		entiendo	entienda						
ENVIAR	'to send'			envío	envíe						
ERGUIR	'to raise'	ie/i		irgo/yergo	irga/yerga			irguió			irguiendo
ERRAR	'to wander'	ie		yerro	yerre						
ESCRIBIR	'to write'			escribo	escriba					escrito	
ESPIAR	'to spy'			espío	espíe						
ESQUIAR	'to ski'			esquío	esquíe						
ESTABLECER	'to establish'			establezco	establezca						
ESTAR	'to be'			estoy	esté			estuvo	está		
EVALUAR	'to evaluate'			evalúo	evalúe						
EXCEPTUAR	'to except'			exceptúo	exceptúe						
FAVORECER	'to favour'			favorezco	favorezca						
FIAR	'to trust'			fío	fíe						
FLORECER	'to flourish'			florezco	florezca						
FORZAR	'to force'	ue	z becomes c before e	fuerzo	fuerce						
FOTOGRAFIAR	'to photograph'			fotografío	fotografíe						
FREGAR	'to rub'; 'to wash up'; 'to annoy' (L. Am.)	ie	g becomes gu before e	friego	friegue						
FREÍR	'to fry'	i/i		frío	fría			frió		frito	friendo
GEMIR	'to wail'	i/i		gimo	gima			gimió			gimiendo
GOBERNAR	'to govern'	ie		gobierno	gobierne						
GRADUAR	'to graduate'			gradúo	gradúe						

Infinitive	Meaning	Stem change	Notes	Present	Present subjunctive	Future	Imperfect	Preterite	Imperative	Past participle	Gerund
GUIAR	'to guide'			guío	guíe						
HABER	perfect auxiliary			he	haya	habré		hubo			
HABITUAR	'to accustom'			habitúo	habitúe						
HACER	'to do'; 'to make'			hago	haga	haré		hizo	haz	hecho	
HELAR	'to freeze'	ie		3sg. hiela	hiele						
HERIR	'to wound'	ie/i		hiero	hiera			hirió			hiriendo
HERVIR	'to boil'	ie/i		3sg. hierve	hierva			hirvió			hirviendo
HOLGAR	'to rest', 'be idle'	ue	g becomes gu before e	huelgo	huelgue						
IMPEDIR	'to prevent'	i/i		impido	impida			impidió			impidiendo
INQUIRIR	'to enquire'	ie		inquiero	inquiera			inquirió			inquiriendo
INTRODUCIR	'to introduce'			introduzco	introduzca			introdujo			
INVERTIR	'to invest'	ie/i		invierto	invierta			invirtió			invirtiendo
IR	'to go'			voy	vaya		iba	fue	ve	ido	yendo
JUGAR	'to play'	ue	g becomes gu before e	juego (but jugamos)	juegue (but juguemos)			jugó			jugando
LEER	'to read'		unstressed i becomes y in some forms	leo	lea		leía	leyó		leído	leyendo
LLOVER	'to rain'	ue		3sg. llueve	llueva						
MANIFESTAR	'to show'; 'to demonstrate'	ie		manifiesto	manifieste						
MEDIR	'to measure'	i/i		mido	mida			midió			midiendo
MENTIR	'to lie'	ie/i		miento	mienta			mintió			mintiendo
MERECER	'to deserve'			merezco	merezca						
MERENDAR	'to picnic'	ie		meriendo	meriende						
MORDER	'to bite'	ue		muerdo	muerda						
MORIR	'to die'	ue/u		muero	muera			murió		muerto	muriendo
MOSTRAR	'to show'	ue		muestro	muestre						
MOVER	'to move'	ue		muevo	mueva						
NACER	'to be born'			(nazco)	nazca						
NEGAR	'to deny'	ie	g becomes gu before e	niego	niegue						
NEVAR	'to snow'	ie		3sg. nieva	nieve						
OBEDECER	'to obey'			obedezco	obedezca						
OFRECER	'to offer'			ofrezco	ofrezca						
OÍR	'to hear'			oigo	oiga			oyó			oyendo
OLER	'to smell'	ue	o becomes hue initially	huelo	huela						
OSCURECER	'to grow dark'			oscurezco	oscurezca						

APPENDIX

Verb (including compound forms)	Meaning	Radical-changing	Orthographic-changing	1sg. Present	3sg. Pres. Subj.	1sg. Future	1sg. Imperfect	3sg. Preterite	2sg. Imperative	Past participle	Gerund
PADECER	'to suffer'			padezco	padezca						
PARECER	'to seem'			parezco	parezca						
PEDIR	'to ask for'	i/i		pido	pida			pidió			pidiendo
PENSAR	'to think'	ie		pienso	piense						
PERDER	'to lose'	ie		pierdo	pierda						
PERMANECER	'to stay'			permanezco	permanezca						
PERPETUAR	'to perpetuate'			perpetúo	perpetúe						
PERTENECER	'to belong'			pertenezco	pertenezca						
PODER	'to be able'	ue		puedo	pueda	podré		pudo			pudiendo
PONER	'to put'			pongo	ponga	pondré		puso	pon	puesto	
PORFIAR	'to persist'			porfío	porfíe						
PREFERIR	'to prefer'	ie/i		prefiero	prefiera			prefirió			prefiriendo
PROBAR	'to prove'; 'to try'	ue		pruebo	pruebe						
PRODUCIR	'to produce'			produzco	produzca			produjo			
PUDRIR	'to rot'			3sg. pudre	pudra					podrido	
QUEBRAR	'to break'	ie		quiebro	quiebre						
QUERER	'to wish', 'want'	ie		quiero	quiera	querré		quiso			
RECOMENDAR	'to recommend'	ie		recomiendo	recomiende						
RECORDAR	'to remember'	ue		recuerdo	recuerde						
REDUCIR	'to reduce'			reduzco	reduzca			redujo			
REFERIR	'to refer'	ie/i		refiero	refiera			refirió			refiriendo
REGIR	'to rule'	i/i	g becomes j before a or o	rijo	rija			rigió			rigiendo
REÍR	'to laugh'	i/i		río	ría			rio			riendo
RENDIR	'to yield'	i/i		rindo	rinda			rindió			rindiendo
REÑIR	'to quarrel'	i/i		riño	riña			riñó			riñendo
REPETIR	'to repeat'	i/i		repito	repita			repitió			repitiendo
REPRODUCIR	'to reproduce'			reproduzco	reproduzca			reprodujo			
RESFRIAR	'to cool'			resfrío	resfríe						
RESOLVER	'to solve'	ue		resuelvo	resuelva					resuelto	
REUNIR	'to reunite'			reúno	reúna						
ROGAR	'to ask'	ue	g becomes gu before e	ruego	ruegue						
ROMPER	'to break'			rompo	rompa					roto	
SABER	'to know'			sé	sepa	sabré		supo			

Infinitive	Meaning	Stem change	Spelling note	Pres. 1sg	Pres. Subj.	Future	Imperfect	Preterite	Imperative	Past Part.	Gerund
SALIR	'to go out'			salgo	salga	saldré			sal		
SATISFACER	'to satisfy'			satisfago	satisfaga	satisfaré		satisfizo	satisfaz	satisfecho	
SEDUCIR	'to seduce'			seduzco	seduzca			sedujo			
SEGUIR	'to follow'	i/i	gu becomes g before a or o	sigo	siga			siguió			siguiendo
SENTAR	'to seat'	ie		siento	siente						
SENTIR	'to regret'	ie/i		siento	sienta			sintió			sintiendo
SER	'to be'			soy	sea		era	fue	sé	sido	siendo
SERVIR	'to serve'	i/i		sirvo	sirva			sirvió			sirviendo
SITUAR	'to situate'			sitúo	sitúe						
SOLER	'usually to'	ue		suelo	suela						
SOLTAR	'to release'	ue		suelto	suelte						
SONAR	'to sound'	ue		sueno	suene						
SOÑAR	'to dream'	ue		sueño	sueñe						
SONREÍR	'to smile'	i/i		sonrío	sonría			sonrió			sonriendo
SUGERIR	'to suggest'	ie/i		sugiero	sugiera			sugirió			sugiriendo
TEMBLAR	'to tremble'	ie		tiemblo	tiemble						
TENDER	'to spread out', 'to tend'	ie		tiendo	tienda						
TENER	'to have'	ie		tengo	tenga	tendré		tuvo	ten		
TENTAR	'to tempt'	ie		tiento	tiente						
TORCER	'to twist'	ue	c becomes z before a or o	tuerzo	tuerza						
TRADUCIR	'to translate'			traduzco	traduzca			tradujo			
TRAER	'to bring'			traigo	traiga			trajo			trayendo
TROCAR	'to exchange'	ue	c becomes qu before e	trueco	trueque						
TRONAR	'to thunder'	ue		3sg. truena	truene						
TROPEZAR	'to stumble'	ie		tropiezo	tropiece						
VACIAR	'to empty'			vacío	vacíe						
VALER	'to be worth'			valgo	valga	valdré					
VARIAR	'to vary'			varío	varíe						
VENIR	'to come'			vengo	venga	vendré		vino	ven		
VER	'to see'			veo	vea		veía	vio		visto	
VERTER	'to pour'	ie		vierto	vierta			virtió			virtiendo
VESTIR	'to dress'	i/i		visto	vista			vistió			vistiendo
VOLAR	'to fly'	ue		vuelo	vuele						
VOLCAR	'to overturn'	ue	c becomes qu before e	vuelco	vuelque						
VOLVER	'to turn'; 'to return'	ue		vuelvo	vuelva					vuelto

Bibliography

Alarcos Llorach, A., *Gramática de la lengua española*, Real Academia Española/Espasa-Calpe, Madrid, 1994.

Batchelor, R.E. and Pountain, C.J., *Using Spanish*, Cambridge University Press, 1992.

Bosque, I. and Demonte, V., *Gramática descriptiva de la lengua española*, Espasa, Madrid, 1999.

Butt, J. and Benjamin, C., *A New Reference Grammar of Modern Spanish*, 3rd edn., Arnold, London, 2000.

De Bruyne, J., *A Comprehensive Spanish Grammar*, adapted with additional material by Christopher J. Pountain, Blackwell, Oxford, 1995.

De Devitiis, Mariani, L. and O'Malley, K., *English Grammar for Communication*, Longman, London, 1989.

Fernández, Jesús Cinto, *Actos de habla de la lengua española*, EDELSA Grupo Didascalia, S.A., Madrid, 1991.

Gelabert, José M.ª, Martinell, E., Herrera, M. and Martinell, F., *Repertorio de funciones comunicativas del español, niveles umbral, intermedio y avanzado*, Sociedad General Española de Librería, S.A., Madrid, 1996.

Gili Gaya, S., *Curso superior de sintaxis española*, 11th edn., Biblograf, S.A., Barcelona, 1973.

González Hermoso, A., Cuenot, J.R. and Sánchez Alfaro, M., *Gramática de español lengua extranjera*, EDELSA Grupo Didascalia, S.A., 3rd edn., Madrid, 1995.

Kattán-Ibarra, J. and Howkins, A., *Spanish Grammar in Context*, Arnold, London, 2003.

Leech, G. and Svartvik, J., *Communicative Grammar of English*, Longman, London, 1975.

Matte Bon, F., *Gramática comunicativa del español*, Tomo I, De la lengua a la idea, Difusión S.L., Madrid, 1992.

Matte Bon, F., *Gramática comunicativa del español*, Tomo II, De la idea a la lengua, Difusión S.L., Madrid, 1992.

Muñoz, P. and Thacker, M., *A Spanish Learning Grammar*, Arnold, London 2001.

Quilis, A., Hernández, C. and De la Concha, V., *Lengua española*, Valladolid, 7th edn., 1976.

Sánchez, A., Martín, E. and Matilla, J.A., *Gramática práctica de español para extranjeros*, SGEL, 1980.

Slagter, J.P., *Un nivel umbral*, Consejo de Europa, Estrasburgo, 1979.

Spinelli, E., *English Grammar for Students of Spanish*, Arnold, London, 1998.

Stewart, M., *The Spanish Language Today*, Routledge, London, 1999.

Van Ek, J.A., for The Council of Europe, *The Threshold Level for Modern Language Learning in Schools*, Longman, London, 1977.

Index of words and topics